Using PFS:® WindowWorks™

SEAN CAVANAUGH

with DEANNA BEBB

Using PFS:WindowWorks

Screens reproduced in this book were created by using Collage Plus from Inner Media, Inc., Hollis, NH.

This book is based on Versions 1.0 and 1.1 of PFS:WindowWorks.

Publisher: Lloyd J. Short

Acquisitions Manager: Rick Ranucci

Product Development Manager: Thomas H. Bennett

Managing Editor: Paul Boger

Book Designers: Scott Cook and Michele Laseau

Production Team: Jeff Baker, Scott Boucher, Michelle Cleary, Keith Davenport, Mark Enochs, Brook Farling, Audra Hershman, Carrie Keesling, Betty Kish, Laurie Lee, Anne Owen, Juli Pavey, Caroline Roop, Louise Shinault, John Sleeva, Bruce Steed, Allan Wimmer, Phil Worthington, Christine Young

CREDITS

Product Director
Shelley O'Hara

Production Editor
H. Leigh Davis

Editors
Jo Anna Arnott
Tracy L. Barr
Barbara Koenig
Heidi Weas Muller
Diane L. Steele

Technical Editor
Sheryl Sandberg

Composed in Cheltenham and MCP Digital by Que Corporation

SEAN CAVANAUGH

Sean Cavanaugh has been working in the software industry since graduating in 1984 from Montana State University. He is an original member of the PFS:WindowWorks development team for Ancier Technologies, Inc., the Southern California-based developer of PFS:WindowWorks and Publisher's Powerpak. Sean is 28 years old and lives between San Diego and his family's ranch in southwestern Montana. When not developing software, or writing about it, Sean spends his time surfing and skiing. This is Sean's first book.

DEANNA BEBB

Deanna Bebb is a writer and educator based in San Diego. Since receiving her master's degree from the University of Rochester, she has been writing about and providing training for software and computer systems. Deanna also teaches literature and composition at the college level and works part-time teaching tap and jazz dance to children.

TRADEMARK ACKNOWLEDGMENTS

ACKNOWLEDGMENTS

I would like to extend special thanks to:

Sheri Sandberg of Spinnaker Software for her technical expertise and endless patience.

Lee Ancier of Ancier Technologies, the developer of PFS:Window-Works and Publisher's Powerpak, for being so cool when I needed the extra time to write.

Deanna Bebb for stepping in and saving this project.

Thanks also to everyone at Que who helped make this book happen: H. Leigh Davis, production editor; Shelley O'Hara, product director; Lloyd Short, Que Publisher; and Diane L. Steele, Terrie Lynn Solomon, Jo Anna Arnott, Tracy L. Barr, Barbara Koenig, and Heidi Weas Muller.

CONTENTS AT A GLANCE

CONTENTS

I   The Word Processor

5 Using Advanced Document Features **139**

II The Spreadsheet

IV Other Modules

Introduction

I f Microsoft Windows is a pizza, then PFS:WindowWorks is a pizza
with everything on it: *the works*. PFS:WindowWorks is a collection
of commonly used applications: word processor, spreadsheet,
chart editor, database, terminal, address book, and label maker. But
PFS:WindowWorks is more than a group of separate applications.
PFS:WindowWorks is a set of commonly used applications that work
with each other. This type of software is called *integrated software*.

What Is Integrated Software?

Different applications specialize in creating different document items.
Although word processors have become very sophisticated, for
example, they still are concerned primarily with such text items as
characters, words, and paragraphs. Spreadsheets handle numbers and
other pieces of information that are best stored in tables. Chart editors
work with graphic objects, such as pie charts, bar graphs, lines, and
patterns.

If you buy three separate programs to perform these tasks, they may or
may not be capable of working together and sharing data. If the programs could be integrated, intermediate steps would invariably be required before such sharing could occur. Integration requirements
could include the following: installing special import and export filters;
updating certain options you did not purchase when you initially installed the software; or entering special codes that instruct the different programs to communicate.

The applications—or *modules*—that constitute PFS:WindowWorks already are integrated and are capable of communication; they can handle and manipulate the different types of data, so you don't need to. The seven WindowWorks modules are described in the following section.

Word Processor

The Word Processor module is the central module of PFS:Window-Works. You use the word processor to create documents, such as letters, memos, reports, newsletters, and brochures. The word processor contains commands and features for creating simple and sophisticated documents.

You have complete formatting control over characters (font, size, and style); paragraphs (indentation, tabs, and line height); and whole documents (margins and page size). Documents you create by using the word processor can include headers and footers, multiple columns, and footnotes. You also can add page and chapter numbers and force manual page breaks.

You can draw graphics, such as lines, rectangles, and ovals, by using the word processor's own tools; insert graphics created by other programs, such as Windows Paintbrush; or link charts and graphs created by the Chart Editor module.

A 100,000-word spell checker and 60,000-word thesaurus enable you to check for spelling mistakes, correct them, and search for synonyms, which are words with similar meanings. You also can add your own words to a customized user dictionary, which is useful for personal names and acronyms.

Spreadsheet

The Spreadsheet module is designed for managing information—usually numerical data—that is best stored in tables of rows and columns. Budgets, expense reports, inventory and price lists, and statistics are good examples of the types of information you may want to store in a spreadsheet.

The spreadsheet contains many useful functions and mathematical operators that enable you to quickly and accurately perform calculations with your data. You can easily add a column of numbers or perform projections by multiplying a number by a certain amount and for a specified number of times. The PFS:WindowWorks Spreadsheet module enables more than 40 mathematical, statistical, financial, and date functions.

Changing the appearance of your spreadsheet is easy. You can format numbers and text contained in your spreadsheets by selecting different fonts and styles, adjust the width and height of cells, add borders and shades, or change alignment options.

Cells or groups of cells can be moved to different locations in a spreadsheet or to different spreadsheet files. By using the mouse, you can quickly select a range of cells, copy it, and paste it in a new location.

Chart Editor

Use the Chart Editor module to create and format charts and graphs. You can create charts from data you enter directly into the chart editor or from data entered into the Spreadsheet module. You can choose from nine different chart types: vertical, horizontal, and stacked bar charts; pie charts and exploded pie charts; line charts, point charts, area charts, and high-low-close diagrams (stock charts).

With the click of the mouse, you can add legends, titles, or borders to your charts. You can change the patterns used to fill chart segments, choose different fonts and sizes for all chart text, add grid lines to improve readability, and change the size and scale of your charts.

You can print charts directly from the chart editor, or you can copy the charts to the word processor and print them in your word processor documents.

Database

The Database module enables you to create database files and design custom data-entry screens and reports. Databases store information in records. Records comprise fields. Consider the phone book as a database. Your name, street address, and telephone number combine to constitute a single record. Your telephone number is one of the fields in that record.

When you design a database, you can create and design fields exactly where you want them to appear, add text identifiers, and specify the type of data to be contained in the fields. You create databases by clicking the mouse where you want fields to appear and specifying field type and size. Because the process is so simple, you can design a database and begin entering records within minutes. You can redesign existing databases, add new fields, or delete existing ones.

Database reports are created in the same manner that you create data entry screens: by clicking the mouse and selecting the fields to be displayed. You can view database reports on-screen or send them to your printer. Database search and selection features enable you to locate specific records quickly.

Terminal

Use the Terminal module in conjunction with a Hayes-compatible modem and normal telephone lines to communicate with other computers or subscription services, such as CompuServe, GEnie, or other electronic bulletin-board services.

You can transfer files to and from other computers and converse in real time by using the keyboard. *Real time* refers to the letters appearing on another computer screen as you type them; likewise, letters typed on the other computer appear on your screen as they are typed. You also can capture your communications sessions for later review or printing. The Terminal module supports several transfer rates and communications protocols, which are different methods of communicating.

The Terminal module provides features for automating common communications tasks, such as a scripting feature that enables you to create automatic log-on scripts. You also can store the phone numbers and communications settings of other computers or services you call regularly.

Label Maker

The Label Maker module is a useful utility for printing mailing labels and envelopes of virtually any size or type. You can enter addresses in defined From and Send To fields that enable you to print labels or envelopes one at a time or merge data from the Address Book or Database modules for printing several labels or envelopes simultaneously.

Address Book

The Address Book module is a specialized database for storing names, addresses, company names, telephone numbers, and notes. It comes with a defined data-entry screen, so you can start using it immediately. Address book records can be viewed individually or in list fashion. You can search for specific information, print the entire address book, or print selected records.

Integration

The PFS:WindowWorks integration features prove the adage, *the whole is greater than the sum of the parts*. The Word Processor module, for example, is as useful and sophisticated as many stand-alone word processors, but it becomes even more powerful when linking tables and charts created in the Spreadsheet and Chart Editor modules or when print merging with data records from the Database or Address Book modules.

WindowWorks supports several types of integration. The following list comprises the direct types of integration tasks available among WindowWorks modules:

- Design charts in the Chart Editor module by using data from the Spreadsheet module.

- Create tables in the Word Processor modules by using data from the Spreadsheet module.

- Insert charts from the Chart Editor module into the Word Processor module; this type of integration enables a three-way link from the Spreadsheet module to the Chart Editor module to the Word Processor module.

- Print-merge Word Processor module documents by using data from the Database module.

- Print-merge Word Processor module documents by using data from the Address Book module.

- Create mailing labels with the Label Maker module by using data from the Address Book or Database modules.

Suppose that you have been working on a spreadsheet by using the PFS:WindowWorks Spreadsheet module to compare your monthly expenses to your different sources of income. To better understand the relationship between these numbers, you need to create a graph. You believe a pie chart would best show this relationship. Simply select the information in the spreadsheet, copy it, click the Chart Editor module, and paste. A chart appears.

By using the chart editor, you can change such elements as the chart type (pie chart in this example) and size, add titles and legend, and place a border around it. If you decide to include the chart in a report for presentation to a bank to help you secure a business loan, you select the chart, copy it, click the Word Processor module, and paste. If you have entered some text into the word processor document, the text automatically flows around the new chart. By using tools in the word processor, you can move the chart, stretch it, shrink it, or add a caption.

Copying the information from the spreadsheet, creating a chart, and placing it into the word processor document require only a few seconds to complete. You don't need to use other programs, and you don't need to enter any special codes or instructions. You can view the spreadsheet, the pie chart, and the finished report at the same time by displaying each module side-by-side. To move from one module to another, click the mouse.

If some of the figures you entered in the spreadsheet are out of date, your income may actually be greater than you initially reported. You already created a chart, formatted it to look just the way you want, and placed it in an exact position next to text in the word processor. Although the process for creating a chart is a quick one, you probably will not want to repeat it.

You don't need to.

You simply click the Spreadsheet module and change the income figure accordingly. When you are satisfied with the change, click the Chart Editor module, and the pie chart is adjusted to reflect the change. This option is called Auto Refresh, and WindowWorks gives you the option of turning it on or off when you paste data from one module into another.

Even if you turn off Auto Refresh, you can perform a manual Refresh Now action at any time. To update the chart as it appears in the word processor, simply click the Word Processor module. By performing a Refresh Now action, you complete a sophisticated data exchange by simply clicking the mouse.

Who Should Use This Book?

If you are a computer novice, this book guides you through the steps for creating a document and integrating charts, graphics, and other elements into your document. You learn to create and use a database, to enter and manipulate data in a spreadsheet, and to use data to create a chart. You also learn to use the Terminal module to communicate with your modem and to use the address book and label maker to simplify your contact list and mailings.

If you are a PC and Windows expert and are comfortable with all types of software, this book provides you with advanced tips for getting the most out of PFS:WindowWorks. You learn to format even the most intricate multi-chapter, multi-column documents that integrate data from the WindowWorks modules and other programs. You learn shortcuts for performing the functions you use most frequently, and you learn to make the WindowWorks Hot-Links work for you.

How To Use This Book

Start by reading Chapter 1, "Getting Started." If you are new to the Microsoft Windows environment, this chapter helps you review some Windows basics. If you are comfortable with Windows, you should review Chapter 1 for some tips on manipulating the WindowWorks modules.

What This Book Contains

Using PFS:WindowWorks contains five parts, 18 chapters, and one appendix. Because PFS:WindowWorks may be the only Windows software you ever need to buy, this book may be the only reference tool you ever need.

Chapter 1, "Getting Started," reviews Windows basics and provides tips for manipulating the WindowWorks modules.

Part I, "The Word Processor," details all facets of document creation with the WindowWorks Word Processor module.

Chapter 2, "Creating a Document," covers basic word processing functions, including entering and selecting text, basic editing skills, and saving and printing.

Chapter 3, "Formatting Your Document," provides instructions and suggestions for formatting your document with character and paragraph formatting, including tabs and indentations.

Chapter 4, "Using Advanced Formatting Techniques," discusses other methods for formatting text, including using styles, designing templates, adding graphics, and creating a multiple column format.

Chapter 5, "Using Advanced Document Features," teaches you to divide your document into multiple chapters and add headers and footers, footnotes, and page numbers. You also learn to use the Outline feature to manage long documents, to create a document template, and to merge text or styles into new documents. This chapter also covers print-merging with fields from a database.

Chapter 6, "Working with Objects and Frames," covers the possibilities for creating and manipulating rudimentary graphics by using the WindowWorks drawing tools.

Part II, "The Spreadsheet," provides instructions for creating and editing a Spreadsheet, and generating a chart from a spreadsheet.

Chapter 7, "Creating a Spreadsheet," covers the basics of formatting the spreadsheet and entering data into your spreadsheet cells.

Chapter 8, "Entering Formulas and Functions," explains the many formulas and functions you can use in creating your spreadsheet.

Chapter 9, "Creating Charts," shows you how to use data from your spreadsheet or other data to create a chart in the Chart Editor module.

Part III, "The Database," covers the WindowWorks Database module, from the basics of how to design and create a database form to the advanced techniques involved with generating database reports.

Chapter 10, "Creating a Database," teaches you to design, create, and edit the best form for your database records.

Chapter 11, "Entering and Editing Data," teaches you to enter, edit, and manipulate the data in the records.

Chapter 12, "Creating Database Reports," details the steps for generating reports from the databases you have created.

Part IV, "Other Modules," describes the use of the Terminal module and the Address Book and Label Maker modules.

Chapter 13, "Setting Up Your System for Terminal," teaches you everything you need to know to use a modem to communicate with another computer.

Chapter 14, "Communicating with the Terminal," provides a hands-on example of using the Terminal module.

Chapter 15, "Using the Address Book," introduces you to the WindowWorks Address Book module, which is a simple database designed for maintaining a list of contacts.

Chapter 16, "Using the Label Maker," gives step-by-step instructions for printing labels and envelopes with the Label Maker module, by using addresses from your Address Book or Database modules.

Part V, "Integration," explains how the WindowWorks modules share data and how to use WindowWorks with other programs.

Chapter 17, "Integrating Data from Program Modules," covers the integration and Hot-Linking of data among the seven modules.

Chapter 18, "Importing Data," describes the process for importing and exporting data of other programs.

Appendix, "Installing PFS:WindowWorks," provides detailed instructions for installing PFS:WindowWorks.

Version 1.0 and Version 1.1

This book covers PFS:WindowWorks Versions 1.0 and 1.1, and the full-screen figures are derived from Version 1.1. The few variances between the versions of the program are noted in the text. Although the procedures for both versions are the same and Version 1.1 offers few new features, Version 1.0 users should consider upgrading because Version 1.1 is a more stable program. Contact Spinnaker Software to receive a free program upgrade.

Getting Started

PFS:WindowWorks offers many sophisticated options. With a little study and practice, however, you quickly can become a WindowWorks power user. Because the windows for all seven modules look similar and work the same way, you need to learn only a few simple conventions to work comfortably with all the modules. The PFS:WindowWorks conventions are the same as the conventions for other Microsoft Windows applications.

Before you can become a WindowWorks power user, you first must be comfortable with a few basic skills. This chapter describes installing and opening PFS:WindowWorks, working with multiple WindowWorks modules, setting up your WindowWorks desktop, and working with windows and menus.

If you are well versed in the operation of Microsoft Windows, you can apply your knowledge to the similar operation of WindowWorks. A little time spent becoming proficient in Windows brings you hours closer to being a PFS:WindowWorks power user.

Starting the Program

Remember to install Microsoft Windows Version 3.0 on your hard disk before attempting to install PFS:WindowWorks. Consult your Microsoft Windows documentation for installation instructions.

You should make duplicates of the WindowWorks program disks by using the DOS DISKCOPY command or the Microsoft Windows File Manager. After making copies, put the original disks away for safekeeping.

Installing PFS:WindowWorks

To install the program, insert Disk 1 of PFS:WindowWorks into drive A or drive B. Next, use one of the following methods:

- If you prefer using the DOS environment, type **a:install** or **b:install**, and press Enter from a DOS prompt or from the DOS icon on your Microsoft Windows Program Manager.

- If you prefer using your Windows environment, start from the Microsoft Windows Program Manager. Choose the Run option on the File menu, type **a:install** or **b:install** on the command line, and press Enter.

- If you want to know the names of all the files on the installation disk, open the Microsoft Windows File Manager, choose drive A or B, and double-click the INSTALL.EXE file.

The PFS:WindowWorks installation program first prompts you to identify the drive from which you are installing the program. If the PFS:WindowWorks disk is in drive A, press Enter. If the PFS:Window-Works disk is in drive B, use the arrow keys to move to the Drive B option and press Enter.

The program then prompts you to identify the drive to which you are installing PFS:WindowWorks. Press Enter to install the program on drive C, or use the arrow keys to move to the appropriate drive letter and press Enter.

 NOTE   PFS:WindowWorks requires approximately 4M of disk space. If the selected drive does not have that much space available, delete unnecessary files or choose another drive before installing PFS:WindowWorks.

Next, the installation program asks you whether you want your AUTOEXEC.BAT file changed as part of the installation. Although this proposition may sound frightening if you monitor every line in your AUTOEXEC file, the change involves only the addition of the WINWORKS directory to your path statement. When a program is in the path, you can start the program from any directory.

If you want WindowWorks to make this addition, press Enter. If you want to use a text editor to edit the AUTOEXEC.BAT file yourself, or if you do not want WINWORKS listed in your path statement, move the cursor to NO and press Enter.

If you choose YES when asked whether you want to change your AUTOEXEC.BAT, WindowWorks renames AUTOEXEC.BAT to AUTOEXEC.BAK. You always can restore your original file by deleting the one WindowWorks created and renaming the backup file to AUTOEXEC.BAT.

The installation program then copies the program files into a directory called WINWORKS on the drive that you chose. When prompted, re-place Disk 1 with Disk 2 and press a key to continue the installation. If, for some reason, you opt not to finish the installation at this point, press Esc to abort the process.

Installing Publisher's Powerpak

If you use Bitstream Facelift, you must choose between it and Publisher's Powerpak. Windows enables only one of these products to be the active printer driver. Therefore, you cannot use Powerpak with WindowWorks and Facelift with another Windows application without making some changes. If you use Adobe Type Manager, it can exist with Powerpak if you install ATM *after* you install Powerpak.

If you install Powerpak and later decide not to use it—or if there is a conflict with another printer and screen driver—delete the file SYSTEM.INI from your Windows directory and rename SYSTEM.BAK to SYSTEM.INI. You also should consider deleting the files in the Powerpak directory to regain disk space.

After all PFS:WindowWorks files have been copied, a prompt asks whether you want to install Publisher's Powerpak. If you haven't dis-covered this software gem, Publisher's Powerpak is a superb printer and screen driver package that includes an outstanding font selection. Powerpak includes three type families; a large variety of additional fonts are available from Atech software. Installing Powerpak is a great way to start building a superlative font library. You should install Publisher's Powerpak unless you already are using a comparable product with which you are satisfied.

To install Publisher's Powerpak, press Enter. Next, replace Disk 2 with Disk 3 and press a key. The Powerpak files copy into a POWERPAK subdirectory in your WINDOWS directory. The Powerpak installation also adds some files to your WINDOWS directory and makes some modifications to your Windows SYSTEM.INI file.

Customizing Your Desktop

When the installation process is complete, a PFS:WindowWorks group window appears on your Program Manager. If you installed Window-Works from a DOS prompt outside of Microsoft Windows, open Windows and find the PFS:WindowWorks group window. This group window contains the icon for the WindowWorks program.

If you want to move the WindowWorks icon to another window, simply drag the icon into that group window. You then can delete the PFS:WindowWorks group window by selecting the window and pressing Del. (To select the group window, click anywhere in the window or select PFS:WindowWorks from the Program Manager's Window menu.) Deleting the group does not affect the program itself—as long as you have moved the WindowWorks icon to another group.

Deleting icons and groups does not delete the actual files from your hard disk; the icon or group is deleted only from the desktop. You always can create another icon or group by choosing New from the Program Manager's File menu.

You also can change the name of the WindowWorks group. To rename the PFS:WindowWorks group, minimize the group window by clicking the control menu box at the left of the title bar and selecting Minimize; alternatively, click the Minimize arrow at the right of the title bar. When you minimize the group window, the main window in your Program Manager becomes the active window. You must click the PFS:Window-Works group icon to make the group active again.

When the icon is active (and the title is highlighted), choose Properties from the Program Manager's File menu. Press Del to delete the name *PFS:WindowWorks*, and then type the new name for the group window. Press Enter or click the OK button to complete the process.

To change the WindowWorks icon's label (or name) or the icon itself, open the PFS:WindowWorks group window and select the WindowWorks icon. Choose Properties from the Program Manager's File menu. Press Del to delete the word WindowWorks, and then type the new label for the icon.

To select a different icon for the program, click the Change Icon button. In the Select Icon dialog box, click View Next to cycle through the three icon choices. When the icon you want to use appears as the Current Selection, press Enter or click the OK button. To put the changes into effect, click the OK button in the Program Item Properties dialog box, or press Enter.

Opening PFS:WindowWorks

To open PFS:WindowWorks, double-click the PFS:WindowWorks icon. The Word Processor module appears with a blank area where you can create a new document. Icons at the bottom of the window (see fig. 1.1) represent the six other modules: Chart Editor, Spreadsheet, Database, Terminal, Address Book, and Label Maker.

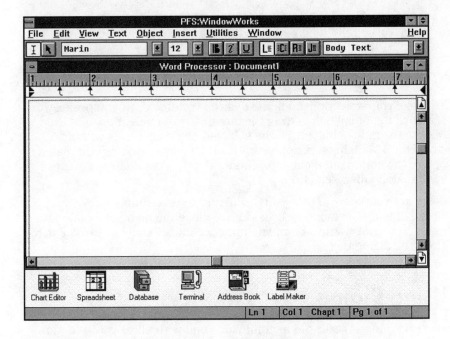

FIG. 1.1

The basic
PFS:WindowWorks
desktop.

Selecting Menu Commands

WindowWorks organizes commands, like all Windows programs, in menus listed across the top bar of the program window. The menu names vary depending on the active PFS:WindowWorks module. If you are working on a document in the Word Processor module, WindowWorks displays the Word Processor menu bar (see fig. 1.2). When you open a different module, a different menu bar appears.

FIG. 1.2

The Word
Processor menu
bar.

PFS:WindowWorks

File Edit View Text Object Insert Utilities Window   Help

To make a selection, you first must open a WindowWorks menu. To open a menu, click the menu name in the menu bar; WindowWorks displays the menu's commands. Figure 1.3 shows the Word Processor module's File menu.

Commands that currently are not available for selection appear in gray on the menu. The selection of available commands changes as you work.

T I P

If a command you want to choose appears in gray, you probably have not completed a necessary step. If, for example, you want to paste something into a document, but the Paste command is grayed, you know that the clipboard contains nothing to paste. You first must cut or copy some data to store on the Windows clipboard.

To make your selection, click the desired command. (If you prefer, you can click the menu name, drag the cursor to your selection, and then release the mouse button.) If the selected command ends with an ellipsis (...), a dialog box appears. This dialog box must be completed before the command can be executed. All other commands execute immediately upon selection.

If you activate a menu that you decide not to use, simply click anywhere outside the menu or press Esc to close the menu. If a dialog box that you do not want to complete appears, click Cancel or press Esc to close the dialog box.

Using Dialog Boxes

Several WindowWorks menu commands end with ellipses (...) to indicate that you must provide more information before the selected command can be executed. You enter the information in a window, or *dialog box*, that appears after you select the command. This window is called a *dialog* box because you enter into a dialog with the program—the program asks you a series of questions that you must answer. The dialog box may require you to enter text, choose settings or options, or confirm or edit a list of settings. The appearance of the dialog box varies depending on the command selected.

When you open a dialog box, the currently selected item is highlighted or surrounded by a dotted box. Edit or accept that item and move to the next item by clicking the next item or pressing the Tab key. (Pressing Shift-Tab moves the cursor to the preceding item.) Because each item may require a different type of selection process, you should be familiar with the elements described in the following sections.

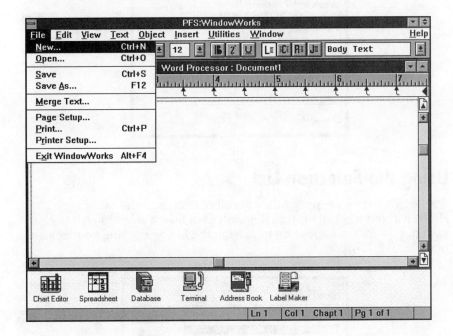

FIG. 1.3

The File menu in the Word Processor module.

Using Drop-Down List Boxes

You use a scroll button to display a short list of selections. The default selection appears to the left of a scroll button. To accept the default selection, move to the next item in the dialog box, or select OK if no additional items exist.

To view the remaining selections, click the scroll button. To select an item from the list, click the item. The selected item is highlighted and appears in the text box to the left of the scroll button (see fig. 1.4). If you want to use the keyboard, use the arrow keys to select, or type the first letter of the selection.

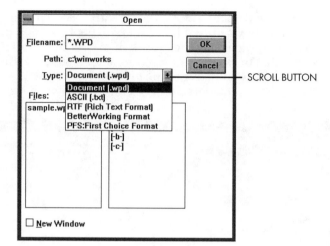

SCROLL BUTTON

FIG. 1.4

A document type
scroll button in
the Open dialog
box.

Using the Selection List

A selection list can appear with a scroll button or, if the list is very
short, without a scroll button. Regardless of how a selection list is generated, you always choose an item from the list by clicking your selection (see fig. 1.5).

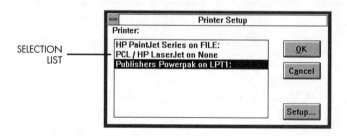

SELECTION
LIST

FIG. 1.5

The Printer Setup
dialog box with
the Printer
selection list.

Using the Text Box

You use a text box for entering text or numbers. A default entry usually
appears in the text box. To change the default entry, click the cursor in
the box and edit the text. To delete an entry, press the Backspace key
to erase each character, or drag the cursor over the entire entry to
highlight the text and then press the Del key. You then can type your
entry and click the OK button in the dialog box.

In some cases, a selection list accompanies a text box. You can type
your entry or click an option from the list (see fig. 1.6).

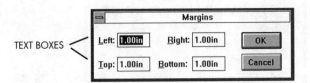

TEXT BOXES

FIG. 1.6

The Margins
dialog box with
text boxes for
Left, Right, Top,
and Bottom.

Using the Check Box

A check box is an on/off switch for an option. To turn an option on,
click its corresponding check box. When you click a check box, an X
appears to indicate that the option is activated. If a check box is empty,
the option is turned off. If more than one check box appears in a dialog
box, you can turn on as many options as you want—the options are not
mutually exclusive. You do not choose between options—you choose
whether you want to select each individual option (see fig. 1.7).

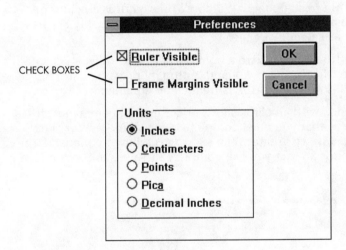

CHECK BOXES

FIG. 1.7

Preferences
dialog box with
Ruler Visible
check box
toggled to the
ON position.

Using the Option Button

You use an option button to choose among items in a group. To select
an option, click the option button. A dot appears in the button to indicate that the option is selected. Although an option button may seem
to work like a check box, a fundamental difference exists: you cannot
activate more than one option button at a time and you *must* select one
option button (see fig. 1.8). When you select one option button, all
other option buttons in the group become deselected. If you prefer, you
can use the arrow keys (rather than the mouse) to move among option
buttons.

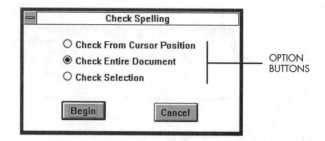

FIG. 1.8

Check Spelling dialog box with the Check Entire Document option selected.

Using the Command Button

A command button is a rectangular button labeled with its associated action. To initiate the action, simply click the button. Every dialog box has the OK and Cancel command buttons. Clicking the OK button activates any options selected in the dialog box and returns to the main screen. Selecting the Cancel button returns to the main screen as if the dialog box had not been opened; WindowWorks ignores any new options that you may have selected in the dialog box. (Pressing Esc has the same effect as selecting Cancel.)

A command button outlined with a bold border is the default selection. You can activate the default command button by pressing Enter. In most dialog boxes, the OK button is the default command.

If a command ends with an ellipsis (...), selecting that command activates a dialog box that you must complete before WindowWorks executes the action. If two greater than signs (>>) follow a command, the dialog box expands so that you can complete further information (see fig. 1.9).

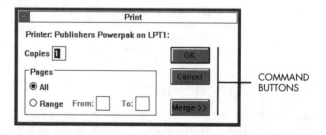

FIG. 1.9

The Print dialog box with sample command buttons.

Using a Scroll List

You can use a scroll list for selecting an item from a long list. The scroll list has a scroll bar, scroll box, and scroll arrows that you use to move through the list. Click the bottom scroll arrow to move down through the list one item at a time. Click the scroll bar below the scroll box to move down one screen at a time. You also can drag the scroll box down to move through the list a few items at a time. Reverse these instructions to move up through the list.

To select an item from a scroll list, click the item. When you press OK, the highlighted item is selected—even if you have moved through the list so that the item is not visible on-screen (see fig. 1.10).

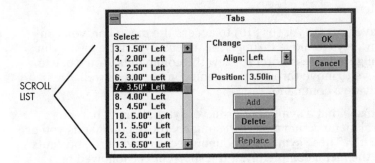

SCROLL LIST

FIG. 1.10

The Tabs dialog box contains a good example of a scroll list.

Using Shortcut Keys

You can select menus and commands by using the keyboard rather than the mouse. As you become an experienced user, you discover that sometimes using the keyboard is faster and more convenient than reaching for the mouse. You should be comfortable, however, with both selection methods. The following sections describe various keyboard shortcuts.

Using Shortcut Keys in Dialog Boxes

Press the Tab key or Shift-Tab to move among fields in a dialog box. To accept the default command button, press Enter. Press Esc to cancel all changes made in the dialog box. Use the arrow keys to move among option buttons and to move to the next item in a scroll or selection list.

Using Shortcut Keys in Menus

Each menu title on the menu bar contains one underlined letter. This letter is the keyboard shortcut you use to access the menu. To access the menu bar, press Alt or F10. When the menu bar is accessed, the control menu button is highlighted. To access the highlighted menu, press Enter. To access another menu, press that menu's underlined letter; WindowWorks displays the menu commands.

Each menu command also contains one underlined letter. Press the underlined letter when the menu is visible, and WindowWorks executes the option. To save your document, for example, you can press Alt-F (or F10-F) to access the File menu, and then press S to save your document. This type of keyboard shortcut applies to every menu command and requires no memorization of shortcut keys—just look for the underlined letter.

After you have pressed Alt (or F10) to access the menu bar, you can use the arrow keys to move through the menus. When the menu you want is highlighted, press Enter to view the commands. You can use the arrow keys to move through the menu commands as well. Press Enter to activate a command.

You also can see that a symbol or group of symbols and characters follow several menu commands—presumably those commands you use most frequently. These symbols are menu-access keyboard shortcuts that bypass the menu completely. If the shortcut is F followed by a number (F1, F2, F3, for example), you can press the corresponding function key to execute the command. To start the spelling checker, for example, you can press F9 instead of opening the Utilities menu and choosing Spell Check.

Some keyboard shortcuts contain a character preceded by a caret or hat (^). In this case, you press and hold the Ctrl key while you press the character to activate the command. To save a document, for example, you can press Ctrl-S much faster than you can open the File menu and choose Save.

If the keyboard shortcut is a group of keys connected with plus signs (+), you press and hold all the keys in the group to activate the command. To exit WindowWorks, for example, press and hold Alt while you press F4. This shortcut has the same effect as choosing Exit from the File menu.

Using Shortcut Keys with Modules

You can press Ctrl-Tab or Ctrl-F6 to move from the current module to the next open module or icon.

Several keyboard shortcuts enable you to move around within each module. The WindowWorks on-line Help system includes a comprehensive list of these shortcuts, as does Appendix C in the WindowWorks User's Guide. To access the list of shortcuts, choose the Index option from the Help menu, and click Keyboard on the Index list. You then can click a module name and review a list of keyboard shortcuts for the selected module. If you find that you need to refer often to the shortcut list, you can print the list by choosing Print from the File menu in the Help window.

Working with Windows

An on-screen window works much like a window in your house. Think of each of your computer's programs and files as a room in the computer house. If you open a window to a room, you can look at and touch parts of the room. You can have many windows open at one time, and you can move back and forth among windows as you work. When you finish looking at one room, you simply close the window.

This approach is too simplistic, however, because an on-screen window has much more versatility than a window in your house. You can move an on-screen window, change its size, and change its contents. You also can open a window within a window, which is what you see when you open WindowWorks.

The initial WindowWorks screen displays two windows: the Window-Works window and the Word Processor window. If you close or minimize the Word Processor window, the WindowWorks window remains unchanged. Closing the WindowWorks window closes all the module windows, however, because the WindowWorks window contains the windows for all seven modules. (The WindowWorks window is a container for the seven modules; the modules cannot exist outside their container.)

Each WindowWorks module appears in its own window within the WindowWorks window. You simultaneously can open multiple module windows, which makes for easy copying of graphs, charts, or text from one module to another.

The beauty of integrated software becomes obvious when you see the edits you make in one module reflected instantly in other related modules. If, for example, you insert a spreadsheet created in the Spreadsheet module into a Word Processor module document, you can revise the spreadsheet in one window and view the spreadsheet side-by-side with a window containing the revised document. (The Auto Refresh feature enables you to view your changes immediately.) With Window-Works, your documents always can contain up-to-date data—without constant cross-checking, copying, and pasting.

Defining the Elements of a Window

Each WindowWorks window has a title bar, a control menu box, window-sizing buttons, a menu bar, and the workspace. Many windows also have horizontal and vertical scroll bars.

When you work in a WindowWorks module, you actually work in a window within a window. WindowWorks is a window that contains the module window. You need to examine your screen and be able to identify which elements belong to the WindowWorks window and which elements belong to the module window.

The minimize and maximize buttons, and the control menu box appear on the title bar of the window that they affect (see fig. 1.11). If you want to minimize the Word Processor module and open another module, you have to find the minimize button on the Word Processor title bar. The minimize button always completely minimizes and returns you to the Program Manager or another open application. The maximize/restore button alternately minimizes or restores WindowWorks to its last size.

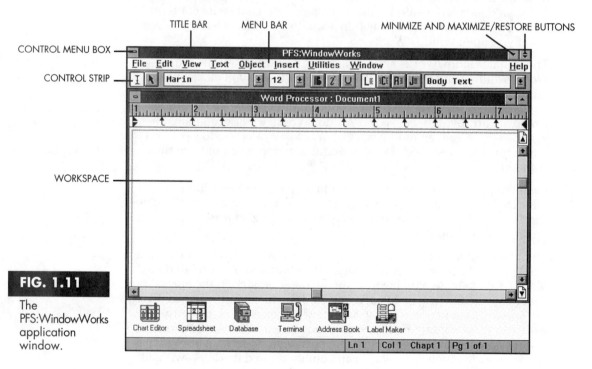

FIG. 1.11

The PFS:WindowWorks application window.

The title bar displays the name of the application or module that appears in the window. The control menu box to the left of the title bar displays commands for changing the active window. You use the window-sizing buttons to the right of the title bar to shrink the window to an icon, restore the window to its previous size, or enlarge the window to full screen. The menu bar contains the command menus available in the active window. The workspace is the area for text and data entry. Horizontal and vertical scroll bars are used to view sections of the window that currently do not appear.

Activating a Module

To activate a module, double-click the icon that appears at the bottom of the WindowWorks window, or choose the module name (or number) from the Window menu. To activate a window when multiple windows are open, click anywhere in the window you want to activate or choose the module name (or number) from the Window menu. You can cycle to the next active window by opening the control menu box for the currently active window and choosing Next. This process makes the next open window the active window. A check mark indicates the currently active module on the Window menu.

If you use the keyboard to activate a module from the Window menu, don't waste time memorizing the numbers that correspond to the modules. The next time you open WindowWorks, the order probably will be different.

T I P

Arranging the Desktop

The desktop is the on-screen area that displays open windows, menus, and icons. You can rearrange your desktop by sizing windows and moving windows. You also can customize your WindowWorks desktop to display the modules you use most frequently. (For more information, see the section "Saving the Desktop Setup" later in this chapter.) The following sections discuss desktop setup tasks.

Using the Mouse

When you move the mouse, a cursor moves on-screen. If your cursor disappears off the edge of the screen, move the mouse around until you see the cursor again. If you move your hand to the edge of the desk and need to continue moving the mouse in that direction, pick up the mouse and put it back in your workspace. Picking up the mouse does not move the cursor.

As you move the mouse to different areas on-screen, the cursor may change shape from an I-beam to an arrow or an hourglass. Window-Works uses the I-beam to enter text and data into an application window, a single-headed arrow to move a window and select menus and commands, and a double-headed arrow to resize windows. An hourglass indicates that the system is processing information and that no other operation can be performed. (The cursor returns to its previous shape when processing is complete.) You most often see the hourglass when you open a program, save a file, or print a file.

Sizing a Window

You can resize windows as necessary to fit open windows neatly on-screen. You can size a window by using your cursor to drag the window borders, by using the control menu box commands, or by using the minimize and restore buttons.

To size a window by dragging the cursor, move the mouse until the cursor reaches the window's edge and changes to a double-headed arrow. Click and hold the mouse button as you drag the cursor in the direction you want to size the window. The window does not change shape, but a shadow border appears to show you the changes you are making. Release the mouse button when the window reaches the desired size.

If you change your mind and want to return the window to its previous size, click the restore button to the right of the title bar.

You also can size a window from the keyboard by using the control menu box. Press Alt-hyphen (-) to view the control menu box commands for the window, and then press S for Size. Use the arrow keys to move the edges of the window. The border appears as a shadow until you press Enter; then the window adjusts to fill the shadow border.

Minimizing a Window

To change an open window into an icon, click the minimize button to the right of the title bar. You can restore the window by double-clicking on the icon or by clicking once on the icon and choosing Restore from the control menu box.

Maximizing a Window

To enlarge an open window to fill the entire screen, click the maximize button. When a window reaches its maximum size, the maximize button changes to a restore button, which is displayed as a two-headed arrow. Click the restore button to return the window to its previous size and placement on-screen.

Moving a Window

You can move a window by dragging the window with the mouse. If you want to arrange open windows for easy viewing, however, you may prefer using the Tile and Cascade options.

To move a window with the mouse, place the cursor in the window's title bar, click and hold the mouse button, and drag the window to its new location. A shadow border indicates the new position for the window. When you release the mouse button, the window moves to fill the shadow border.

You also can move a window from the keyboard by using the control menu box. Press Alt-hyphen to view the window's control menu box commands, press M for Move, and then use the arrow keys to move the shadow border. When you press Enter, the window moves to fill the shadow border.

Tiling the Windows

The Tile option places all currently open WindowWorks modules into evenly sized windows, arranged neatly on-screen for easy viewing (see fig. 1.12).

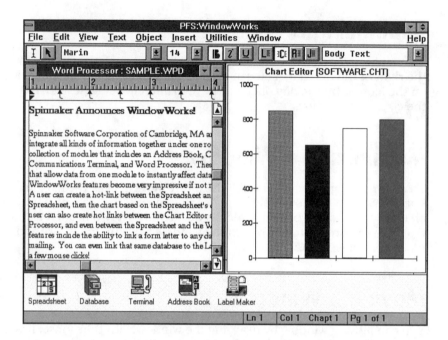

FIG. 1.12

Tiled Word
Processor and
Chart Editor
modules.

To tile open windows, choose the Tile option from the Window menu. The window that was active before you tiled the windows remains the active window and becomes the top-left window in the tile pattern. To switch to another window, select the Next option from the active module's control menu box, or simply click in another window.

You can tile as many windows as you want; however, with all seven modules open, you don't have room to work comfortably in any of the modules.

Cascading the Windows

The Cascade option places all currently open WindowWorks modules into evenly sized windows, stacked in a staggered line with the currently active window at the front (see fig. 1.13).

To cascade the open windows, choose the Cascade option from the Window menu. The currently active window appears at the front. To switch to another window in the cascade, select Next from the active module's control menu box, or click anywhere in the desired window.

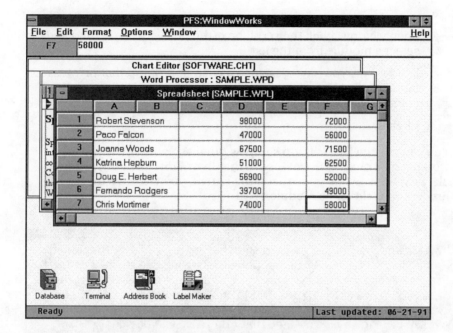

FIG. 1.13

Cascaded Chart
Editor, Word
Processor, and
Spreadsheet
modules.

Saving the Desktop Setup

By moving and resizing the window modules, you can create a desktop
arrangement that suits your work needs. If, for example, you use the
Spreadsheet more frequently than the Word Processor, you can minimize the Word Processor module and open the Spreadsheet module in
a large window.

When you have designed the perfect desktop, you can save the setup
so that your personalized desktop arrangement appears each time you
open WindowWorks.

To save your desktop setup, perform the following steps:

1. Choose the Save Setup command from the active window's Window menu.

   WindowWorks displays a dialog box that prompts you to save a
   single module or the entire desktop arrangement.

2. Click the option button next to Single Module to have the module
   listed in the box to the right of the prompt replace the Word Processor as the large window when you open WindowWorks.

If the module title listed is not the module you want to save as the open window, click the scroll box (the box with the arrow) and select a module from the list.

If, however, you have designed a custom desktop that involves multiple modules, choose the Save Desktop option to save the complete arrangement.

3. Click OK.

You can change the desktop setup as often as you want. If you are working on a chart this week, save the Chart Editor as the open module; next week, when you are writing letters, you can save the Word Processor as the open module.

T I P   The Maximize PFS:WindowWorks on Startup option also is included in this dialog box. Select this option unless you need to view your Program Manager while you are using WindowWorks. Selecting the Maximize PFS:WindowWorks option enables the program to fill the complete screen on startup. This feature provides you with ample workspace and saves you time that otherwise will be spent resizing and maximizing the window.

Getting Help

Help for using WindowWorks is available from any module whenever you need assistance. The program's Help system is thorough and great to have when you need a quick reminder (and this book is out of reach). In all WindowWorks modules, the Help menu is on the far right of the menu bar.

The Help menu has options for getting assistance with the active module, commands, and keyboard shortcuts. The Help menu also has an option that explains the Help system itself (see fig. 1.14).

Usually, you need help with the module in which you are working. To get help with the current module, you can choose the Active Module option from the Help menu. This option works, however, only if you are not stuck in a dialog box.

FIG. 1.14

The Help
window.

Press F1 as a shortcut to get help. Pressing F1 works even if you are
in a dialog box and takes you directly to a Help index concerning the
current module.

T I P

When you are inside the Help Index window, you can scroll or use the
Tab key or arrow keys to move through the list of topics. Double-click a
topic with the mouse, or highlight it, and press Enter. The best way to
use the Help system is by using the mouse. As you move the mouse
around within the Help window, the cursor changes to a hand when it
reaches underlined items associated with help. Just click the item, and
the associated Help screen or box appears. If an item has a solid underline, clicking the item retrieves a new screen with more detailed information. If an item has a dotted underline, you need to click and hold
the mouse button to view an information box that defines the item.

In addition to information about the current module, the index enables
you to access a command reference, a catalog of keyboard shortcuts,
and an extensive glossary of terms used in WindowWorks.

The command buttons come in handy if you find yourself stuck several
levels deep in a detailed Help screen, and you want to see an index
again. The Index command button returns you to the main Window-
Works Help Index, so that you can start working your way down
through the myriad screens again. If you have gone one level too far,
the Back command button returns you to the preceding screen. The
Browse forward and Browse back command buttons enable you to
move quickly through subtopics. If any button is grayed, you are not in
the right place in the Help system to use that button.

The menu bar gives you a great deal of control over the information in the Help screens. If you find yourself repeatedly needing help with the same topics, you have several options to make the process more convenient. You can select a printer with the Printer Setup option on the File menu, and then print the current Help screen with the Print option. Alternatively, you can copy the information to any Windows application by using the Windows clipboard. To begin the process, choose Copy from the Edit menu; the information currently on-screen copies to the clipboard. You then can use the Paste command in any application to add the information. You also can create a WindowWorks document that contains a master list of most frequently used help topics from all your applications.

When you are in the Help window, you can use the Open option in the File menu to switch to any Windows Help system. This feature can be convenient for making a master list of common help topics and for referring to the Windows Help screens for a basic Windows refresher.

You even can personalize your Help system with annotations and bookmarks. You can add a note to yourself about the current topic by choosing the Annotation option from the Edit menu. A dialog box appears for entry of your personal note. When you click OK, the current topic reappears with a Paper Clip icon next to the title to indicate an annotation. Each time you access this topic, the paper clip appears. You can review the annotation with a click on the Paper Clip icon.

If you want to use bookmarks with frequently used topics, choose Define from the Bookmark menu. Enter the topic to be bookmarked, and click OK. The topic then appears as bookmark number 1 on the Bookmark menu, so that you can quickly and easily find the topic next time. When you choose the bookmark from the menu, the screen appears. You also can use the Define option to delete bookmarks you no longer use.

If you forget all these hints, you can get on-line assistance with the Help system by choosing the Using Help option from the Help menu. The Windows Help system is an advanced program in its own right. If you want to get the most from this convenient information source, delve into your Microsoft Windows manual.

T I P

If you have limited disk space, and you plan never to open a Help screen, you can free up substantial space by deleting your Help files. All Windows applications have Help files that end with the extension HLP, which make Help files identifiable for easy deletion.

Exiting the Program

Before you close WindowWorks, remember to save any changes you have made in any module. You do not have to close each module before closing WindowWorks.

To close WindowWorks, choose Exit WindowWorks from the File menu. If you have made changes in any module since you last saved your files, the program displays a prompt that reminds you to save your changes.

If you already are familiar with the Windows control menu box, you may prefer to exit the program by choosing Close from the control menu box.

If you are putting WindowWorks aside for a short period of time, you can minimize the program instead of closing it. Restoring a minimized program is much faster than opening WindowWorks from the Program Manager. This feature comes in handy if you need to return to the Program Manager for quick reference. To minimize the program, use the minimize button on the WindowWorks title bar or the control menu's Minimize option, which also is on the WindowWorks title bar.

When you minimize the program, WindowWorks becomes an icon below your Program Manager. Minimizing the program preserves all your work until you return—even if you did not save your work.

> **CAUTION:** Minimizing a program without saving your work can be dangerous. You should save your work—even if you are going to minimize the program without exiting.

The program still is active (using memory) when minimized. Minimizing, therefore, is different from closing, which makes the program inactive. To return to the minimized program, double-click the Window-Works icon. To return to the program after you exit, you must open the PFS:WindowWorks group window and double-click the WindowWorks icon.

Chapter Summary

The key to minimizing the learning curve when becoming a Window-Works power user is your command of the Microsoft Windows environment. WindowWorks is intuitive, and its operation involves no surprises for anyone comfortable with Windows. The beauty of Windows and its applications is that you have to learn operations only once; then you can apply these operations to all Windows programs.

This statement is true particularly with WindowWorks; each WindowWorks module is just another window. If you can work with a window in your Windows Program Manager, you can work with a module in WindowWorks. If you spend some time experimenting, you quickly will be referring to yourself as a WindowWorks power user.

PART

The Word Processor

I

OUTLINE

Creating a Document

C hapter 2 opens Part I, "The Word Processor." In this chapter, you
learn to create a document. You learn to start the Word Processor, enter text, edit text, copy and paste text, and check for spelling
errors. Finally, you learn to save and print your work.

Starting the Word Processor

When you start the program, WindowWorks opens a new document in
the Word Processor module by default (see fig. 2.1). You can use the
Save Setup option to change the default start-up module; if you have
done so, or if you started the program and subsequently opened a different module, double-click the Word Processor icon to re-open the
Word Processor. Alternatively, you can choose the Word Processor
option from the Window menu.

The word processor is the one WindowWorks module that enables you
to have open more than one document at the same time—up to four
document windows at once. When you open the first new document
window, WindowWorks displays the temporary title, Document1, in
the title bar. Each subsequent new document is named Document2,
Document3, and Document4. As soon as you save each document,
the title bar displays its permanent name.

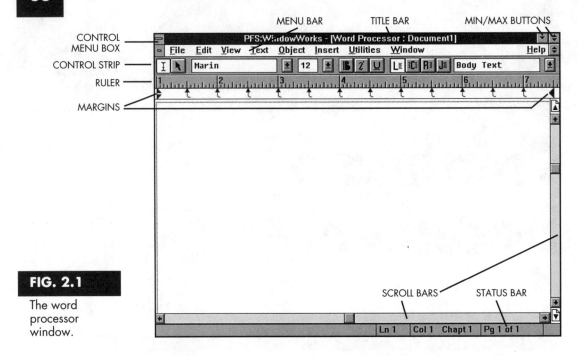

FIG. 2.1

The word processor window.

If you have been working for a while and notice that the title bar is still displaying a temporary title, you probably should save your work. Refer to the section "Saving your Work" in this chapter for more detailed information on saving a document.

After reading Chapter 1, "Getting Started," you already are familiar with most of the WindowWorks Word Processor module on-screen elements: the menu bar, the control menu box, the minimize and maximize buttons, and the scroll bars. You learn in detail about the ruler and the tabs and paragraph indent markers on the ruler in Chapter 3, "Formatting a Document."

Entering Text

The blinking vertical line on the left side of the document window is the *cursor*. The cursor, also referred to as the *text cursor*, *I-beam*, or *insertion point*, indicates the position at which text you type from the keyboard is entered. For new documents, the cursor is positioned in the upper-left corner of the document, unless you do something to move the cursor. The cursor blinks while waiting for you to type text.

You enter text into the word processor by pressing keys on the keyboard. Words you type appear on-screen to the left of the cursor. The word processor knows how many characters and words can fit on a line based on the size of the page, the left and right margin settings, and the size of the current font. When the word processor cannot fit any more text on a line, the cursor moves down to the next line. You do not need to press Enter to move the cursor to the next line, unless you want to end the current paragraph and start a new one.

Pressing the Enter key at the end of a line creates a *hard line break*. Text that wraps automatically to the next line is called a *soft line break* or *word wrap*.

Inserting Text

After you type some text, you may realize that you left out a letter or a word. You can move the cursor to any position within the text by using the mouse or arrow keys, and type the missing characters. New text is inserted at the cursor, which pushes existing text to the right or down to the next line.

If, however, you want to replace existing text rather than insert new characters within existing text, press the Ins (Insert) key on your keyboard. Pressing the Ins key turns the overtype feature on and off. When the overtype feature is on, OVR is displayed on the right side of the status bar.

If you want to replace existing text with new text, the easiest method is to highlight the text to be replaced, and then type. The highlighted text is deleted as soon as you press any key. Be careful, however, because unlike text deleted with the Del or Backspace keys, text you replace by using this method cannot be restored.

T I P

To move the cursor by using the mouse, move the mouse until the insertion point appears at the desired point on-screen. To move the cursor by using the keyboard, you can use the key combinations listed in Table 2.1.

Table 2.1. Cursor Movement Keys

Cursor Movement	Keys
Move left one character	Left Arrow
Move right one character	Right Arrow
Move to the beginning of the line	Home
Move to the end of the line	End
Move up one line	Up Arrow
Move down one line	Down Arrow
Move up one screen	Page Up
Move down one screen	Page Down
Move up one paragraph	Ctrl-Up Arrow
Move down one paragraph	Ctrl-Down Arrow
Move to the beginning of the document	Ctrl-Home
Move to the end of the document	Ctrl-End

Several handy keyboard shortcuts enable you to move to another place in the document without moving the cursor. In other words, you can look through the document without losing your marked place. These keyboard shortcuts are listed in Table 2.2.

Table 2.2. Keyboard Shortcuts

Screen movement	Keys
Move up one screen without moving cursor	Minus sign (-) on the the number keypad
Move down one screen without moving cursor	Plus sign (+) on the number keypad
Move up one page without moving cursor	Ctrl-minus sign (-) on the number keypad
Move down one page without moving cursor	Ctrl-plus sign (+) on the number keypad

Correcting Typing Errors

You can deal with typos and misspellings in at least two ways: finish typing and use the spell checker to find and correct mistakes, or correct errors as you make them. The first option—using the Word Processor module's built-in spell checker—is discussed later in this chapter.

The second option—correcting mistakes as you type—is easy to implement by using the Backspace and Del keys. Press the Backspace key to delete text to the left of the cursor, and press the Del key to delete text to the right of the cursor. You can backspace over one character at a time by pressing and then releasing the Backspace key. Alternatively, holding down the Backspace key deletes characters quickly until you release the key. Using the Backspace key is the most common method of deleting small amounts of text. If you need to delete a whole page of text, however, backspacing over one character at a time can be tedious. (For more information on quick and easy text deletion, see the section "Selecting Text" later in this chapter.)

The Del key functions like the Backspace key, except that pressing Del deletes text to the right of the cursor without moving the cursor itself.

Text you delete by using the Backspace or Del keys can be un-deleted, if you have not moved the cursor or pressed any other key since deleting the text. To restore text deleted with the Backspace or Del keys, select the Undelete command from the Edit menu. If, for example, you deleted a five-character word by pressing the Backspace key five times, choose Undelete from the Edit menu, and the whole word reappears. If, however, you deleted the word and then typed another character or moved the cursor, the Undelete command is *grayed* (unavailable for selection), and your deleted text cannot be recovered.

Editing Text

The best feature in word processing software is that you can create and edit documents simultaneously. In other words, you don't have to complete a document, print it, and then go back and edit your work. You can move text, delete or replace text, and change the font at the same time that you're entering new text. Unless you're just correcting typos, serious editing also involves selecting a group of text. The word processor editing functions are discussed in the following sections.

Selecting Text

You can select text in two ways: by dragging the mouse or by pressing the direction keys (arrow keys, PgUp, PgDn, Home, and End) in conjunction with the Shift key. You probably will want to use both methods at different times; therefore, you should take time to familiarize yourself with the two text selection methods.

To select text by using the mouse, follow these steps:

1. Move the I-beam pointer to the beginning or end of the text you want to select.

2. Click and hold down the left mouse button and drag in any direction.

   WindowWorks highlights the selected text by displaying it in *reverse video*, which is white on black. When the text you want to select is highlighted, release the mouse button. The text remains highlighted until you perform an operation on the text or click the mouse button.

T I P   You can select an entire word by double-clicking anywhere in the word.

At this point, you can edit the selected text. Be careful, however, because selected text is vulnerable. If you type anything from the keyboard, the selected text is replaced by whatever you type. Text you replace in this manner cannot be retrieved.

To select text by using the keyboard, follow these steps:

1. Move the cursor to the beginning or end of the text you want to select.

2. Press and hold the Shift key.

3. Press the arrow, PgUp, PgDn, Home, or End keys to highlight the text.

T I P

If you prefer using the keyboard to using the mouse, WindowWorks provides several keyboard shortcuts for selecting text. With the Word Processor module open, choose Keyboard from the Help menu. Then choose Selection Keys to see a complete list of text selection shortcuts. Notice that these shortcuts are the movement shortcuts listed in Table 2.1 and are executed while holding down the Shift key.

To select all the text in your document, press the Ctrl key and the number five key on the numeric keypad with NumLock on. You may want to select your entire document to change the document's font size, for example. (A better way to change font styles, however, is to format your document by using the Styles option, which is discussed in Chapter 4.)

If you have selected text by using the mouse, you can extend your selection in any direction by using the keyboard. Whether the selection is extended or shortened depends on which side of the selection you began. If, for example, you select text from left to right by using the mouse, you can extend the selection one character at a time to the right by holding down the Shift key and pressing the right-arrow key; pressing the left-arrow key deselects one character at a time.

Likewise, if you select text from the right to the left with the mouse, holding down the Shift key and pressing the left-arrow key extends the selection to the left; pressing the right-arrow key deselects characters to the right. Unfortunately, if you select text with the keyboard, you cannot extend your selection with the mouse.

 Double-clicking a word to select it is the same as selecting from left to right.

Pressing the right-arrow key moves the cursor to the end of the selected text block; pressing the left-arrow key moves the cursor to the beginning of the selected text block.

To deselect text, click the mouse button anywhere outside the selection, or press an arrow key.

Cutting, Copying, and Pasting Text

The Edit menu's Cut, Copy, and Paste commands are among the most frequently used editing options. You can use these commands to rearrange text; you also can move selected text to a different document, to different modules, such as the Spreadsheet or Database, or to different Windows programs.

The Copy and Cut commands copy, or duplicate, selected text and place it on the Windows clipboard. The Windows *clipboard* is a temporary holding area; text you copy or cut remains on the clipboard until you again choose Copy or Cut or until you exit Windows.

The difference between the Copy and Cut options is that Copy leaves the selected text in your document after moving a copy of the text to the clipboard; the Cut command deletes the selected text from your document after moving the text to the clipboard.

To copy text to another place in your document, perform the following steps:

1. Select the text by using the mouse or the Shift and arrow keys.

2. Choose Copy from the Edit menu.

3. Use the mouse or arrow keys to move the cursor to the point at which you want to place the duplicated text.

4. Choose Paste from the Edit menu.

   The text now appears in two places in your document.

The Copy command can be a great time-saver. Suppose that you are writing a paper about mathematics and you need to make several references to Guillaume François Antoine de l'Hôpital, a French nobleman who wrote the first calculus text. Instead of typing *Guillaume François Antoine de l'Hôpital* each time, select the name, choose Copy from the Edit menu, and then choose Paste to make a duplicate. Notice that when you copy text, all formatting information is copied as well.

T I P   Instead of choosing Copy or Paste from the Edit menu, you can use the keyboard shortcut keys Ctrl-Ins for Copy and Shift-Ins for Paste.

Moving Text

To move text, you can use the Cut command. If you want to move one paragraph above another paragraph, for example, follow these steps:

1. Select all the text in the second paragraph.

2. Choose Cut from the Edit menu (see fig. 2.2). (The keyboard short-cut for Cut is Shift-Del.)

3. Move the cursor to a position above the first paragraph.

4. Choose Paste.

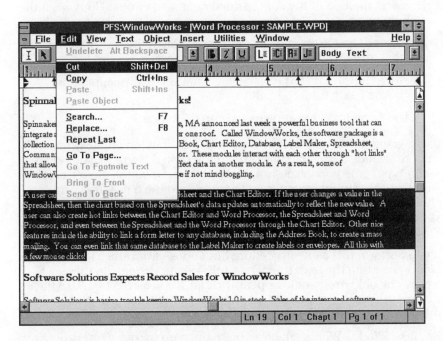

FIG. 2.2

The Cut com-mand on the Edit menu and a word processor document with selected text ready to be cut.

CAUTION: Cut text maintains only a temporary existence on the clipboard. If you choose Cut or Copy again before pasting cut text, the text is gone and is replaced by the newly cut or copied text. If you exit Windows, all information on the clipboard is lost.

Moving Text between Documents

If you find yourself about to type a lengthy text selection used in a previous document, you can save time by using the Copy command to duplicate the text in your new document. If you want to use almost all of the old document, copying the entire document to a new file name may be best. To learn this procedure, refer to the section "Saving Your Work" later in this chapter.

To copy text from one WindowWorks word processor document to another, follow these steps:

1. Select the text in the source document, and choose Copy from the Edit menu.

2. Choose Open from the File menu, and select the destination document into which you want to paste the text.

3. Move the cursor to the place you want the text to appear, and choose Paste from the Edit menu.

   The same text now appears in both documents.

If, for example, you are writing a cover letter for a job application and want to include a previously written paragraph describing your current job, retyping the paragraph is a waste of time. Open the old letter, select the paragraph that you want to insert into the new letter, and choose Copy. Then choose Open to open the new letter, move the cursor to the point at which you want to insert the paragraph, and choose Paste.

If you perform this same procedure but choose Cut rather than Copy before inserting the text, the paragraph will appear only in the new letter. The old letter would appear without the selected text. Use the Cut feature when you need to move text from one document to another.

Because WindowWorks enables you to open up to four word processor documents at once, you can display the old and new documents in a *tiled*, or side-by-side, fashion (see fig. 2.3). Moving text between tiled documents is almost the same as moving text within the same document. To learn how to tile two documents, refer to the "Opening Documents" section later in this chapter.

If you exit WindowWorks and return to the Program Manager, you can open the clipboard to see whether the text you copied is available to other applications, such as Write and Notepad (see fig. 2.4). By default, the clipboard icon appears in the Main group.

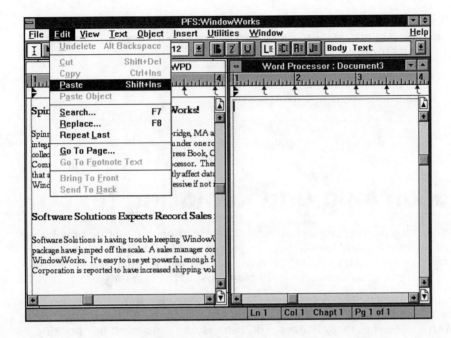

FIG. 2.3

Two documents tiled.

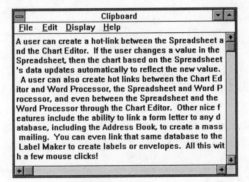

FIG. 2.4

Clipboard indicating copied text.

Because the text you copy remains on the clipboard until you cut or copy something else, you can paste WindowWorks text into other Windows programs. Formatting information is not retained when you paste text between different programs. In other words, if you copied italicized text from WindowWorks and pasted the text into Windows Write, the characters would not be italicized. If, however, you pasted the selection back into the WindowWorks Word Processor, the text would be italicized.

To become more familiar with copying, cutting, and pasting between Windows programs and with using the Windows clipboard, review your Microsoft Windows documentation.

Because you are likely to use the Cut, Copy, and Paste commands frequently, you may want to memorize and use the following keyboard shortcuts for these three commands:

Command	Keyboard Shortcut
Copy	Ctrl-Ins
Cut	Shift-Del
Paste	Shift-Ins

Searching and Replacing Text

You can save yourself a great deal of aggravation and editing time by knowing when and how to use the Search and Replace commands. Instead of looking line by line through a document for text that you want to edit, you can use Search or Replace to find the text for you.

The Search command searches through the document, finds the first occurrence of the desired text, and then selects the text so that you can make necessary changes. You can resume the search by choosing Repeat Last from the Edit menu. The Replace command finds the desired text and replaces it with new text that you specify.

To search for a word, a group of words, or text embedded within words, perform the following steps:

1. Move the cursor to the beginning of the document. (Pressing Ctrl-Home is the easiest way to move the cursor to the beginning of the document.)

2. Choose the Search command from the Edit menu (or press F7) to display the Search dialog box (see fig. 2.5).

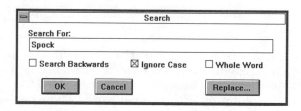

FIG. 2.5

The Search dialog box.

3. In the Search For box, type the text you want WindowWorks to find.

4. Click OK.

WindowWorks scans the document for the text and highlights the first occurrence. To find the next occurrence of the search text, choose the Edit menu's Repeat Last command, which repeats the most recent Search or Replace command using the same text. Alternatively, choose the Search command (F7) again; the last search text you entered appears in the Search For box as a default.

WindowWorks can search for any text that can be entered from the keyboard (up to 51 characters) but cannot locate tabs or carriage returns. The program can recognize spaces, which enables you to search for groups of words such as *We the people*.

Suppose that while writing a lengthy report on Chinese customs, you decide to add a few paragraphs to the section titled "Cuisine." Rather than looking for the "Cuisine" section by moving through the entire document, you can select Search, type **Cuisine** in the Search For box, and click OK. WindowWorks finds the word for you, and you can begin editing.

Setting Search Options

WindowWorks can search forward to the end of a document or backward to the beginning of a document from the cursor location. By default, WindowWorks searches forward, and the search always begins at the current cursor location. If you want to search a document from beginning to end, place the cursor at the beginning of the document before selecting Search. If you are well into the creation of your document and want to search for something you have typed, you can leave the cursor at its current location, select Search, and click the Search Backwards check box in the Search dialog box.

By default, the Search command is not case sensitive. If, for example, you typed **Cuisine** in the Search For box, WindowWorks locates *cuisine*, *CUISINE*, or any case combination unless you turn off Ignore Case by clicking the Ignore Case check box. With Ignore Case unchecked, WindowWorks locates the exact text that you type in the Search For box by looking for exact matches of uppercase and lowercase letters. Using the preceding example—with **Cuisine** entered in the Search For box and Ignore Case unchecked—Cuisine would be found, but *cuisine* and *CUISINE* would be ignored.

You can search for whole words or text embedded within other words. If you typed **win** in the Search For box, for example, WindowWorks locates *windows*, *winter*, *Irwin*, and any other word containing *win* unless you turn on the Whole Word option by clicking the Whole Word check box. If you select the Whole Word check box, WindowWorks locates the word *win* only.

WindowWorks does not search for text in text frames or tables.

If WindowWorks cannot find the text typed in the Search For box, the program displays an explanatory message. If WindowWorks does not find the search text, you may want to choose Search again and change the direction of the search. If the text you are seeking still isn't found, the text doesn't exist in your document.

T I P   You can paste text into the Search For box to search for text that you copied to the Windows clipboard. When the Search dialog box is open, however, you cannot choose Paste from the Edit menu; the program beeps if you click outside the dialog box. Instead, press Shift-Ins (the keyboard shortcut for Paste) to paste the text into the Search For box.

Replacing Text

Suppose that after writing your report on Chinese customs, you realize that throughout the paper you typed *Peking* rather than the more modern spelling *Beijing*. Deleting every occurrence of *Peking* and typing in *Beijing* is quite a task—even with the help of the Search command. The Replace function can make this change for you.

To replace text with new text that you specify, perform the following steps:

1. Move the cursor to the beginning of the document. (Ctrl-Home is the easiest way to move the cursor to the beginning of the document.)

2. Choose Replace from the Edit menu (or press F8). You also can choose Replace by clicking the Replace button in the Search dialog box, if you already have typed in your search text and want to specify replacement text.

   The Replace dialog box appears (see fig. 2.6).

3. Type the text you want WindowWorks to find in the Search For box.

4. In the Replace With box, type the text that is to replace the Search For text.

5. Click Start.

```
┌──────────────────────────────────────────────────┐
│ ─                      Replace                      │
├──────────────────────────────────────────────────┤
│ Search For:                                         │
│ │Peking                                          │  │
│ Replace With:                                       │
│ │Beijing                                         │  │
│ ☐ Search Backwards   ☒ Ignore Case   ☐ Whole Word  │
│ ☐ Replace All   [ Start ]  [ Replace ]   [ Cancel ] │
└──────────────────────────────────────────────────┘
```

FIG. 2.6

The Replace
dialog box.

WindowWorks searches the document for the text you typed in
the Search For box and stops at the first occurrence of the text.
You then have to decide whether you want to replace this occurrence with the text you typed in the Replace With box or if you
want to move on to the next occurrence.

To replace the selected text with the Replace With text, click Replace. To leave the highlighted text unchanged and continue the
search, click Skip. Continue this process until the search is complete.

The Replace dialog box's Search Backwards, Ignore Case, and Whole
Word options work like their counterparts in the Search dialog box.

In the preceding example, you wanted to replace every occurrence of
Peking with *Beijing*. Therefore, clicking Replace for every occurrence of
Peking is a waste of time. If you type **Peking** in the Search For box,
Beijing in the Replace With box, and turn on the Replace All option by
clicking the Replace All check box, WindowWorks automatically
changes every occurrence of *Peking* to *Beijing* without prompting you
to select Replace or Skip.

> **CAUTION:** Using Replace All can be dangerous if the search
> string and replace string are not exactly correct.

WindowWorks will substitute your Replace With string exactly as you
typed it. If you happen to have a paragraph of all capital letters, for
example, WindowWorks will not convert the Replace With string to all
caps unless you typed it in that way.

Checking Your Spelling

As you write, you occasionally encounter words that are difficult to
spell, and you may make errors that you don't catch immediately. The
WindowWorks spell checker can help you solve these problems. By
using the Spell Check command, you can check for misspellings in an
entire document, a portion of a document, or a single word.

Using the spell checker is not a substitute for proofreading your document. If you have typed *Just Say On* rather than *Just Say No*, for example, the spell checker will not find any errors, because *on* is a correctly spelled word. WindowWorks has no way of knowing what you really meant to say; the program can identify only non-standard words.

To check for misspelled words, perform the following steps:

1. Choose Spell Check from the Utilities menu (or press F9).

   The Check Spelling dialog box appears (see fig. 2.7).

FIG. 2.7

The Check Spelling dialog box.

2. Select one of the three options in the dialog box by clicking a button.

   To check the spelling of your entire document, click Begin or press Enter. Check Entire Document is the default option and is selected when the Check Spelling dialog box appears.

If you already have checked the beginning of your document and want to save time by checking only the remainder, place the cursor at the beginning of the section to be checked, choose Spell Check, select Check From Cursor Position, and click Begin. All text from the cursor position to the end of the document is checked for spelling errors.

If you need to check the spelling of a word or a small section of your document, highlight the text to be checked, choose Spell Check from the Utilities menu, select Check Selection in the dialog box, and click Begin. The highlighted text is checked for spelling errors. A grayed Check Selection option indicates that you have not selected any text to check. Click Cancel (or press Esc), select the text to be checked, and try again.

The only difference among these options is the portion of the document checked for spelling errors. If no spelling errors are found in the section or document being checked, an on-screen message informs you that the spelling check is finished.

If WindowWorks finds a group of characters that cannot be identified as a standard English word, the Spell Check dialog box appears. The Spell Check dialog box displays the questionable word and offers you several options (see fig. 2.8).

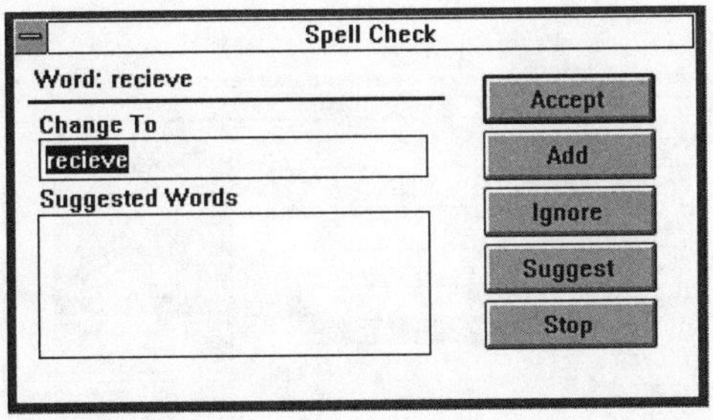

```
┌─────────────────────────────────────────┐
│ ─            Spell Check                 │
│ Word: recieve                            │
│ ──────────────────────────  ┌─────────┐  │
│ Change To                   │ Accept  │  │
│ ┌─────────────────────────┐ └─────────┘  │
│ │recieve                  │ ┌─────────┐  │
│ └─────────────────────────┘ │  Add    │  │
│ Suggested Words             └─────────┘  │
│ ┌─────────────────────────┐ ┌─────────┐  │
│ │                         │ │ Ignore  │  │
│ │                         │ └─────────┘  │
│ │                         │ ┌─────────┐  │
│ │                         │ │ Suggest │  │
│ │                         │ └─────────┘  │
│ │                         │ ┌─────────┐  │
│ └─────────────────────────┘ │  Stop   │  │
│                             └─────────┘  │
└─────────────────────────────────────────┘
```

FIG. 2.8

The Spell Check dialog box.

The word in question appears in the Change To box. At this point, you have several options. These options are discussed in the following sections.

Ignoring a Word

Don't be surprised if the word selected actually is a correctly spelled word. WindowWorks may not recognize the name of your company (or even your name) as a standard English word. You can, however, teach WindowWorks to recognize certain words. If the selected word is spelled as you want it to appear, click Ignore; WindowWorks continues checking. After you click Ignore, WindowWorks does not stop at other occurrences of that word in the document. If, however, you want to leave this single occurrence unchanged but need to correct future oc-currences of the same word, click Accept to accept the word without affecting the rest of the spelling check.

Typing the Correct Spelling

If the selected word is spelled incorrectly and you know the correct spelling, type the correct spelling in the Change To box, and click Ac-cept to proceed.

54

Listing Suggestions

If the word is spelled incorrectly and you are not sure of the correct spelling, click Suggest. A list of correctly spelled words appears in the Suggested Words box (see fig. 2.9).

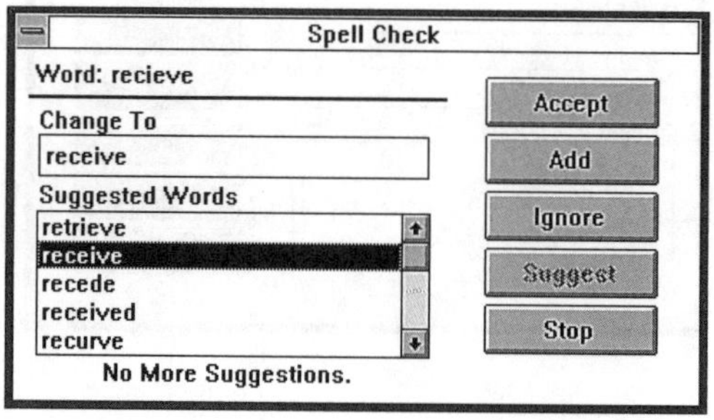

FIG. 2.9

Possible replacements in the Version 1.0 Suggested Words box.

```
┌─────────────────────────────────────────────────┐
│ ─                    Spell Check                  │
│ Word: recieve                                     │
│ ─────────────────────────────      ┌──────────┐  │
│ Change To                           │  Accept  │  │
│ │receive                      │     └──────────┘  │
│ Suggested Words                     ┌──────────┐  │
│ │retrieve                   ↑│      │   Add    │  │
│ │receive                     │      └──────────┘  │
│ │recede                      │      ┌──────────┐  │
│ │received                    │      │  Ignore  │  │
│ │recurve                    ↓│      └──────────┘  │
│        No More Suggestions.         ┌──────────┐  │
│                                     │ Suggest  │  │
│                                     └──────────┘  │
│                                     ┌──────────┐  │
│                                     │   Stop   │  │
│                                     └──────────┘  │
└─────────────────────────────────────────────────┘
```

WindowWorks compiles this list from all words similar to the word in the Change To box. If your initial spelling is way off, however, the word that you intended may not appear in the Suggested Words list. If this situation occurs, you can take another guess at the spelling, type the word into the Change To box, and click Suggest again. WindowWorks displays a different list of words from which you can choose.

When you see the spelling that you intended, select that word from the list. The selected word appears in the Change To box. Click Accept to replace the originally misspelled word with the correct spelling and continue with the spelling check. WindowWorks will keep suggesting alternate spellings until you choose one of the words or its dictionary is exhausted. When WindowWorks runs out of words to suggest, the words No More Suggestions appear below the Suggested Words list.

Adding Words to the Dictionary

If WindowWorks does not recognize certain correctly spelled words, such as your name, your company name, or the name of a product, you can add the words to the WindowWorks user dictionary so that the spell checker no longer selects them. To add a word to the user dictionary, click Add when the word appears in the Change To box. The word is no longer selected as misspelled, unless you delete the word from the user dictionary.

The user dictionary containing your personal list of words for the spell checker is stored in a file called USER.DCT. This file is located in the

EXEC subdirectory of your WINWORKS directory. To keep your dictionary from taking up unnecessary disk space, you can edit the USER.DCT file and delete words that you no longer need.

To edit the USER.DCT file, perform the following steps:

1. Choose Open from the File menu.

2. Select ASCII(.TXT) from the Type scroll list.

3. Select the WINWORKS directory, and then select the EXEC subdirectory in the Directories list box.

4. Type **USER.DCT** in the Filename box or select USER.DCT in the Files scroll list so that USER.DCT appears in the Filename box.

5. Click OK.

   The USER.DCT file appears in the word processor window (see fig. 2.10).

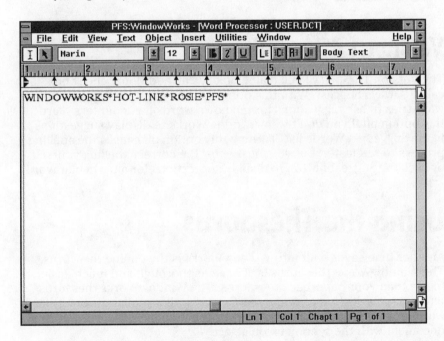

FIG. 2.10

USER.DCT file listed in the word processor window.

The USER.DCT file appears as a list of words (all in capital letters) with an asterisk (*) after each word. No spaces or commas exist between words. You can delete words from the list, but you must be certain that the list maintains the same format.

6. Delete words that you no longer need, and be certain that the last word on the list is followed by an asterisk (*).

7. Choose Save As from the File menu.

8. Select ASCII(.TXT) from the Type scroll list.

9. Be certain that C:\WINWORKS\EXEC appears in the Path field. If this is not the case, select WINWORKS and then EXEC from the Directories scroll list.

10. Type **USER.DCT** in the Filename box and click OK.

11. Click YES when the prompt asks whether you want to overwrite the existing file.

You can delete words from the user dictionary more easily by using the Spell Check command. Use the method described in the preceding steps only if your user dictionary is getting very large and is using an inordinate amount of disk space.

Version 1.1 Variations

The Version 1.1 Spell Check dialog box has an additional check box called Always Suggest. With this option turned on, WindowWorks always tries to list suggestions for unknown words it encounters. Turn this option off if you don't want WindowWorks to display suggestions in the Suggested Words list. Turning this option off causes the spelling process to run faster, but you must enter the correct spelling yourself, or click the Suggest button to display suggestions for a particular word.

Using the Thesaurus

Another time-saver built into WindowWorks is the on-line thesaurus. The WindowWorks thesaurus is at least as thorough and much easier to use than your paperback thesaurus. The WindowWorks thesaurus offers you a selection of synonyms (words with a similar meaning) for a word in your document. The thesaurus then replaces the word in your document with the synonym you select.

To replace a word with a synonym, perform the following steps:

1. Place the cursor anywhere in the word that you want to replace with a synonym.

2. Choose Thesaurus from the Utilities menu, or press Shift-F9.

The Thesaurus dialog box appears. In Version 1.1, the selected word appears in a text box to the left of a list of synonyms (see fig. 2.11). In Version 1.0, the selected word appears directly above the list of synonyms.

3. Select a synonym from the list.

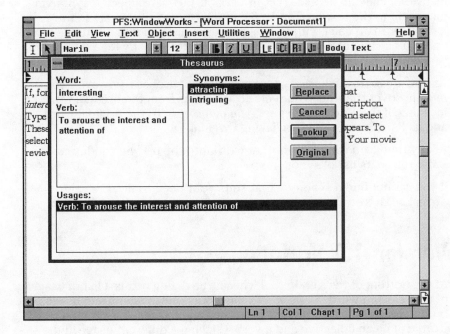

FIG. 2.11

The Thesaurus dialog box for Version 1.1.

4. Click Replace to replace the original word with the selected synonym in Version 1.1. Click OK in Version 1.0.

   Your document reappears with the synonym substituted for the original word.

You can use the thesaurus in many situations. If, for example, you are writing a review of an interesting movie but you think that *interesting* is too mundane, you can use the thesaurus to find a more suitable description. Type **interesting** into your document, move the cursor anywhere in the word, and select Thesaurus from the Utilities menu (or press Shift-F9). A list of two synonyms appears in Version 1.1 (four in Version 1.0). To select *intriguing* to replace *interesting*, click the word intriguing and click Replace. Your movie review reappears with the word intriguing substituted for interesting.

Synonym Swapping

If none of the synonyms on the selection list is quite what you want, you can see a list of synonyms of the synonyms. Select a synonym from the selection list, and click Lookup in Version 1.1 (Swap in Version 1.0) instead of clicking Replace (OK in Version 1.0). The selected synonym moves up to the text box, and a list of its synonyms appears in the selection list. You can continue this process until you find a suitable synonym. You can click Replace (OK in Version 1.0) at any time during this procedure to place the currently selected synonym into the document.

As you move through the synonym swapping process, however, you may discover that the synonyms stray too far from the original word's meaning. If this situation occurs, you can return to the original word and its list of synonyms by clicking Original.

At any time, you can type another word into the text box and press Enter to see its list of synonyms.

If you cannot find a synonym that suits your needs, click Cancel (or press Esc) to return to your document without changing any words.

Version 1.1 Variations

At the bottom of the Version 1.1 Thesaurus dialog box is a list of usages of the selected word. Some words have only one meaning and usage, but many words have different meanings and usages. For example, a word can be an adjective and a verb. Clicking a different usage in the Usage list changes the list of synonyms for that word.

Saving Your Work

You need to save your document if you want to retrieve it for future use. The saving process includes naming the document and copying the document to your hard disk, where the file remains until being opened again or deleted. You also can save your document to a floppy disk rather than your hard disk; however, saving to your hard disk and later copying the document to a floppy disk usually is more efficient.

Until saved with a file name, your work is extremely vulnerable. Any number of incidents, such as a power failure, the fatal `Unrecoverable Application Error` that you occasionally encounter in Windows programs, and others, can result in the loss of your entire document, which leaves you with no record of your work and no option but to retype every word.

When you save a document, the file name appears on the title bar of the document window. The file name's display is helpful if you have multiple word processor documents open at the same time. If the title bar of your word processor window displays Word Processor:Document1, you are working on a document that has not been saved. *Document1* is the name that WindowWorks assigns to the document in the first word processor window you open. The default document title in the second window opened is *Document2*, and so on. If you have done more work than you are willing to retype and your document still is named *Document1*, save your work with a file name.

To save a new document, follow these steps:

1. Choose Save from the File menu (or press Ctrl-S).

   The Save As dialog box appears (see fig. 2.12).

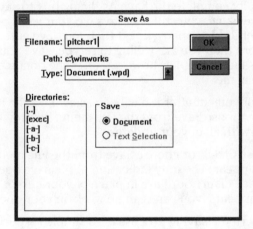

FIG. 2.12

The Save As
dialog box.

2. In the Directories selection list, select the drive letter and directory name for the directory in which you want to store the document. The currently selected drive and directory appear in the Path field. WINWORKS is the default directory; if you want to store your document in the WINWORKS directory, proceed to Step 3.

3. Type the file name for your document in the Filename text box. The file name should be fewer than eight characters. Do not type an extension (the three characters after the dot), because WindowWorks automatically gives all documents a WPD extension to indicate that the file is a word processor document.

T I P For each WindowWorks module, files are given an extension that indicates the module: WPD for the Word Processor, CHT for the Chart Editor, WPL for the Spreadsheet, and WDF for the Database. Although you can save a file with a different extension, allowing WindowWorks to save files with the automatic extension enables the program to find files more quickly.

4. Click OK.

The document now is saved on your hard disk with the file name you selected, and you can resume work on your document. The next time you want to open the document, look for the file name that you selected in the preceding process.

After you initially complete the Save As dialog box to save your document with a file name, you still need to save your work periodically. The same general rule applies: if text that you have entered since your last save is more than you are willing to retype, save your work again. The process is much simpler, however, after the document has been assigned a file name.

To save your document after it has been assigned a file name, simply press Ctrl-S or choose Save from the File menu. WindowWorks saves the document with all of your updates.

When you press Ctrl-S (or choose Save from the File menu), a dialog box does not appear. The only indication of the save operation is the brief appearance of an hourglass in place of your cursor. When the hourglass disappears, you can resume work on your document.

Because the periodic saving process is so simple (especially if you use the Ctrl-S keyboard shortcut), you should save your work frequently. Get into the habit of pressing Ctrl-S every time you take a break from working on your document.

Saving a Document with a New File Name

At some point, you may want to rename an existing file. This procedure is valuable if you want to edit an existing document and keep a copy of the original version as well. If you were to open and edit a document and then use the Save command, the edited version would overwrite the old version, and you would have no copy of the original, unedited document. The Save As command enables you to save copies of both versions with different names.

The process of saving an existing document with a new name is similar to saving a document for the first time. To save a document with a new name, perform the following steps:

1. Choose Save As from the File menu, or press F12.

   The Save As dialog box appears.

2. The current file name is selected in the Filename text box. Type a new file name for the document.

3. Click OK.

You don't need to save the copy on your hard drive. The Save As command is a convenient way to make a copy on a floppy disk without going to DOS. Be certain that you change back to the C drive (if that's your hard drive) before removing the floppy disk from its drive. Windows remembers the last drive you saved to when you try to save again.

When the dialog box disappears, the document reappears with its new name. Your old document is safely on your hard disk, unchanged from the last time it was saved. You now have two identical documents with two different file names; they will not be identical if you made changes before selecting Save As. To access the original file with the original file name, you must open the document from the File menu.

Suppose that you have written a letter (saved as PITCHER1.WPD) to Nolan Ryan asking for pitching tips. You want to send the same letter with minor modifications to Roger Clemens. You can open the Nolan Ryan letter (PITCHER1.WPD), choose Save As from the File menu, type **PITCHER2.WPD** in the Filename box, and click OK. You can edit and save the new file (PITCHER2.WPD) for Mr. Clemens. You then have two different letters with two different filenames, and you need only type a few words rather than the whole letter.

Saving a Text Selection as a New File

You do not need to save an entire document with a new name. You may want to save only a selection if you are working on a large document, such as a book, and you want to save part of it to a separate file, such as a chapter. If you want to create a new document that contains only an excerpt from an existing document, perform the following steps:

1. Open the existing document.

2. Select the portion of text that you want to use as a new document.

3. Choose Save As from the File menu.

4. Select the Text Selection option by clicking the button next to Text Selection. (If the button is grayed, you need to press Cancel or Esc, return to the document, and select some text.)

5. Type a name for the new file containing the text excerpt in the Filename text box.

6. Click OK.

The original document appears and is unchanged. Unlike saving an entire document with a new name, saving a text selection with a new name returns you to the old document. To access the new document containing the text selection, you must open the document from the File menu.

Saving a Document in Another File Format

If you need to save your document as a WindowWorks template or export your document for use in another program or computer, you can use the Save As option.

Usually, when you save a document in WindowWorks, the Type field in the Save As dialog box displays Document(.wpd). This setting is the default file format and is the normal format for WindowWorks files.

If you are planning to open the file in another program, you can save the file in an ASCII(.TXT) format, ASCII Breaks(.TXT) format, or RTF (Rich Text Format). ASCII (American Standard Code for Information Interchange) is a file format that can be used by most word processors and your Windows Notepad. If you save your file in ASCII format, all text is saved; however, no graphics, objects, styles, or formatting are saved. WindowWorks can save two types of ASCII files: plain ASCII and ASCII text with line breaks every 80 characters. WindowWorks also can save RTF (Rich Text Format) files, which contain all text, graphics, styles, and formatting. RTF files can be used in many programs, including programs on the Apple Macintosh.

To save a WindowWorks document in an alternative file format, perform the following steps:

1. Choose Save As from the File menu.

2. Click the scroll button in the Type text box, and select a file format from the list (see fig. 2.13).

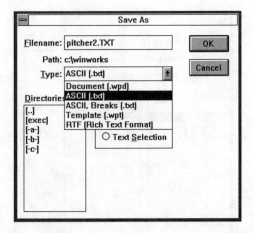

FIG. 2.13

Format selection
list in the Save As
dialog box.

3. When you select a file format, WindowWorks changes the extension on the current file name to the standard extension for the selected format. You can modify the file name if necessary.

4. Click OK.

The file is saved in the selected format with the new file name. The new file appears when the Save As dialog box closes. Your original document still exists in WindowWorks standard format, just as it was saved last.

You also can use this option to save a document as a WindowWorks document template. You learn how to create and use document templates in Chapter 4.

Opening Documents

When you first open WindowWorks or the WindowWorks Word Processor module, no document appears in the word processor workspace. You can start work on a new document or open an existing document.

To open a previously created document, follow these steps:

1. Choose Open from the File menu, or press Ctrl-O.

   The Open dialog box appears (see fig. 2.14).

2. Select the drive and directory that contain the file to be opened by clicking the drive letter and directory name in the Directories selection list.

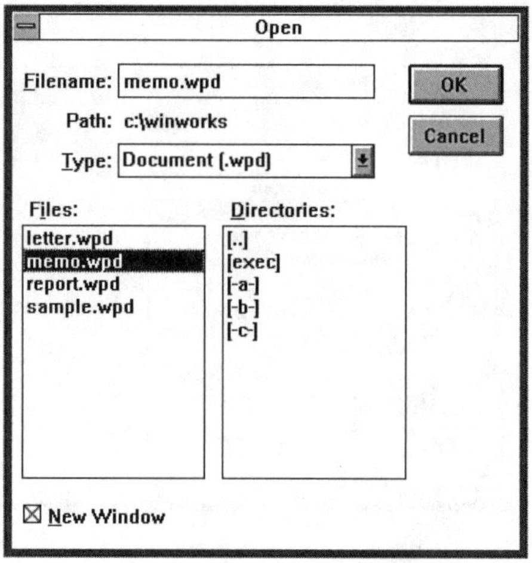

FIG. 2.14

The Open dialog box.

3. Select the file to be opened from the Files selection list, or type the file name in the Filename text box.

4. Click OK.

The selected document appears in the word processor window. If you have not saved the document that was in the word processor window before you opened a new file, a prompt reminds you to save the existing document, because the document that you just opened is about to replace the previously opened document in the word processor window.

Opening Multiple Documents

The WindowWorks word processor enables you to open up to four documents at a time in four separate windows. If you do not want the document that you are opening to replace the current document in the word processor window, you can open the document in its own window. To open a document in a new window, select the New Window check box in the Open dialog box (refer to fig. 2.14).

You can repeat this process until four documents are open. You then can use the Tile or Cascade command from the Window menu to arrange the document windows. Alternatively, you can minimize all but the document that you currently are using; the other documents still are on-screen as icons handy for editing. If you are going to be doing a great deal of cutting, copying, and pasting among documents, opening documents in multiple windows is easier than closing and opening documents each time you want to perform an editing operation.

Opening Documents in Other File Formats

You also can open documents created in other programs. You can open documents that have been saved as ASCII(.TXT), RTF (Rich Text Format), BetterWorking format for documents created in Spinnaker BetterWorking Eight-in-One and BetterWorking Word Publisher, and PFS:First Choice format for documents created in PFS:First Choice.

To open a document saved in another format, perform the following steps:

1. Choose Open from the File menu, or press Ctrl-O.

2. Select the appropriate format in the Type selection list.

3. Select the appropriate drive and directory in the Directories selection list.

4. Select the file to be opened from the Files selection list, or type the file name in the Filename text box.

5. Click OK.

The document appears in the word processor window. If you save the document without changing the file name, the original format is overwritten with the normal WindowWorks document format. If you want to edit the document but maintain the other format, you must use the Save As option to save the file as ASCII or RTF. You cannot save a file in BetterWorking or PFS:First Choice format.

Printing

After you have created, edited, and saved your document, you are ready to print a hard copy of your work. Check to see that your printer is connected properly and turned on.

Setting Up the Printer

Before you actually print your document, you must set up the printer properly. To set up the printer, perform the following steps:

1. Select Printer Setup from the File menu.

   The Printer Setup dialog box appears (see fig. 2.15).

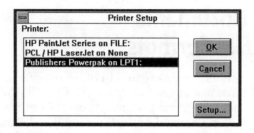

FIG. 2.15

The Printer Setup
dialog box.

2. Select from the Printer selection list the printer or printer driver
   that you want to use. (If you installed Publisher's Powerpak when
   you installed WindowWorks, you probably want to select Publish-
   ers Powerpak from the Printer list).

3. Click the Setup button.

   The Setup dialog box for the selected printer appears. (The layout
   of this dialog box varies with each printer driver. Figure 2.16
   shows the Publisher's Powerpak setup dialog box.)

```
┌─────────────────────────────────────────────────────────┐
│                   Publisher's Powerpak                    │
│  Printer:     HEWLETT-PACKARD,LASERJET,STANDARD           │
│  Font Set:   basic                                        │
│  ┌─Paper──────────────────┐ ┌─Orientation──┐ ┌────────┐  │
│  │ ◉ Letter    ○ A3        │ │ ○ Portrait   │ │   OK   │  │
│  │ ○ Legal     ○ A4        │ │ ◉ Landscape  │ └────────┘  │
│  │ ○ Ledger    ○ B5        │ └──────────────┘ ┌────────┐  │
│  │ ○ Executive ○ Custom    │ ┌─Resolution───┐ │Printers...│ │
│  └─────────────────────────┘ │ ○ Draft      │ └────────┘  │
│  ┌─Paper Size─────────────┐  │ ◉ Quality    │ ┌────────┐  │
│  │ Width: 8.5   ◉ inch.   │  └──────────────┘ │ Fonts...│  │
│  │ Height: 11.0 ○ cm.     │  Copies  1        └────────┘  │
│  └────────────────────────┘            ┌──Screen Fonts...─┐│
│                                                            │
│  Output Filename:              □ Print to File             │
│  ┌──────────────────────┐      □ Compatibility Mode        │
│  └──────────────────────┘      □ Output for Typesetter     │
│        ⊠ Use Powerpak Screen Driver                        │
│  Copyright (c) 1990, Atech Software - v1.2                 │
└─────────────────────────────────────────────────────────┘
```

FIG. 2.16

The Publisher's
Powerpak setup
dialog box.

4. Select the page orientation that corresponds to the orientation of
   your document. *Portrait* produces a standard 8 1/2-by-11-inch vertical page layout. *Landscape* indicates an 11-by-8 1/2-inch horizontal page layout.

5. Click OK to return to the Printer Setup dialog box.

6. Click OK to exit the Printer Setup dialog box.

Now that WindowWorks knows which printer you want to use, you should check to see that your document is ready to print. Select Page from the View menu to see how your document will look when printed.

Printing Your Document

After your printer is selected, you are ready to print your work. To print your document, perform the following steps:

1. Choose Print from the File menu, or press Ctrl-P.

    The Print dialog box appears (see fig. 2.17).

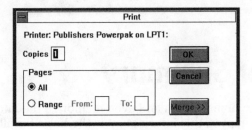

FIG. 2.17

The Print dialog box with Publisher's Powerpak as the selected printer.

2. Check that the printer displayed in the Printer field is the printer you want to use. You cannot edit the printer selection in the Print dialog box. If the printer listed is not correct, click Cancel or press Esc and use the Printer Setup option to select the right printer.

3. If you want to print more than one copy of the document, enter the number of copies that you want in the Copies text box. By default, WindowWorks prints one copy.

4. If you do not want to print all pages of the document, select the Range button and type the desired starting and ending page numbers in the From and To text boxes. If, for example, your document is 10 pages and you need to print only the first two pages, select Range, enter 1 in the From box, and enter 2 in the To box. WindowWorks prints the first two pages of your document.

WindowWorks presumes that you want to print all pages of your document; therefore, All is the default option.

5. Click OK.

The document prints. During the printing process, a dialog box appears. If you want to abort the printing process, click Cancel (or press Esc). Your document stops printing, and you have to select Print from the File menu to print the document again.

T   I   P   If your document does not print, your Windows Print Manager may be stalled for some reason. This situation usually occurs if your printer is off-line, turned off, not properly connected, or out of paper. If this is the case, you do not need to select Print again to print the document.

First try to isolate and correct the problem. Then minimize or put WindowWorks in the background (Alt-Esc), and open the Windows Print Manager from the Windows Program Manager. You should see the print job that you attempted listed in the Print Manager dialog box. If the status of the Print Manager is *stalled*, click Resume. If you successfully have corrected the printer problem, your document prints, and you can return to your WindowWorks document.

Chapter Summary

You should take time to learn and even memorize the information presented in this chapter; this information is the basis for all the advanced Word Processing features that you learn about in later chapters. A little time spent learning these techniques and shortcuts will make you much more efficient and effective in using the WindowWorks Word Processor module.

Although you can move the cursor one character at a time with the arrow keys, for example, memorizing the keyboard shortcuts that enable you to move throughout the entire document saves time. Although you can delete text one character at a time by using the Del or Backspace keys, selecting blocks of text with the mouse or with the Shift and cursor-movement keys is much faster.

You also can save a great deal of time by making frequent use of the Cut, Copy, Paste, Search, and Replace commands and by knowing how to save an existing file or existing text as a new document. If you can perform these functions easily, you will not find yourself typing text more than once. (*Frequent use of the Save feature may save you from a major retyping job.*) You also can save time when working with multiple documents if you understand how to open a new document window and how to arrange the windows on-screen.

Proofreading time can be shortened drastically if you are comfortable using the spell check and thesaurus features. These features—if used correctly—can be a tremendous improvement on your old-fashioned desktop companions.

If you make use of the features explained in this chapter, you will be ready to print a presentation-quality document in a very short time.

Formatting Your Document

W indowWorks provides many powerful formatting tools. In Chapter 2, you learned to enter and edit text. In this chapter, you learn to manipulate the appearance of text on-screen and in print.

The following three basic types of formatting exist:

- *Character formatting*—includes changing fonts, point sizes, and type styles, which also are called font attributes.

- *Paragraph formatting*—enables you to control alignment, indents, line spacing, tabs, and other attributes.

- *Page formatting*—enables you to specify page dimensions and orientation and to change the size of all four margins.

Another type of formatting—*chapter formatting*—controls headers, footers, and page numbers. The details of chapter formatting are discussed in Chapter 4.

Selecting a Formatting Method

You can enter text only by typing characters from the keyboard; however, you can format text in several ways. You can choose formatting options from the control strip, menus, dialog boxes, or by using keyboard shortcuts (see figs. 3.1-3.4).

If, for example, you want to bold selected text, you have several methods available. You can click the Bold button on the control strip; you can choose Bold from the Text menu; you can choose Character from the Text menu and click the Bold option in the Character dialog box; or you can press Ctrl-B on your keyboard.

The method you choose is not important—the result is the same. The control strip contains the most widely used formatting options. The Text menu contains the control strip options plus a few more features. The dialog boxes contain all formatting options.

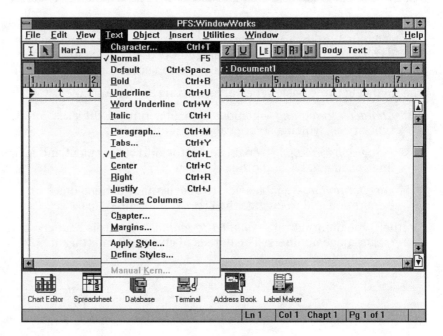

If you are changing a single formatting option, such as making text bold or centering a paragraph, the quickest method is to use the control strip or a keyboard shortcut. If, however, you want to make several formatting changes, such as choosing a different font, increasing the font size, and changing the style to bold and italics, using a dialog box is faster than using the options on the control strip.

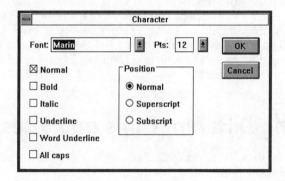

The Character dialog box.

The Paragraph dialog box.

You can format text before or after you type. Choosing formatting options before you type determines how text appears as soon as typing begins. Formatting options, such as the Bold command or the Hyphenation command remain in effect until you turn them off or choose another option that affects the original setting. One example of this situation is changing alignment from left to justified; both options cannot be active simultaneously.

To format existing text, you first must select the text. You select characters for formatting by highlighting them; you select paragraphs by placing the cursor within the paragraph.

Formatting Characters

If you didn't care how your documents looked, you wouldn't need a graphical operating system, such as Windows; powerful application software, such as WindowWorks; or screen and printer font software, such as Publisher's Powerpak. You could use a simple DOS text editor and print your documents by using a single font on a low-resolution dot-matrix printer. But mediocrity isn't what WindowWorks is about; you want your documents to look good. The following sections discuss ways to enhance your text.

Choosing Different Fonts and Sizes

WindowWorks lists the fonts available on your printer in the Character dialog box and the Font pull-down menu located on the control strip. The available fonts are determined by your printer or printer driver software. If, for example, you are using an HP DeskJet printer and the standard HP DeskJet printer driver that comes with Windows, you can choose only one font—Courier—in a limited number of point sizes.

If you are using a PostScript printer or an enhanced printer driver, such as Publisher's Powerpak, which works with just about any printer, you can choose from several fonts and enter any point size between 4 and 127. Figure 3.5 shows examples of fonts you can select if you are using Publisher's Powerpak as your printer driver. You can mix and match fonts, sizes, and styles.

The default font is selected when you start the word processor. If you use Publisher's Powerpak, the default font probably is Marin 12 point. If you don't use Publisher's Powerpak, the default font is Times Roman 12 point.

You can change fonts before or after you type text. If text is selected, changing the font applies only to the selected text; no other text is affected. If no text is selected, a newly chosen font affects text you type following the cursor location where the font was selected. You can change fonts at any time.

To select a different font, perform the following steps:

1. Click the button to the right of the Font menu.

2. Select a font from the list.

   Figure 3.6 shows the Font pull-down menu with Powerpak fonts.

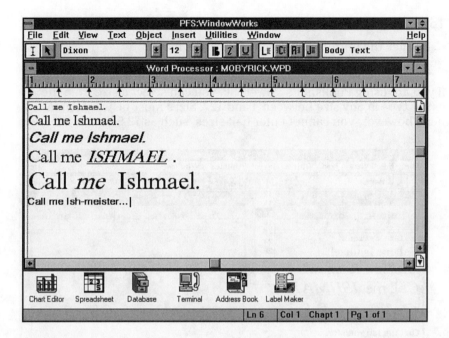

FIG. 3.5

Several
Powerpak fonts
in different sizes
and styles.

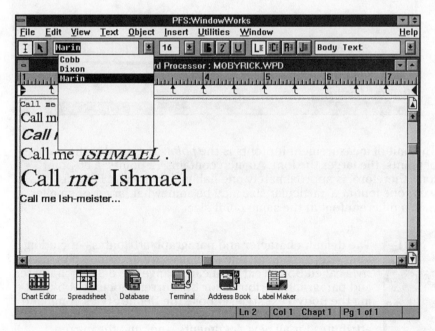

FIG. 3.6

The Font pull-
down menu with
Powerpak fonts.

To select a different font size, perform the following steps:

1. Click the button to the right of the Size menu.

2. Select a size from the list (see fig. 3.7).

If you are using Publisher's Powerpak, you can select a size from the list or type in any size between 4 and 127. Sizes must be whole numbers, however; you cannot enter half-sizes, such as 72.5.

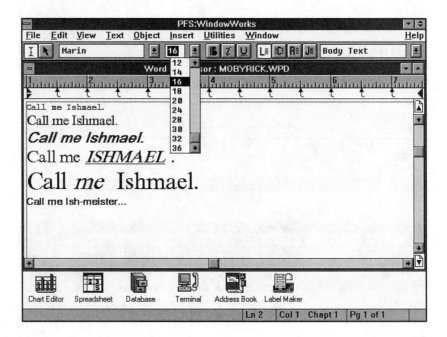

The Size pull-down menu.

The unit of measurement for fonts is the *point*. The greater the number of points, the larger the font. An inch contains 72 points; a 36-point font, therefore, is approximately one-half inch in height. Font designs vary; one font at a particular size may be somewhat larger or smaller than a different font at the same point size.

NOTE The default character and paragraph attributes—including font, size, alignment, line spacing—are determined by the *style* called Body Text. You can change the default character and paragraph attributes for the current document by editing the Body Text style; choose the Define Styles command from the Text menu. You also can specify different default attributes for all new documents—not just the current document—by creating a document *template* that contains an edited Body Text style. (See Chapter 4 for information on working with styles and Chapter 5 for information about using templates.)

Depending on your printer type, the way text appears on-screen may differ somewhat from its printed appearance. Your monitor's resolution probably is lower than your printer's. Therefore, on-screen text usually is not as smooth as printed text. If you are using standard Windows screen fonts, such as Times Roman, Helvetica, or Courier, you are limited to certain point sizes, such as 8, 10, 12, and 24. You can choose non-standard sizes, such as 16 or 20 point, and depending on your printer, the characters may print adequately; however, on your monitor the fonts still appear rough. In WindowWorks, however, line breaks occur on-screen as they will occur when printed.

A better solution is using an enhanced screen and printer driver, such as Adobe Type Manager or Publisher's Powerpak, which is distributed free with WindowWorks. These products provide WYSIWYG (What You See Is What You Get) capability for Windows. Figure 3.8 shows Tms Rmn in 10, 12, 16, 24, and 32 point. Compare the screen fonts in figure 3.9 with those in figure 3.8.

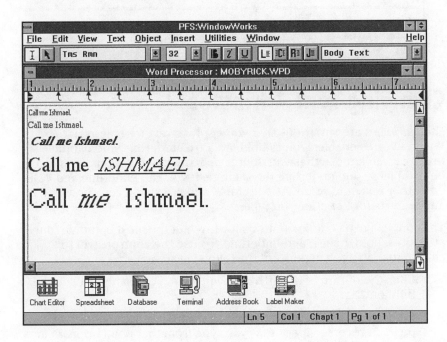

FIG. 3.8

Times Roman in 10, 12, 16, 24, and 32 point.

If you select text that contains more than one font, the Font menu is empty. If, for example, you select text that contains the fonts Dixon and Marin, the Font menu appears blank. You still can pull down the menu and select a font, but the font you select is applied to the entire selection. The Size menu also appears blank if the current text selection contains text of different sizes.

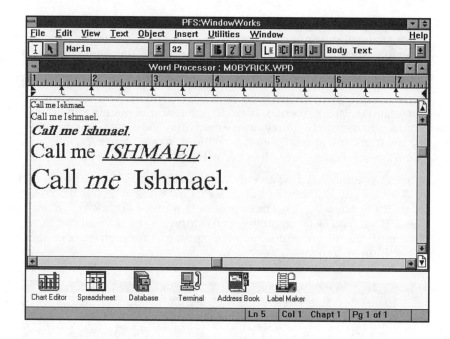

FIG. 3.9

Marin in 10, 12, 16, 24, and 32 point.

Changing Font Attributes

Font attributes are variations that you apply to text for emphasis. WindowWorks enables you to bold, italicize, underline, and capitalize text. You can choose these attributes in many combinations. You can bold, italicize, and underline the same text; you can underline and italicize other text, and so on. As with fonts and sizes, you can change font attributes before or after you type.

The control strip contains buttons for three of the most common font attributes: bold, italics, and underline. To use the control strip to change font attributes, perform the following steps:

1. Click the button of the attribute you want. For example, click the Bold button.

   When you click a button to turn on an attribute, the button appears in reverse video. Text you type from that point appears in the selected attribute. If text is selected, any changed attributes apply only to the selected text (see fig. 3.10).

2. Click the button again to turn off the attribute.

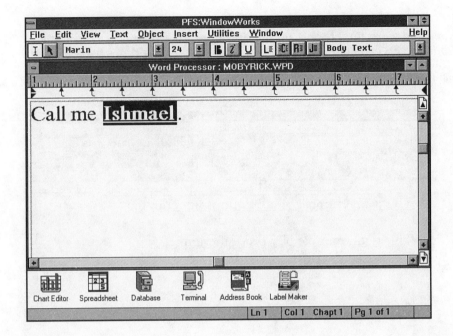

Selections that contain normal and emphasized text (bold, italics, and so on) are called *ambiguous* selections. If text that you select is ambiguous, the B in the Bold button is grayed, and the same rule applies to the Italic and Underline buttons. If you press an attribute button that is grayed, that attribute is applied to the entire selection; pressing the button again turns the attribute off for the entire selection. You cannot, however, return a selection to an ambiguous state.

You also can change font attributes from the Text menu by following these steps:

1. Click Text to open the Text menu.

2. Click the attribute you want.

When you choose an attribute from the Text menu, a check mark appears and indicates that the attribute is on, or active. Choose the attribute again to turn it off; the check mark disappears.

Choose the Normal command to turn off all font attributes. If, for example, text is bold and italicized, check marks appear next to the Bold and Italic commands. To turn these attributes off, you can choose Bold from the Text menu and then choose Italic from the Text menu. Rather than choosing two different commands, however, you can choose Normal to turn off both attributes simultaneously.

Two different types of underlining attributes exist: continuous underline and word underline. Continuous underline—the only underlining option you can choose from the control strip—underlines text, spaces, and tabs. Word underline does not underline spaces or tabs. Figure 3.11 shows examples of each underlining option.

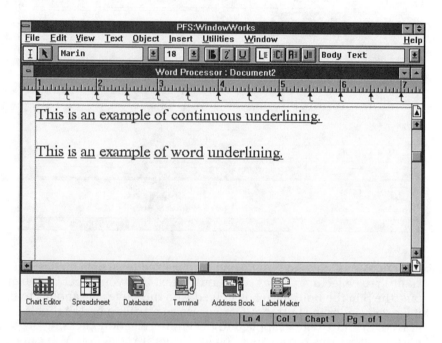

FIG. 3.11

Text using
Continuous
Underline and
Word Underline.

You can select one (but not both) of these underlining styles.

The Character dialog box enables you to control all character formatting options. To display the Character dialog box, choose Character from the Text menu (see fig. 3.12).

To make selected text bold, for example, or to make new text that you type appear bold, select the Bold check box by clicking it with the mouse.

The following are the keyboard shortcuts for character formatting:

Ctrl-B	Bold
Ctrl-I	Italic
Ctrl-U	Underline
Ctrl-W	Word Underline
Ctrl-K	All Caps
F5	Normal

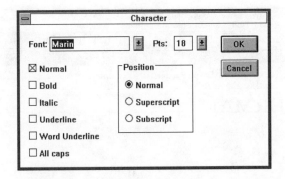

FIG. 3.12

The Character
dialog box.

Two attribute options have not yet been discussed: All caps and Position. Neither option can be changed from the control strip.

Choose the All caps attribute to display text in all uppercase letters. This command is different from pressing the Shift or Caps Lock keys on your keyboard, because the All caps attribute can be turned off to return text to lowercase. If you press the Shift key while typing, turning off this option will not make that text lowercase.

If you type *Sean*, for example, by pressing Shift-S then e, a, and n, the All Caps option would *not* be on if you selected the S and opened the Character dialog box. But you could select e, a, and n and capitalize them by selecting them and choosing all caps.

In the Character dialog box, the three position options are Normal, Superscript, and Subscript. The Normal option positions text on the baseline; Normal is the default attribute. The Superscript option decreases the size of the text and positions it above the baseline. The Subscript option decreases the size of the text and positions it below the baseline. To return text to its normal position on the baseline, select the text and click the Normal option in the Character dialog box. Figure 3.13 shows examples of superscript and subscript text.

Kerning Text

You can adjust manually the amount of space between two characters, which is a process called *kerning*. Kerning text is a fine-tuning process that is not required for most documents. You may find kerning useful to adjust the space between certain letter pairs, such as *Ta*, *Tw*, *Te*, *WA*, *Wa*, *We*, *Wo*, *Ya*, and *Yo*, for example, but usually only at sizes of 20 points and higher. Kerning is useful especially for fine-tuning headlines.

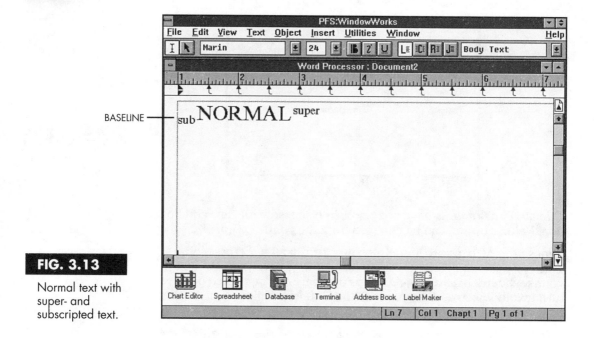

BASELINE ——

FIG. 3.13

Normal text with super- and subscripted text.

To kern text manually, perform the following steps:

1. Select two characters. (If greater or fewer than two characters are selected, the Manual Kern command is grayed).

2. Choose the Manual Kern command from the Text menu.

   The Kern dialog box appears and indicates the characters you selected.

3. Enter a positive number to increase the amount of space between the two characters; enter a negative number to decrease the amount of space between characters. Whether positive or negative, the number you enter is expressed as a percentage. (Zero percent is the normal amount of space between two characters.)

4. Click OK.

The space between the pair of letters is adjusted by the amount you entered. To change or return the spacing to normal, you must select the same two characters and choose the Manual Kern command. You can enter any decimal number between -50.0 and 50.0. Enter 0 to return the spacing to the default. Figures 3.14 and 3.15 show the difference between kerned and unkerned 36-point characters.

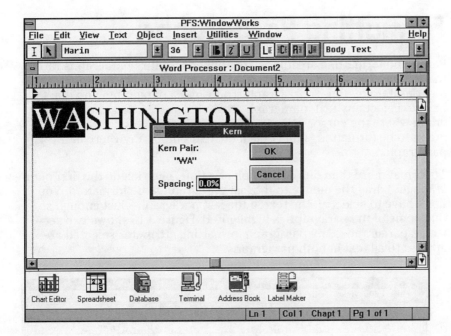

FIG. 3.14

The letters W
and A unkerned.

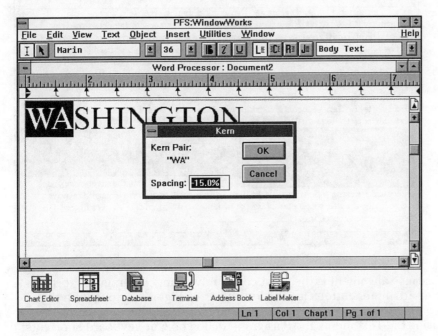

FIG. 3.15

The letters W
and A kerned.

Formatting Paragraphs

Paragraph formatting attributes are applied to entire paragraphs rather than single characters or words. You can apply paragraph formats before or after you type a paragraph. To format a paragraph, you don't have to select any text; paragraph attributes are applied to the paragraph where the cursor is located. In other words, to select a paragraph to be formatted, simply click the text cursor anywhere in the paragraph.

To format more than one paragraph at a time, click inside the first paragraph and drag the mouse to the last paragraph to be formatted. You don't have to select all the text in the last paragraph—just enough so that some of the paragraph is highlighted. Figure 3.16 shows two selected paragraphs. Any paragraph formatting attributes selected are applied to all text in both paragraphs.

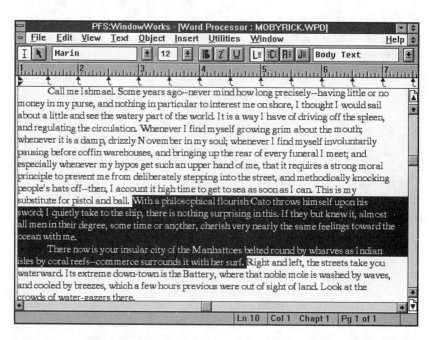

FIG. 3.16

Two selected paragraphs.

Because alignment is the most commonly changed paragraph formatting attribute, buttons for the four types of alignment appear on the control strip. You also can change paragraph alignment options by using the Text menu, the Paragraph dialog box, or keyboard shortcuts. You can change some paragraph formatting options, such as indents and tabs, from the Paragraph dialog box or by clicking and moving the indent and tab markers on the ruler.

Using Tabs

You can use tabs to move the cursor to a specific location without using the space bar. Tabs are useful for aligning text or numbers in tables or for aligning text to a specific location in a document. In WindowWorks, left-justified tab stops initially are positioned every one-half inch from the left margin to the right margin. You can change the justification of the default tab stops, move or delete them, or add new tab stops.

When you type text and want to move the cursor to a tab stop, press the Tab key. The cursor jumps to the right to the nearest tab. If no tabs currently are set or if the cursor is positioned at the last tab on the ruler, pressing the Tab key moves the cursor down to the next line. Tabs are similar to spaces; tabs that you insert in a document can be deleted by pressing the Backspace or Del keys.

Tab settings are paragraph attributes, which means that each paragraph in your document can have different tab settings. Some paragraphs may need only one tab stop, such as a decimal-aligned tab for entering numbers near the right side of the page. Remove any tab markers positioned before the decimal tab so that you need to press the Tab key only once to move the cursor to the tab stop. Some paragraphs, such as a table of numbers, may require multiple tab stops.

WindowWorks enables you to create four types of tab stops: left, right, centered, and decimal-aligned. Figure 3.17 shows how text lines up to the four tab types.

You can create and edit tab stops on the ruler by using the mouse or the Tabs dialog box. Editing tabs on the ruler is the faster method, but you have less control over the type and placement of each tab.

Setting Tabs on the Ruler

You easily can create, delete, and move tab stops on the ruler by using the mouse. When you start a new document, left-justified tab markers appear on the ruler at one-half inch intervals. These markers are the default tabs, which can be modified easily.

To add a tab to the ruler, click the mouse where you want to create a tab marker. A left-justified tab marker appears at the position you clicked.

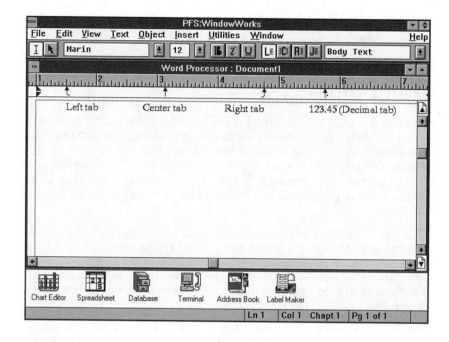

FIG. 3.17

Ruler with text aligned at the four tab types.

 **NOTE** You can add only left-justified tabs to the ruler by using the mouse. You cannot add right, centered, or decimal-aligned tabs to the ruler by clicking the mouse; however, you can add a left-justified tab to the ruler and then change its type in the Tabs dialog box. (To access the Tabs dialog box, choose the Tabs command from the Text menu).

To move a tab on the ruler, perform the following steps:

1. Click and hold the mouse button on the tab you want to move.

   The tab marker is highlighted (see fig. 3.18).

2. Move the tab anywhere on the ruler between the left and right indent markers by dragging the mouse. The ruler displays tick marks every 1/8 inch; however, tabs can be positioned on the ruler at 1/16-inch intervals.

To delete a tab on the ruler, perform the following steps:

1. Click and hold the mouse button on the tab you want to delete.

   The tab marker is highlighted.

2. Holding down the mouse button, drag the tab above or below the ruler.

   When you release the mouse button, the tab is deleted.

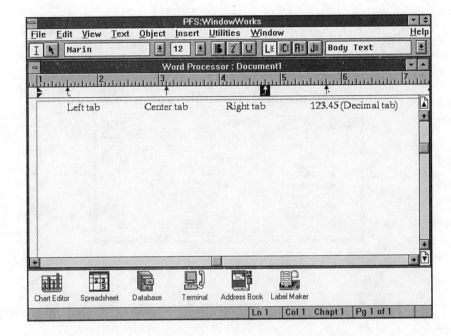

FIG. 3.18

Highlighted tab
marker on ruler.

Setting Tabs from the Tabs Dialog Box

The Tabs dialog box provides the most control for creating and editing tabs. You access the Tabs dialog box by choosing the Tabs command from the Text menu or by clicking the Tabs button in the Paragraph dialog box. Figure 3.19 shows the Tabs dialog box.

The Select box lists the position and alignment of each tab and numbers the tabs from the left. A tab's position is measured from the left margin. If, for example, your left margin is set at 1.0 inch and you create a tab stop at 1.0 inch, the tab appears on the ruler at the 2.0 inch mark, which is 1 inch from the left margin. If you change the left margin, all tab stops automatically are adjusted.

To add a new tab in the Tabs dialog box, perform the following steps:

1. Choose the Tabs command from the Text menu, or click the Tabs button in the Paragraph dialog box.

   WindowWorks displays the Tabs dialog box with the first tab highlighted (refer to fig. 3.19).

2. Move the cursor to the Position box by using the mouse or by pressing the tab key until the Position field is highlighted. Enter a number for the tab's position in the Position box. (You do not need to type **in**, for inches, after the number.)

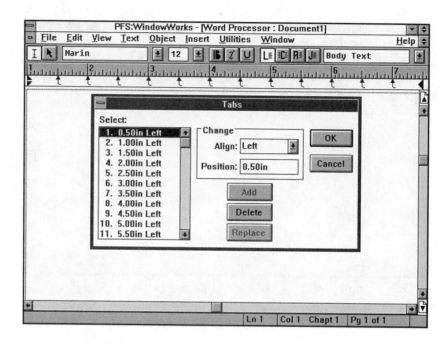

FIG. 3.19

The Tabs dialog
box with default
tabs set.

You can specify a tab's position to 1/100 inch. The number you
enter must be between 0.00 and 22.00 inches.

3. Choose an alignment type from the Align pull-down menu. The
default is Left, but you can choose Center, Right, or Decimal.

4. Click the Add button to add the tab to the Select list.

5. Repeat Steps 2, 3, and 4 to add as many tabs as you want.

6. Click OK to close the dialog box and add the new tabs to the ruler.
Click Cancel to close the dialog box without changing the current
tab settings.

You also can change the position and alignment of existing tabs in the
Tabs dialog box. You may need to modify a tab if, for example, you
added a left-justified tab to the ruler by using the mouse and need to
change its alignment.

To change a tab in the Tabs dialog box, perform the following steps:

1. Click the tab you want to change in the Select list.

    Remember that tab stop positions are measured in inches from
    the left margin. The selected tab's current alignment and position
    is indicated in the Align and Position fields.

2. Select a different type of alignment from the Align pull-down menu, and enter a new position in the Position field if necessary.

3. Click the Replace button to change the tab.

   Using the position you entered, the tab is renumbered within the Select list. The tab remains highlighted so that you can make additional changes if necessary.

4. Repeat Steps 1, 2, and 3 to change the alignment and position of other tabs.

5. Click OK to close the dialog box and update the ruler with your changes. Click Cancel to close the dialog box without changing the ruler.

To remove tabs from the Tabs dialog box, highlight the tab to be removed in the Select list and click the Delete button. The tab is removed, and the list of tabs is renumbered. You can remove as many tabs as you want; you even can remove all tabs. If you change your mind about tabs that you removed, click the Cancel button to close the Tabs dialog box without deleting any tabs.

Tab changes are saved for that document but not for new documents or any other documents. You can change the default Body Text style, however, if you want tab changes to occur in new documents.

Changing Paragraph Indents

Paragraph indentations control the amount of space between a paragraph and the left or right margin. By default, paragraph indentations are aligned on the margins, which causes some people to think that they are margin indicators. A key difference, however, exists between margins and indents: margins control page size and remain the same for each page in the document; indents control paragraph width and can change from paragraph to paragraph. In other words, margins are a page formatting attribute, and indents are a paragraph formatting attribute.

Paragraph indentations appear on the ruler as inward pointing black triangles. You can change the triangles' positions on the ruler by clicking and dragging the triangles with the mouse or by entering new positions in the Indents section of the Paragraph dialog box. Indents can be moved inward from the margins but cannot be moved outside the margins.

The right indent is a single triangle. You can click and drag the right indent left, away from the right margin. The position of the right indent marks the paragraph's right boundary. When text you type reaches the right indent, the text wraps down to the next line.

The left indent actually is two indents and is indicated by two triangles. The top triangle marks the left boundary of the first line of a paragraph; the bottom triangle marks the left boundary of the paragraph's remaining lines. Initially, these two boundaries are the same; therefore, the triangles appear directly above one another. To move both indents, click and drag the bottom triangle. Click and drag the top triangle if you want to change only the first line indent.

Using First Line Indents

A first line indent often is used to indent paragraphs (see fig. 3.20). Rather than setting a tab and pressing the tab key each time you want to start a new paragraph, create a first line indent. You can create a first line indent in two ways: click and drag the top triangle inward to the point where you want the first line of your paragraph to begin, or choose Paragraph from the Text menu and enter in the First box the number of inches you want the first line indented. Therefore, each time the reader presses enter, the next line is indented automatically.

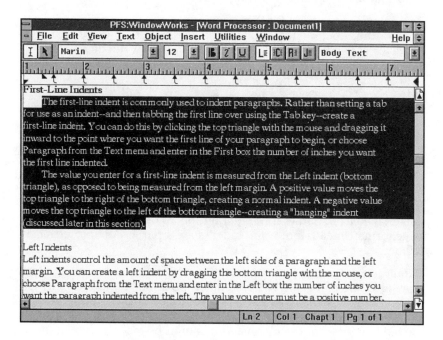

FIG. 3.20

Several unedited first-line indented paragraphs.

The value you enter for a first-line indent is measured from the left indent (the bottom triangle) rather than from the left margin. A positive value moves the top triangle to the right of the bottom triangle to create a normal indent. A negative value moves the top triangle to the left of the bottom triangle to create a *hanging indent*. Hanging indents are discussed later in this chapter.

Using Left Indents

Left indents control the amount of space between the left side of a paragraph and the left margin (see fig. 3.21). You can create a left indent by dragging the bottom triangle with the mouse or by choosing Paragraph from the Text menu and entering in the Left box the number of inches you want the paragraph indented. The value you enter is measured from the left margin and must be a positive number.

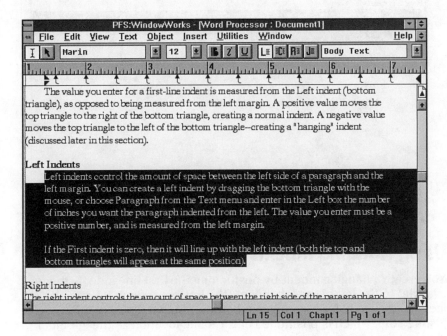

FIG. 3.21

Two left-indented paragraphs.

If the first indent is zero, then it aligns with the left indent; the top and bottom triangles appear at the same position. A first indent setting of zero indicates no first indent. The first line of the paragraph will be at the same position as all following lines.

Using Right Indents

The right indent controls the amount of space between the right side of the paragraph and the right margin (see fig. 3.22). You can change the right indent by dragging the right indent marker by using the mouse or by entering its position in the Paragraph dialog box.

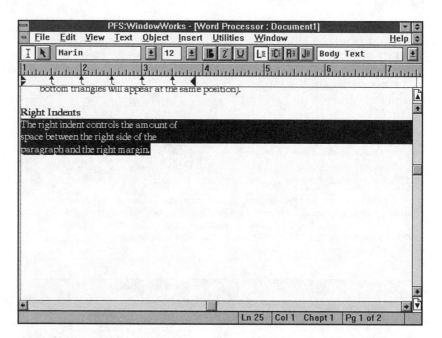

FIG. 3.22

A right-indented paragraph.

Using Hanging Indents

You create a hanging indent by positioning the first line indent (the top triangle) to the left of the left indent (the bottom triangle). Hanging indents are useful for creating numbered or bulleted paragraphs. A left-justified tab, which is positioned at the same location as the left indent, usually is used with hanging indents.

For numbered or bulleted paragraphs, the number or bullet character is entered and is followed by a tab (see fig. 3.23). Subsequent lines of text are aligned automatically to the left indent. In figure 3.23, the tab and left indent are in the same position.

Creating a hanging indent is a two-step process. To create a hanging indent on the ruler, perform the following steps:

1. Click and drag the left indent (the bottom triangle) to the right (see fig. 3.24). Moving the bottom triangle also moves the top triangle; the bottom triangle cannot be moved by itself.

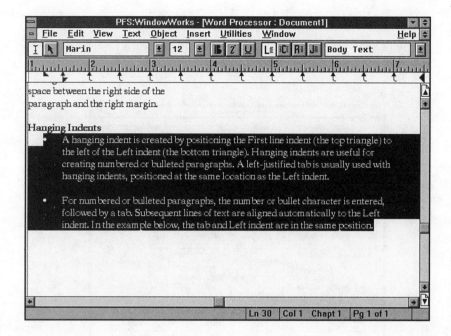

FIG. 3.23

Two examples of bulleted hanging indents.

FIG. 3.24

Both triangles in the same spot on the ruler.

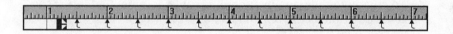

2. Click and drag the first line indent (the top triangle) to the left of the bottom triangle. The top triangle can be moved independently of the bottom triangle.

   The ruler now looks like the one shown in figure 3.25.

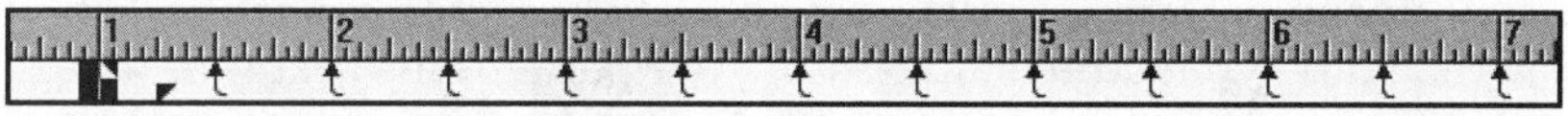

FIG. 3.25

A hanging indent on the ruler.

You also can create a hanging indent by entering values into the Paragraph dialog box. Perform the following steps:

1. Choose Paragraph from the Text menu.

2. Enter in the Left box the number of inches from the left margin that you want the second and subsequent lines of the paragraph indented.

3. Enter the same value in the First box, but make the value negative.

The position of the First indent always is measured relative to the Left indent. Figure 3.26 shows values entered in the Paragraph dialog box.

Paragraph

Tabs...   Shades...

Border
Style: None
Separation: 0.10in   Lines...

OK   Cancel

Indents
First: -0.25in
Left: 0.25in
Right: 0.00in

Spacing
Above: 0pt
Below: 0pt
Leading: 120% [Normal]

Columns
Number: 1
Gutter: 0.30in
Height: 1.00in
Increment: 0.25in

Hyphenation: None
Auto Number Style: None
Outline Level: 0

Alignment
● Left ○ Center ○ Right ○ Justify

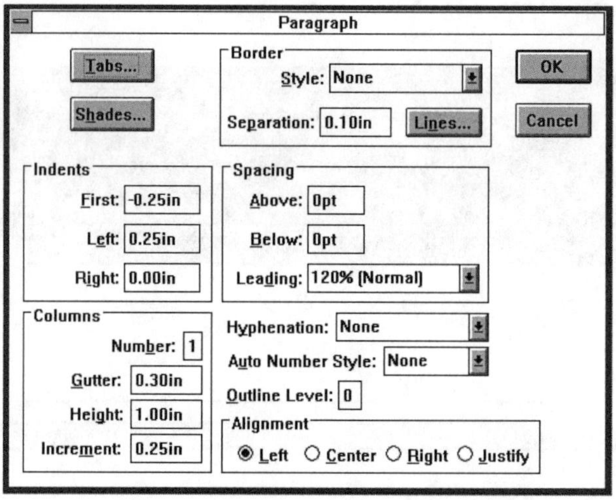

FIG. 3.26

Paragraph dialog box with entries in the First and Left boxes.

FIG. 3.27

A hanging indent and tab on the ruler.

4. To complete the hanging indent, create a left-justified tab at the same position as the bottom triangle, or drag over an existing tab marker (see fig. 3.27).

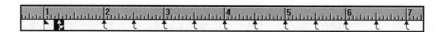

5. Click OK to close the paragraph dialog box and return to the document window.

In your document, type a number or bullet character, press the Tab key, and start typing the main text of your paragraph. Text that wraps down to the next line is lined up with the tab and left indent marker.

You should not create hanging indents using only the Tab key or space bar without moving the indent markers. If you do not move the indent markers but rather use the Tab key or space bar to indent subsequent lines of text, you may think that your paragraph looks fine. But if you later add text to the first line, change fonts, adjust margin settings, or do anything that adjusts the width of the paragraph, the result is a tangled mess of text and tabs. By creating hanging indents with the indent markers, you can change fonts, add text, change the page size, and so on without having to do a major formatting repair job.

WindowWorks provides a bullet character— ■ —that is useful for starting indented paragraphs, lists, and so on. You can type this character by pressing Ctrl-Shift-8. For more variety, use the dingbats font to create bullet-type characters. Instead of beginning all your indented paragraphs with numbers, asterisks, or the generic bullet character, use dingbats. In particular, the letters *n* and *o* in the dingbats font are useful as bullet-type characters.

T I P

The following table lists other useful dingbats characters. With the dingbats font chosen in the Font menu, press the character on the left to get the dingbats character on the right.

Key	Dingbats Font
n	■
o	❑
+	☞
v	❖

Several other good dingbats characters can be used. In addition, several variations of the Dingbats font itself are available; each variation offers different types of characters that are suitable for almost any task (see fig. 3.28). If you installed Publisher's Powerpak, you can purchase several different types of dingbats fonts directly from Atech Software. If you have a PostScript printer, the dingbats font already is available in your Font menu.

Aligning Text

The four paragraph alignment options are Left, Center, Right, and Justified. Left-aligned paragraphs have an even left edge and an uneven, or *ragged*, right edge. Left alignment is the default setting for new paragraphs. Center-aligned paragraphs are centered between the left and right paragraph indents—not between the left and right margins of the page. Center alignment is useful for titles and headlines. Right-aligned paragraphs are set even with the right paragraph indent and have a ragged left edge. Justified paragraphs have an even left and right edge. Figure 3.29 shows examples of each type of alignment.

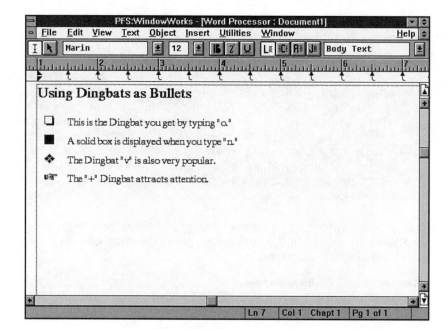

FIG. 3.28

Examples of hanging indent paragraphs with dingbats characters.

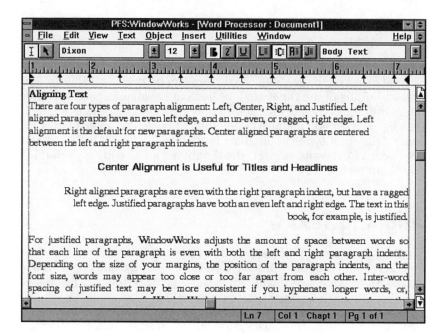

FIG. 3.29

Examples of the four paragraph alignment types.

Left-aligned and justified paragraphs are used most often. Center and right alignment are used in special cases. You probably would not want to write a letter using only right-aligned paragraphs, because such a letter would be difficult for the reader to follow. Centered and right-aligned text calls too much attention to itself for use in normal body text. But for this same reason, centered and right-aligned text is useful for headlines, titles, page numbers, headers, and footers.

You can change the alignment of the current or selected paragraph by clicking one of the alignment buttons on the control strip with the cursor anywhere in the paragraph (see fig. 3.30).

FIG. 3.30

Control strip
alignment
buttons.

You also can change paragraph alignment by choosing Left, Center, Right, or Justify from the Text menu. A check mark appears next to the active alignment setting.

An easy way to select paragraph alignment options is to use the key combinations in the following table.

Key Combination	Alignment
Ctrl-L	Left
Ctrl-C	Center
Ctrl-R	Right
Ctrl-J	Justify

To change alignment from the Paragraph dialog box, choose Paragraph from the Text menu, and click the appropriate option button in the Alignment section.

Remember that paragraph alignment is relative to the paragraph indents—not the page edges and not necessarily the margins. If you need text to be aligned to a fixed position on the page (such as centered between the left and right edges of the paper), you may find setting appropriately aligned tabs easier. Figure 3.31 shows an example of centering text between the page edges. Create a center-aligned tab at 4.25 inches on the ruler, which is the width of the page—8.50 inches—divided by two.

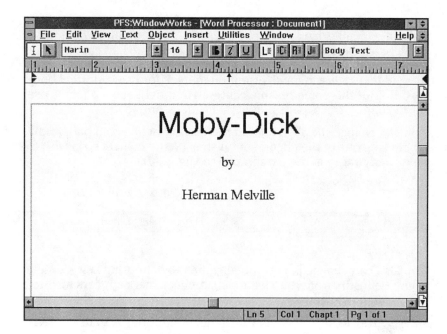

FIG. 3.31

Text centered at tab at 4.25 inches on ruler.

Paragraph alignment options apply to all the text in a paragraph. If you need different text selections within the same line (or paragraph) to be left justified, centered, and right justified, you have to set special tabs. In figure 3.32, the paragraph is left aligned, but center and right-justified tabs are used.

Hyphenating Text

In justified paragraphs, WindowWorks adjusts the amount of space between words so that each line of the paragraph is even with the left and right paragraph indents. Depending on the size of your margins, the position of the paragraph indents, and the font size, words may appear too close or too far apart. Spacing between the words in justified text may be more consistent if you hyphenate longer words or—better yet—if you choose one of the automatic hyphenation options from the Paragraph dialog box.

You can hyphenate words manually by pressing the hyphen (-) followed by a space at the position you want the word to break. If, for example, you type the word *obstreperous* near the end of a line, but the word wraps to the next line, try pressing the hyphen followed by a space between *obstrep* and *erous*. The first part of the word fits at the end of one line and the second part of the word begins the next line. Unfortunately, this method of manually hyphenating text can take a long time, especially in a long document. Another drawback also exists: if you delete or add text and cause line lengths to change, manually hyphenated words may occur before the end of a line in the edited paragraph.

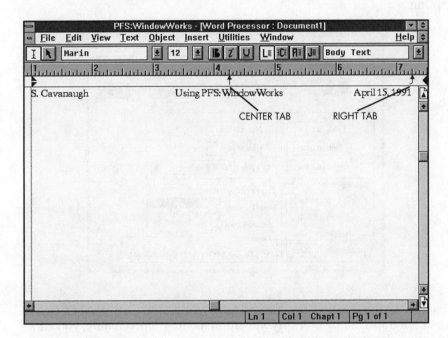

FIG. 3.32

Center and right-justified tabs.

WindowWorks can hyphenate eligible words in a paragraph to improve line breaks. By choosing one of the three types of automatic hyphenation, you don't have to worry about words being hyphenated before the end of a line. With the Hyphenation option on, if you cause a hyphenated word to wrap to the next line by inserting text, WindowWorks automatically removes the hyphen and, if necessary, adds a hyphen to the next eligible word.

To turn on the Hyphenation option for the current paragraph or selected paragraphs, choose Paragraph from the Text menu. By default, Hyphenation is set to None; the option is turned off. You open the Hyphenation menu from the Paragraph dialog box. You can choose one of three types of hyphenation from the Hyphenation menu: Adjacent Lines, 2 Line Separation, or 3 Line Separation (see fig. 3.33).

The Adjacent Lines option hyphenates eligible words at the end of each line, if necessary. The 2 Line Separation and 3 Line Separation options hyphenate eligible words but ensure that at least 2 or 3 non-hyphenated lines appear between each hyphenated line. In most cases, Adjacent Line hyphenation provides the best paragraph hyphenation. But for some paragraphs—depending on the text—too many consecutive lines may be hyphenated, creating an awkward look. If this situation occurs, try using the 2 Line Separation or 3 Line Separation option.

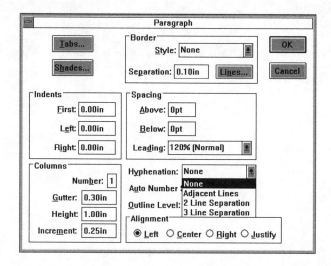

FIG. 3.33

The Hyphenation menu in the Paragraph dialog box.

To turn off the Hyphenation option for a paragraph, choose None from the Paragraph dialog box's Hyphenation menu. Unfortunately, you cannot turn off the Hyphenation option for a single word and still apply hyphenation to the rest of the paragraph. Hyphenation is something of an all-or-nothing feature.

Setting Line Spacing

Line spacing is the vertical distance between lines of text in a paragraph. Line spacing is controlled by two factors: the size of the font and the Leading option selected for the paragraph. WindowWorks automatically maintains the optimal line spacing for a paragraph by setting the distance at the current font plus 20 percent.

To change line spacing for the current paragraph or selected paragraphs, perform the following steps:

1. Choose Paragraph from the Text menu to open the Paragraph dialog box.

2. Pull down the Leading menu in the Spacing box and choose the line spacing option you want (see fig. 3.34).

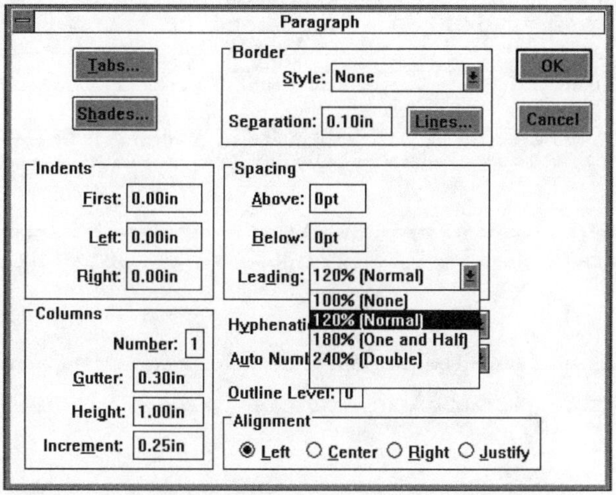

FIG. 3.34

The Leading menu in the Paragraph dialog box.

The Leading menu contains four line spacing options: 100% (None), 120% (Normal), 180% (One and Half), and 240% (Double). The Leading option default is 120% (Normal). This option adds 20% to the current font size. If the font size of the paragraph text is 10 point, for example, the default line spacing is 12 point—10 point multiplied by 120%.

The four paragraphs in figure 3.35 show the following four leading settings: None, Normal, One and Half, and Double.

When you change font sizes, line spacing for the whole line changes. If the font size of a paragraph's text is set to 10 point, for example, and you change the size of one word or even one character to 12 point, the normal spacing for the line changes to 14.4 point, which is 12 multiplied by 120 percent. The Leading options calculate line spacing based on the largest font in each line of the paragraph. However, an aesthetically sound paragraph usually should not mix text of different point sizes. Text combining different point sizes usually looks awkward and is difficult to read, because too much attention is drawn to the larger text.

You also can add spacing—measured in points—between paragraphs. To add extra space between paragraphs, enter in the Above or Below box the amount of space that you want above or below the current paragraph or selected paragraphs. These values do not affect the amount of space between lines within a paragraph, and you can choose to add space above and below a paragraph. The values you enter are measured in points; 72 points are contained in one inch. The default setting in the Above and Below spacing boxes is 0.

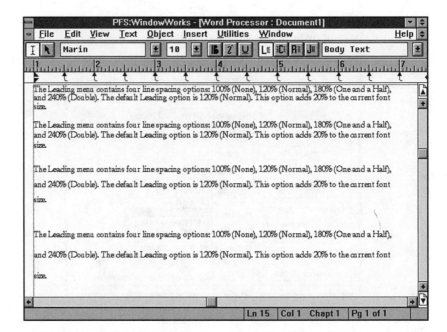

FIG. 3.35

Four paragraphs with different leading options.

Some people use the Above and Below spacing options instead of adding blank lines (by pressing Enter) after each paragraph. Using 10-point text, the normal blank line contains 12 points of vertical space. If you enter 12 in the Above or Below box and then press Enter after a paragraph, a blank line appears to be added—as if you pressed Enter twice.

Adding Borders and Shades

Paragraph borders and shades provide a great way to emphasize important paragraphs. Although you can draw objects and apply background shading by using the drawing tools (discussed fully in Chapter 6), you also can add border lines, shading, and fill patterns as paragraph attributes; therefore, the size and dimensions of the borders and shades are dependent on the size of the paragraph. Borders and shades shrink and grow with the paragraph. Figure 3.36 shows examples of paragraphs with borders and shades.

Adding Borders

To add border lines to the current paragraph or selected paragraphs, perform the following steps:

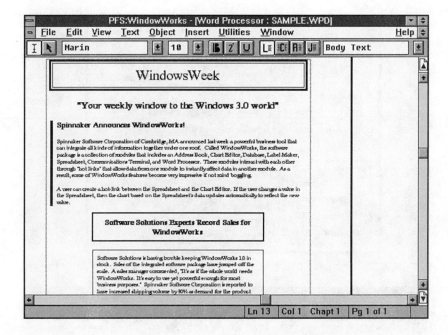

FIG. 3.36

Paragraphs formatted with borders and shades.

1. Choose Paragraph from the Text menu to open the Paragraph dialog box.

2. Choose the type of border you want from the Style pull-down menu in the Border box (see fig. 3.37). The default selection, None, specifies no border. The options in the Style menu describe where the border lines are drawn in relation to the paragraph. Box, for example, draws a border around all sides of the paragraph; Above draws a border line only above the paragraph; and so on.

3. In the Separation box, enter a value (in inches) for the amount of space you want placed between the border line and the text. The default is 1/10 inch of separation. Border lines are drawn outside the paragraph indents according to the amount of space you enter. Border lines are never drawn above or below the top and bottom margins but may be drawn outside the left and right margins (see fig. 3.38).

   A separation of zero places the border line directly on the left and right paragraph indents. The amount of leading (line spacing) affects the placement of top and bottom border lines.

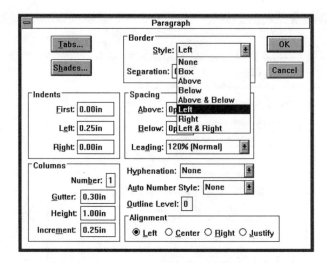

FIG. 3.37

The Style menu in the Paragraph dialog box.

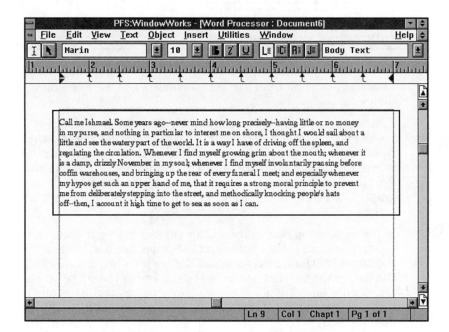

FIG. 3.38

A sample border box drawn within top and bottom margins but outside left and right margins.

4. Press the Lines button to select a line type for the border. WindowWorks provides several different line widths ranging from Hair Line (the thinnest line your printer can generate) to 12 point (see fig. 3.39). You also can choose from three multi-line styles. You can select one of the single lines or one of the multi-lines—but not both.

Click the line you want to select. A box appears around the line to indicate your current selection.

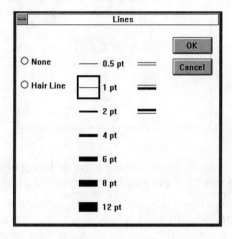

FIG. 3.39

The Lines dialog box.

5. Choose OK to close the Lines dialog box and return to the Paragraph dialog box. Choose OK again to close the Paragraph dialog box and draw the border for the selected paragraphs.

You can create border lines before or after you type text. To turn off border lines for a paragraph, place the cursor anywhere in the paragraph and choose Paragraph from the Text menu and then None from the Border box's Style menu.

Adding Shades

You can add background shades or cross-hatch patterns to paragraphs. Except for the solid black shade, text always is displayed and printed on top of the shade or pattern.

To add a background shade or cross-hatch pattern to the current paragraph or selected paragraphs, perform the following steps:

1. Choose Paragraph from the Text menu to open the Paragraph dialog box.

2. Press the Shades button for a list of background shades and patterns (see fig. 3.40). Select a shade or pattern by clicking it. A box appears around the current selection.

3. Choose OK to close the Shades dialog box and return to the Paragraph dialog box.

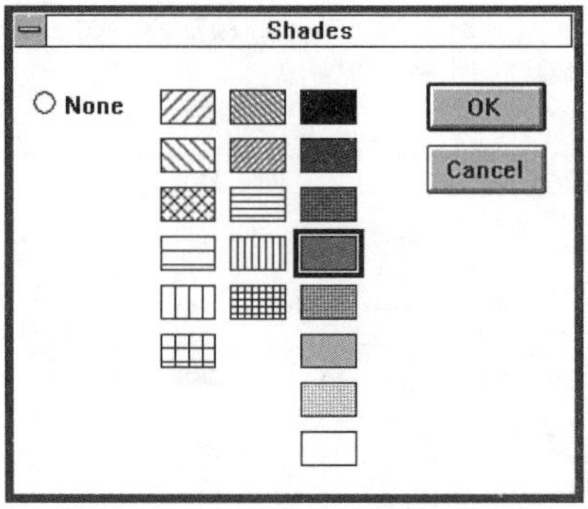

FIG. 3.40

The Shades
dialog box.

4. Choose OK again to close the Paragraph dialog box and add the background shade or pattern to the selected paragraphs.

If the paragraph also has a border, the shade or pattern is drawn to the edge of the border so that the separation space is shaded. If the paragraph does not have a border, the shading extends to the left and right paragraph indents.

T I P If you don't want a paragraph border but you want the background shade or pattern to extend past the paragraph by the amount of space specified in the Separation box, turn on the border feature anyway by selecting a border style, but set the line width to None in the Lines dialog box.

Setting Margins

Margins are the amount of white space separating the top, bottom, left, and right edges of the page from the text. Margins are measured from each page edge. In other words, the left margin is measured from the left edge of the page, the right margin is measured from the right edge of the page, and so on.

To increase or decrease the size of any of the four margins, perform the following steps:

1. Choose Margins from the Text menu (see fig. 3.41).

2. Enter specific values for Left, Right, Top, and Bottom. The default margin settings are one inch for each margin.

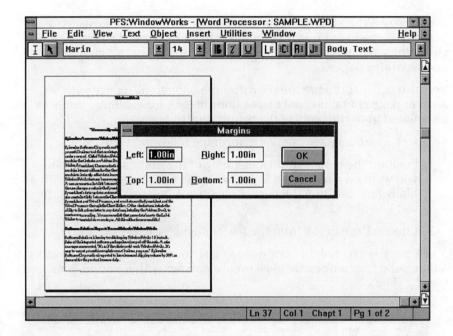

FIG. 3.41

Document with corresponding margins indicated in Margins dialog box.

Margin settings apply to each page in a document. A single document cannot include one page with a two-inch left margin and another page with a one-inch left margin.

Many laser and inkjet printers require a minimum margin between 0.25 and 0.50 inches. Most dot-matrix printers, on the other hand, can print to the edge of the page. You need to consider these requirements when setting your margins.

Margins are represented in your document as dotted lines. Only left and right margins are visible in Continuous view. Of course, these margin lines do not print. Margins also are indicated on the ruler. Zero on the ruler is the left edge of the paper.

Although paragraph indents align on the ruler with the left and right margins, paragraph indents and margins are different. Paragraph indents determine the boundaries of individual paragraphs and can be moved inward—but not past—the margins. Margins determine the boundary for all text and graphics on a page.

Inserting Page Breaks

WindowWorks determines where page breaks occur based on page size, page orientation (specified using the Page Setup command), and margin size. When text you type fills a page, WindowWorks inserts a page break, and your text continues on the next page. If you are in Page view, a new blank page is created; in Continuous view, a thin dotted line separates pages.

You also can insert page breaks without having to fill a page with text. A cover page containing only a few lines of text, for example, needs to be isolated from the body of the report it introduces.

To insert a manual page break, perform the following steps:

1. Position the cursor at the beginning of the first line of text that you want on a new page. If you want the new page to begin with a blank line, position the cursor on a blank line or at the end of the last line of text.

2. Choose Page Break from the Insert menu, or press Ctrl-Enter.

A new page is created. In Continuous view, hard page breaks appear as a thin, solid line; automatic page breaks appear as thin dotted lines (see fig. 3.42).

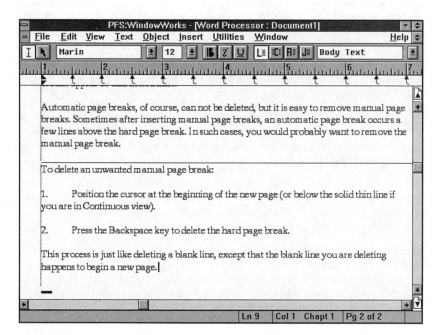

FIG. 3.42

Automatic and manual page breaks in Continuous view.

Automatic page breaks cannot be deleted, but removing manual page breaks is easy. To delete an unwanted manual page break, perform the following steps:

1. Position the cursor at the beginning of the new page or below the solid thin line if you are in Continuous view.

2. Press the Backspace key to delete the hard page break.

This process is just like deleting a blank line, except that the blank line you are deleting happens to begin a new page.

Viewing Your Document

You can edit your document in three different view modes and in five different magnifications. A *view mode* is a way of looking at your document. Each view mode has its own capabilities and limitations. Of the three view modes—Page, Continuous, and Outline—only Page and Continuous view are discussed in this chapter. See the section "Using the Outliner" in Chapter 5 for information about the Outline view mode.

When you start WindowWorks, Page view is the default. Page view displays your document as it will appear when printed. All margins are visible in Page view; each page appears as a single entity. Page view is the only view in which you can create and edit graphics and frames.

Continuous view is best suited for text editing. Continuous view displays text as a continuous stream; top and bottom margins are not visible and page breaks are displayed as thin lines. If you think of Page view as stacked sheets of paper, Continuous view is a scroll of paper. Shaded boxes representing your graphics are visible—not the actual graphics themselves—in Continuous view, but you cannot create or manipulate them.

To choose a document view mode, choose one of the three modes from the View menu (see fig. 3.43). A check mark appears next to the active mode.

You can view and edit your document in several different sizes, or magnifications. In Page view, all view magnifications are available from the View menu. Actual Size, the default, displays your document at its printed size. The 200% Size option displays your document at twice its actual size; the 50% Size option displays your document at half its actual size; and so on.

In Continuous view, all magnifications are available except Fit Page In Window. In Continuous view, no concept of pages exists; Continuous view treats text as an uninterrupted stream.

Turning off the ruler display gives you more room to view your document. You may find this feature helpful in the Fit Page In Window view. Choose Ruler from the View menu to turn the display of the ruler on or off.

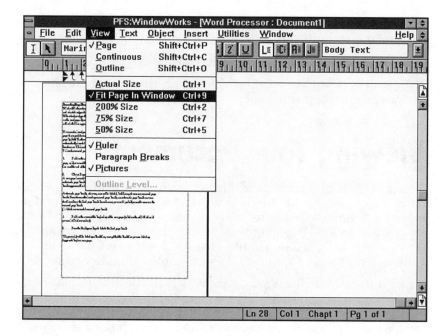

FIG. 3.43

The View menu and a document displayed in Fit Page in Window size.

You'll probably also want to maximize the Word Processor window. Fit Page in Window does exactly that; if the ruler is visible and the Word Processor window is not maximized, the document will appear smaller than if there is no ruler and the document is maximized.

Choose Paragraph Breaks from the View menu to turn the display of paragraph marks on or off. Paragraph marks show where lines break (see fig. 3.44).

Chapter Summary

In this chapter, you learned about the three types of formatting: character, paragraph, and page. You can format text by choosing options from the control strip, the Text menu, and dialog boxes. The Character command controls all character formatting; the Paragraph command controls all paragraph formatting. You also can control certain paragraph formatting options, such as tabs and indents, from the ruler.

You can specify formatting options before or after typing text. Setting formatting options before typing sets the attributes that determine how text is displayed as soon as you type. To format existing text, you must first select it. You select paragraphs by positioning the cursor anywhere within the paragraph.

The following chapter, "Using Advanced Formatting Techniques," covers advanced topics, such as using styles and templates, and teaches you to create complex, multi-column layouts.

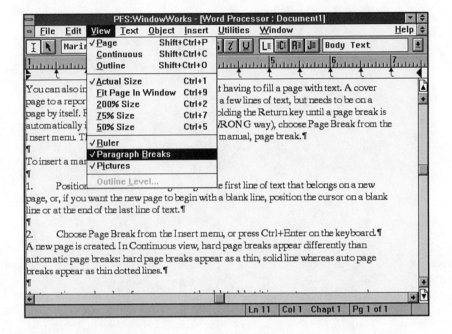

FIG. 3.44

Document with paragraph marks and the View menu's Paragraph Breaks option.

Using Advanced Formatting Techniques

In this chapter, you learn to create and use styles, use templates to transfer styles between documents, and create multi-column layouts.

Formatting documents by using such items as styles and templates is considered rather progressive. Formatting text without using styles or templates, is a one-time procedure. You format individual words and paragraphs until they look just the way you want. But if you want to use that format again, you must remember how you formatted the text, and then apply that formatting to new text.

Many people are perfectly satisfied formatting text this way. But any power user will tell you that using styles is the best way to format text. By creating and using styles, you avoid repetitive tasks, such as applying numerous formatting attributes and choosing typeface, point size, justification, and line spacing; instead, you apply them all at once.

Formatting with Styles

In Chapter 3, "Formatting Your Document," you learn to format text by changing attributes of individual characters and paragraphs. You can format text by selecting it, opening the Character or Paragraph dialog box, and changing the existing—or default—settings. These new setting changes are called *overrides*. But what is being overridden? What determines how text is formatted in the first place? The answer is *styles*.

A style is a collection of character attributes (font, size, and type style) and paragraph attributes (alignment, indents, tabs, and leading) that you can name, save, and apply to text. Think of a style as a set of instructions that tells WindowWorks how to format selected text. When you choose a style, all the attributes that the style comprises are applied to the selected text.

Because all the formatting changes appear simultaneously when you select a style, you don't need to apply several formatting attributes individually to each paragraph in a document. If you want all titles in a document to be bold, italic, and centered, for example, you can define all those attributes in one style. When you apply the style, you avoid applying each attribute to every title. Figure 4.1 shows three different styles.

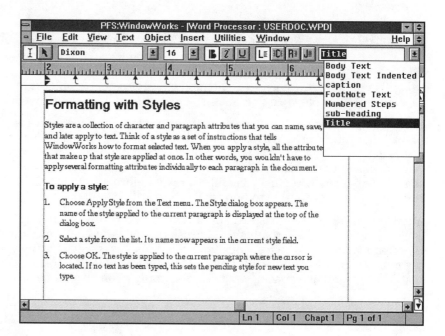

FIG. 4.1

A title style, a subhead style, and a body text style.

You can save styles you define as document templates to make them available for use with other WindowWorks documents. Refer to the sections "Creating Templates" in this chapter and "Working with Templates" in Chapter 5.

When you use styles, you quickly and easily can make formatting changes that affect the entire document. If you format each paragraph in a document individually without using styles, you must select and reformat *each* paragraph that you want to modify. In a lengthy document, this process requires much time. Format the same document by using styles, and any modifications you make to the styles change *all* paragraphs formatted with those styles.

You may decide, for example, that you want to indent the first line of every paragraph in the body of your document. If you have formatted the document with styles, you can modify the paragraph indent attributes of the Body Text style (or whatever style you use for the main text) to indent, in one step, the first line of every paragraph using that style.

All WindowWorks word processor documents contain two defined styles—Body Text and FootNote Text—that you can modify but not rename or delete. Assuming that you are not yet using document templates, WindowWorks selects the Body Text style when you start the word processor, which determines the default character and paragraph attributes of text you type. The pull-down menu on the right side of the control strip is the Style menu (see fig. 4.2). You select defined styles from this menu just as you select fonts from the Font pull-down menu.

The Style menu always displays the name of the style applied to the *currently selected paragraph*, the paragraph in which the cursor is positioned. The control strip indicates the name of the style selected in the menu.

Defining Styles

If you know how to open the Character and Paragraph dialog boxes and how to select formatting options, you already know most of what you need to define styles. (If you are not familiar with the Character and Paragraphs commands, review Chapter 3, "Formatting Your Document.") Before you actually create new styles, read the following section about defining the Body Text style and modifying it and other existing styles.

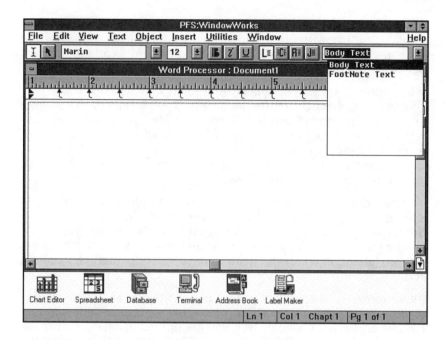

FIG. 4.2

The Style menu.

Modifying Existing Styles

Several methods exist for modifying styles. To modify an existing style by using the Define Style command, perform the following steps:

1. Choose Define Styles from the Text menu. The Define Style dialog box appears (see fig. 4.3) and lists two styles, Body Text and FootNote Text; only Body Text is highlighted (selected). Only one style can be applied to a paragraph at a time, but all styles can be modified.

    Body Text is the default style for text you type in the word processor. FootNote Text is the default style for text you type when you insert footnotes.

2. Click the Character button to view or change the character attributes of the Body Text style. The Character dialog box that appears is the same dialog box you retrieve when you choose the Character command from the Text menu.

    If you are using Publisher's Powerpak, the default character attributes for Body Text are Marin 12 point. If you are using a different printer driver, the default attributes are Tms Rmn 12 point.

3. Change any or all of the options (Font, Pts, and so on) and click OK. The Character dialog box closes and WindowWorks returns to the Define Style dialog box, with the Body Text style still selected.

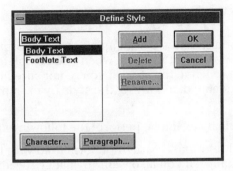

FIG. 4.3

The Define Style
dialog box.

To save the changes, you can click OK in the Define Style dialog
box. Any changes you made to character attributes in step 3 become the new defaults for Body Text. If you want to make additional changes, you can click the Character button and follow
step 3 again.

NOTE   Version 1.0 users should not choose a different style from
the list before clicking OK from the Define Style dialog box
to save the changes made. If you do so, you cancel the
changes you made to the previously selected style.

4. Click the Paragraph button to view or change the paragraph attributes of the Body Text style. The Paragraph dialog box that
   appears is the same dialog box you retrieve when you choose the
   Paragraph command from the Text menu.

5. Change any or all of the paragraph formatting options (Tabs, Indents, Spacing, and so on) and click OK. The Paragraph dialog box
   closes and WindowWorks returns to the Define Style dialog box,
   with Body Text still highlighted.

NOTE   Version 1.0 users should not choose a different style before
clicking OK in the Define Style dialog box. If you move to
another style first, any changes you made—including character changes made in step 3—are lost.

6. When you complete all the changes you want to make to the Body
   Text style, click OK. WindowWorks closes the Define Style dialog
   box and saves any character and paragraph formatting changes
   you made.

   WindowWorks applies all the changes you made in steps 3 and 5
   to all paragraphs formatted with the Body Text style. You can
   modify any style you create by using the preceding procedure.

Modifying Styles by Example

You also can modify styles by example. First you format the text until it looks exactly as you want it. Then, when you complete the paragraph formatting, you redefine the style. If you're not sure how you want an existing style redefined, modifying the style by example is the best method.

To modify a style by example, perform the following steps:

1. Select and reformat a paragraph formatted with the style you want to change. If you also want to change the style's character attributes, be sure to select (highlight) at least the first word in the paragraph before you change font, size, and type style. WindowWorks uses the character formatting of the first word to determine the character attributes for a style.

2. Click inside the style menu on the control strip, and press Enter.

   WindowWorks displays a dialog box asking whether you want to redefine the style based on its current attributes (see fig. 4.4).

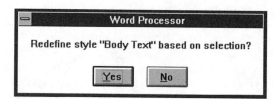

FIG. 4.4

Redefine style dialog box.

3. Click Yes to redefine the style. WindowWorks reformats all other paragraphs currently assigned the same style.

   If you click No, the example does not redefine the style, and the reformatted paragraph returns to its original formatting.

Paragraph attributes return to their original settings, but character formatting remains. You can select the text and choose Default from the Text menu to return the character formatting back to the current style.

Creating New Styles

Creating new styles is almost as easy as redefining existing styles. You can create a style from scratch, or first format text with the attributes you want in the new style, which is defining by example.

To create a new style by using the Define Style command, perform the following steps:

1. Choose Define Style from the Text menu. The Define Style dialog box appears (see fig. 4.5). The style applied to the currently selected paragraph is highlighted.

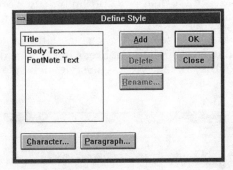

FIG. 4.5

Define Style dialog box.

2. Click the Add button to clear the style name displayed in the text box at the top of the dialog box.

3. Enter a unique name for the style. A style name can be a maximum of 17 characters long. You may find it useful to choose a name that describes the part of the document the style is formatting, such as *Bulleted List*, *Title*, or *Subheading*.

4. Change the character and paragraph formats by first clicking the Character and Paragraph buttons, then selecting the attributes you want. The character and paragraph dialog box settings initially reflect the attributes of the currently selected paragraph, the paragraph where the cursor was located when you chose Define Styles.

   Repeat steps 2 through 4 for each additional style you want to create, and enter a unique name for each.

5. Click OK when you are finished creating styles. This closes the Define Style dialog box and returns you to the document but does not apply any styles just created.

   The style just created is added to the style pull-down menu on the control strip.

Creating New Styles by Example

You can create new styles by example. If you first format a paragraph the way you want a new style to be defined, you can skip the steps in the preceding section.

To create a style by example, perform the following steps:

1. Select and format a paragraph the way you want the style defined. If you want to define a style for headlines, for example, select the headline text, and format it accordingly. You would probably choose a large font, make it bold or underlined, and center it.

2. With the paragraph selected, click inside the style menu. The current style name is highlighted. Press Backspace or Del to delete the name of the current style. The style menu is now blank (see fig. 4.6).

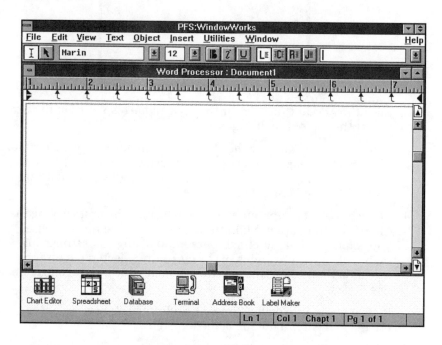

FIG. 4.6

Blank style menu.

3. Type a new name, such as *headline*, and press Enter.

   WindowWorks displays a dialog box (see fig. 4.7) asking whether you want to create a new style based on the current selection.

4. Click Yes to create a new style.

Creating styles by example is the easiest way to create new styles, because you can see the effect of your character and paragraph formatting choices as you make them.

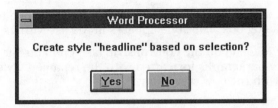

FIG. 4.7

Create style
dialog box.

Renaming and Deleting Styles

Other than Body Text and FootNote Text, you can rename or delete any styles you define in WindowWorks. If you transfer styles from one document to another by using a document template, you may not need all the styles in the new document, or you may want to change the names of styles. Deleting unneeded styles, or renaming existing ones is a snap.

To delete a style, perform the following steps:

1. Choose Define Styles from the Text menu.

2. Select the style you want to delete from the list.

3. Click the Delete button. WindowWorks displays a dialog box asking whether you want to delete the style.

4. Click OK to delete the style.

Any paragraphs formatted with the style just deleted are returned to the Body Text style. The character overrides of the deleted style, however, are not removed. If a paragraph is formatted with a style that is bold and centered, for example, and you delete the style, the paragraph would no longer be centered, assuming that your Body Text style is not centered, but would still be bold.

> **CAUTION:** Paragraphs with the deleted style are returned to body text, but in name only; the paragraph settings do not return to those of body text as they should. Selecting body text on one of these paragraphs does not actually reformat the paragraph with the attributes of body text.

To rename a style, perform the following steps:

1. Choose Define Styles from the Text menu.

2. Select the style you want to rename from the list.

3. Click the Rename button. WindowWorks displays a dialog box where you can enter a new name for the style (see fig. 4.8).

4. Type a unique name and click OK. You are returned to the Define Style dialog box. The style appears in the list with its new name.

The style menu on the control strip also contains the new name, and any paragraphs formatted with the renamed style are updated with the new style name.

Rename	
New Name: Level 4 Heading	OK
	Cancel

Applying Styles

Applying a style is a single action that applies several formatting attributes simultaneously. You can apply styles to selected paragraphs by two methods: select a style from the style pull-down menu on the control strip, or choose Apply Style from the Text menu and select a style from the dialog box that appears. Both methods work the same, but selecting a style from the control strip is quicker. By using the Apply Style command, however, you can modify or redefine a style before applying it.

To apply a style, perform the following steps:

1. Select the paragraph or paragraphs you want to format with a style. If you only want to apply a style to a single paragraph, you don't need to select the entire paragraph. Place the cursor anywhere within the paragraph and proceed with step 2.

2. Choose a style from the style pull-down menu on the control strip, or choose Apply Style from the Text menu, and select a style from the list (see fig. 4.9).

The selected text is formatted by using the applied style's character and paragraph formatting instructions.

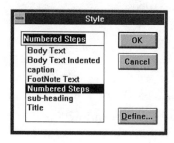

Style	
Numbered Steps	OK
Body Text	Cancel
Body Text Indented	
caption	
FootNote Text	
Numbered Steps	
sub-heading	
Title	Define...

When you apply a style, individual character overrides are not turned off. Overrides are character attributes you selected from the control strip or the Text menu, but which are not defined in the style itself. For example, a selected paragraph contains some italicized words, but the character attributes of the style you are going to apply uses the Normal (non-italicized) type style. When you apply the style, all the attributes of the style are applied to the text, but the italicized text would remain italicized. The italics override is not turned off.

You can remove character overrides, however, without actually opening the Character dialog box and turning them off individually. To remove character overrides, select the text and choose Default from the Text menu. This procedure formats the characters exactly as specified in the current style and removes any additional character formatting attributes you may have chosen. If the current style uses the Normal type style, for example, but some words in the paragraph are underlined, selecting all the text in the paragraph and choosing Default turns off the Underline attribute.

Reviewing Style Samples

Following in table 4.1 are some sample styles you may find useful. For styles you use on a regular basis, you may want to save them in a *template* so they can be available in new documents you create. See the following section, "Copying Styles to New Documents," for information about creating style templates. Using document templates also is discussed in Chapter 5.

Table 4.1. Sample Styles

Style Name	Description	Comments
Body Text [*]	Marin 10 point normal, 120% leading, Left aligned	Default style for normal body text
FootNote Text [*]	Same as Body Text, italicized	Default style for footnote text
Bullet Text	Body Text plus first line indent: -0.25"; left indent: 0.25"; left tab at 0.25	Use for hanging indents, such as bulleted or numbered lists

continues

Table 4.1. continued

Style Name	Description	Comments
Indent Text	Body Text plus left indent: 0.25"	Use for indented lines
Title	Dixon 24 point bold, Center aligned; Outline Level: 1	Use for report titles, article headlines, etc.
Section	Dixon 14 point bold, Left aligned; Outline Level: 2	Use for section headings
Sub-section	Dixon 12 point bold, Left aligned; Outline Level: 3	Use for sub-headings
Caption	Marin 8 point normal, 100% leading, Left aligned	Use for captions or callouts to graphics and imported pictures
3 Column	Body Text plus Number of Columns; Gutter: 0.25", Height: 4.0"	Use for creating three column layout, minimum 3; column height is four inches; distance between column is 1/4 inches

*These WindowWorks default styles can be modified but not renamed or deleted; the font size in the example was changed from 12 point to 10 point.

Copying Styles to New Documents

Styles you create usually are available only in the document where they were defined. If you have defined a set of styles in a WindowWorks document that you plan to use often, you can save the document as a template to make the styles and many other items available to new documents. If you save a document as a template, you can choose the template when you create new documents.

Saving a document as a template enables you to use that document's page setup attributes, margins, and styles as the basis for new documents. Using templates is useful if you need to create consistently formatted documents, such as newsletters, proposals, or forms. Essentially, templates contain everything a document contains.

Saving Documents as Templates

The following steps demonstrate how to create style templates; style templates contain styles and page setup information but no text or graphics.

To save a document as a style template, perform the following steps:

1. Open the document containing the styles you want to save in a template.

2. Choose Save As from the File menu. The Save As dialog box appears. The document's name is displayed in the Filename field. You can change it to *MYSTYLES*, for example, or keep the document's name as the name of the template.

3. Choose Template (.wpt) from the Type pull-down menu (see fig. 4.10). The extension WPT is automatically appended to the filename you entered in step 2. WindowWorks only recognizes templates by their extensions, so don't enter a different one.

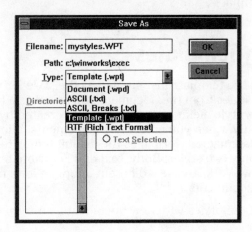

FIG. 4.10

Save As dialog box.

4. Click OK. You are returned to what appears to be the document. Notice, however, the filename displayed on the word processor title bar; it has the extension WPT, which indicates that it is not a document but rather a template.

Everything that composes a document is saved with the template—text, graphics, page dimensions, margins settings, footnotes, headers, and footers. Even View menu settings are saved with templates. Because you are interested only in creating a template of styles, however, you should delete all text and objects.

5. Select all the text in the template, and press the Del key on your keyboard. An easy way to select all text is to press the Ctrl key and the 5 key on the numeric keypad at the same time; Num Lock must be on. Any graphic objects, frames, headers, or footers should be deleted too.

   Be certain that the current view setting is the one you want for new documents. For example, if you save the template at 75 percent size, new documents you create with this template also will appear at 75 percent size. If you're not sure which view is appropriate, choose Actual Size from the View menu.

   At this point, your template should be blank. The status bar at the bottom of the screen should say Ln 1, Col 1, Chapt 1, and Pg 1 of 1.

6. Choose a style from the style menu that you want to be the initial style for new documents. For example, choose Body Text from the style pull-down menu. This is probably the style you will use the most.

7. Choose Save from the File menu to save all the changes you made to the template.

Selecting Templates

You can select the template just created as the style for new documents. All the styles from the document you saved as a template will be available in the style menu of new documents created by using this template. Initially, when you create new documents, WindowWorks uses the template named Normal as the default template. The Normal template has only two styles: Body Text and FootNote text. But you can instruct WindowWorks to use a different template for a new document or for all new documents.

To use custom templates with new documents, perform the following steps:

1. Choose New from the File menu. The New dialog box appears.

2. Select a template from the Use Template list box: for example, the template you created in the preceding section (see fig. 4.11).

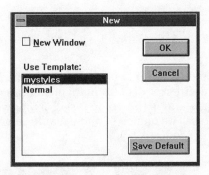

FIG. 4.11

New dialog box.

If you want this template to be automatically selected every time you create a new document, click the Save Default button. Otherwise, when you start up the Word Processor, new documents will continue to use Normal as the default template.

3. Click OK to create a new document that uses the custom template.

By following these steps, you can use the styles stored in a template with *new* documents. But what if you wanted to use styles from one template with an existing document, with a document that wasn't initially created using a particular style template, or a document created using the Normal template? You can merge templates and documents as discussed in the next section.

Copying Styles to Existing Documents

WindowWorks enables you to merge styles from templates or other documents with the current document. Suppose, for example, that you wrote the text for a company newsletter in a WindowWorks document but have not yet formatted it. In fact, you haven't defined any styles. But you remember that you created a newsletter template containing a number of useful styles for last month's newsletter called newsletr. You can merge this template with the current document to copy all the template's styles into your unformatted, unstyled document.

To transfer styles from a template into an existing document, perform the following steps:

1. Open the document you want to merge the styles into.

2. Choose Merge Text from the File menu. The Merge dialog box appears.

3. Choose Template (.wpt) from the Type pull-down menu.

4. Double-click the [exec] directory in the Directories list box if not already selected.

   All WindowWorks templates are stored in the Exec subdirectory. The Exec subdirectory is automatically created when you install WindowWorks and is the home for all WindowWorks program files and templates. The names of all available templates appear in the Files list box (see fig. 4.12).

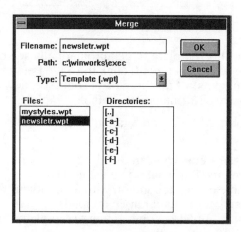

FIG. 4.12

Merge dialog box containing the Files list box.

5. Select a template from the Filename field, and click OK.

   All the styles from the template are added to the current document. If the current document and the template contain styles with the same name, styles in the current document are replaced with those from the incoming template.

NOTE The Merge Text command also can be used to merge entire documents—not just templates. When you merge documents or templates containing text, all text from the merged document or template is appended to the current document beginning at the cursor location. However, graphic objects, frames—including text frames—charts, and tables do not merge.

Working with Columns

Putting text into multiple columns in WindowWorks is a simple task—unlike many word processing programs on the market. When you use WindowWorks to create columns, you don't need to perform the following tasks: create special sections within your document for columns, define multi-column grids in a separate layer, or use spreadsheet-like tables to thread your text into. If anything, the columns feature in WindowWorks errs on the side of being simplistic.

Columns in WindowWorks are a paragraph attribute, which you define and control by using the Paragraph command under the Text menu. One benefit to this approach is that you can easily combine single column text with multi-column text. Because columns are a paragraph attribute, putting multi-column text within single column text is no different than putting a left-justified line of text after a centered line of text.

WindowWorks enables you to control the number of columns, eight maximum; the gutter, which is the amount of space between columns; and the height of columns. The program also has a Balance Columns command, which makes all the columns in a selection the same height, to ensure that one column doesn't run the length of the page, while another column is only two lines high.

One drawback of the WindowWorks column feature, however, is that you cannot create columns of different widths within the same selection. For example, you cannot set the first column within a three-column selection to be three inches wide, while the other two columns are one and one-half inches wide. They all must be the same width. You can create such a layout by combining text frames with columns, however. Using text frames is discussed in detail in Chapter 6.

Like all other paragraph attributes, you can create multiple columns before or after you type text. If you specify multiple columns before entering text, new text you type is entered within the confines of the columns; or you can select existing paragraphs and reformat them into multiple columns. WindowWorks columns are *snaking* columns, which means that text fills one column, continues at the top of the next, fills it, and continues at the top of the next, for the number of columns you specified. Figure 4.13 shows an example of snaking columns.

To create a multi-column layout, perform the following steps:

1. Select the paragraphs you want formatted in columns; or position the cursor where you want new text to be typed in columns.

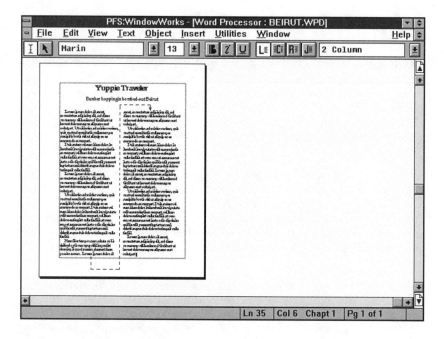

FIG. 4.13

Two-column text with snaking columns indicated.

2. Choose Paragraph from the Text menu. The Paragraph dialog box appears.

3. Select the Number field in the Columns section of the dialog box, and enter the number of columns you want to create. One is the default that turns the columns feature off. You can create up to eight columns.

4. Select the Gutter field, and enter the amount of space you want separating each column. The default is 0.3 inches (see the following section).

5. Select the Height field and enter a value for the minimum column height. The Height field determines how high a column will be before text fills it and flows into the next column. The default is one inch.

6. Select the Increment field and enter the additional amount you want the column height increased if your text exceeds the existing column height (see fig. 4.14). The default is one-quarter inch.

7. Click OK to accept the column settings and close the Paragraph dialog box.

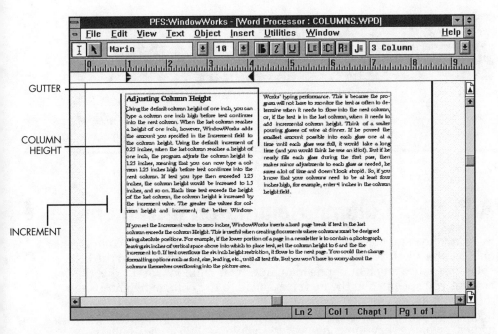

FIG. 4.14

Two columns of text.

Adjusting Column Width

WindowWorks automatically determines the width of each column by dividing the printable area of the page by the number of columns you specify. If you need to create columns of a certain width, you can adjust values, such as the gutter, left and right margins, or even the page size, by using the following formula for calculating column width:

$$\text{column width} = \frac{p - m - (g(n - 1))}{n}$$

The printable area is determined by subtracting the sum of the left and right margins (*m*) and the total gutter width—gutter (*g*) times number of columns (*n*) minus one—from the page width (*p*).

For example, assuming a page width of 8.5 inches, left and right margins of one inch each, and a gutter width of 0.25 inches, each column in a three-column layout would be two inches wide; each column in a two-column layout would be 3 1/8 inches wide. Using the same page size and margins with a gutter width of 0.375 inches, each column in a five-column layout would be one inch wide. Table 4.2 gives examples of determining column width.

Table 4.2. Determining Column Width

Page Width	L&R Margins	Total Gutter		Printable Area	# Col	Column Width
8.5"	– (1" + 1")	– (0.25" x (3 - 1))	=	6.0"	/3	= 2.0"
8.5"	– (1" + 1")	– (0.25" x (2 - 1))	=	5.75"	/2	= 3.125"
8.5"	– (1" + 1")	– (0.375" x (5 - 1))	=	5.0"	/5	= 1.0"

Adjusting Column Height and Increment

By using the default column height of one inch, you can type a column one inch high before text continues into the next column. When the last column reaches a height of one inch, however, WindowWorks adds the amount you specified in the Increment field to the column height. Using the default increment of 0.25 inches, when the last column reaches a height of one inch, the program adjusts the column height to 1.25 inches, meaning that you can now type a column 1.25 inches high before text continues into the next column.

If text you typed then exceeded 1.25 inches, the column height would be increased to 1.5 inches, and so on. Each time text exceeds the height of the last column, the column height is increased by the increment value.

The greater the values for column height and increment, the better WindowWorks' typing performance. This is because the program will not need to monitor the text as often to determine when it needs to flow into the next column, or, if the text is in the last column, when it needs to add incremental column height.

Consider a waiter pouring glasses of wine at dinner. If he poured the smallest amount possible into each glass one at a time until each glass was full, it would take a long time. But if he nearly fills each glass during the first pass, then makes minor adjustments to each glass as needed, he saves a lot of time—not to mention social embarrassment. If you know that your columns need to be at least four inches high, therefore, enter 4 inches in the column height field.

T I P

If you set the Increment value to zero inches, WindowWorks inserts a hard page break if text in the last column exceeds the column Height. This feature is useful when creating documents where columns must be designed by using absolute positions. For example, if the lower portion of a page in a newsletter is to contain a photograph, which leaves six inches of vertical space to place text, set the column height to 6 and the increment to 0. If text overflows the six inch height restriction, it flows to the next page. You could then change formatting options, such as font, size, and leading, until all text fits; but you won't have to worry about the columns themselves overflowing into the picture area.

Positioning Text within Columns

Unfortunately, WindowWorks does not have a mechanism for inserting hard column breaks that enable you to end columns at a place other than the end of the column. If you end the first column half-way down the height of the column, for example, no keyboard shortcut exists for starting the second column before the first column has ended. You need to insert blank line feeds by pressing the Return or Enter keys until the cursor wraps text to the beginning of the second column.

Balancing Columns

The value you enter for column height is the minimum value WindowWorks is going to reserve for your columns. For example, if you specified three columns with a height of five inches, but text only flowed half-way into the second column, the area reserved for the third column would be left empty. If the paragraph was only one line in length, five inches would still separate it from the single-column text in the document.

Figure 4.15 shows a three-column layout with a height of four inches but only a few lines of text in the first column. Single-column text appears below and is separated by the unused column height. Figure 4.16 shows the column settings in the Paragraph dialog box.

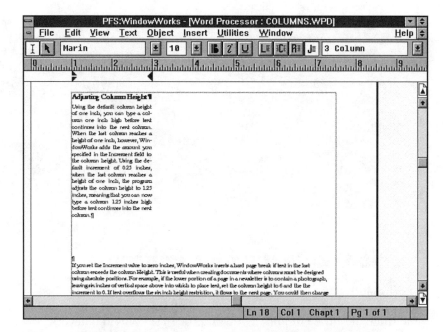

FIG. 4.15

Three-column
layout with
single-column text
below.

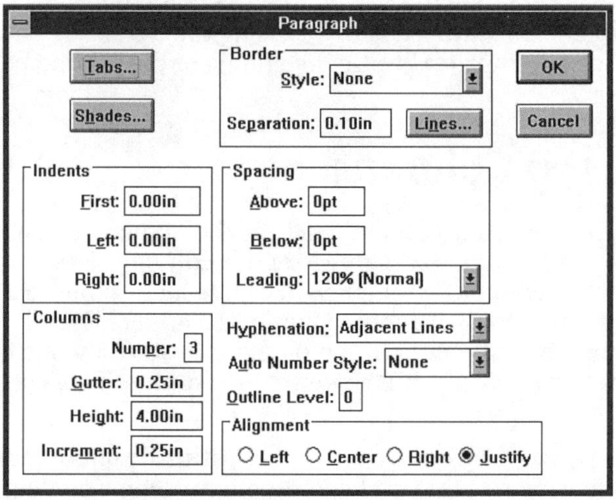

FIG. 4.16

The Paragraph
dialog box
indicating
column settings.

If you want all the text to spread equally between the columns, choose
the Balance Columns command from the Text menu. The Balance Columns command ignores the value you entered for column height and
adjusts the columns so that each one contains approximately the same
amount of text (see fig. 4.17). Figure 4.18 is the Paragraph dialog box
with the column settings indicated.

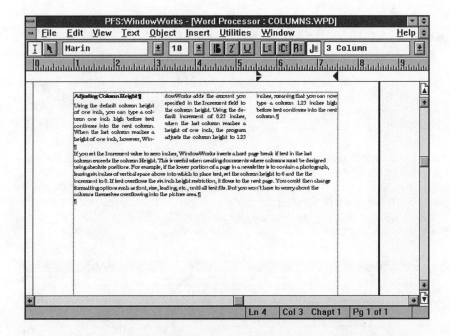

FIG. 4.17

A balanced three-column layout.

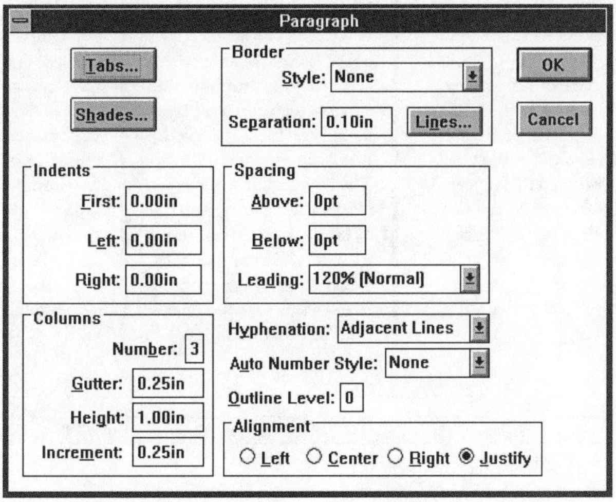

FIG. 4.18

Paragraph dialog box indicating the revised column settings.

Depending on the number of lines of text, the last column may have fewer lines than the preceding columns even after choosing Balance Columns. To be more exact, the last column can have up to *n-1* fewer lines, where *n* is the total number of columns, than the preceding columns.

T I P Use the Right style border to display vertical lines between columns of text. Choose a border style and line type from the Paragraph dialog box. Remember to insert a hard return at the end of the next to last column so that you can turn the border lines off so that the last column will display border lines only to the right of the first, second, third, etc., columns, but not to the right of the last column.

In figure 4.19, a hard return was inserted at the end of the second column. Paragraphs in the first two columns were selected and formatted with border lines to the right. The third column, which starts a new paragraph because of the hard line return, is not formatted with a border line. Paragraph Breaks were selected from the View menu to show the ends of paragraphs.

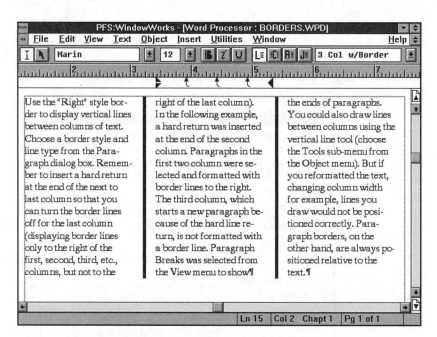

FIG. 4.19

Three columns with border lines in between.

You also can draw lines between columns by using the vertical line tool; choose the Tools submenu from the Object menu. If you reformatted the text, changing column width, for example, your drawn lines would not be positioned correctly. Paragraph borders, on the other hand, always are positioned relative to the text.

Turning Off Multiple Columns

To turn columns off, first select the multi-column text, then choose Paragraph from the Text menu and enter 1 for the number of columns. Text is reformatted into a single column between the left and right paragraph indents.

Because the columns feature is a paragraph attribute, you can define a style for multi-column text. If you created a style named 3 Col, for example, which formats text in three columns, simply choose 3 Col from the style menu on the control strip whenever you need a three-column layout. You also can create a special variation of the style for putting border lines to the right: 3 Col w/Border, for example.

T I P

Chapter Summary

In this chapter, you learned to format text by using styles. In Window-Works, a style is a collection of character and paragraph formatting attributes that you define and apply to selected paragraphs. All the attributes that compose the style are applied simultaneously. Formatting with styles can save considerable time and ensure that your documents are formatted consistently.

Styles are defined by using the Define Styles command under the Text menu. You also can format text first by setting the character and paragraph formatting options until it looks just the way you want it; then you define a style based on the text by entering a new name in the style pull-down menu on the control strip. This method is called defining a style by example.

You learned to copy styles between WindowWorks documents by creating style templates. Templates determine the initial document settings and styles. You also can store other information in a template, such as text, graphics, tables, and charts. Using templates to store information other than styles is discussed in Chapter 5.

Finally, you learned to format text into multiple columns. In Window-Works, column formatting is a paragraph attribute. You control the number, size, and space between columns by using the Paragraph command under the Text menu. Because column formatting is a paragraph attribute, you easily can combine single-column text with multi-column text on the same page. You also can define a style for formatting text into multiple columns.

Using Advanced Document Features

You probably are accustomed to thinking of the techniques covered in this chapter as tedious and time-consuming. Footnotes, tables of contents, indexes, headers and footers, and page numbers have caused headaches and missed deadlines for many writers. With WindowWorks, however, you can rest easy and put aside your preconceived notions about these text elements. If you are comfortable with using the other functions of the WindowWorks Word Processor, these advanced document techniques are a natural progression of the operations you already use.

Although these elements can be added at any time during the document creation process, they generally serve as the finishing touches. Skilled application of these techniques can help you to produce a professional-looking document. When you have created the perfect document, you can save it as a template so that you can reuse the professional touches you have added.

Most of these elements use a feature that enables you to divide your document into chapters. As you learn these techniques, you become familiar with the Chapter dialog box, which you access by choosing Chapter from the Text menu. You add headers, footers, and footnotes to one chapter at a time. If you do not divide your document into multiple chapters, your entire document is called Chapter 1; you add headers, footers, and footnotes to this one chapter, and these elements appear throughout the document.

After you master the techniques associated with dividing text into chapters, WindowWorks becomes a powerful desktop publishing tool. You can specify that your headers and footers change with each chapter to reflect the chapter number and title. Your pages can be numbered by chapter, which makes referencing a long document simple. And you can make footnote references appear at the end of the appropriate chapter rather than together at the end of the document, which makes footnotes much easier to use as a reference tool.

Adding Footnotes

With WindowWorks, entering footnotes is not the horrible process that you remember from the days of typed term papers. WindowWorks enables you to enter the footnote marker and its corresponding text as you type or after you type your document; choose the method that suits your writing style. WindowWorks even numbers the footnotes for you, so that you can add or edit footnotes in the middle of a document without renumbering.

 **NOTE** The footnote reference numbers always appear as superscript characters. Footnote numbers are standard superscript character size, which are 30 percent of the current text size. If your text is particularly small, the superscript characters are tiny, and WindowWorks may not be able to display the characters on-screen. If this is the case, WindowWorks substitutes a gray block for the on-screen footnote reference number. If you want to view the footnote reference, switch to the 200% Size view. Even when the numbers are too small to be displayed, the numbers print normally.

Footnote text always is printed at the end of the chapter in which the corresponding footnotes occur. If your document is all one chapter, the footnotes appear at the end of the document and are preceded by a footnote separator line. (For details on dividing your document into chapters, refer to the section "Working With Chapters" later in this chapter.)

After you enter footnote markers and text, you can edit the font, size, and other attributes just as any document text. You also can edit the line that separates the body of your document from your footnotes. The following sections discuss these tasks.

Inserting Footnotes

To insert a footnote, perform the following steps:

1. In your document, place the cursor where you want the footnote reference to appear.

2. Choose Footnote from the Insert menu, or press Shift-Ctrl-F.

   A footnote reference number appears at the cursor location. A line, which is the *footnote separator*, appears at the end of the chapter or document followed by the footnote number. Footnote text appears at this location (see fig. 5.1).

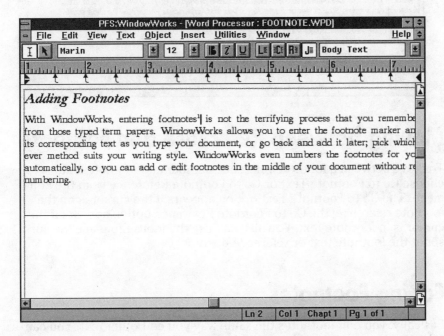

FIG. 5.1

Text with footnote reference added.

3. Move the cursor to the footnote number at the end of the chapter, or choose Go to Footnote Text from the Edit menu.

4. Type the text for the footnote (see fig. 5.2).

The footnote text appears formatted in the default font and size for the style called Footnote Text. As you type footnote text, the Style indicator on the control strip indicates that the current style is Footnote Text. Refer to the section "Editing Footnotes."

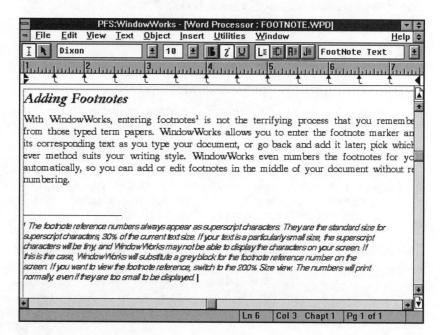

FIG. 5.2

Footnote text added.

Moving between Reference and Footnote

To move between a footnote reference number and footnote text, choose Go to Footnote Text or Go to Footnote Reference from the Edit menu. The Go to Footnote Text option appears if the cursor is on the footnote reference; the Go to Footnote Reference option appears if the cursor is in footnote text. You also can use the mouse to place the cursor at the footnote text or reference position.

Editing Footnotes

Basically, you edit footnotes the same way you edit other text. You can select footnote text and change its font, size, placement, or character attributes. Such changes, however, are a good idea only if you are editing individual words or phrases within footnote text. If you want to change the appearance of all your footnotes, you should modify the Footnote Text style. (See Chapter 4 for detailed instructions on editing a style.)

You also can use the cursor to select reference numbers in a document and to modify the font, size, position, and character attributes of the numbers. You cannot, however, change or delete a footnote number unless you want to remove the footnote entirely. Your footnotes, therefore, cannot be marked with an asterisk or any character other than the number that WindowWorks assigns automatically.

Changing the Footnote Separator

The footnote separator, which is the line between the body of a chapter and the footnote text, can be modified or removed. To modify or remove the footnote separator, perform the following steps:

1. Enter at least one footnote so that the footnote separator line appears at the end of the chapter.

2. Choose Chapter from the Text menu.

   The Chapter dialog box appears (see fig. 5.3).

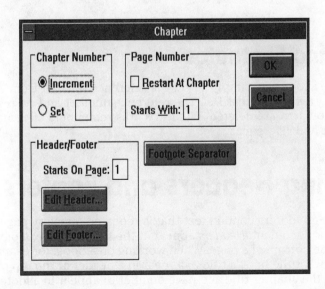

FIG. 5.3

Chapter dialog box.

3. Click the Footnote Separator button.

   The Lines dialog box appears (see fig. 5.4).

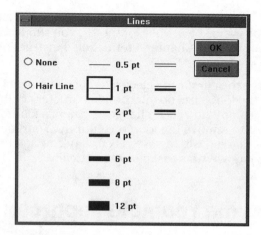

FIG. 5.4

Lines dialog box.

4. Select None to remove the separator that precedes the footnotes. If you want a separator to appear, select Hairline or another line style, and click OK.

5. Click OK again to close the Chapter dialog box.

When you return to your document, the new line style for the footnote separator appears; if you have chosen the None option, no separator appears.

Deleting Footnotes

To delete a footnote, simply select the reference number from the document text, and press Del. The reference number and corresponding footnote text are deleted. WindowWorks renumbers all remaining footnotes and references.

Adding Headers and Footers

Headers and footers contain text that is repeated on every page of a chapter or document. *Headers* appear at the top of a page; *footers* appear at the bottom of a page. When working on a book, for example, you may want the book's title to appear in a header at the top of each page and the chapter title and page number to appear in a footer at the bottom of each page.

WindowWorks makes entering headers and footers simple. You can enter headers and footers for the entire document or for one chapter at a time. Your headers and footers can include automatic chapter and page numbering and can be formatted with any font, size, and character attributes.

Creating Headers and Footers

You can create headers and footers with any text you choose, including page and chapter numbers. For more information, refer to the "Working with Chapters" section. To insert a header or footer into your document, perform the following steps:

1. Choose Chapter from the Text menu.

   The Chapter dialog box appears (refer to fig. 5.3).

2. Click the Edit Header button to create a header for your document, or click the Edit Footer button to create a footer.

   The Define Header or Define Footer text entry box appears (see fig. 5.5).

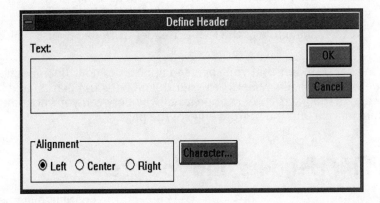

FIG. 5.5

Define Header dialog box.

3. Type into the Text box the text that you want to appear in the header or footer.

   Header or footer text is limited to the line width of the Text entry box. When you reach the end of the first line in the Text entry box, the text automatically wraps to the second line. If you want to force a line break, which is called a *hard line break*, press Ctrl-Enter to start a new line. You can enter a maximum of three lines of text in a header or footer.

4. Select an alignment—Left, Center, or Right—for your header or footer text.

5. Click the Character button to format the header or footer text.

   The Character dialog box appears (see fig. 5.6).

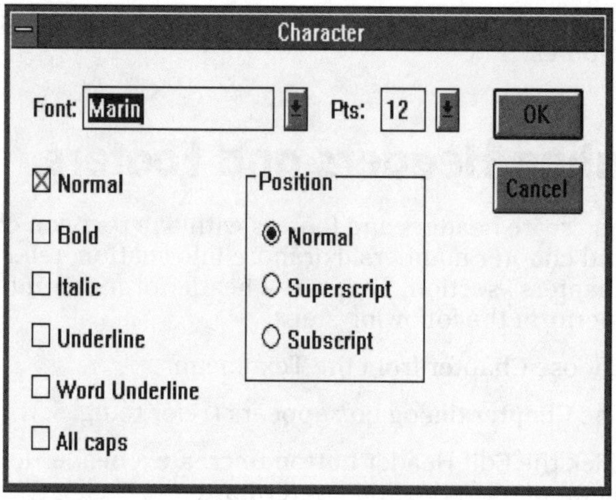

FIG. 5.6

Character dialog
box.

6. Choose a font from the Font selection list, a point size from the
   Size selection list, and any desired character attributes. Then
   click OK.

7. Click OK again to exit the Define Header or Define Footer dialog
   box.

The header or footer that you specified appears in your document.
Headers appear halfway between your document's top margin and the
top edge of the page. Footers appear halfway between your document's
bottom margin and the bottom edge of the page.

Editing Headers and Footers

After you enter a header or footer, you can edit the content, alignment,
starting page, or text format at any time. Just click anywhere in the
header or footer text, and the Define Header or Define Footer dialog
box appears; you must be in Page View to be able to see headers and
footers on-screen. You then can make modifications to the header or
footer content or characteristics. When you click OK, the changes appear in the document.

You also can edit existing headers and footers by choosing Chapter
from the Text menu and clicking the Edit Header or Edit Footer button.
This method, however, requires more time than simply clicking once
on the header or footer text.

Starting on Different Pages

Quite often, you do not want headers and footers to appear on the first few pages of a document or chapter—especially when these pages are title pages, prefaces, and so on. If you want headers and footers to start on a later page in a document or chapter, enter the desired starting page number into the Starts on Page box in the Text menu's Chapter dialog box. Any headers and footers that you have defined appear on the selected page and every subsequent page until the end of the document or the next chapter break. The following section explains more about working with chapters.

Working with Chapters

You may want to divide your WindowWorks document into multiple chapters for the following three reasons:

- You want headers and footers to reflect different chapters of a document. For example, you may want the footers in each chapter to contain the chapter title.

- You want page numbers to reflect the chapter number or to re-start with each chapter. For example, you may want to use a numbering style such as 1-1, 1-2, 1-3 ... 2-1, 2-2.

- You want your footnotes to appear at the end of each chapter rather than at the end of the document.

To create a chapter, you enter a chapter break. When you enter a chapter break, you create 2 chapters: Chapter 1 precedes the break, and Chapter 2 follows the break. You can enter a chapter break anywhere in your document.

To enter a chapter break, choose Chapter Break from the Insert menu or press Shift-Ctrl-Enter. A horizontal divider appears in your document at the position of the chapter break (see fig. 5.7). The horizontal divider is shown only in Continuous View. In Page View, of course, the document will show the correct pagination. This divider does not appear when you print your document. The chapter break also creates a page break; in other words, each new chapter starts a new page. You cannot have a chapter start in the middle of a page.

The current chapter number is displayed on the status line at the bottom of the Word Processor window. When you create multiple chapters, headers and footers apply to the current chapter and footnotes appear at the end of each chapter. If you have not created multiple chapters, WindowWorks considers the entire document to be Chapter 1, and footnotes appear at the end of the document.

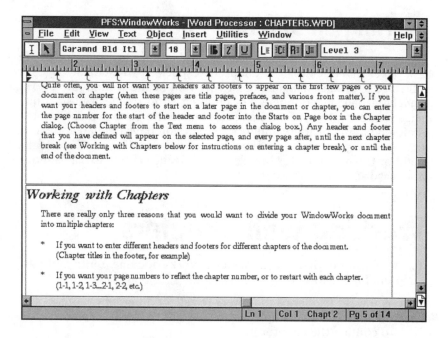

FIG. 5.7

Document with
chapter break.

Any headers and footers that you enter before creating a chapter break appear in every chapter. Headers and footers that you enter after adding chapter breaks appear only in the chapter in which they are created.

Deleting a chapter break is just like deleting a page break. To delete a chapter break, place the cursor at the beginning of the chapter and press the Backspace key. When you delete a chapter break, you don't change any text. The text that follows the chapter break simply becomes part of the preceding chapter. The preceding chapter's headers and footers apply to all the newly merged text. Footnotes are renumbered to advance sequentially through the document instead of restarting with the second chapter, and all footnote text appears at the end of the document.

Adding Page Numbering

You can insert page numbers automatically in your document's header or footer. To specify automatic page numbering, you simply insert a code for page numbers rather than text in the Define Header or Define Footer dialog box.

To add page numbers, perform the following steps:

1. Choose Chapter from the Text menu.

    The Chapter dialog box appears (refer to fig. 5.3).

2. Click Edit Header if you want page numbers to appear at the top of each page; click Edit Footer if you want page numbers to appear at the bottom of each page.

    The Define Header or Define Footer dialog box appears (refer to fig. 5.5).

3. Enter the number sign (#) by pressing Shift-3 in the Text box (see fig. 5.8). You also can enter any text that you want displayed with the page number. If, for example, you want page numbers to appear in your document as *page 1*, *page 2*, *page 3*, and so on, enter **page #** in the Text box.

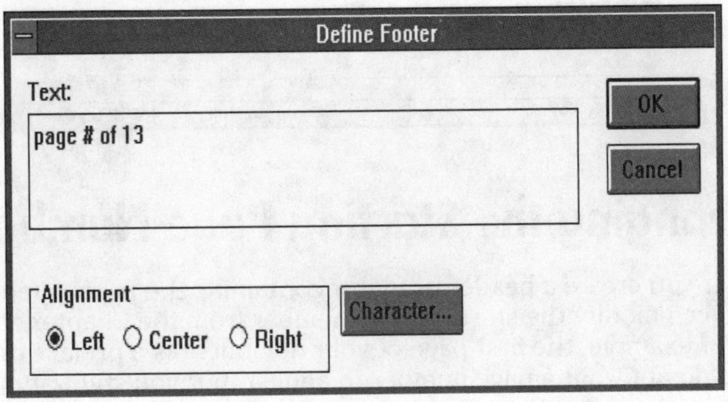

FIG. 5.8

Define Footer dialog box with page number entered.

4. Select an alignment—Left, Center, or Right—for the page number.

5. Click the Character button and select a font, size, and any character attributes that you want to apply to the page number.

6. Click OK to return to the Chapter dialog box.

7. Click OK to return to the document.

Page numbers appear as headers or footers in your document (see fig. 5.9).

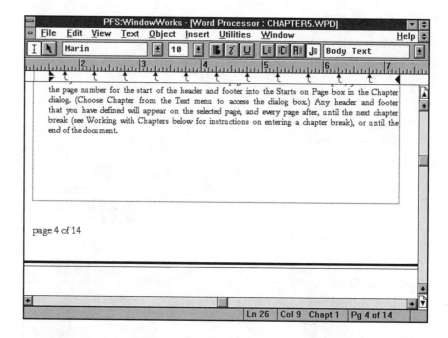

FIG. 5.9

Document with page number in footer.

Changing the Starting Page Number

After you create a header or footer containing the page number code, you can modify the starting page number from the Chapter dialog box. If, for example, the first page of your document is a preface on which you do not want a page number to appear, but you still want the next page to be called Page 2, change the Header/Footer Starts On Page number to 2. The header or footer then is prevented from appearing on the first page. If left at that, however, the footer on Page 2 will appear as Page 1. You also must edit the page number in the Page Number Starts With box. In this box, enter a 2 so that the first page number displayed will be Page 2.

Another option is to restart the page numbering at the beginning of each chapter. If you select the Page Number Restart At Chapter option in the Chapter dialog box, the header or footer restarts the page number at 1—if 1 is selected in the Page Number Starts With box—at the beginning of each chapter.

Adding Chapter Numbering

If you want page numbers to restart at the beginning of each chapter, you also may want to include a chapter number. Page numbers can appear as 1.3; 1,3; 1-3; or any other variation indicating that the current page is Page 3 of Chapter 1. Alternatively, you may want the chapter number to appear in the header and the page number to appear in the footer. You can include chapter numbers and page numbers in a variety of useful ways in headers and footers.

To add a chapter number, follow the steps for adding a page number but use the at character (@) by pressing Shift-2 rather than the code for page numbers.

The header definition in figure 5.10, for example, displays the header in figure 5.11.

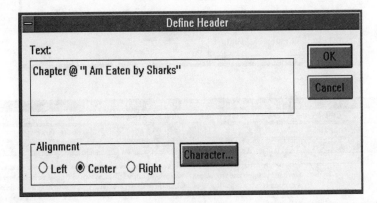

FIG. 5.10

Define Header dialog box with chapter @ reference.

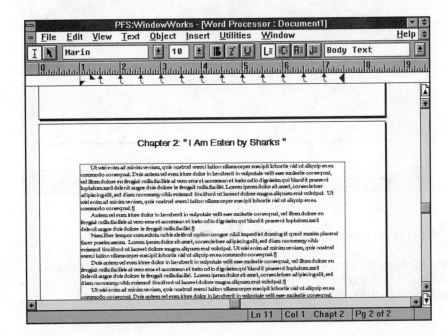

FIG. 5.11

Document with header from figure 5.10.

If you want to include the chapter number and page number in the same footer, define the footer as shown in figure 5.12. The footer appears in your document as shown in figure 5.13.

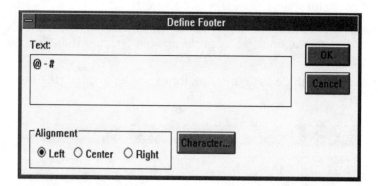

FIG. 5.12

Define Footer
dialog box with
@ – # reference.

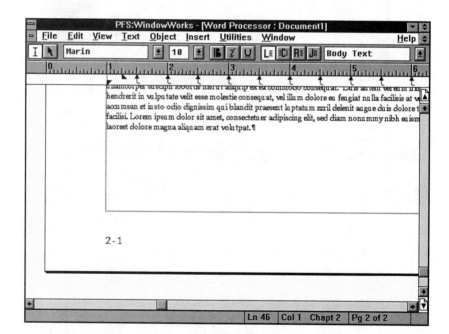

FIG. 5.13

Document with
footer from
figure 5.12.

Setting the Chapter Number

You can tell WindowWorks to number chapters sequentially (the first chapter is Chapter 1, the second chapter is Chapter 2, and so on), or you can set the number for each chapter manually. The chapter number that you set is the number that appears in any headers and footers that include a chapter number reference.

If you want the chapter numbers to increment automatically through-out the document, select Chapter Number Increment in the Chapter dialog box.

Select Chapter Number Set if you if you want to specify the chapter number yourself, and type the number that you want to assign to the current chapter. You can repeat this process for each chapter.

Creating an Index

Creating an index for your WindowWorks document is easy. The pro-cess involves choosing the words you want to reference and selecting how you want the references to appear in the index. WindowWorks creates the index for you with alphabetized entries and page numbers. You can edit, add, or delete index entries at any time during the docu-ment creation process. You do not have to mark words to be indexed as you write; you can go back to the document and add the indexing later.

Although you don't have to wait until you finish your document to gen-erate the index, you should not waste time formatting an index that becomes obsolete every time you make edits that change the pagina-tion of index entries. You should finalize pagination and editing before creating a comprehensive version of your index.

Marking Index Entries

When you decide that you want a particular occurrence of a word or phrase to appear in the index, you must mark the selection for indexing by following these steps:

1. Place the cursor in the word, phrase, or location—space, word, letter, or blank line—that you want to appear referenced in the index.

2. Choose Mark Index Entry from the Utilities menu.

   The Index Entry dialog box appears with the current word or phrase selected in the Index Entry text box (see fig. 5.14).

3. Edit the selection in the Index Entry text box to read exactly as you want the corresponding text in the index to read.

   If you want a phrase rather than a single word to appear in the index, edit the text so that the phrase is displayed.

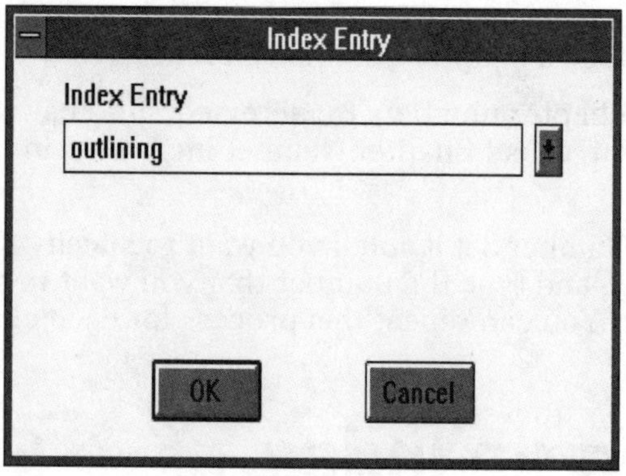

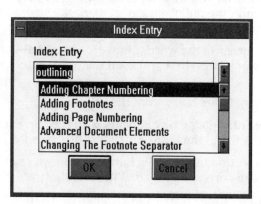

FIG. 5.14

Index Entry
dialog box.

4. Click OK to mark the cursor location.

   A reference will appear in the index listed exactly as entered with the page number of the current cursor location.

   Repeat this process for each word or phrase in the document that you want to appear in the index.

After creating a few index entries, you may find that you want new references to appear under already created index listings. If this is the case, you do not need to retype the entry. In fact, you shouldn't retype the entry; if a new index entry differs even slightly from an existing entry, you end up with two index listings when you only need one.

Simply click the scroll button next to the Index Entry dialog box instead of typing an index entry. A scroll list appears with all the entries that you have created (see fig. 5.15). Select the entry that you want to use to index the current mark and click OK. The entry will appear in the index followed by two page numbers: one for the original reference with that name and one for the reference that you just marked.

FIG. 5.15

Index Entry
dialog box
with scroll list
displayed.

When you are marking an index entry, you are not marking a particular word or phrase; you are marking a cursor location. WindowWorks does not search for particular words when creating your index; Window-Works finds each index marker, makes a reference based on the text that you typed in the Index Entry dialog box, adds the current page number, and alphabetizes the entries. Therefore, you do not need to enter a reference that exactly matches the text that appears at the current cursor location.

If, for example, you are writing a report on financial management software products and you want the index entry *Check Writing Capabilities* to refer the reader to a particular paragraph, you can mark the beginning of the paragraph and enter **Check Writing Capabilities** in the Index Entry dialog box. The index then refers the reader to the page on which the paragraph appears—even if the paragraph doesn't contain the words *check writing capabilities*. If, instead, you wanted this reference to appear alphabetically under H for *Home Finances*, you can enter **Home Finances, check writing**.

Because you are not limited to the exact words and phrases that appear in the text, you can determine how your readers can best locate information in the index and write entries that are clear and useful. Keeping this fact in mind, you can create a thorough and helpful index.

Unfortunately, because you are marking a location rather than a word for indexing, WindowWorks inserts only that particular occurrence of the word into the index. The program does not search through the entire document for every occurrence of a word—you must do that yourself.

If you know that a particular word or phrase occurs many times in your document, find each occurrence by using the Search option from the Edit menu, choose Mark Index Entry each time you find the word or phrase, and select the same index entry from the list of already created entries. When you create the index, that index entry is repeated multiple times, with each entry followed by one page number.

After the index is created and inserted in your document, you should delete repetitive entries and create one entry followed by a list of page numbers separated by commas, with each page number referring to one of the marks you have inserted. To do this, use your basic text editing techniques to delete the recurrences of the key word, and combine the page numbers into a list.

Creating the Index

After you have marked all the places in your document to be indexed, you are ready to create, or generate, a WindowWorks index.

WindowWorks does all the organizational work; you simply tell the program how to format the index.

To generate an index, perform the following steps:

1. Place your cursor where you want your index to appear— probably at the end of your document.

2. Choose Generate Index from the Utilities menu.

   The Index dialog box appears (see fig. 5.16).

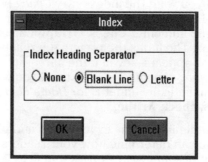

The Index dialog box offers you a selection of index separators; a *separator* divides each alphabetical section of index entries. If you select None, your index appears one line after another. This method works well only with very short indexes, unless you intend to format the index yourself by adding spacing, tabs, and dividers.

A better option for longer indexes is the Blank Line option, which uses a blank line to separate the A entries from the B entries and so on through the alphabet.

If your index is very long and detailed, you may want to select the Letter option, which introduces the A entries with an A, the B entries with a B, and so on.

3. Select a separation format for your index, and click OK.

The index appears at the current cursor location. You can edit and format text in the index just as any other text in your document. The appearance of the index can be tailored so that the entries are easy to read.

You may want to create a style for your index entries. You may want to format the index in multiple columns; set a tab for page numbers; and insert commas, dashes, lines, and so on. You can look at various books for examples of indexes; figure 5.17 shows one such example.

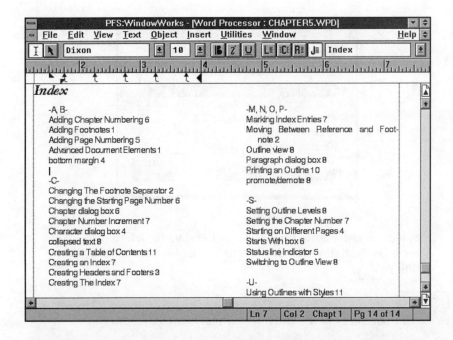

FIG. 5.17

A sample index.

The index figure shows:

Index

-A, B-
Adding Chapter Numbering 6
Adding Footnotes 1
Adding Page Numbering 5
Advanced Document Elements 1
bottom margin 4

I

-C-
Changing The Footnote Separator 2
Changing the Starting Page Number 6
Chapter dialog box 6
Chapter Number Increment 7
Character dialog box 4
collapsed text 8
Creating a Table of Contents 11
Creating an Index 7
Creating Headers and Footers 3
Creating The Index 7

-M, N, O, P-
Marking Index Entries 7
Moving Between Reference and Footnote 2
Outline view 8
Paragraph dialog box 8
Printing an Outline 10
promote/demote 8

-S-
Setting Outline Levels 8
Setting the Chapter Number 7
Starting on Different Pages 4
Starts With box 6
Status line indicator 5
Switching to Outline View 8

-U-
Using Outlines with Styles 11

T I P

If you make changes in your document and must generate your index again, the formatting and editing that you did in the current index is lost, and you must repeat your formatting work. This process is easier when you create a style for your index entries (see Chapter 4). Simply change all new index entries to your already defined Index style, and the entries will be formatted correctly.

Editing Index Entries

If you decide that you don't need a certain index entry or that you want to go to a specific index entry marker, you can use the Edit Index Entry option.

To edit index entries, perform the following steps:

1. Choose Edit Index Entry from the Utilities menu.

   The Edit Entry Dialog box listing all defined index entries appears (see fig. 5.18).

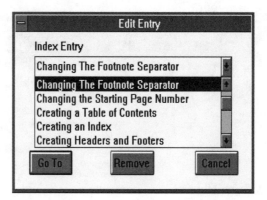

FIG. 5.18

The Edit Entry
dialog box.

2. Select an entry from the list. Click Remove to delete the entry; click Go To to find the first occurrence of a reference for that entry.

 If you remove an index entry, you also remove all index markers in the document that refer to that entry.

Using the Outliner

The term *outliner* sounds like a separate program or module, but the outlining feature in WindowWorks actually is just a different view of the document, like Page view or Continuous view. You switch to Outline view simply by choosing Outline from the View menu.

Any document can be displayed in Outline view; just as any document can be displayed in Page view or Continuous view. Changing to Outline view does not alter your document. Be aware, however, that any changes you make while in Outline view are there when you return to Page view.

If you are creating a complex document that uses the index, chapter, and footnote features, you probably can benefit from viewing your document in outline form.

Defining an Outline

An outline is a tool for viewing only the main ideas of a document. You probably learned to create outlines in school. The most important ideas are identified with Roman numerals—I, II, III, IV, V, and so on. Each of these top-level ideas acts as an umbrella for subtopics identified with letters of the alphabet: A, B, C, D, and so on. Each subtopic likewise can be broken down further using Arabic numbers: 1, 2, 3, 4, 5, and so on.

Traditional pen-and-paper outlines are extremely logical and straight-forward but generally not useful. The reason that creating outlines in grade school was such a futile exercise—most of us created them after we wrote our papers—was that outlines were inflexible and existed separately from the documents they were supposed to help organize.

With WindowWorks, you can outline a document before, during, or after you have created it. In addition, you always can have an up-to-date outline; you can get a quick overview of where you have been and where you are going with your document.

Outlining is a method of organizing your ideas by assigning them different levels. An idea is contained in a paragraph, and each paragraph can be assigned an outline level between 0 and 9. By reexamining your grade school outlines, you can see that Roman numeral headings correspond to level one ideas, uppercase letters to level two ideas, Arabic numbers to level three ideas, and so on. The ideas to which you assign these levels serve as headings. The rest of the text is the document's body text.

Usually when you are creating a document and using an outline, you create the headings in the Outline view and assign the headings a level; you then write the body text in Page or Continuous view.

Outlining makes revising and editing your documents easy, because you can change the level by promoting or demoting any outline paragraph simply by clicking a button. You also can use the outline to get a quick overview of your document's organization.

You can choose to view your entire document organized as an outline, or you can choose to view only certain outline levels. If, for example, you want to revise top-level headings only, you can *collapse*, hide from view, all but the level one paragraphs so that only the Roman numeral headings are visible. The other paragraphs still exist, but they remain collapsed until you expand the outline or exit Outline view.

In Outline view, you cannot create or edit graphics or use Utility menu functions, such as creating an index, spell checking, or opening the thesaurus. Other functions are unavailable in Outline view as well, but you don't have to memorize them; WindowWorks grays unavailable menu commands.

Switching to Outline View

You can view new or existing documents in Outline view by choosing Outline from the View menu. You also can create documents entirely in Outline view without switching into Page or Continuous view.

To change to Outline view, perform the following steps:

1. Open the document you want to outline by choosing Open from the File menu. Alternatively, you can create a new document by choosing New from the File menu.

2. Choose Outline from the View menu.

To exit Outline view, choose one of the other two view options—Page or Continuous—from the View menu. You can go back and forth from Outline view to Page or Continuous view as frequently as you need to during document creation; changing views does not affect your document.

Setting Outline Levels

You can assign any paragraph an outline level. Paragraphs with outline levels between 1 and 9 are treated as headings, with 1 being the broadest heading level. Paragraphs with an outline level of 0, the default outline level, are treated as body text.

You can use two methods to change a paragraph's outline level: you can change the level in the Paragraph dialog box, or you can change the level in Outline view by clicking the left- or right-arrow buttons on the control strip (see fig. 5.19).

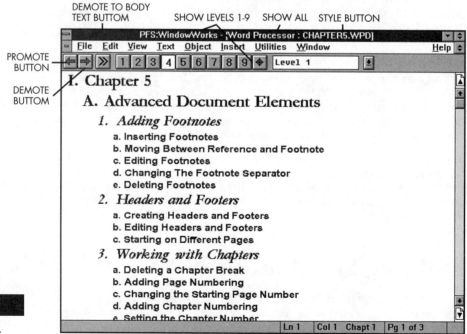

FIG. 5.19

Outline view.

The control strip contains the following promote and demote buttons:

Demote Button. Click the right arrow to demote a paragraph's outline level. This process changes a paragraph's level from 2 to 3 or from 3 to 4, for example. If a paragraph's outline level is 0, clicking the right arrow promotes its level to 1; however, subsequent clicks demote the outline level to 2, 3, and so on.

Promote Button. To promote a paragraph's outline level, click the left-arrow button on the control strip. This process changes the paragraph's level from 4 to 3 or from 2 to 1, for example. If the paragraph's outline level is 0, clicking the left-arrow button has no effect; you first must click the right-arrow button.

Demote to Body Text Button. You can return a paragraph's outline level to 0 (body text) by clicking the double angle-brackets button.

Except for body text, each paragraph in an outline is numbered. The way the paragraph is numbered depends on its level within the outline. The first level 1 paragraph, for example, is preceded by the Roman numeral I, the second level 1 paragraph by the Roman numeral II, and so on. The first level 2 paragraph is preceded by the letter A, the second level 2 paragraph by B, and so on. The first level 3 paragraph is preceded by the number 1, followed by 2, 3, 4, and so on. The first level four paragraph is preceded by the lowercase letter *a*, followed by *b*, *c*, and so on. Levels 5 through 9 alternate between numbers and lowercase letters.

Paragraph numbering restarts each time a paragraph is preceded by a higher-level paragraph. If, for example, you have two level 1 paragraphs (I and II), the level 2 paragraphs under the first level 1 paragraph are preceded by A, B, C, and so on. But the level 2 paragraphs under the second level 1 paragraph do not begin with D, E, F; the level 2 paragraphs restart with A after each level 1 paragraph.

If this sounds like an alphanumeric nightmare—relax. You don't need to track paragraph numbers. WindowWorks renumbers paragraphs automatically when you create, insert, or delete paragraphs. When you press Enter after a paragraph, the new paragraph has the same level, unless you specifically assign a different level. If, for example, the cursor is positioned on a level 4 paragraph and you press Enter, the new paragraph also is level 4; all subsequent paragraphs are renumbered accordingly.

Paragraph numbers are displayed and printed only when you are in Outline view; paragraph numbers don't appear in other views unless you use the Paragraph command to specify that WindowWorks displays them. You can turn on the display of paragraph numbers in Page and Continuous views by opening the Paragraph dialog box and selecting a number style from the Auto Number Style menu. The default setting is None, but you can choose the Legal or Outline number style from the menu; the number styles are defined in the following paragraph. The numbers then appear and print in all views.

The following are levels in Outline number style:

I. Level one

   A. Level two

      1. Level three

         a. Level four

The following are levels in Legal number style:

1. Level one

   1.1 Level two

      1.1.1 Level three

         1.1.1.1 Level four

You can select and format text in Outline view just as you do in other views. You even can apply styles from the Style menu. You cannot choose any paragraph formatting options from the Text menu, however, because the indentation levels are predetermined in Outline view. The only way you can change the indentation is by changing the outline level.

Displaying Specific Outline Levels

After you have assigned different outline levels to paragraphs, you can choose which levels you want displayed in Outline view. This feature is useful for quickly determining the organization of a document. If you are writing a book, for example, you can choose to view only the level 1 paragraphs, which are the chapter titles. All other text temporarily is collapsed, or hidden from view.

The numbered buttons on the control strip determine which levels are displayed. When you click a button corresponding to an outline level, that level and all levels above it are displayed. If you click the 4 button, for example, only levels 4, 3, 2, and 1 are displayed.

To display all outline levels (including body text), click the Show All (snowflake) button on the control strip.

Alternatively, you can choose the Outline Level command from the View menu; Outline Level is available in Outline View only. Clicking one of the numbers in the Outline Level dialog box is the same as clicking the level buttons on the control strip. This method was designed for people who don't have a mouse; you cannot select a button on the control strip without a mouse, but you can select an option from a dialog box.

Unfortunately, WindowWorks does not provide an easy way to reorganize or change the order of paragraphs in Outline view. No mechanism exists for quickly moving one outline level and all its collapsed sublevels up or down within the outline.

You can, however, cut or copy a paragraph and paste it elsewhere in the outline. If you cut or copy a paragraph that is followed by collapsed sublevel paragraphs, the collapsed paragraphs are cut or copied as well. If, for example, you have collapsed all but the level 1 and 2 paragraphs from view by clicking the 2 button on the control strip and you then cut a level 2 paragraph, all the sublevels until the next level 2 paragraph are cut also. When you paste the paragraph, the sublevels are pasted as well.

Printing an Outline

Choosing Print from Outline view prints the document as displayed in Outline view. Only those paragraphs currently in view are printed; any collapsed paragraphs are not printed. Paragraph numbers always are printed in Outline view. You can change the font and style of outline text, but you cannot change the indentation of levels, which are printed as they appear on-screen.

Using Outlines with Styles

When you change outline levels in Outline view, the outline level displayed in the Paragraph dialog box changes as well. In other words, the outline level is a paragraph attribute, which means that an outline level can be defined as part of a style.

Outlining becomes a powerful feature when used in conjunction with styles, because you can combine the way text looks with the way text is organized. You may want a report title, for example, to be formatted using a large, bold font, such as Dixon 24-point bold; a report title also is a good example of a level 1 paragraph. Section titles in the report would be smaller than the report title itself—but still eye-catching—perhaps in Dixon 14-point bold. A section title style may be assigned an outline level of 2.

When you apply styles containing outline levels to text, the text automatically is numbered and indented in Outline view. You don't have to change levels using the buttons unless you want to override the level you defined as part of the style. See Chapter 4 for more information on using styles.

Creating a Table of Contents

After you have created headings and designated their level by using the Outline view or the Outline Level indicator in the Paragraph dialog box, WindowWorks can organize these headings into a table of contents for your document; you must use an outline to create a table of contents.

You can tell WindowWorks to include all headings for which you specified levels, or you can specify that only headings of certain levels be included in the table of contents. If, for example, you included nine levels of headings, your table of contents probably would be incredibly long and complex. Because a complex table of contents is not a particularly practical reference tool, you may want to limit the table of contents to the top two or three levels.

T I P   Wait until you are almost finished with your document before you generate a table of contents. Otherwise, you may find yourself editing, or even deleting and regenerating, your table of contents as you modify your document and the pagination changes.

1. Designate levels for headings in your document. Use the Outline view or specify a level in the Outline Level field in the Paragraph dialog box.

2. Move the cursor to where you want your table of contents to appear.

   NOTE   The table of contents does not appear at the beginning of your document automatically. The table of contents appears at the cursor's location when you select the Table of Contents option from the Utilities menu. Remember to place the cursor at the correct location before creating the table of contents. Usually, the table of contents should appear after any title pages and before the body of your document.

3. Choose Table of Contents from the Utilities menu.

   The Table of Contents dialog box appears (see fig. 5.20).

   In the Table of Contents dialog box, you can indicate which headings you want to include in the table of contents.

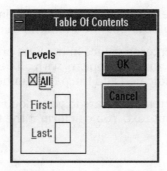

FIG. 5.20

Table Of
Contents dialog
box.

4. If you want to include all the levels that you have defined, click OK. The table of contents appears at the current cursor location.

 NOTE The All option is the default setting. Choose this option if you have defined only a few heading levels. If you have defined more than a few levels, the table of contents may be overwhelming.

5. If you want to include a limited group of headings in the table of contents, click the All toggle box to deselect it. You then can choose the first and last heading levels that you want to include in the table of contents.

When you deselect the All option, the First and Last heading level fields display the values 1 and 9—indicating that the table of contents includes all heading levels from 1 to 9 (see fig. 5.21).

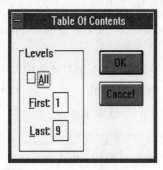

FIG. 5.21

TOC dialog
box with All
deselected.

Edit the First and Last field values so that they represent the group of headings that you want to include. You may need to edit only the Last value so that instead of using heading levels 1 through 9, WindowWorks uses levels 1 through 3, for example.

If you want to use the first 3 heading levels in your table of contents, the First value should be 1 and the Last value should be 3.

When you have entered values in the First and Last fields, click OK. The table of contents appears with all headings of the outline levels that you indicated and the page number for each heading.

After your table of contents appears in your document, its text is just like any other document text. You can format the text, alter the tab settings, and so on.

Working with Templates

You can save a document as a template so that everything contained in the document—text, graphics, styles, and so on—is available to new documents.

Saving a document as a template enables you to use that document's page setup attributes, margins, and styles as the basis for new documents. Templates are useful if you need to create consistently formatted documents, such as newsletters, proposals, or forms. Templates contain everything that a document contains.

Everything that composes a document is saved with the template: text, graphics, page dimensions, margins settings, footnotes, headers, footers, and so on. Even the current View menu setting, such as Outline, Page, and 75%, is saved so that a document created with the template opens to the selected view. Be certain that the current view setting is the view you want for new documents. If, for example, you save the template at 75% Size, new documents you create with this template appear at 75% Size as well. (Of course, you always can change the view later.) If you're not sure which view is appropriate, choose Actual Size from the View menu.

To save a document as a template, perform the following steps:

1. Open the document you want to save as a template.

2. Choose Save As from the File menu.

   The Save As dialog box appears.

3. The document's name is displayed in the Filename field. You can change or retain the document's name as the name of the template.

4. Choose Template(.wpt) from the Type pull-down menu (see fig. 5.22). The extension WPT is added automatically to the filename you entered. WindowWorks recognizes templates only by their extensions, so don't enter a different extension.

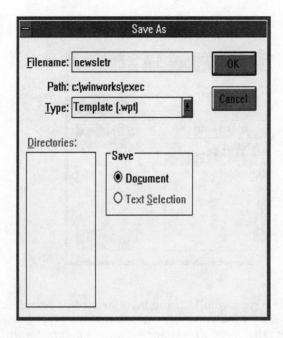

FIG. 5.22

Save As dialog
box with
Template (.wpt)
selected.

5. Click OK.

You are returned to what appears to be the document. Notice,
however, that the filename displayed on the Word Processor title
bar has the extension WPT, which indicates not a document but a
template.

You can choose the style before you initially save the template. To
make and save a change on an already opened template, complete the
following steps:

1. From the Style menu, choose an initial style for new documents.
   Choose Body Text, for example, from the Style pull-down menu.
   Body Text is the style you probably will use most.

2. Choose Save from the File menu to save all changes made to the
   template.

When you open new documents, you can select any template that you
have created. Initially, when you create new documents, WindowWorks
uses the default template, Normal. You can, however, instruct Window-
Works to use a different template for a new document or for all new
documents.

To use custom templates with new documents, perform the following
steps:

1. Choose New from the File menu.

   The New dialog box appears.

2. Select a template from the Use Template list box (see fig. 5.23).

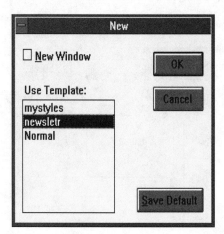

FIG. 5.23

New dialog box
with a template
selected.

3. Click the Save Default button if you want this template to be selected every time you create a new document. Otherwise, when
   you start the Word Processor, new documents continue to use
   Normal as the default template.

4. Click OK to create a new document using the custom template.

By following these steps, you can use the text and graphics stored in a
template whenever you create new documents. Remember, too, that
you can add text items from any WindowWorks document or template.
The document that you use text from need not be created using the
same template as the new document; the template that you use text
from need not be the default template. Transferring the text contents of
one document or template into another document, a process called
merging, is discussed in the following section.

Merging Documents and Templates

WindowWorks enables you to merge the text and styles—but not
graphics—of two documents or templates. Suppose, for example, that
you want to combine text from two documents. You can open that the
first document and then bring in text from the second document. In

many cases, especially with short documents, you may want to use the Copy and Paste features to copy all the text from one document and paste the text into another document.

To transfer text and styles from a document or template into an existing document, perform the following steps:

1. Open the document into which you want to merge text and position the cursor where you want the incoming text to begin. If you put the cursor at the beginning of the document, for example, text from the incoming document begins at that point and pushes down all other text.

2. Choose Merge Text from the File menu.

   The Merge dialog box appears.

3. If you want to merge text and styles from a WindowWorks document, choose Document(.wpd) from the Type pull-down menu; choose Template(.wpt) if you want to merge text and styles from a WindowWorks template. The names of all available documents or templates appear in the Files list box.

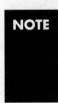 If you want to merge text from a template, double-click EXEC in the Directories list box. All WindowWorks templates are stored in the EXEC subdirectory. The EXEC subdirectory is created automatically when you install WindowWorks; EXEC holds all WindowWorks program files and templates.

4. Select a document or template, and click OK (see fig. 5.24).

   All of the selected document's text and styles are added to the current document.

 If the current document and the merging document contain styles with the same name, styles in the current document are replaced by those from the incoming document or template.

When you merge documents or templates containing text, all text from the merged document or template is appended to the current document beginning at the cursor location. Some elements, such as graphic objects, frames (including text frames), charts, and tables, are not merged.

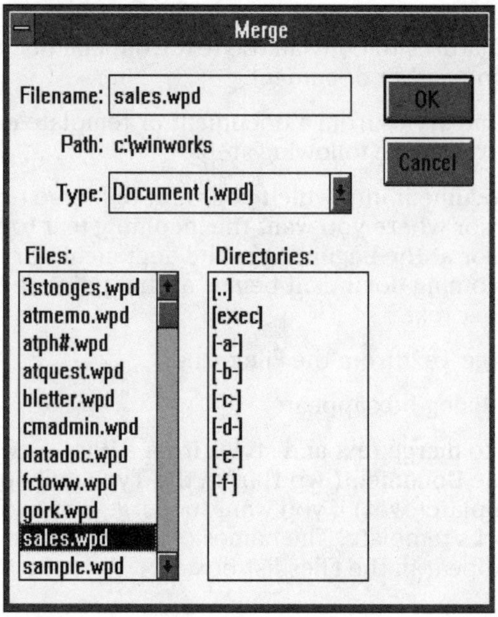

FIG. 5.24

Merge dialog box with Document selected.

Chapter Summary

The techniques and elements discussed in this chapter are optional when you are creating a document. You can write an excellent document that does not include a table of contents, headers and footers, footnotes, an index, or page numbers; in fact, these elements would be inappropriate in some documents. You can, however, use these elements to give lengthier, more detailed documents an extremely professional edge.

A document marked clearly on every page with a header or footer containing a title and page number is easy to read and use. For longer documents, chapter separations and independent page numbering for each chapter may simplify the reader's task of finding information. A table of contents is appropriate in most documents, and a well-formatted table of contents can be a real eye-catcher. If your document is particularly detailed and complex, readers appreciate footnotes and a thorough index.

These elements are tools that you can use to simplify the reader's job; the Outline view, on the other hand, is an outstanding tool for simplifying your job as a writer. You can organize your thoughts quickly or get an overview of an existing document's structure. Use the Outline view to give your document direction and overall cohesion.

Working with Objects and Frames

I n the preceding chapters, you learned to use WindowWorks to enter, edit, and format text. WindowWorks also enables you to create
and manipulate graphic objects. You can draw rudimentary graphics,
such as lines, rectangles, and ovals by using the WindowWorks drawing
tools. You can import bit-mapped, TIFF, and PCX graphics files created
with other programs. Additionally, you can import objects from other
WindowWorks modules, such as tables from the spreadsheet or charts
from the chart editor. You also can create text objects called *text
frames*, which are documents within a document.

This chapter discusses the types of graphic objects you can use in your
documents. These graphic objects share at least one significant charac-
teristic: all objects are independent of the main body of text in a document; the graphics exist on a separate object layer. If you draw a
rectangle in the middle of a blank page, for example, and then type text
on that page, the text will not move or push down the rectangle; rather,
the text will flow over or around the rectangle according to your specification. All objects are anchored to the page—not to the text. In this
respect, WindowWorks is more like a desktop publishing program than
a word processing program.

Comparing Object Mode to Text Mode

WindowWorks has two modes: Text mode and Object mode. You already are familiar with Text mode, in which you enter and format text. You can create and manipulate objects in Object mode, which sometimes is called Pointer mode. Each mode has its own button on the control strip (see fig. 6.1). Click the Object button to enter object mode and the Text button to return to text mode.

Text mode and Object mode buttons on the control strip.

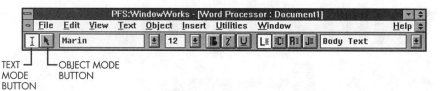

TEXT MODE BUTTON   OBJECT MODE BUTTON

All commands are not available in all modes. Text menu commands, for example, which are not used to manipulate objects, are grayed when you click the Object mode button. Likewise, most of the Object menu commands are unavailable in Text mode. Certain types of objects—specifically text frames and tables—possess attributes you can edit using both modes. You edit the text within a text frame, for example, in Text mode, but you edit the frame itself—size, position, border, and fill attributes—in Object mode.

Drawing Simple Objects

You can create horizontal or vertical lines, rectangles, ovals, and rounded-corner rectangles by using the drawing tools from the Object menu. In Chapter 3, you added border lines to paragraphs. Paragraph borders look similar to lines or rectangles you create with the drawing tools; however, paragraph borders actually are paragraph attributes anchored to the text, which means that the borders move with the paragraph. When the size of the paragraph changes, so does the length of the border lines. Objects you draw with drawing tools, on the other hand, are completely separate from the text in your document.

To draw an object, choose Tools from the Object menu. The Tools menu contains six drawing tools: the frame tool (discussed later in this chapter), vertical and horizontal line tools, rectangle tool, oval tool, and rounded-corner rectangle tool (see fig. 6.2).

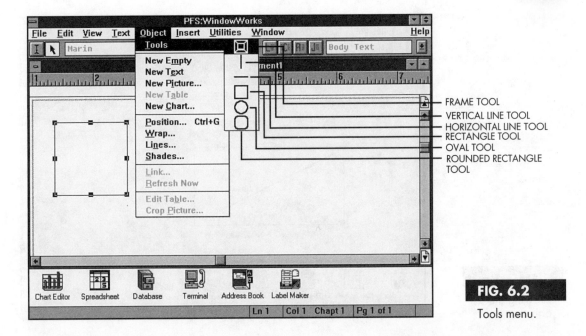

FIG. 6.2

Tools menu.

When you select a drawing tool, the cursor changes to a cross hair containing a representation of the object you are about to create. If you are drawing an oval, for example, the cursor is a cross hair above an oval. Position the cross hair where you want the object to begin, and click and hold the left mouse button while dragging to where you want the object to end (see fig. 6.3).

The outline of the object you are drawing *rubberbands* as you move the mouse; a rubberband is a shadow or outline that shows you what the object will look like. The border of an object that is being resized, stretches or contracts like a rubberband. Release the mouse button when you are satisfied with the object's size and shape.

When you release the mouse, the object is drawn and the cursor is still a cross hair. You can draw another object of the same type, press the right mouse button once to retrieve the Object mode pointer for moving or resizing the object, or double-click the right mouse button to switch to Text mode.

When selecting a tool, instead of choosing the Tools menu from the Object menu, simply double-click the right mouse button. This shortcut displays the Tools menu at the position in the word processor where you double-clicked (see fig. 6.4). The menu disappears after you select a tool.

T I P

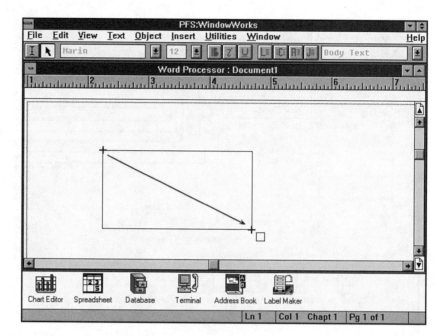

FIG. 6.3

Drawing an object.

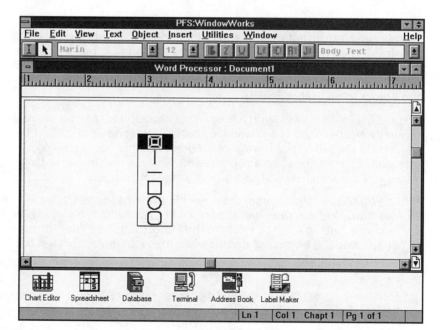

FIG. 6.4

Tools menu positioned in the word processor window.

You can draw a limitless number of objects in a document. You cannot, however, draw objects that extend past the boundaries of the page. Margins, on the other hand, affect text only so that you can draw objects that extend past the margins. In fact, graphics, such as decorative page borders, letterhead designs, and logos, are most useful when placed outside the margins. Remember, however, that most laser and inkjet printers reserve some space—usually between 1/8 and 1/4 inch—as nonprintable area. If you draw an object that extends to the very edge of the page, portions of the object may not be printed. Figure 6.5 shows a page containing several different objects available in WindowWorks.

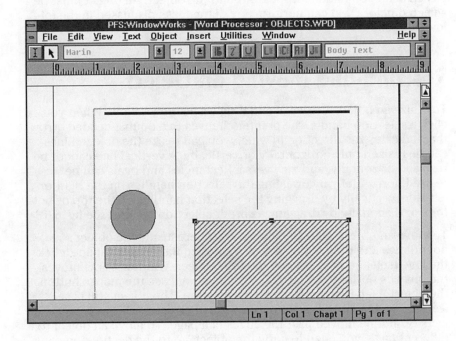

FIG. 6.5

Sample objects.

Immediately after being drawn, an object is surrounded by selection handles. If the object is a horizontal or vertical line, selection handles appear on the end points of the line. Selection handles indicate that an object is selected. Only one object can be selected at a time. You cannot select multiple objects for grouping or for simultaneously changing attributes, such as line width, fill pattern, and text wrap.

Manipulating Objects

After drawing an object, you can modify the object in several ways: you can change the object's size, location, and appearance. All the commands for working with graphic objects are located on the Object menu. Before you can modify an object, however, you must first select it.

Selecting an Object

To select an object, you must be in Object mode. To activate Object mode, click the Object mode (arrow pointer) button on the control strip or click the right mouse button. Next, click the object you want to select. Selection handles appear around the object. An object must be selected before you can perform any of the tasks discussed in the following sections.

Resizing and Moving an Object

To resize an object, you click and drag a selection handle. When you click a selection handle, the pointer changes to a double-headed arrow that indicates the direction in which you can resize the object. Lines can be resized only horizontally or vertically. A vertical line cannot be resized horizontally, and vice versa. Rectangles and ovals can be resized horizontally by dragging the selection handles on the right or left side, vertically by dragging the selection handles on the top or bottom, or diagonally by dragging a corner selection handle (see fig. 6.6).

To move an object, click the mouse anywhere inside the object's boundaries and drag. If the object is a horizontal or vertical line, click the line itself and drag. As you drag the object, WindowWorks moves the object's outline (see fig. 6.7). When you release the mouse button, the object itself is moved to the new location. The object still is selected, which enables you to move, format, or delete the object. Objects cannot be moved past the edges of a page. To move an object to a different page, you need to copy the object, go to the destination page, and then paste the object. (For more information on this process, see the section "Copying and Pasting Objects" later in this chapter.)

Deleting an Object

To delete an object, select the object and then press the Del key, or choose Cut from the Edit menu. This process deletes the object and places a copy of the object on the Clipboard. You later can paste the cut object in another location within the same document or in a different document.

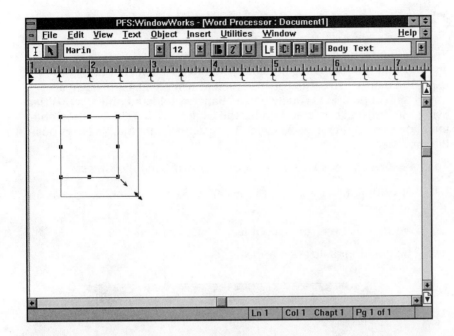

FIG. 6.6

Square being resized.

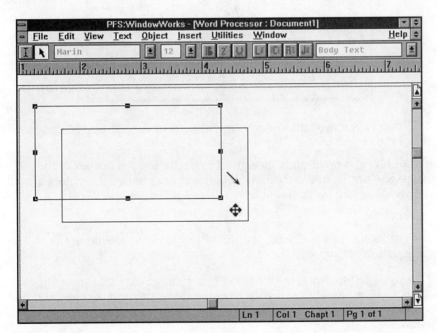

FIG. 6.7

Rectangle being moved.

Changing the Position of an Object

You can use several methods for changing the position of, or moving, an object. In the preceding section, you moved a selected object by using the mouse. This method is sufficient when you can *eyeball* an object's ideal position. You also can change a selected object's position using the Position command under the Object menu. The Position command displays a dialog box in which you can set an object's exact position and size.

To change an object's size or position, perform the following steps:

1. Select the object you want to modify; selection handles appear on the object.

2. Choose Position from the Object menu, or press Ctrl-G.

   The Position dialog box appears (see fig. 6.8).

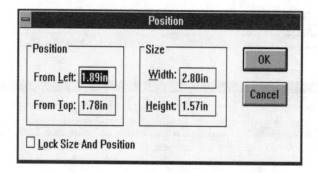

FIG. 6.8

Position dialog box.

3. Enter (in inches) the object's position from the top and left edges of the page.

   An object's position is measured from the top-left corner of the page—not from the margins. If you want to change the object's size, you can enter (in inches) values for Height and Width.

4. Click OK.

   The dialog box is closed and the object is repositioned at the location you specified.

As these steps illustrate, the Position command is useful for moving objects to exact locations. If your document layout requires this kind of accuracy, use the Position command instead of moving objects with the mouse.

Check the Lock Size And Position option in the Position dialog box to prevent the object from being moved or resized accidentally with the mouse. This option also prevents you from deleting the object using the Del key but not from cutting it using the Cut command.

T I P

Copying and Pasting Objects

You can copy a selected object to the Clipboard so that you can later paste the object into a different location within the same document or in a different document. For example, assume you need to create several 1-by-4-inch rectangles. Rather than drawing and resizing the rectangles one at a time, create a single rectangle, copy it to the Clipboard, and then paste as many copies as you need. You also can copy an object in one document and paste it into another document.

To copy and paste an object, perform the following steps:

1. Select the object you want to copy; selection handles appear on the object.

2. Choose Copy from the Edit menu.

    A duplicate of the object—including such attributes as line width and fill pattern—is placed on the Clipboard. If the Clipboard contains another object, that object is replaced by the one you just copied.

    The object remains on the Clipboard until you copy another object or until you exit WindowWorks.

3. Go to the place in the document where you want to place a copy of the object, and choose Paste Object from the Edit menu.

    A copy of the object is pasted into the middle of the current window. Objects always are pasted to the center of the current window but are never pasted past the page edges. In most cases, you need to move the object by using the mouse or the Position command. (See previous sections on moving and positioning an object.)

NOTE Objects can be copied and pasted only in Page view. Page view is the only view that enables you to switch between Text and Object modes; you cannot select or manipulate objects in Continuous or Outline views. Choose Page from the View menu before working with objects.

Changing Line Types, Shading, and Fill Patterns

You can change the line width or style of any object you draw. For *closed* objects—all objects except horizontal and vertical lines—you also can change the shading or fill patterns.

To change the line width or line style of an object, perform the following steps:

1. Select the object whose line width or style you want to change; selection handles appear on the object.

2. Choose Lines from the Object menu.

   The Lines dialog box appears (see fig. 6.9).

   WindowWorks provides several different line widths that range from Hair Line, which is the thinnest line your printer can generate, to 12 point. You also can choose from three multiline styles. You can select a single line width or a multiline style—but not both. The default line width for new objects you draw is Hair Line. For graphics you import from other programs—such as bit-mapped, TIFF, and PCX files, or tables and charts from the spreadsheet and chart editor—the Lines command controls the style or width of border lines for the object. The default border line style for imported graphics is None (no border). You can, however, add border lines to any imported graphic object.

3. To select a line width or style, simply click that option.

   A box appears around the width or style to indicate the current selection.

4. Choose OK to close the Lines dialog box.

The selected object reflects the line width and style you chose in the Lines dialog box.

In addition to changing line width and style, you can add background shades or cross-hatch patterns to objects. Any object that you draw or import (except horizontal and vertical lines) can contain fill patterns or shades.

To add a background shade or cross-hatch pattern to an object, perform the following steps:

1. Select the object whose shade or fill pattern you want to change; selection handles appear on the object.

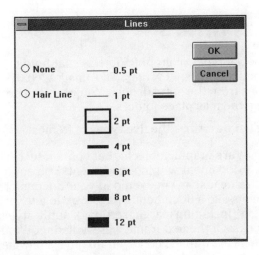

FIG. 6.9

Lines dialog box.

2. Choose Shades from the Object menu.

   The Shades dialog box appears (see fig. 6.10).

3. Select a shade or pattern by clicking it.

   A box appears around the current selection.

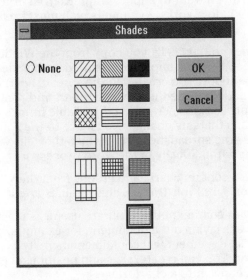

FIG. 6.10

Shades dialog box.

4. Choose OK to close the Shades dialog box.

The selected object is filled with the shade or pattern you designated.

Using Frames

Frames are special types of graphic objects that hold elements, such as text, bit-mapped graphics, PCX files, TIFF images, charts from the chart editor, or tables from the spreadsheet. You even can create empty frames and use them as placeholders.

The following list describes the five types of frames:

- *Text frames* are graphic objects that contain text. Think of a text frame as a document within a document. You enter and edit text in a text frame just as you would in your document. The size of a text frame is like a document's page size. In a text frame, you can format text (including margin settings), apply styles, and even spell check as if the text frame were a distinct WindowWorks document. Text frames, however, do have a few limitations. Text frames cannot contain headers, footers, footnotes, page breaks, or chapter breaks. You also cannot mark index entries or create a table of contents in a text frame.

- *Picture frames* can contain bit-mapped graphics, such as graphics created in Windows Paintbrush, PCX files created in programs such as PC Paintbrush, or TIFF images created in most scanning programs. If you want to import graphics from other programs into your WindowWorks documents, you must create picture frames.

- *Table frames* contain cells you copy from the WindowWorks spreadsheet. If, for example, you wanted to include in a document an expense report you created in the spreadsheet, you can copy the cells that compose the expense report and paste them into the word processor to create a table. Table frames are *linked*, which means that any changes you make to the source of the in-formation—the spreadsheet from which the cells were copied—can appear automatically in the word processor.

- *Chart frames* contain charts and graphs from the WindowWorks chart editor. Like table frames, chart frames are linked.

- *Empty frames* contain nothing but are useful as placeholders. When you are laying out a document, for example, you may know that the final document will contain an uncreated chart from the chart editor. You can create, size, and position an empty frame and later change it to a chart frame.

You can use several methods to create a frame. The first method is to use the frame tool to draw the frame and then specify its type. The second method is to specify the frame type and then draw the frame.

With the first method, you draw the frame by using the frame tool from the Tools menu. With the second method, you choose one of the frame commands from the Object menu and then draw the frame.

A third method exists for creating table, chart, or picture frames: if you copy a table or chart from the spreadsheet or chart editor by using the Copy command, you can create a table or chart frame by choosing Paste Object from the Word Processor's Edit menu and then drawing the frame. You likewise can create a picture frame if you copy to the Clipboard a bit-mapped image from a program, such as Windows Paintbrush.

Using the Frame Tool

To create a frame by using the frame tool, perform the following steps:

1. Choose the Tools menu from the Object menu (or double-click the right mouse button) and select the frame tool (see fig. 6.11).

   The pointer changes to a cross hair.

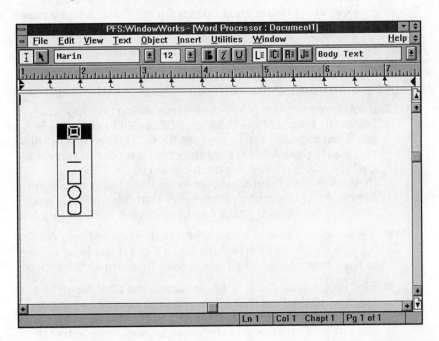

2. Position the cross hair where you want to position one of the frame's corners. Then click and hold the left mouse button while dragging to where you want to position the opposite corner.

3. Release the mouse button when you are satisfied with the size and dimensions of the frame.

The New Frame dialog box appears (see fig. 6.12).

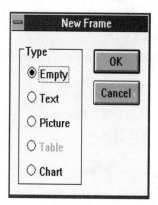

FIG. 6.12

New Frame
dialog box.

The Table option is available only if the Clipboard contains cells copied from the WindowWorks spreadsheet. To create a table frame, therefore, you first must open a spreadsheet, select a range of cells, and copy them to the Clipboard.

4. Choose a frame type—Empty, Text, Picture, Table, or Chart—and click OK.

The frame type you choose determines which dialog box appears:

■ *If you choose Picture*, the New Picture dialog box appears. Select the graphic type (bitmap, PCX, or TIFF) and the file you want to put in the frame (see fig. 6.13). The Files list displays all the available files of the chosen type. Alternatively, if a bit-mapped image has been copied to the Clipboard (from Windows Paintbrush, for example), simply select the Clipboard as the source. Remember that this option is available only if a bitmap image has been copied to the Clipboard.

■ *If you choose Chart*, the New Chart dialog box appears (see fig. 6.14). Select a Chart Editor file. If a chart has been copied to the Clipboard, you can select the Clipboard as the source.

■ *When you create Table or Chart frames*, the Link dialog box appears. In the Link dialog box, you can choose to turn on Auto Refresh (see fig. 6.15). When you turn on Auto Refresh, any changes you make to the information source automatically appear in the Word Processor document. This feature also is referred to as a *hot link*. The Link box appears after you select a chart to go in the frame.

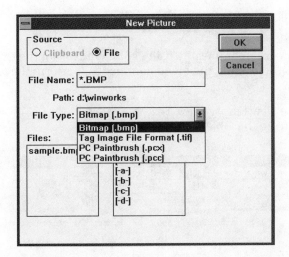

FIG. 6.13

New Picture
dialog box.

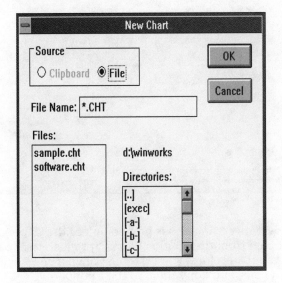

FIG. 6.14

New Chart
dialog box.

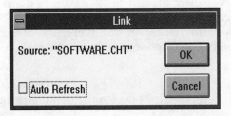

FIG. 6.15

Link dialog box.

Using the Object Menu

You also can create frames by using commands from the Object menu. To create a frame using the menu commands, perform the following steps:

1. Choose New Empty, New Text, New Picture, New Table, or New Chart from the Object menu (see fig. 6.16).

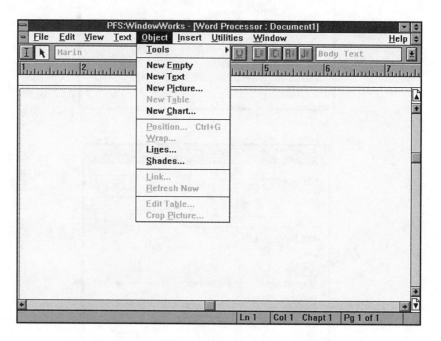

FIG. 6.16

The Object
menu.

The New Table command is grayed unless the Clipboard contains cells copied from the WindowWorks Spreadsheet. To create a table frame, therefore, you first must open a spreadsheet, select a range of cells, and copy them to the Clipboard.

If you choose New Picture, the New Picture dialog box appears. Select the graphic type (bit-mapped, PCX, or TIFF) and the file you want to put in the frame. Alternatively, if a bit-mapped image has been copied to the Clipboard, simply select the Clipboard as the source.

If you choose New Chart, the New Chart dialog box appears (refer to fig. 6.14). Select a Chart Editor file. If a chart has been copied to the Clipboard, you can select Clipboard as the source.

After you select a file command, the frame tool pointer appears.

2. Position the frame tool pointer where you want one of the frame's corners. Click and hold the left mouse button while dragging to the opposite corner. Release the mouse button when you are satisfied with the size and dimensions of the frame.

Using the Paste Object Command

In addition to the methods described in the preceding two sections, you can use the Paste Object command to create table, chart, and picture frames. If you have copied to the Clipboard such an object as a range of cells from the Spreadsheet, a chart from the Chart Editor, or a bit-mapped image from such a program as Windows Paintbrush, you can create a frame simply by choosing Paste Object from the Edit menu. Again, the Clipboard must contain an object—otherwise the Paste Object command is grayed.

To create a table frame, for example, you first must open a WindowWorks spreadsheet in the Spreadsheet module, select the range of cells you want included in a table, and choose Copy from the Edit menu (see fig. 6.17). Next, return to the Word Processor and choose Paste Object from the Edit menu (see fig. 6.18). Next, specify whether you want the Auto Refresh option activated (see fig. 6.19); the frame tool appears, and you can draw the table frame (see fig. 6.20). Figure 6.21 shows a completed table frame based on the information in the spreadsheet in figure 6.17.

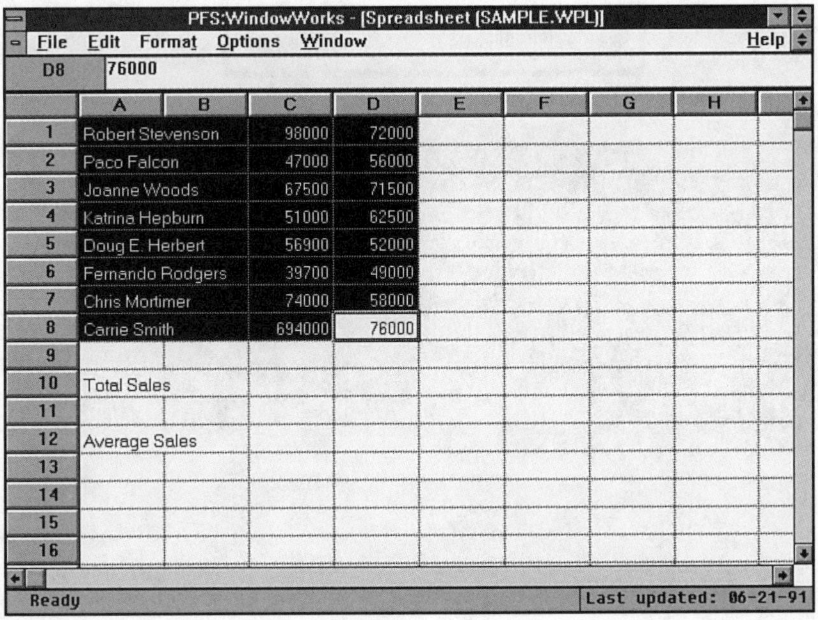

FIG. 6.17

A selected range of cells in the spreadsheet.

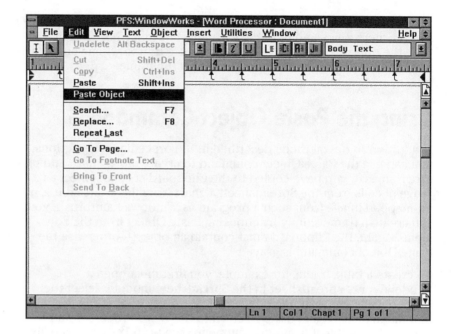

FIG. 6.18

The Paste Object option on the Word Processor Edit menu.

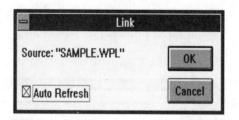

FIG. 6.19

Selecting the Auto Refresh option.

T I P   When you copy cells from the Spreadsheet, you can choose Paste or Paste Object from the Word Processor's Edit menu. You can use the Paste Object command to create a table frame; you can use the Paste command if you just want to paste the text from the cells into the Word Processor. In other words, the Paste command does not create a table. When you paste Spreadsheet data into the Word Processor as text, columns are separated by tabs and rows are separated by line breaks.

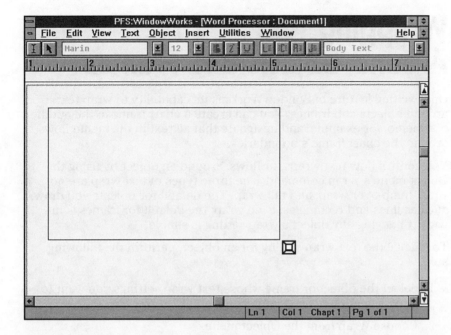

FIG. 6.20

Drawing the frame.

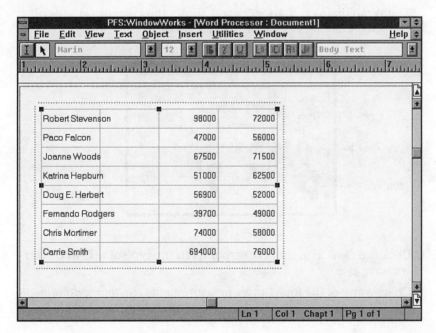

FIG. 6.21

A completed table frame.

Wrapping Text Around Objects and Frames

One exciting feature of WindowWorks is its capability to wrap text around objects and frames. You can create a chart frame in the middle of a memo, for example, and designate that all text in the memo flows around the chart frame's boundaries.

You control how text wraps, or flows, around an object by using the Object menu's Wrap command. The three types of text wrap are no wrap, jump-over wrap, and full wrap. The default for objects you draw, such as lines and rectangles, is no wrap; the default for frames is full wrap. Changing any object's wrap setting is simple.

To change the text wrap setting for an object, perform the following steps:

1. Select the object or frame whose text wrap settings you want to alter; selection handles appear around the object.

2. Choose Wrap from the Object menu.

   The Wrap dialog box appears and shows the current settings of the selected object or frame (see fig. 6.22).

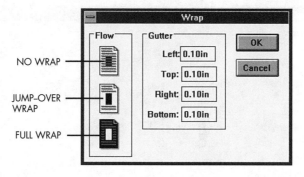

FIG. 6.22

Wrap dialog box.

3. Click the Flow icon that corresponds to the type of text wrap you want.

4. Change any of the four Gutter measurements. *Gutter measurements* are the minimum distances you want separating the object's four sides from the text.

5. Click OK to close the dialog box and apply the text wrap settings you specified.

Clicking one of the following three Flow icons determines how text wraps around an object:

■ *No wrap icon* turns text wrap off. Text flows over the object as though the object didn't exist. You probably would not use this option for frames; however, you may find it useful for lines and other objects you create using the drawing tools.

■ *Jump-over icon* stops text above and continues text below an object. Values entered for the Left and Right Gutter settings are ignored, because no text wraps on the left or right sides of the object.

■ *Full wrap icon* flows text around all four sides of an object.

Figures 6.23–6.25 show examples of each type of wrap.

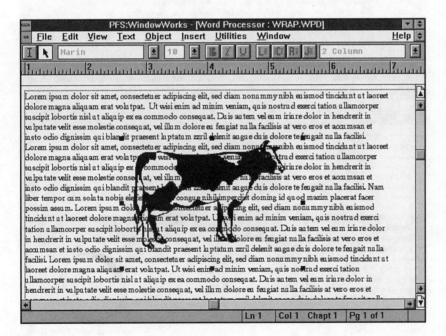

FIG. 6.23

Graphic with no text wrap.

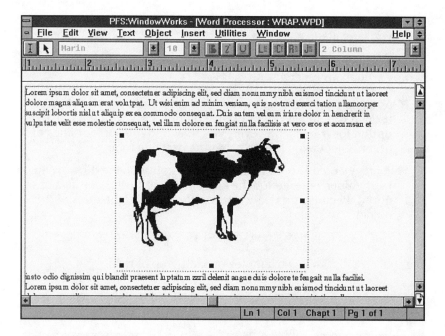

FIG. 6.24

Graphic with jump-over text wrap.

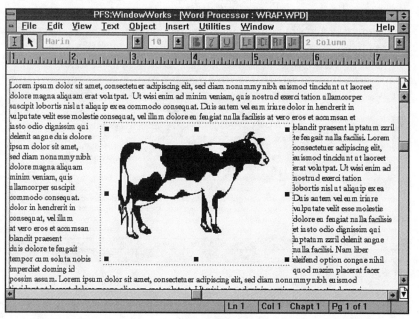

FIG. 6.25

Graphic with full text wrap

Gutter settings are used to control the amount of space between an object and surrounding text. The default gutter is 1/10 inch. In figure 6.26, the top and bottom gutters are set to 0.5 inches; the left and right gutters are set to 0.125 inches.

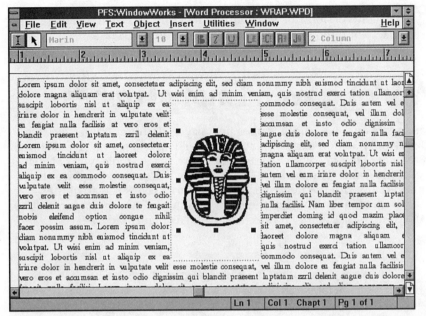

FIG. 6.26

Samples of
different gutter
widths.

If you move or resize an object or frame, the wrap settings remain
intact. Similarly, if you cut or copy an object, its wrap settings
remain intact when you paste the object.

You can wrap text around three sides of an object by increasing one of
the wrap gutters to the page margin or column edge (see fig. 6.27).

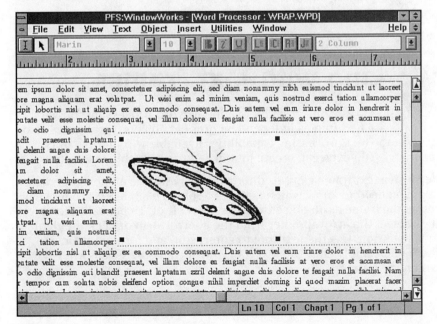

FIG. 6.27

Text wrapped on
three sides with
left, top, and
bottom gutters set
to 1/10 inch and
right gutter
increased to
page margin
or column
boundary.

NOTE In Version 1.0, wrap gutters must be less than one inch. This limitation does not exist for Version 1.1 users.

Working with Empty Frames

You create and use empty frames just as you do other frames. First, specify the position and wrap attributes. Then, when you have decided to replace the frame with a picture or chart, for example, you can select the empty frame, choose New Chart or New Picture, and replace the empty frame with the new one. WindowWorks keeps the attributes— size, location, and wrap—of the empty frame and uses them for the new frame. Therefore, empty frames are useful as placeholders.

T I P You can use the size and position of a selected frame as the basis for a new frame (see fig 6.28). If you choose one of the New frame commands from the Object menu when another frame is selected and surrounded by selection handles, WindowWorks asks whether you want to use the selected frame for the one you are creating (see fig. 6.29). If you choose Yes, the selected frame is replaced by the one you are creating (see fig. 30). Be careful when you use this method. Short of recreating the frame, you cannot undo your action. This method is particularly useful for changing Empty Frames to other types of frames.

Working with Text Frames

Text frames are a truly great innovation in word processing software. Not only are text frames independent graphic objects; text frames also have all the text processing capabilities available with normal document text. You even can create multiple columns within text frames.

Because a text frame can be edited and formatted as an object and as text, you need to know which features apply to each mode. To move or resize the frame as an object, use the object tool. To activate the object tool, select the arrow pointer from the control strip or click the right mouse button. Use the text tool to enter, edit, and format text inside the frame. Simply click the text tool (the I-beam cursor) anywhere within the frame.

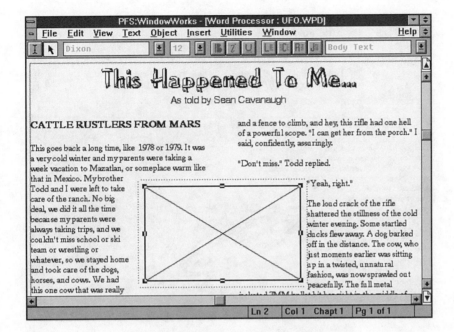

FIG. 6.28

An empty frame in a document.

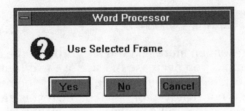

FIG. 6.29

The Use Selected Frame dialog box.

When a text frame is selected as an object, text formatting commands are grayed. Conversely, when text in the frame is selected, object commands are grayed. If you want to spell check a text frame, for example, but the Spell Check command is grayed, you are in Object mode and need to switch to Text mode before selecting text-related commands. If you want to change the text wrap characteristics of a frame but the Wrap command is grayed, you are in Text mode and need to select the frame in Object mode.

An easy way to tell which mode you're in is to check the control strip. If the text tool button (I-beam) is pressed, you're in text mode. If the object tool button (arrow) is pressed, you're in object mode.

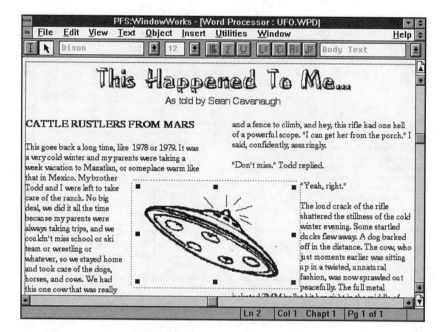

FIG. 6.30

Empty frame
changed to a
picture frame,
where the size
and position
remain the same.

Resizing Text Frames

A text frame may contain more text than is visible in the currently sized frame. If, for example, you decrease the size of a text frame containing several lines of text, less text will be visible. When you resize a frame, text in the frame is not removed or deleted; the text is just hidden from view. You can enlarge the frame by using the object tool or the Object menu's Position command so that all text is visible.

Changes to the font, font size, and other formatting attributes may affect how much text is visible. If a text frame is full of 10-point text and all text is visible, changing the point size to 14 will cause some of the text to be hidden (see fig. 6.31). To see all the text again, you would need to decrease the point size or enlarge the frame size (see fig. 6.32).

Spell Checking Text Frames

When the text cursor is inside a text frame, you can check the spelling of all text in the frame by choosing Spell Check from the Utilities menu. You can spell check only one frame at a time. If the cursor is in the main body of the document when you choose Spell Check, text contained in frames will not be checked.

The WindowWorks thesaurus also is available when you are working in text frames. Simply position the cursor on a word in the text frame, and choose Thesaurus from the Utilities menu.

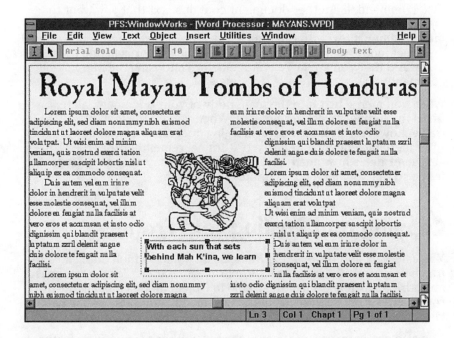

FIG. 6.31

More text is present than is visible in frame.

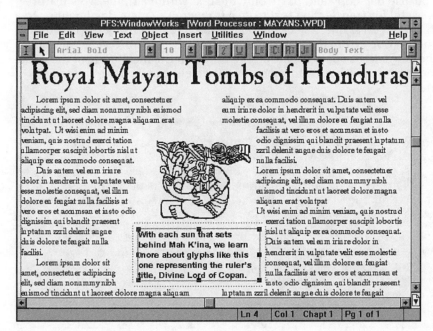

FIG. 6.32

The frame is resized so that all text is visible.

Merging Text from Other Documents

You can merge text into text frames by using the File menu's Merge Text command. If another document contains text that you want to include in a text frame, use the Merge Text command under the File menu to import text into the frame. The Merge Text command is grayed in Object mode; therefore, be certain that the cursor is inside the text frame and that you are in Text mode before choosing the Merge Text command.

When you merge text into the main body of your document, all text items (including styles) are merged. When you merge text into a text frame, however, styles from the merging document *are not* merged. After merging a document into a text frame, remember that the frame's size determines how much text is visible. You may need to enlarge the frame so that all merged text appears on-screen.

Copying and Pasting Text Frames

You can copy and paste a text frame as an object, which duplicates the frame itself and all its text and formatting attributes. To copy and paste an entire text frame, select the frame in Object mode by using the arrow pointer, choose Copy from the Edit menu, and then choose Paste Object. You can duplicate the frame as many times as necessary.

You also can copy and paste only the text within a frame. This feature is useful for transferring text from a frame to the main document or to a different text frame. Select the text in the frame by using the text tool; choose Copy from the Edit menu; position the cursor where you want the new text to appear—within the frame, in the main body of the document, or in another text frame—and then choose Paste from the Edit menu.

T I P   The WindowWorks header and footer capabilities are somewhat limited; for example, you cannot set tabs, use multiple fonts or styles, or paragraph border lines or shades. Headers and footers are useful for including auto-repeating items, such as page numbers and chapter numbers; for page and chapter numbers, no easy alternative exists to using headers and footers.

For shorter documents that require complex headers or footers, however, you can create a text frame to use as a header or footer; copy it; and paste it on each page in the document. In fact, you can combine the header or footer feature with text frames. In figure 6.33, the header is a text frame, and the footer is an actual footer used for page numbering (see fig. 6.34).

The footer feature was used for page numbering. You cannot include auto-repeating and auto-incrementing or chapter numbers in a text frame. You could accomplish these tasks manually, but this procedure would be difficult for long documents.

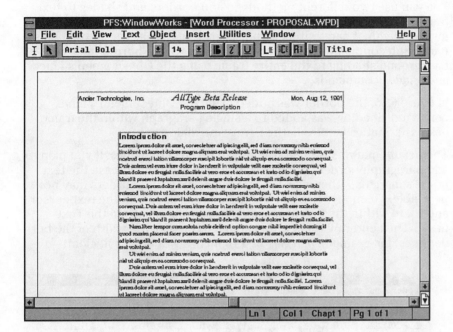

FIG. 6.33

A header in a text frame copied on each page.

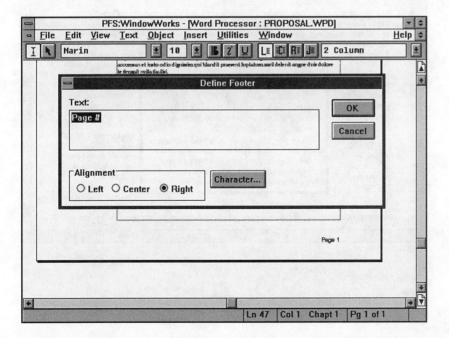

FIG. 6.34

The Define Footer dialog box, which creates the page number in the lower-right corner.

Adding Borders and Shades to Text Frames

You can use two different methods to add borders and shades to text frames. The first method is to add border lines and background shading to individual paragraphs within a text frame using the Text menu's Paragraph command. The second method is to add border lines and background shading to the entire frame using the Object menu's Lines and Shades commands.

In figure 6.35, the border was added using the Object menu's Lines command. Shading was added to a single paragraph within the frame using the Shades feature in the Paragraph dialog box.

The default margins for text frames are set to zero inches. If you plan to add paragraph borders or shades, you may want to increase the text frame's margins; otherwise, left and right paragraph borders may not be visible. To change the text frame's margins, position the text cursor anywhere within the text frame and choose Margins from the Text menu. Then enter margins wide enough to display the width of the border lines; for example, margins of 0.10 inches would be sufficient.

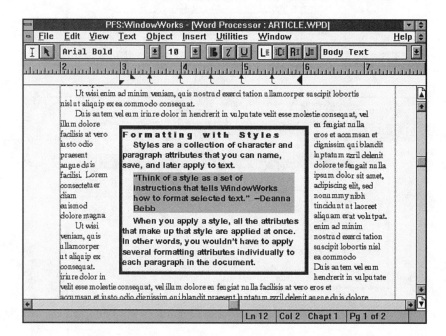

FIG. 6.35

Border and shading added to a text frame.

CAUTION: Although you can use some of WindowWorks' more sophisticated features—such as inserting merge fields from a database file and formatting text into multiple columns—try not to go overboard when using text frames. Text frames make great picture captions, are useful for positioning text outside page margins, and easily can be duplicated using the Copy and Paste commands; in short, text frames have many uses. Text frames do, however, have some limitations and are not well suited for handling large amounts of text.

Working with Picture Frames

Picture frames have qualities and formatting features that other frame types do not. You can resize picture frames, position them, and add borders—but not shades. In addition, you can scale and crop picture frames, which you cannot do to other WindowWorks objects. You also can copy and paste pictures from other programs, such as Windows Paintbrush, into WindowWorks picture frames.

Copying a Picture

To copy a picture from Paintbrush to WindowWorks, perform the following steps:

1. Open Windows Paintbrush, and select an image or part of an image.

2. Choose Copy from the Edit menu (see fig. 6.36).

   Several bit-mapped files are distributed with Microsoft Windows. You can open these bit-mapped files, such as PAPER.BMP, BOXES.BMP, PARTY.BMP, the Paintbrush program. Alternatively, you can create your own bit-mapped files.

 NOTE Although you can create color bitmaps and import them into WindowWorks as picture frames, color is not yet supported by WindowWorks. Color files are displayed in color but always print in black and white. Similarly, color PCX files are not supported and cannot even be opened in WindowWorks.

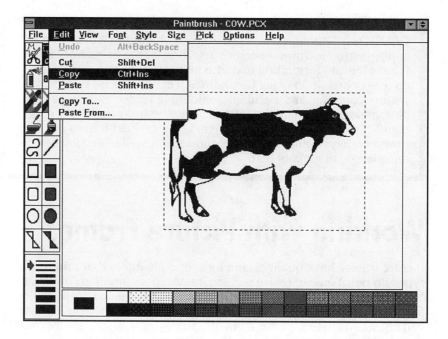

FIG. 6.36

Copying a
Windows
Paintbrush
picture.

3. Open the WindowWorks Word Processor, and choose Paste
   Object from the Edit menu.

   Depending on how much memory your system has and which
   Windows mode you are running, you may be able to run
   WindowWorks and Paintbrush at the same time.

   The frame tool pointer appears.

4. Draw a frame.

   The bit-mapped graphic you copied from Paintbrush appears in
   the frame (see fig. 6.37).

Instead of choosing Paste Object in step 3, you can choose New Picture
from the Object menu. Alternatively, you can use the frame tool from
the Tools menu to draw the frame and then select Picture from the New
Frame dialog box. With either method, when the New Picture dialog
box appears, the Source option defaults to Clipboard (rather than File)
if you have copied a bitmap file to the Clipboard.

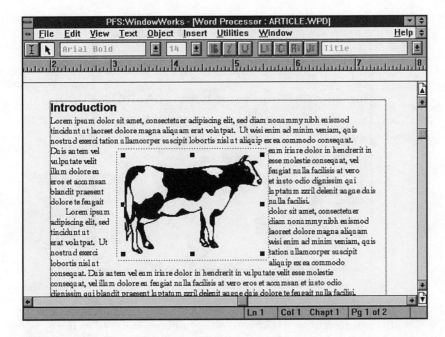

FIG. 6.37

Picture from
Windows
Paintbrush
imported into
WindowWorks.

Scaling a Picture

You can resize a picture with the mouse by dragging one of the picture's selection handles or by selecting the picture and then choosing the Position command. (Both methods were discussed earlier in this chapter.) In addition, you can *scale* a picture. Scaling a picture differs from resizing it, although the net result can be the same. You resize a picture by changing its height and width in inches. You scale a picture by changing its height and width as a percentage of its original size.

To scale a picture, perform the following steps:

1. Select the picture frame you want to scale; selection handles appear on the frame.

2. Choose Crop Picture from the Object menu.

   The Scale & Crop dialog box appears (see fig. 6.38).

3. Enter percentage values for the picture's scale in the Width and Height boxes.

   Click the Full Size option if you want Width and Height to be 100 percent. In other words, click Full Size to set the picture back to its original size. The picture's original size also is displayed for reference.

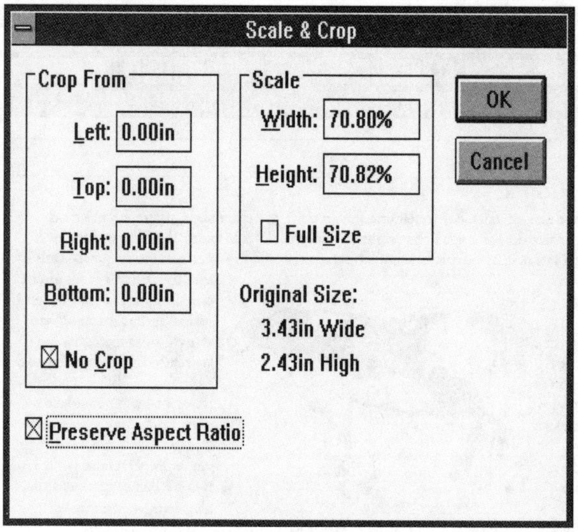

FIG. 6.38

Scale & Crop
dialog box.

Click the Preserve Aspect Ratio option to set the scale values for
Width and Height to whatever value you have entered in the
Height box. If, for example, you enter **122%** in the Width box and
146% in the Height box, clicking the Preserve Aspect Ratio
changes both options to 146%. Preserve Aspect Ratio differs from
Full Size in that Full Size always equals 100% for Height and Width;
Preserve Aspect Ratio assures that the picture's proportions do
not change regardless of the picture's size.

4. Click OK to close the dialog box and to scale the selected picture
   using the values you entered.

When the Preserve Aspect Ratio option is checked, a picture's *aspect
ratio*—the relationship of the horizontal scale to the vertical scale—
always is maintained, even if you resize the picture using the mouse.
Clicking and dragging any of the picture's selection handles changes
the picture's size but does not change its aspect ratio. The aspect ratio
is maintained until you turn off the Preserve Aspect Ratio option.

Cropping Pictures

WindowWorks enables you to *crop* picture parts that you don't want
displayed. Cropping a picture is similar to covering parts of a photograph with masking tape; the unwanted area still exists but cannot be

seen. Suppose that you have created a picture frame containing a scanned photo in TIFF format. The TIFF file is an image of two people, but you want to include only one person in your document. By using the cropping feature, you can crop the unwanted person from the photo.

To crop a picture, perform the following steps:

1. Hold down the Ctrl key and click one of the picture's selection handles.

   The pointer changes to a cropping tool (see fig. 6.39).

2. Drag until only the part of the picture you want displayed remains in the frame (see fig. 6.40).

To enlarge, or un-crop, the picture, hold down the Ctrl key, click a selection handle, and drag away from the picture's edge. When you crop a picture, the size of the image within the picture frame is not changed. You still can resize or scale a cropped image just as you normally would by clicking and dragging a selection handle without holding down the Ctrl key. When you resize or scale a cropped picture, all cropped portions remain cropped. Also, the Preserve Aspect Ratio and Full Size options are not affected when you crop an image, which means that you can resize or scale a picture after cropping it and crop a picture after resizing or scaling it.

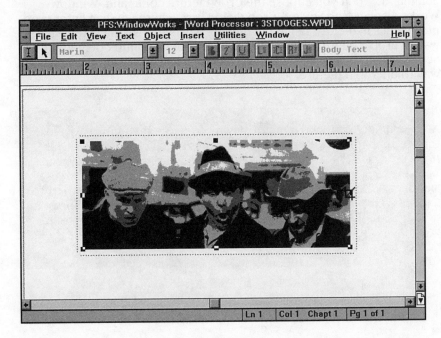

FIG. 6.39

Using the cropping tool.

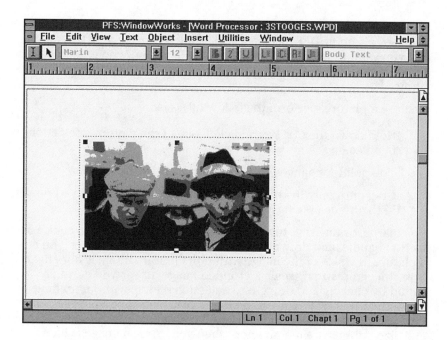

FIG. 6.40

The same picture
as in figure 6.39
but cropped.

You also can crop a picture by using the Object menu's Crop Picture
command. When you choose the Crop Picture command, Window-
Works displays the Scale & Crop dialog box, where you can enter cropping values in inches. Using the mouse, however, usually is the easiest
way to crop a picture. On the other hand, you may find opening the
Scale & Crop dialog box and choosing the No Crop option the easiest
way to uncrop a picture.

T I P

After you have cropped a picture, you can move the picture within
the cropped frame without moving or resizing the frame itself. This
process is called *panning*. To pan a cropped picture, hold down the
Ctrl key, click inside the frame (not on one of the selection handles),
and drag. When you release the mouse, a different part of the picture
is displayed (see figs. 6.41 and 6.42). Unfortunately, WindowWorks
does not enable you to see the picture as you are panning; therefore,
you may have to pan back and forth a few times before you see the
part of the picture you want displayed.

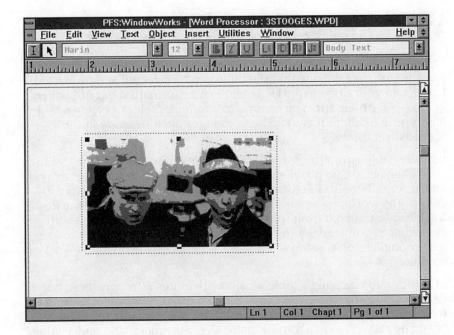

FIG. 6.41

Figure section before panning.

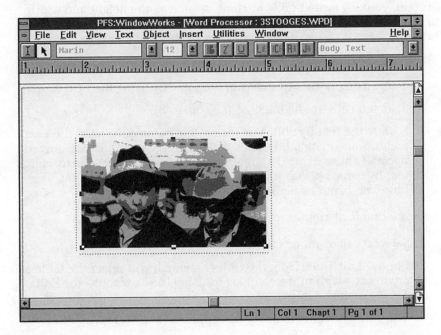

FIG. 6.42

Same figure after panning to a different section.

Working with Table Frames

Table frames, like text frames, can be moved and resized as objects, and the text contained within the table can be selected and formatted like text in your document. Table text can be formatted but not edited in the word processor. You cannot, for example, select a cell in a table and type in a different value. These changes must be made in the Spreadsheet module.

Because tables from the spreadsheet are linked to the word processor, such changes are no problem. You can edit the text in the spreadsheet and, if Auto Refresh is activated, changes you make appear automatically in the word processor. If Auto Refresh is not on, choose the Refresh Now command from the Object menu to update the table with any changes you made in the spreadsheet. (See Chapter 17 for a more complete discussion of integrating data between WindowWorks modules.)

In addition to changing a table's object attributes (size, position, border lines, and shading), you can apply two other types of formatting to tables. First, you can format the text attributes of a table's text by changing elements such as font, point size, alignment, and underlining. Second, you can format table attributes, such as the height and width of rows and columns, the type of numeric display, and the display of table gridlines. You can select and format one cell or a range of cells.

To format text in a table, perform the following steps:

1. Select a cell or range of cells in the table by using the Text tool.

    Selected cells are highlighted (see fig. 6.43).

2. Format the text by choosing formatting commands from the Text menu. Some commands, such as Paragraph and Tabs, are grayed because these items do not apply to tables. You also can format text by using options on the control strip. The Styles menu, however, is not available for formatting table text.

To format table attributes, perform the following steps:

1. Select a cell or range of cells by using the Text tool.

2. Choose Edit Table from the Object menu. If you select the table as an object—without selecting cells using the Text tool—the Edit Table command is grayed.

    The Table Attributes dialog box appears (see fig. 6.44).

    The Numeric Format option determines how numbers are displayed. Numbers can be displayed as percentages, dates, dollar amounts, etc. Choose the option that best fits your needs. Options in this menu do not change the display of text—only the numbers.

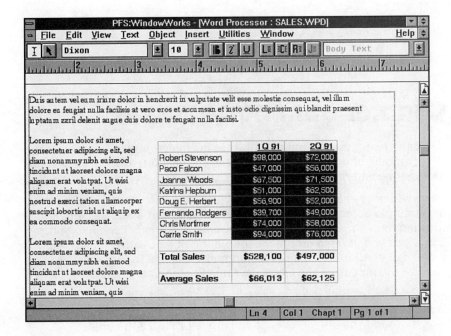

FIG. 6.43

Table with cells
selected and
formatted.

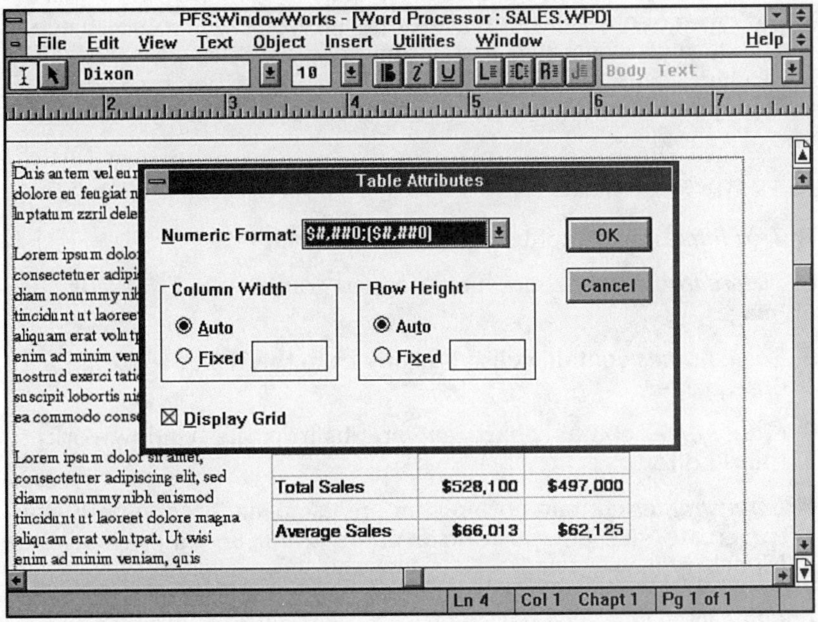

FIG. 6.44

Table Attributes
dialog box.

For the Column Width and Row Height options, you should
choose Auto to enable WindowWorks to determine the optimal
size. When Auto is selected, Row Height is adjusted automatically
when you change the font or point size. You can manually adjust
these values by selecting Fixed and entering sizes in inches.

The Display Grid option turns the display of table grid lines on or off.

3. Click OK to close the dialog box and apply your changes.

Chapter Summary

You can create, select, and edit objects in Object mode. To activate the Object mode, choose the arrow pointer on the control strip. Commands for creating and manipulating objects are located on the Object menu.

WindowWorks enables you to work with a variety of graphics. You can draw simple objects, such as lines, rectangles, and ovals by using the drawing tools located on the Object menu. You easily can change the line width and style of an object and fill the object with a background pattern or shade. You can move and resize objects in two ways: you can use the mouse or the Object menu's Position command.

You can choose how document text wraps around objects by using the Wrap command. When you turn Text Wrap on for an object, text always wraps around the object, even if you move or resize the object.

WindowWorks enables you to create frames into which you can place different types of objects. Frames are special types of graphic objects that contain such element as text, bit-mapped graphics, PCX files, TIFF images, charts from the WindowWorks Chart Editor, and tables from the WindowWorks Spreadsheet. You also can create empty frames to use as placeholders.

The five types of frames and their functions include following:

- *Text frames* are graphic objects that contain text.

- *Picture frames* can contain bit-mapped graphics, PCX files, or TIFF images.

- *Table frames* contain cells you copy from the WindowWorks Spreadsheet.

- *Chart frames* contain charts and graphs from the WindowWorks Chart Editor.

- *Empty frames* contain nothing but are useful as placeholders. You can create, size, and position an empty frame and later change the frame's type.

Although each frame type has special characteristics, all frames are objects, which means that you can add border lines, add background shades, and make text wrap around them.

The Spreadsheet

PART II

OUTLINE

Creating a Spreadsheet

A *spreadsheet* is a table used for recording and managing numerical information. You can use spreadsheets to perform cost analyses, calculate profits and losses, and monitor and graph stock trends. Spreadsheets also can be used as a computerized alternative to an accounting ledger book.

In the WindowWorks Spreadsheet module, you can enter spreadsheet data into rows and columns, perform calculations, format the spreadsheet for printing or exporting to the Word Processor module, and even create a chart in the Chart Editor module by using the spreadsheet data.

Starting the Spreadsheet

To start the WindowWorks Spreadsheet module, double-click the Spreadsheet icon or choose Spreadsheet from the Window menu. The spreadsheet window appears containing a blank worksheet for entering your spreadsheet data (see fig. 7.1).

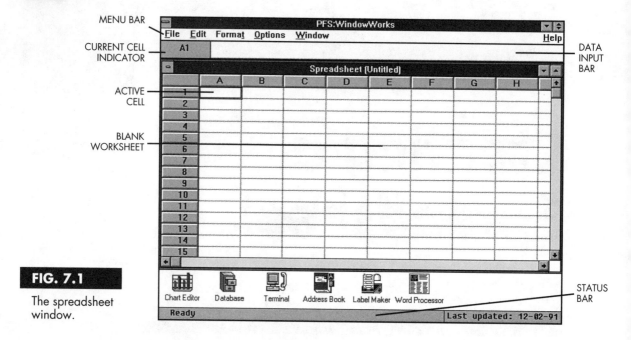

MENU BAR
CURRENT CELL INDICATOR
ACTIVE CELL
BLANK WORKSHEET
DATA INPUT BAR
STATUS BAR

FIG. 7.1

The spreadsheet window.

Understanding the Spreadsheet Window

The Spreadsheet window contains a menu bar and a status bar. Where you would find the control strip in other modules, however, the Spreadsheet module displays a data entry bar, which indicates the current cell and has a space for entering cell data. The workspace is the blank *worksheet*—a simple matrix of rows identified by numbers and columns identified by letters.

A *cell* is the area of intersection between a row and a column. You enter each piece of information for your spreadsheet into a cell. Each cell can contain one piece of numerical data, a text entry (such as a title or label) or a formula.

Each cell has a name, or a cell *address*. The address is the cell's column letter followed by the cell's row number. For example, D7 is the cell where Column D intersects Row 7.

To enter data into a cell, you select the cell and type the data. As you type, the data appears on the data entry bar. The address of the currently selected cell appears to the left of the cell data on the data entry bar.

NOTE Theoretically, you can enter up to 10,000 columns and 32,000 rows of data in the WindowWorks Spreadsheet module. You are limited, however, by your system resources: your computer's memory and disk space.

Selecting Cells

Before entering data into a cell, you first have to designate the cell as *active* by selecting it. You can select one cell one at a time, or you can select a range or contiguous group of cells. Even if you select a range of cells, however, only one is the currently active cell.

Selecting a Single Cell

You select a single cell by clicking it. A thick border appears around the cell, indicating that the cell is currently active. The address of the active cell appears in the current cell indicator, and any associated data, text, or formula appears in the data entry bar.

Selecting a Range of Cells

Quite often, you may find selecting multiple cells more efficient than repeating the same operation, such as formatting, on single cells. You can select simultaneously any group of contiguous cells: you can select an entire row, an entire column, or a block.

To select a row of cells, simply click the row heading number. The entire row is highlighted, which indicates that all cells are selected (see fig. 7.2). The cell A13 in the selected row is active, as indicated by its thick border. To select multiple rows, click the heading of the first row to be selected, and drag the cursor to the heading of the last row to be selected.

Similarly, to select a column of cells, click the column heading letter. The column is highlighted, and the cell in Row 1 is active (see fig. 7.3). To select multiple columns, click the heading of the first column to be selected and drag the cursor to the heading of the last column to be selected.

To select a block, or *range*, of cells, click a corner of the block and drag the cursor to the far corner of the block. The cell in which you start the block is active (see fig. 7.4). If the block is particularly large and extends off-screen, you may want to use the keyboard to select the range of cells. To select a range of cells from the keyboard, click the first cell in the range, scroll to the last cell in the range, and hold down the Shift key while you click the last cell. To select the range from cell C10 to cell D13, for example, click cell C10, and then press the Shift key as you click cell D13. Cell C10 remains the currently active cell.

You can select all cells on the worksheet by clicking the blank box, the *global select cell*, directly above the row heading numbers. When you select all the cells, cell A1 is the active cell.

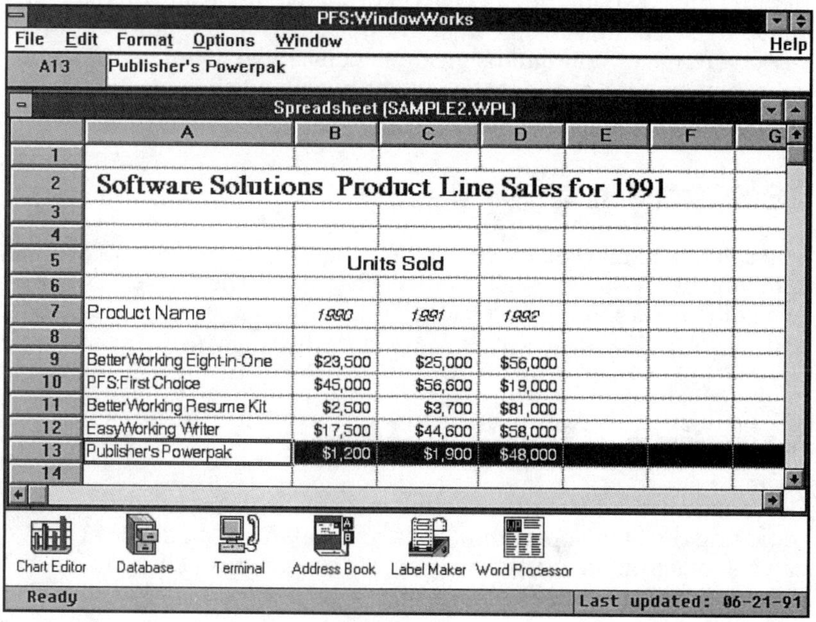

FIG. 7.2

A selected row of data with A13 as the active cell.

Moving to a Specific Cell

To move to a cell that does not appear on-screen, you can use the scroll bars to move right, left, up, or down. If the desired cell is more than approximately 10 rows or columns away from your current position, however, this method is not practical.

To move to and activate a specific cell with the Go To command on the Edit menu, perform the following steps:

1. Choose Go To from the Edit menu.

   The Go To Cell dialog box appears (see fig. 7.5).

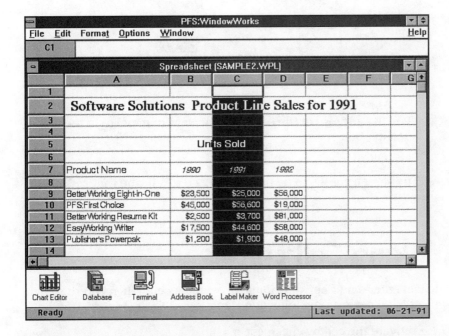

FIG. 7.3

A selected column of data with C1 as the active cell.

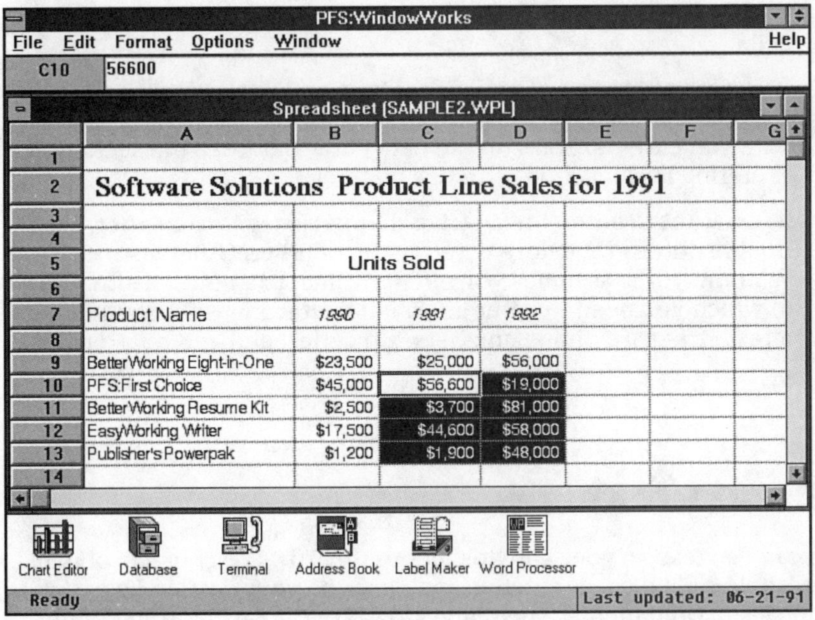

FIG. 7.4

A selected range with C10 as the active cell.

FIG. 7.5

Go To Cell
dialog box.

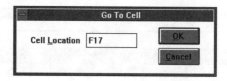

2. Type the address of the cell that you want to move to in the Cell
   Location box.

3. Click OK.

   The screen scrolls to display the selected cell, and that cell is
   active.

Making Cell Entries

You can enter a number, a formula, or text in a cell. When entering each
type of data, perform the following steps:

1. Activate the cell by clicking it.

2. With the cell selected, type a value, text string, or formula for the
   cell.

   If you are entering a formula, first type an equals sign (=) or an at
   sign (@). As you type the number, text, or formula for the cell, the
   data you enter appears on the data entry bar. (See the section
   "Entering Formulas" later in this chapter.)

   If you want to enter a text string that begins with a number, type
   double quotes (") before entering the number. Otherwise,
   WindowWorks assumes you enter a value. Examples of situations
   in which you need to enter information starting with a number as
   a text string are phone numbers, zip codes, and 2nd quarter.

3. Press Enter to place the data in the cell.

Entering Text

You can use text on your spreadsheet to title rows or columns of data.
Text labels can be used to define and describe your data. In figure 7.6,
all entries in Column A are text labels—as are the headings in Row 7.

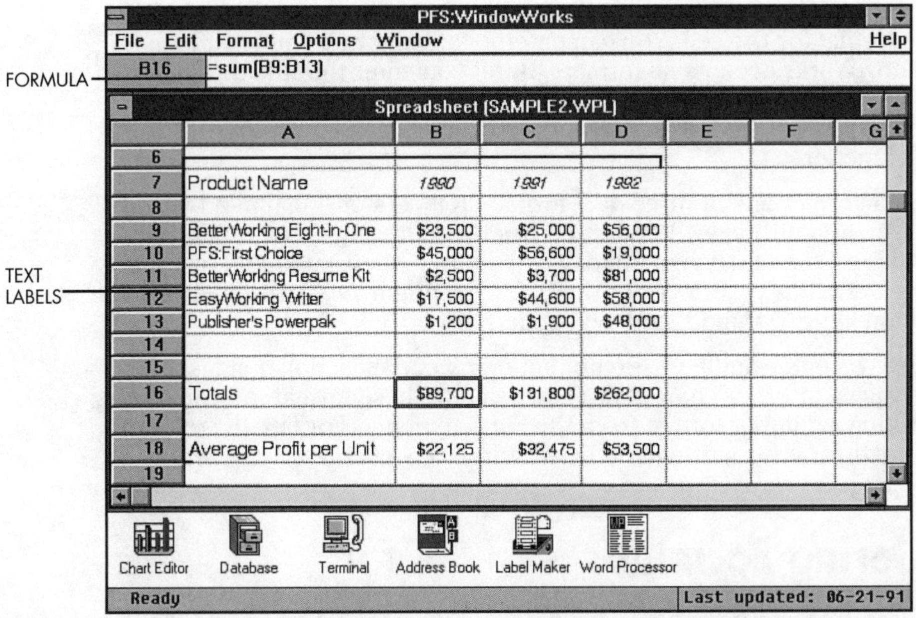

FORMULA

TEXT LABELS

	PFS:WindowWorks						
File Edit Format Options Window							Help
B16	=sum(B9:B13)						

Spreadsheet (SAMPLE2.WPL)

	A	B	C	D	E	F	G
6							
7	Product Name	1990	1991	1992			
8							
9	BetterWorking Eight-in-One	$23,500	$25,000	$56,000			
10	PFS:First Choice	$45,000	$56,600	$19,000			
11	BetterWorking Resume Kit	$2,500	$3,700	$81,000			
12	EasyWorking Writer	$17,500	$44,600	$58,000			
13	Publisher's Powerpak	$1,200	$1,900	$48,000			
14							
15							
16	Totals	$89,700	$131,800	$262,000			
17							
18	Average Profit per Unit	$22,125	$32,475	$53,500			
19							

Chart Editor   Database   Terminal   Address Book   Label Maker   Word Processor

Ready   Last updated: 06-21-91

FIG. 7.6

Sample spreadsheet with text labels.

With the cell selected, type the text label. When the text appears correctly and completely on the data entry bar, press Enter. The text appears in the cell.

If the text that you enter does not fit, the label overflows into the cell to the right of the selected cell. The text nevertheless is considered part of the cell that was active when you entered the label. In other words, when you again select the original cell, all the text appears in the data entry bar. If you select an overflow cell, no text appears in the data entry bar.

If no data is in the cell(s) that text overflows into, your data will look good on-screen and in print. However, if you enter data into the overflow cell, data in the previous cell will appear to be missing. You must change the width of that cell to see all of the data.

Entering Numbers

In a spreadsheet, you have to enter values on which you later can perform calculations. The numbers you enter can be positive or negative. (You use a minus sign (-) to indicate a negative number.) You can enter numbers with or without decimal points, in scientific notation (2e5), or as dates. You can enter a percentage as a decimal (.20 = 20%).

If you want to use dates as part of a calculation, you must specify a date format for the cell. You can enter a date any way you want to; WindowWorks accepts all formats. But if you enter the Julian value for the date, WindowWorks displays the date in the specified format. WindowWorks uses Julian dates when making calculations or utilizing date functions.

You can select one of three date formats for Version 1.0: mm-dd-yy, dd-month, or month-yyyy. Version 1.1 has the following date formats: m/d/yy; m-d-yy; mmm d, yy; mmm d, yyyy; mmmm d, yy; mmmm d, yyyy; m/yyyy; d/m; d/m/yy; d/m/yyyy; d mmm yy; d mmm yyyy; d mmmm yy; d mmmm yyyy; yymmdd; and yyyymmdd.

When you enter numbers, do not enter any commas, dollar signs, percent signs, or other characters. You can add these format indicators by selecting a number format from the Format menu. (For details, refer to the section on formatting numbers later in this chapter.)

Entering Formulas

To perform a mathematical calculation, you first must enter an equation or formula. All equations must be preceded by an equal sign (=). You can type an equation using the basic mathematical operators, such as plus (+) and minus (-) used for addition and subtraction; you also can use one of the many WindowWorks functions.

Using Mathematical Operators

The simplest formulas are those that use the standard mathematical operators, as the following table indicates:

Operator	Symbol
Addition	+
Subtraction	-
Multiplication	*
Division	/
Exponentiation	^

If, for example, you want to display the sum of cell B2 and cell B3, enter the following equation:

=B2+B3

If you enter spaces, WindowWorks strips them. When you press Enter, the sum appears in the cell that contains the equation.

Of course, you can perform other mathematical calculations. You can use the equation =B2-B3, for example, to display the difference between the values in cells B2 and B3, the equation =B2*B3 to display the product, and =B2/B3 to display the quotient.

 NOTE When you click a cell that contains an equation, the equation appears on the data entry bar. The result of the equation appears in the cell itself. If you want to edit the equation, place the cursor in the equation on the data entry bar and make any necessary changes. When you press Enter, the result of the revised equation appears in the cell.

Using Functions

In addition to entering simple functions using the mathematical operators, you can use a set of functions for more complex and advanced calculations. If, for example, you want to add the values in Column B—starting with cell B3 and ending with cell B10—you would need to type the following equation:

=B3+B4+B5+B6+B7+B8+B9+B10

As you can imagine, this process can become quite tedious if you have a large spreadsheet. You can, however, substitute the SUM function and enter the following equation:

=SUM(B3:B10)

For details about the various functions, refer to Chapter 8.

Editing a Spreadsheet

To edit a single cell, you can edit any value, label, or equation simply by clicking the cell and modifying the cell contents on the data entry bar. You also can use the standard editing techniques to cut, copy, and paste cell contents.

TIP As you edit cells in a spreadsheet, remember that apparently empty cells may contain formatting information from data previously located in the cell. If data that you enter or edit seems to be formatting in an unusual way, click the cell, choose Number from the Format menu, and select the correct entry format to replace the one currently existing in the cell. This process erases any errant formatting codes in the cell.

Copying and Pasting Cells

You can copy or cut the text, number, or formula contained in any cell or range of cells. You then can paste the contents into any other cells.

To copy and paste the contents of a cell, perform the following steps:

1. Click the cell to select it. Alternatively, click and drag to select a range of cells.

2. Choose Copy from the Edit menu (or press Ctrl-Ins) to copy the contents. To move the contents, choose Cut from the Edit menu (or press Shift-Del).

3. Click the cell into which you want to paste the contents. (If you are pasting the contents of a range of cells, click the cell that is to be the upper-left corner of the pasted block.)

4. Choose Paste from the Edit menu (or press Shift-Ins).

   The new location now contains the cut or copied information.

NOTE If you paste the contents of a cell into a cell that already contains data, the existing data is replaced by the pasted data. If you are trying to reformat your spreadsheet and want to avoid losing existing data, you may need to insert new rows or columns into the spreadsheet. (For more information, refer to the sections on inserting rows and columns later in this chapter.)

Understanding Fixed and Relative Cell References

You should be aware that unless you specify otherwise, WindowWorks uses *relative* cell addresses for the data that is pasted into a new location. If, for example, cell B10 contains a sum formula that adds the values in cells B1 through B9, you can copy the contents of B10 (the equation) to Column E. The equation in Column E, however, is adjusted so that it adds the values in cells E1 through E9.

You can prevent WindowWorks from making this adjustment by specifying Column B as an *absolute* reference for the equation in cell B10. If Column B is an absolute reference, the sum always will represent the total of the cells in Column B—no matter where in the spreadsheet the cell contents are copied.

For more information on relative and absolute cell references, refer to Chapter 8.

Clearing Cells

Clear does not remove any formatting. Clear removes data from a cell but does not place it on the clipboard. Therefore, the information that was cleared cannot be pasted to another location.

Inserting and Deleting Rows and Columns

You can add blank rows or columns at any location in your spreadsheet. This process can be the simplest method of reformatting your spreadsheet. If you find yourself copying and pasting the contents of column after column—just to move several columns over—you should learn to add a new column instead. You also can save a great deal of effort by deleting an entire column rather than one cell at a time.

To add a row to your spreadsheet, perform the following steps:

1. Select the row heading that you want to be immediately below the new row.

   When you select the row heading, the entire row is selected, and the Column A cell is the active cell (see fig. 7.7).

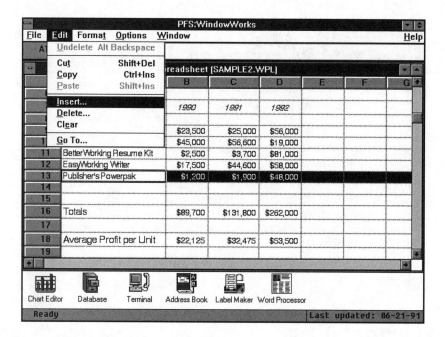

FIG. 7.7

Selected row
with Insert option
highlighted.

2. Choose Insert from the Edit menu.

   A blank row appears above the selected row. All information
   below the selected row moves down one line (see fig. 7.8).

You also can insert more than one row. Before choosing Insert, simply
select the number of rows that you want to add. If, for example, you
want to insert two rows, select the two rows that are to be immediately
below the new rows. Then choose Insert from the Edit menu.

To add a column to your spreadsheet, perform the following steps:

1. Select the column heading that you want to be immediately to the
   right of the new column.

   When you select the column heading, the entire column is selected, and the Row 1 cell is the active cell.

2. Choose Insert from the Edit menu.

   A blank column appears to the left of the selected column. All
   information to the right of the selected column is moved one
   column to the right.

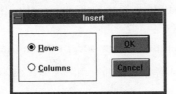

	PFS:WindowWorks						
File Edit Format Options Window							Help
A13							

Spreadsheet [SAMPLE2.WPL]

	A	B	C	D	E	F	G
6							
7	Product Name	*1990*	*1991*	*1992*			
8							
9	Better Working Eight-in-One	$23,500	$25,000	$56,000			
10	PFS:First Choice	$45,000	$56,600	$19,000			
11	Better Working Resume Kit	$2,500	$3,700	$81,000			
12	EasyWorking Writer	$17,500	$44,600	$58,000			
13							
14	Publisher's Powerpak	$1,200	$1,900	$48,000			
15							
16							
17	Totals	$89,700	$131,800	$262,000			
18							
19	Average Profit per Unit	$22,125	$32,475	$53,500			

Chart Editor   Database   Terminal   Address Book   Label Maker   Word Processor

Ready   Last updated: 06-21-91

FIG. 7.8

A new row is inserted.

The preceding steps represent the easiest way to insert rows and columns into your spreadsheet. WindowWorks does, however, provide you with a "long-cut" for inserting rows and columns. If you do not select a row or column heading prior to choosing the Insert option, the new row or column is inserted above or to the left of the currently active cell. When using this method, however, you have to tell WindowWorks whether you want to insert a row or a column.

When you choose Insert with only one cell selected, the Insert dialog box appears (see fig. 7.9). When you select Row or Column and click OK, the new row or column appears.

```
┌──────────── Insert ────────────┐
│                                 │
│   ◉ Rows          ┌────────┐   │
│                   │   OK   │   │
│   ○ Columns       └────────┘   │
│                   ┌────────┐   │
│                   │ Cancel │   │
│                   └────────┘   │
└─────────────────────────────────┘
```

FIG. 7.9

The Insert dialog box.

To remove a row or column from your spreadsheet, select the row or column heading for the row or column to be removed and choose Delete from the Edit menu. The row or column—along with all of its cells and their contents—is removed. You can select and delete as many rows or columns as necessary.

When you delete a row, all of the cells below the deleted row are moved up to fill the gap. Likewise, cell contents of columns to the right of a deleted column are moved left to fill the gap.

If you inadvertently delete a row or column, you can restore it—but only if you act right away. *Immediately* after you delete a row or column, choose Undelete from the Edit menu to restore the row or column to its original position. If you perform any other operation after deleting a row or column, however, you cannot use the Undelete function. Undelete will undo a delete action. To undo something that you cut, use the Paste option. You cannot undo a Clear action.

Formatting Cells

After you enter data, you can set formatting attributes so that your spreadsheet is a useful resource and a professional-looking document that you can print or export to the Word Processor module. For your spreadsheet to accurately reflect its numeric values, for example, you must select a numeric format for each cell containing a number. In addition to setting numeric format options, you can set justification, character attributes, such as font, type size, and type style, cell borders, column width, and row height.

Formatting Numbers

Numbers you enter into your worksheet are formatted in a general numeric format—right-justified. By default, text is formatted left-justified, Dixon 10 point (if using Publisher's Powerpak). You can change this default to specify a particular type of number—a dollar value, percentage, date, scientific expression, and so on. If a cell is formatted with one of these options, its contents are displayed with the appropriate formatting characters, such as commas, decimal points, dollar signs, dashes, or exponents.

To format a cell containing a number, perform the following steps:

1. Select the cell or range of cells.

2. Choose Number from the Format menu.

   WindowWorks displays the Numeric Formats dialog box that lists available number formats (see fig. 7.10).

3. Select a format from the list, and click OK.

   The cell or range of cells is displayed in the selected format.

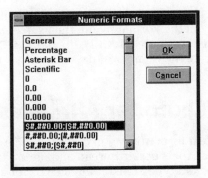

FIG. 7.10

Numeric Formats
dialog box.

The following list contain the number formatting options:

- *General*. This option is the default format. Numbers are right-justified and leading zeros are dropped.

- *Percentage*. A percentage is displayed with a percent sign (%) and is 100 times the value in the cell.

- *Asterisk Bar*. This option displays a quantity of asterisks equal to the value in the cell. If the cell's value is too large to be expressed with asterisks, the expression #DATA appears in the cell.

- *Scientific*. This format displays the cell's value as exponential notation.

The formats in the following list display the value in the cell with the number of decimal places shown. Any additional decimal places are retained in the spreadsheet and are used in calculations; but additional decimal places do not appear in the cell.

- *$#,###.##*. This option is the common financial "dollars and cents" format. A dollar sign is displayed to the left of the value, a comma is placed to the right of the thousands place, and two decimal places are shown.

- *#,###.##*. This format is the same as the "dollars and cents" format—without the dollar sign.

- *$#,###*. The dollar format displays the dollar sign and a comma to the left of the thousands place. No decimal places are displayed, and all values are rounded to the nearest dollar.

- *Date*. The three date formats are mm-dd-yy, dd-month, and month-yyyy.

  The date *August 12, 1991* would appear in these formats as *08-12-91*, *12-Aug.*, and *Aug-1991*, respectively.

If you want 8/12/91 to appear in a cell, you must enter =**date(91,8,12)**; choose Number from the Format menu; then select m/d/yy from the list. If you simply enter =**date(91,8,12)**, the number 33461 will display in the cell to indicate the number of days since Jan. 1, 1900.

Changing Character Attributes

With some basic text formatting, you can customize your spreadsheet and make data and labels easier to read and understand. You can set the font, type size, and type style for any cell or for a range of cells by following these steps:

1. Select a cell or range of cells.

2. Choose Character from the Format menu.

    The Character dialog box appears (see fig. 7.11).

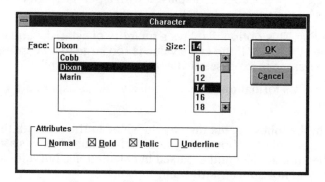

FIG. 7.11

Character dialog box.

3. Select a font, size, and any desired character attributes. Then Click OK. Fonts and sizes are determined by the selected printer. Attributes available are Normal, Bold, Italic, Underline.

The text or numbers in the selected cells are formatted with the new type specifications. If you selected a cell containing text that extends over several cells, all the text is formatted.

Adding a Border

You may want to draw attention to certain cells in your spreadsheet, or you may need to isolate one group of cells. The easiest way to make these impressive changes is to add a border to some of the cells in your spreadsheet. You can add lines above, below, and to the sides of any or all cells. You also can shade a cell or a group of cells.

To add borders or shading, perform the following steps:

1. Select a cell or a range of cells.

2. Choose Borders from the Format menu.

    The Borders dialog box appears (see fig. 7.12).

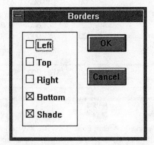

FIG. 7.12

Borders dialog box.

3. Choose the border lines that you want to appear around the selected cells.

    The Left option displays a line along the left edge of each cell; the Right option displays a line along the right edge of each cell; the Top option displays a line above each cell; and the Bottom option displays a line below each cell. You can select all four options to create a box around each cell. Check the Shade box to add gray shading to selected cells.

4. When you have made your selections, click OK (see fig. 7.13).

Changing the Alignment

When you enter a formula, a number, or text into your worksheet, your entry is formatted and aligned according to the WindowWorks defaults. Text for labels and titles is aligned to the left of the cell; numbers are aligned to the right of the cell.

You can modify the alignment of these elements. You may, for example, want column labels aligned in the center of each cell. To align the text or number in a cell or range of cells, select the cells and choose an alignment (Left, Center, or Right) from the Format menu. The formatting attributes you assign remain assigned to the cell—even if you edit the text or value in the cell.

FIG. 7.13

Spreadsheet
containing
bordered and
shaded cells.

If you are not satisfied with your alignment changes, choose Default
from the Format menu. When you choose Default, the selected cells
return to the text or numeric default format.

Using Fill

The Align menu's Fill option enables you to enter text or numbers and
specify that they be repeated to fill the entire cell. You can use this
option to create a line of dollar signs or asterisks dividing one cell or
row from another (see fig. 7.14). Simply enter the text that you want
repeated across each cell width, select a cell or group of cells, and
choose Fill from the Format menu.

Changing the Size of Cells

Another formatting function that WindowWorks enables you to control
is cell size. You can adjust the width of each column to suit the text or
values that fill the column. You also can adjust the height of each row,
which enables you to use large font sizes. Remember that if you installed Publisher's Powerpak, you can scale your fonts to any size.

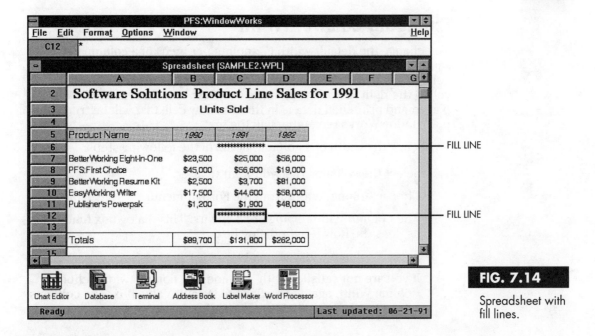

FIG. 7.14

Spreadsheet with fill lines.

Changing Row Height

WindowWorks determines the default row height based on the current font size. To change the height of a row or rows, perform the following steps:

1. Select the rows that you want to alter.

2. Choose Row Height from the Format menu.

   The Row Height dialog box appears (see fig. 7.15).

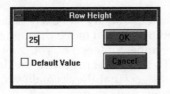

FIG. 7.15

Row Height dialog box.

3. Enter a row height in points. The row height must be greater than the font size for the selected rows.

   If you are not satisfied with the modified row height, choose Row Height again and click the Default Value box. The rows return to the default height.

Changing Column Width

You change the default width (72 points per inch) of a column in the same manner as changing a row height. If a cell contains more than the column can display, the contents of the cell appear to overflow into the cell to the right. If no data is in the overflow cell, the text will be displayed and printed. If data is in the overflow cell, text will be truncated, but WindowWorks remembers all the text.

To change the width of a column, perform the following steps:

1. Select the columns that you want to alter.

2. Choose Column Width from the Format menu.

   The Column Width dialog box appears. This dialog box functions as does the Row Height dialog box.

3. Enter a column width in points.

   If you are not satisfied with the modified column width, choose Column Width again and click the Default Value box. The columns return to the default width (50 points).

Viewing the Spreadsheet

Because the WindowWorks Spreadsheet module enables you to create a large spreadsheet, you should be comfortable moving around in and viewing the spreadsheet. You can use the scroll bars to move vertically and horizontally through the spreadsheet.

Locking Titles

Because your spreadsheet quickly can exceed several screens, you may want to see your headings as you move through the data. Without headings, you may become confused as you view column after column, screen after screen. To solve this problem, the Spreadsheet module enables you to *lock* titles so that they remain visible as you scroll through the data on your worksheet.

To lock the column titles so that they appear on-screen as you move through the data, click anywhere in the row *below* the titles (because your titles are not necessarily in Row 1, and you must tell Window-Works in which row the data starts). Then choose Lock Horizontal Titles from the Options menu.

To lock the row titles so that they appear on-screen as you move through the data, click anywhere in the column to the *right* of your titles. Then choose Lock Vertical Titles from the Option menu.

Removing the Grid

You can remove your spreadsheet's on-screen grid lines. Simply choose Display Grid from the Option menu, and the grid lines disappear. To make the grid lines reappear, choose Display Grid again.

Setting Calculation Options

If your spreadsheet contains any formulas or equations, your spreadsheet must be calculated to give accurate responses in the equation cells. You can control several aspects of the calculation process, as described in the following sections.

Setting Number of Iterations

When a WindowWorks spreadsheet is calculated again, the spreadsheet actually is calculated twice—to account for any formulas that depend on other calculations within the spreadsheet. This process is referred to as two *iterations* of the calculation cycle. If your spreadsheet does not contain formulas that refer to other formulas, you can modify this setting so that WindowWorks performs only one iteration with every recalculation. Alternatively, you can increase the number of iterations if your spreadsheet contains many formulas that depend on other calculations within the spreadsheet.

To change the number of iterations, perform the following steps:

1. Choose Calculation from the Options menu.

   The Calculation Options dialog box appears (see fig. 7.16).

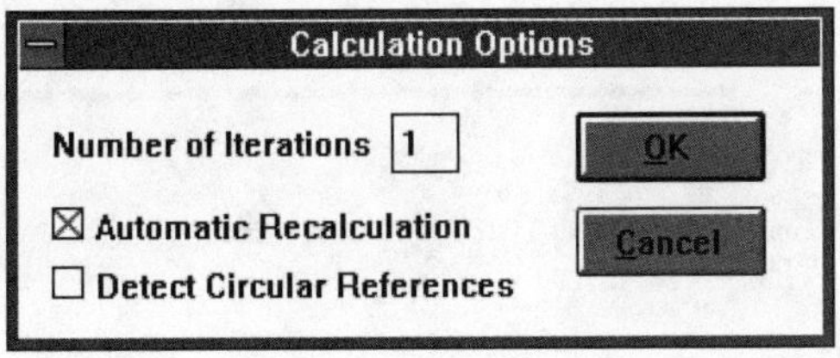

Calculation Options

Number of Iterations [1]
☒ Automatic Recalculation
☐ Detect Circular References

[OK] [Cancel]

FIG. 7.16

Calculation Options dialog box.

2. Edit the Number of Iterations field, or type in a number so that it contains any one or two digit number, and click OK.

Using Automatic Recalculation

WindowWorks automatically recalculates your spreadsheet every time you open the spreadsheet and every time you enter data into a cell. If you are working with a particularly large spreadsheet, this calculation process can be time consuming. To solve this problem, simply turn off the Automatic Recalculation option in the Calculation Options dialog box. (To re-enable the Automatic Recalculation option, choose Calculation from the Options menu and turn the option on.)

If the Automatic Recalculation option is turned off, you must manually recalculate the spreadsheet when you want formula cells updated with accurate values. When you want to update the formula cells, choose Recalculate from the Options menu.

Saving a Spreadsheet

To avoid having to enter data twice, you should save your spreadsheet often. To save your spreadsheet, perform the following steps:

1. Choose Save from the File menu.

   The Save As dialog box appears (see fig. 7.17).

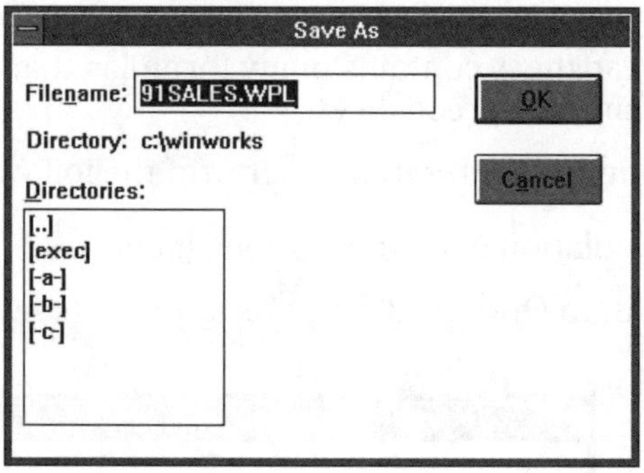

FIG. 7.17

Save As dialog box.

2. Type a file name into the Filename field. (Your spreadsheet should have a WPL extension.)

3. Click OK.

After you have saved the spreadsheet once, you can select Save or press Ctrl-S as often as you like to save the document. You do not have to repeat the file naming process. To save a spreadsheet with a different name, choose Save As from the File menu.

Importing Information from Other Sources

If you have been working in a different spreadsheet program and are making the transition to WindowWorks, you can import documents created in the other program. WindowWorks can import spreadsheets that have been created with Lotus 1-2-3 WKS, Lotus 1-2-3 WK1, and Spinnaker Eight-in-One TPL. You also can import any file that has been saved as an ASCII Comma Separated Value (CSV) type file.

To import a spreadsheet file, perform the following steps:

1. Choose Import from the File menu.

   The Import Worksheet dialog box appears (see fig. 7.18).

Import Worksheet dialog box.

2. Select a file type from the pull-down Type menu.

3. Select a file name from the Files list. When the correct file appears in the Filename box, click OK.

Most formatting and formulas will be translated perfectly. However, 1-2-3 offers some formatting options and formulas that WindowWorks does not support. If WindowWorks encounters such a situation in an imported worksheet, the calculated value will be imported as a number, not as a formula. The formula must be rebuilt in WindowWorks. The file is saved in whatever format the user chooses. Simply saving the file will make it a WindowWorks WPL file. If the user wants to save it as a different file type, follow the steps outlined in the following section "Exporting a Spreadsheet in a Different Format."

Exporting a Spreadsheet in a Different Format

You also can export the current WindowWorks spreadsheet for use with another spreadsheet program. The exporting process is similar to the importing process.

To export a spreadsheet in a different format, perform the following steps:

1. Choose Export from the File menu.

   The Export Worksheet dialog box appears.

2. Select a file type from the pull-down Type menu.

3. Enter a file name with the appropriate extension for the program to which you are exporting. (Use WKS or WK1 for Lotus 1-2-3, TPL for Spinnaker Eight-in-One, or CSV for Comma Separated Value.)

4. Click OK.

The file is ready to open with the spreadsheet program you selected from the Export Type menu.

Printing a Spreadsheet

Before you print your spreadsheet, be sure that you are satisfied with the page setup and spreadsheet formatting settings by following these steps:

1. Choose Page Setup from the File menu.

   The Page Setup dialog box appears (see fig. 7.19).

2. Enter margins for the left, right, top, and bottom of the page. (You may want to leave these options at the one inch default setting.)

3. Click the Page Numbers option if you want page numbers to appear on each page of your spreadsheet.

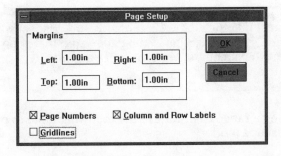

FIG. 7.19

Page Setup
dialog box.

4. Click the Column and Row Labels option if you want the titles for your spreadsheet columns and rows to appear on each page.

5. Click the Gridlines option if you want the gridlines to appear on your printed spreadsheet.

6. Click OK.

When you are satisfied with the options you have selected, you are ready to print your spreadsheet. Perform the following steps:

1. Choose Print from the File menu.

   The Print Worksheet dialog box appears (see fig. 7.20).

FIG. 7.20

Print Worksheet
dialog box.

2. Enter the number of copies that you want to print, and click OK.

If you want to print your spreadsheet in landscape mode, choose Printer Setup from the File menu. Be certain that your printer is selected, and click the setup button. Choose Landscape from the Orientation section.

You can select a range of cells to print if you don't want to print the entire worksheet. Highlight the range of cells you want to print, and choose Print from the File menu.

T I P	To get the maximum printable area in your spreadsheet when using page numbers, set the margins in the Page Setup dialog box to .75 inch. To print the maximum area without page numbers, set the margins to .25 inch.

When marking a range to print, use the following table to print an entire page in landscape mode:

Row Height	Maximum Number of Rows
8	50
10	40
13	40
15	29
18	24

If your row height is 8 points, for example, you can print up to 50 rows on a page.

Chapter Summary

With the WindowWorks Spreadsheet module, you can build a powerful spreadsheet quickly and easily, which enables you to create a spreadsheet to suit almost any need at home or office. You can enter formulas that the computer calculates much faster and more accurately than you can by hand or with a calculator.

In addition to the control you gain over numbers, you gain control over the format and appearance of your worksheet. Experiment with fonts, row and column sizes, borders, shading, and alignments. You also can select the appropriate numerical format for your data.

After creating the perfect spreadsheet, you have several options: you can print the spreadsheet, export it to another spreadsheet program, copy and paste it into a WindowWorks Word Processor document, or copy the data into the WindowWorks Chart Editor to make a graph.

Entering Formulas and Functions

WindowWorks provides a variety of functions that enable you to create unique documents in the Spreadsheet and Database modules. This chapter explains how to create formulas by constructing functions and operators. This chapter also describes the different types of functions you can use in WindowWorks.

Learning the Construction of Functions

Spreadsheet functions are made up of two parts: the function name and an argument. The argument is enclosed within the parentheses following the function. Some functions, such as TODAY( ) or PI( ), do not use arguments. Other functions use multiple arguments. The function AVG( ), for example, returns the average of a list of numbers or range of cells and needs at least two arguments. Multiple arguments must be separated by commas.

Entering Function Arguments

An *argument* is the information a function uses to perform a calculation. An argument can be a value or a reference to another cell. When the argument is a reference to another cell, the value of the referenced cell is substituted for the argument. With the AVG( ) function, for example, you can enter =AVG(10,20) or =AVG(A7,C4), in which A7 and C4 are cells containing values. You also can mix values and references in an argument by entering =AVG(10,A7,20,C4), for example.

Following Function Syntax

To be correctly interpreted by the spreadsheet, functions must be entered according to the established rules—or *syntax*. Some functions require special syntax, but the following general rules apply to all functions:

- All functions that start a cell entry must begin with an equals sign (=). Because the AVG( ) function in =AVG(A1:A10) begins the cell entry, the function is preceded by an equals sign. No equals sign is required for functions that do not begin a cell entry. The AVG( ) function in =SUM(AVG(A1:A10)+B1), for example, is not preceded with an equals sign because AVG( ) does not begin the cell entry.

- You must spell functions correctly.

- Do not enter spaces between the function name and the left parenthesis.

- Functions that don't require arguments don't require parentheses. Typing =PI( ) or =PI produces the same result because the PI function does not require an argument.

- You must enter all required arguments.

- For functions using multiple arguments, you must separate the arguments with commas.

Functions are not case sensitive. No differentiation is made between SUM(A1:A10), sum(a1:a10), and Sum(A1:a10), for example.

If a function argument references a cell with text, the cell with text is treated as a blank cell. If you enter =AVG(A1,A2), in which A1 contains the number 26 and A2 contains the text *Year*, the result is 26 because the average of 26 alone (because the text cell is blank) is 26. Treating text cells as blank is considerably different from treating text cells as zero. In this example, for instance, if text cells were treated as zero rather than as blank, the result would be 13 because the average of 26 and 0 is 13.

Using Ranges in Function Arguments

Many functions can reference a range of cells as their argument. The AVG( ) and SUM( ) functions are functions that frequently use ranges as their arguments. To calculate the sum total of a column of numbers, for example, use the SUM( ) function with the coordinates of the column as the range.

You enter a range by typing the first cell location of the range, a colon (:), and the last cell of the range. The following examples use the AVG( ) function to illustrate how to enter ranges:

Function	Range
=AVG(A1:A7)	References cells in a single column
=AVG(A1:D1)	References cells in a single row
=AVG(A1:D7)	References a block of cells (multiple rows and columns)

A range also can consist of *noncontiguous cells*, cells that don't border each other. Use commas to separate noncontiguous cells or ranges in an argument. The following examples show how to create arguments referencing noncontiguous cells:

Function	Explanation of Argument
=AVG(A1, B17, C4)	References a list of noncontiguous cells
=AVG(A1:A7,B17,C4)	References a range of cells and two noncontiguous cells
=AVG(A1:A7,D1:D7)	References two separate ranges

Using Absolute and Relative Cell References in Functions

WindowWorks uses both absolute and relative cell references. To illustrate the differences between absolute and relative cell addressing, perform the following exercise:

1. Enter **1** in cell A1, **2** in cell A2, and so on, through **5** in cell A5.

2. Enter **=A1+5** in cell B1.

   The value 6 is returned in B1 (see fig. 8.1).

3. Select cell B1; copy B1 by choosing Copy from the Edit menu.

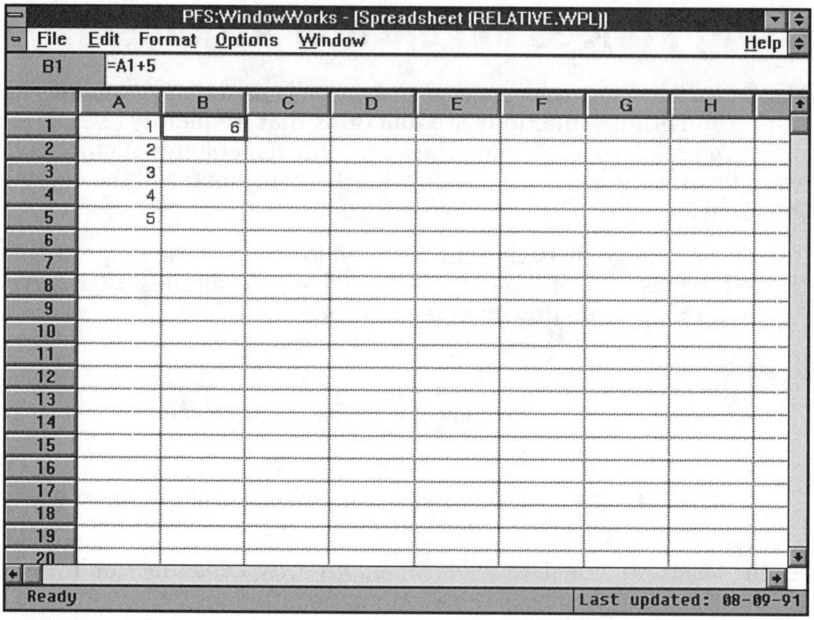

FIG. 8.1

The result of entering 1 in cell A1 and =A1+5 in cell B1.

4. Highlight cells B2 through B5, and choose Paste from the Edit menu.

   Although the value of B1 equals 6, this value is not the value pasted into cells B2 through B5. If you select cell B2, you notice that the formula in B2 is =A2+5. However, the formula you copied and pasted was =A1+5. This difference is the result of *relative cell addressing*. With relative cell addressing, the direction and distance of the reference from the equation do not change, but the cell to which the reference points does change if you paste an equation, such as =A1+5.

   If you paste the equation within the same column as the original equation, the column reference (B in this example) does not change, but the row reference does (see fig. 8.2). Inversely, if you paste the equation within the same row as the original equation, the row reference (1 in this example) does not change, but the column reference does (see fig. 8.3).

5. Highlight cells C1 through E1, and choose Paste from the Edit menu.

   By default, WindowWorks uses relative cell addressing when you paste equations from one cell into another. You can override this, however, and tell WindowWorks to use *absolute cell addressing*, also called *fixed cell addressing*. Enter a dollar sign ($) before the column and/or row reference to create an absolute reference.

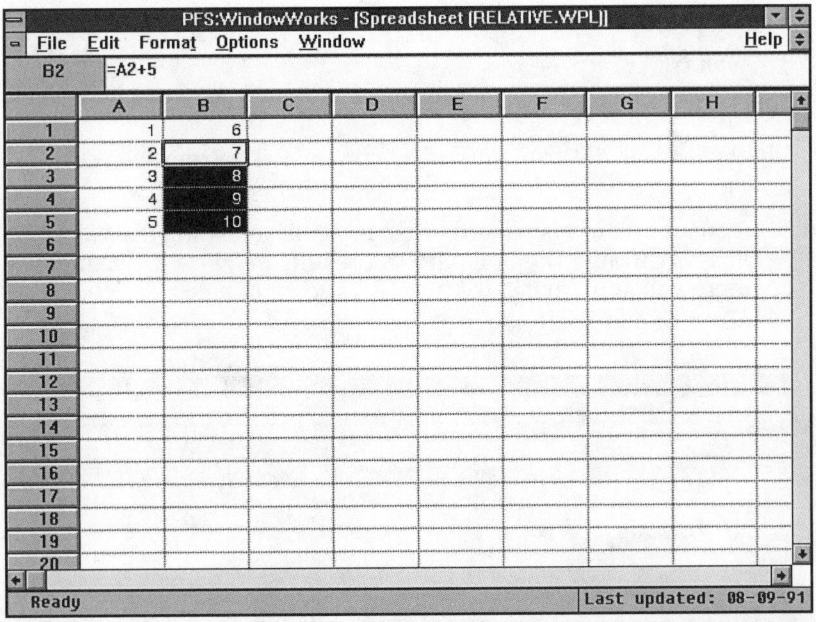

FIG. 8.2

The column reference remains the same, but the row reference has changed.

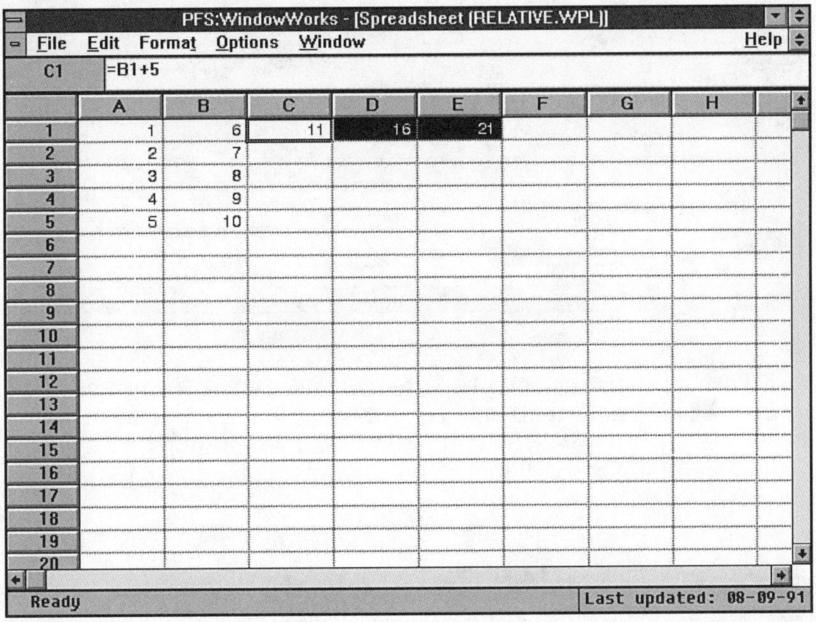

FIG. 8.3

The row reference remains the same, but the column reference has changed.

244

6. Type **=A1+5** in cell B1.

The value **6** is returned.

7. Select and copy cell B1.

8. Highlight cells B2 through B5, and choose Paste from the Edit menu.

The same equation is pasted into each cell, returning the value 6 in cells B2 through B5. Compare the results in figure 8.4, using absolute cell addressing, to the cells, shown in figure 8.2, that use relative cell addressing.

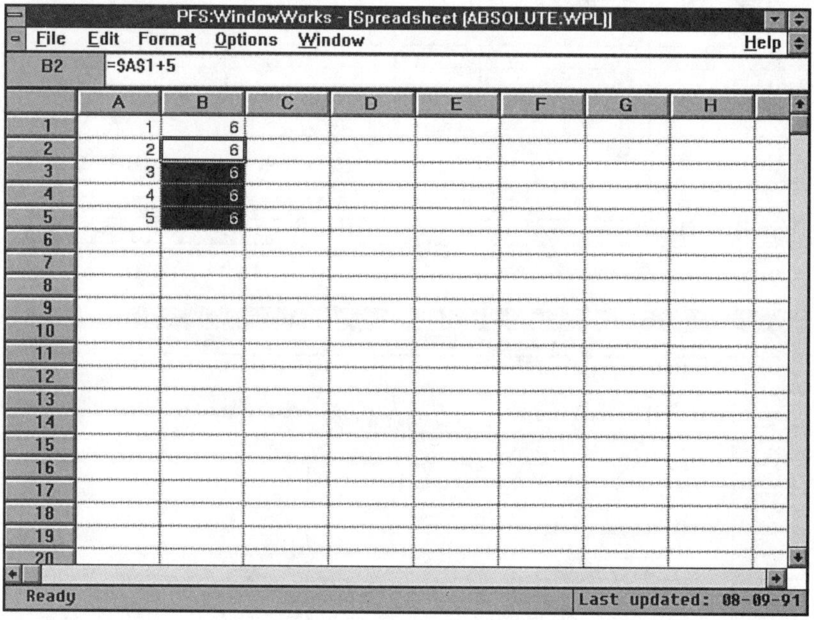

FIG. 8.4

Absolute cell addressing.

You can mix relative and absolute cell addressing. If you want the column address to remain fixed, but the row reference to remain relative, for example, you enter **=$A1+5**. If you want the row reference, but not the column, to be absolute, you enter **=A$1+5**.

Detecting Circular References in Functions

A *circular reference* occurs if an argument within a function refers to itself, causing the spreadsheet to go into a loop when it attempts to interpret the argument. For example, if you enter **1** in cell A1, **2** in cell A2, and **=SUM(A1:A3)** in cell A3, WindowWorks totals A1 and A2 but becomes confused when attempting to add the contents of cell A3—the cell where the function exists. In this example, WindowWorks returns 6, but if you change the values of A1 or A2 or recalculate the spreadsheet, the results you get in A3 will vary.

> WindowWorks can check for circular references, alerting you with a warning message if you inadvertently enter one. If you want WindowWorks to check all functions you enter for circular references, choose Calculation from the Options menu; then check the Detect Circular References option.
>
> **T I P**

If you activate the Detect Circular References option, WindowWorks displays a warning message when an argument that refers to itself is entered (see fig. 8.5).

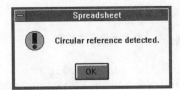

FIG. 8.5

Circular reference detected dialog box.

Click OK to close the dialog box; then correct the circular reference.

Using Operators

You use operators to tell WindowWorks the type of mathematical or logical operation you want to perform. Mathematical operators are used to make simple calculations used in a spreadsheet. Logical operators create conditional expressions that evaluate cells in a spreadsheet.

Using Mathematical Operators

The following mathematical operators are the same operators used on calculators to add, subtract, multiply, divide, and exponentiate numbers:

Operation	Operator
Addition	+
Subtraction (also used for negation)	-
Multiplication	*
Division	/
Exponentiation	^

Operators can be used alone or with other spreadsheet functions. Remember to precede entries with an equals sign (=). To add the contents of two cells by using the addition operator, for example, type **=A1+B1** into the cell.

WindowWorks uses standard mathematical conventions for determining operational hierarchy: exponentiation is solved first, multiplication and division are solved next, and addition and subtraction are solved last. Use parentheses to group parts of an equation you want evaluated separately. If you enter **=2*2+3** into a cell, for example, the result is 7; however, if you enter **=2*(2+3)**, the result is 10.

Using Logical Operators

Logical operators are used to create conditional expressions returning a value of 1 if true, a value of 0 if false. You can evaluate the contents of two cells, comparing them with one of the operators listed here. If **10** is entered in A1 and **100** is entered in B1, and the function **=A1<B1** is entered in cell C1, the result is 1, indicating the value is true because the value of cell A1 (10) is less than the value of cell B1 (100).

Use the following operators to create your expressions:

Operator	Operation
=	Equal to
>	Greater than
<	Less than
>=	Greater than or equal to
<=	Less than or equal to
<>	Not equal to

Use the IF( ) function with logical operators to perform sophisticated comparisons on cell contents. The IF( ) function uses the results of a logical comparison to determine which of two possible values should be returned. Using the preceding example, if you enter **=IF(A1<B1,1000,20)** in cell C1, the result is 1000. The first part of the formula is the logical condition (are the contents of A1 less than the contents of B1?); the second part of the formula is the value that is returned if the condition is true; the third part of the formula is the value that is returned if the condition is false. In this example, the condition is true (10 is less than 100), and so 1000 is returned.

T I P

Listing Mathematical Functions

Mathematical functions are used to perform calculations on values contained within the parentheses. Two mathematical functions, PI( ) and RAND( ), neither require nor accept additional values or arguments; these functions simply return a value.

NOTE Trigonometric functions—sin, cosine, tangent, arc sine, arc cosine, and arc tangent—accept and return values in radians, not degrees. To calculate the tangent of 30 degrees, for example, enter **=TAN(0.523)**. Thirty degrees ($\pi/6$) equals 0.523 radians.

Table 8.1 lists the mathematical functions.

Table 8.1. Mathematical Functions

Function Name	Action
ABS(*number*)	Returns the absolute value of *number*. Absolute value is the distance between *number* and 0 and is always expressed as a positive number. For example, ABS(1-5) and ABS(5-1) both return 4.
ACOS(*number*)	Returns the arc cosine of *number* in radians (*number* must be a number between -1 and 1).
ASIN(*number*)	Returns the arc sine of *number* in radians (*number* must be a number between -1 and 1).

continues

Table 8.1. continued	
Function Name	**Action**
ATAN(*number*)	Returns the arc tangent of *number* in radians.
COS(*number*)	Returns the cosine of *number* in radians.
EXP(*number*)	Raises the constant e (2.71828183) to the power of *number*. This function is the inverse of the natural logarithm function, LN().
INT(*number*)	Returns the integer value of *number*. This function does not round number but instead truncates any decimals. For example, =INT(3.9) returns 3; =INT(-3.9) returns -3.
LN(*number*)	Returns the natural logarithm—the logarithm base e (2.71828183)—of *number*.
LOG(*number*)	Returns the base 10 logarithm of *number*.
MOD(*number1*, *number2*)	Returns the remainder (modulus) of *number1* divided by *number2*.
PCT(*number*)	Returns the value of *number* divided by 100; in other words, converts *number* to a percentage value.
PI( )	Returns the value of pi, accurate to 8 decimal places.
RAND( )	Returns a random number between 0 and 1 that changes every time the spreadsheet is recalculated.
ROUND(*number*, *number-of-decimals*)	Rounds *number* to *number-of-decimals*.
SGN(*number*)	Returns 1 if *number* is positive, 0 if it is zero, or -1 if it is negative.
SIN(*number*)	Returns the sine of *number* in radians.
SQRT(*number*)	Returns the square root of *number*.
TAN(*number*)	Returns the tangent of *number* in radians.

Listing Statistical Functions

All statistical functions work on a range of cells or values. Blank cells, or cells containing text, are ignored when used as arguments in the following functions. Entering =AVG(1), although not syntactically incorrect, for example, is useless. See table 8.2 for a list of statistical functions:

Table 8.2. Statistical Functions

Function	Action
AVG(*values-1,values-2,...*)	Returns the average of values in a list or range of cells by adding all the values and dividing the total by the number of values.
CNT(*values-1,values-2,...*)	Returns the number of items in the list. Enter numbers or cell references.
MAX(*values-1,values-2,...*)	Returns the maximum value in a list or range of cells.
MIN(*values-1,values-2,...*)	Returns the minimum value in a list or range of cells.
STD(*values-1,values-2,...*)	Returns the standard deviation of values in a list or range of cells. *Standard deviation* is calculated using the formula SQRT(VAR(values-1,values-2,...)).
SUM(*values-1,values-2,...*)	Returns the sum total of a list or range of cells.
VAR(*values-1,values-2,...*)	Returns the statistical variance of values in a list or range of cells.

Listing Financial Functions

Table 8.3 provides a list of financial functions used by WindowWorks.

Table 8.3. Financial Functions

Function	Action
DDB(*cost,salvage-value,life,prd*)	Computes the depreciation allowance of an asset by using the double declining balance method.

continues

Table 8.3. continued	
Function	**Action**
FV(*pmt,int,nper*)	Computes the future value of an investment, given the payment amount (*pmt*), interest rate per period (*int*), and the number of regular payments (*nper*).
NPER(*pmt,int,prn*)	Computes the number of periods required to repay a loan given the payment amount (*pmt*), the interest rate per period (*int*), and the amount of principal (*prn*).
NPV(*int,list*)	Returns the net present value of a loan, given the interest rate (*int*) and a list of cash receipts or payments due. The *list* can be any range.
PMT(*prn,int,nper*)	Returns the periodic payment amount, given the principal amount (*prn*), interest rate per period (*int*), and the number of regular payments (*nper*).
PV(*pmt,int,nper*)	Returns the present value of payment, given the regular payment amount (*pmt*), interest rate per period (*int*), and the number of regular payment periods (*nper*).
SLN(*cost,salvage-value,lf*)	Calculates the straight-line depreciation of an asset for a single period. This method evenly depreciates initial *cost* to *salvage-value* over the useful life (*if*) of the asset.

Listing Date Functions

The spreadsheet represents each day—beginning January 1, 1900—with a number. January 1, 1900 is day 1. The numeric format of the cell determines how the date is displayed. If you enter =**DATE(62,8,12)** into a cell, for example, 8-12-62 is returned if the cell's numeric format is set to General (the default). If the cell's numeric format is set to any other type (such as ####), however, the Julian date is returned. In this case 22869 would be returned, representing the number of days passed since January 1, 1900.

 NOTE If you enter **8/12/62** into a cell formatted as General, WindowWorks does not recognize this format as a date; WindowWorks interprets it as a text string. To indicate to WindowWorks that you are entering a date, you must enter it as **=date(91,8,12)**, where 91 is the year; 8 is the month; and 12 is the day. You can then choose one of the date formats available in the Numeric Formats dialog box.

The function TODAY( ) returns the *system date* (the date set by your computer's system clock). Again, if the cell's numeric format is set to General, the date is returned as 8-8-91; otherwise, a number is returned representing the number of days that have passed since January 1, 1900 and today. *Today* also can be used as an argument for any of the date functions that accept arguments. For example, you can enter =DATE(today), or =MONTH(today), and so on into a cell. See table 8.4 for a list of date functions.

Table 8.4. Date Functions

Function	Action
DATE(*yy,mm,dd*)	Returns the Julian date.
TODAY( )	Returns today's Julian date as set in the system clock.
DAY(*Julian date*)	Returns the day of the Julian date.
MONTH(*Julian date*)	Returns the month of the Julian date.
YEAR(*Julian date*)	Returns the year of the Julian date.

TODAY( ), like PI( ), does not require parentheses ( ) because it does not accept an argument. The user can choose whether to enter them. However, when referring to them in the text (tables, figures, etc.), always include the parentheses because they indicate a function.

Listing Other Functions

Table 8.5 lists other functions used by WindowWorks.

Table 8.5. Other Functions

Function Name	Action
CHOOSE(*integer, case0, case1,...*)	Uses *integer* to select value from list.
HLOOKUP(*lookup-number, compare-range,index-number*)	Selects value in table, according to *lookup-number.*
VLOOKUP(*lookup-number, compare-range,index-number*)	Selects value in table, according to *lookup-number.*
IF(*condition,number-if-true, number-if-false)*	Returns *number-if-true* if *condition* is true; returns *number-if-false* if *condition* is false.

Chapter Summary

WindowWorks offers a wide range of functions for use in the Spreadsheet and Database modules. These functions perform mathematical, statistical, financial, date, and logical calculations on the arguments you specify. Arguments can be values you enter directly or the addresses of cells containing values. These functions are the key to creating complex and sophisticated spreadsheets or database reports.

Creating Charts

The Chart Editor module enables you to create charts and graphs from numbers you enter directly or from data you paste from the Spreadsheet. When you paste information from the Spreadsheet, the information is *linked*; therefore, any changes you make to the Spreadsheet data also appear in your chart. You can modify and print charts directly from the Chart Editor, or you can copy (and link) charts to the Word Processor to modify and print them. This module is very simple to use.

NOTE The terms *chart* and *graph* are interchangeable. This module may well have been named the Graph Editor.

Nine chart types are available to enable you to graph almost any kind of data. Certain chart types, however, are best suited for particular kinds of data. Experimenting to determine which chart best suits a particular need is simple. After you enter your data or paste it from the Spreadsheet, changing chart types is simply a matter of clicking a button. You also click a button to add a legend to your chart. If you decide you don't need a legend, click the button again.

Starting the Chart Editor

To start the Chart Editor, double-click the Chart Editor icon or choose Chart Editor from the Window menu. The Chart Editor becomes the active window.

The Chart Editor window consists of the menu bar, control strip, and work area (see fig. 9.1).

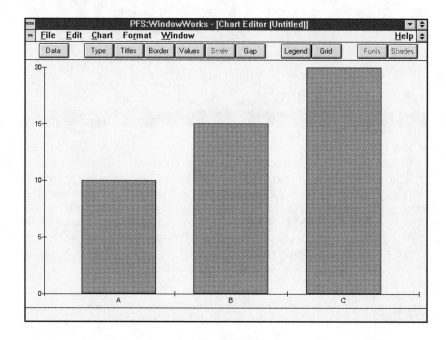

FIG. 9.1

The Chart Editor window.

When you start the Chart Editor, the work area is blank. This area is where the Chart Editor displays your charts as soon you enter some data or paste data from the Spreadsheet.

The menu bar contains the Chart Editor's menus, which enable you to access menu commands. The control strip also enables you to use most of these menu commands. Each button on the control strip corresponds to a menu command. For example, clicking the Data button on the control strip produces the same result as choosing the Chart Data command that enables you to enter chart data from the Edit menu. Table 9.1 lists each button and its menu-command equivalent.

When possible, this book refers to the control strip buttons because they provide the easiest way to access the Chart Editor's options; however, you can substitute menu commands.

Table 9.1. Menu Equivalents for Control Strip Buttons

Button	Menu/Command
Data	Edit/Chart Data
Type	Chart/Chart Type
Titles	Chart/Titles
Border	Chart/Border
Values	Chart/Data Values
Scale	Chart/Scale
Gap	Chart/Cluster Gap
Legend	Chart/Legend
Grid	Chart/Grid
Fonts	Format/Fonts
Shades	Format/Shades

You can choose from the following chart types: Bar, Stacked Bar, Horizontal Bar, Line, Pie, Exploded Pie, Point, Area, and High-Low-Close (see figs. 9.2–9.10).

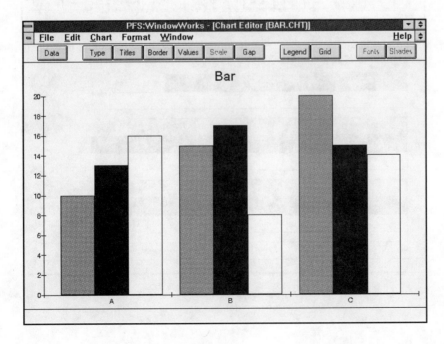

FIG 9.2

A sample bar chart.

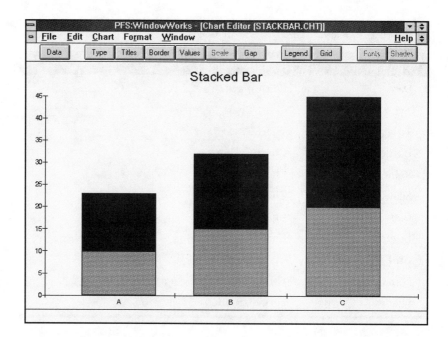

FIG. 9.3

A sample stacked bar chart.

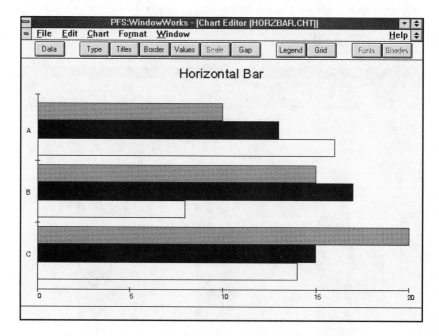

FIG. 9.4

A sample horizontal bar chart.

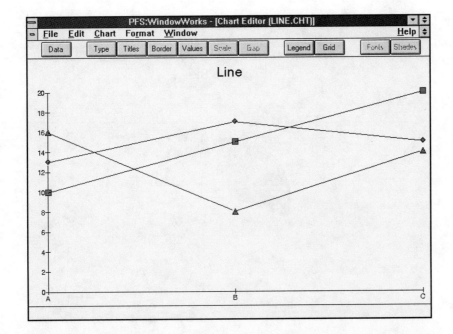

FIG. 9.5

A sample line chart.

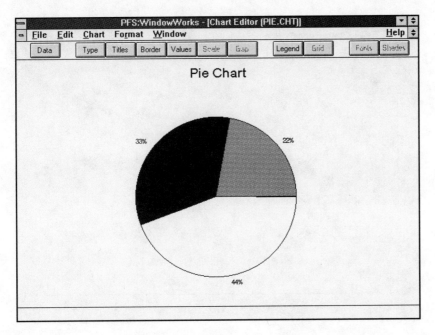

FIG. 9.6

A sample pie chart.

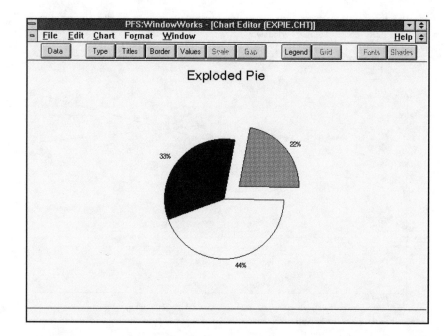

FIG. 9.7

A sample exploded pie chart.

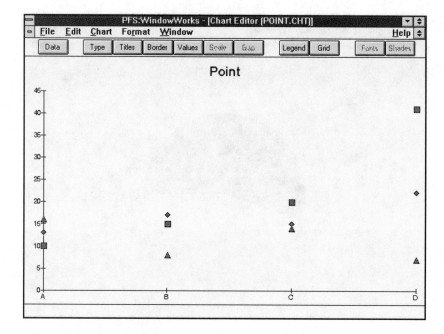

FIG. 9.8

A sample point chart.

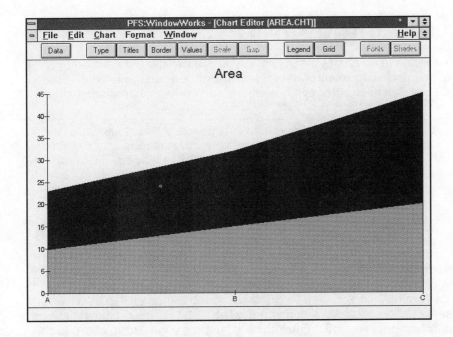

FIG. 9.9

A sample area chart.

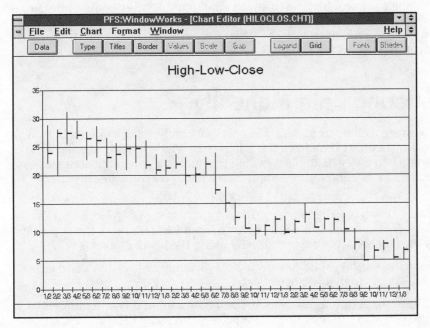

FIG. 9.10

A sample high-low-close chart.

Creating a Chart

You can create charts in two ways: you can use the Data button from the control strip to enter data manually, or you can import data from the Spreadsheet. Although both methods produce charts, some differences do exist.

Data you paste from the Spreadsheet is linked; if you change the spreadsheet, you quickly can update your chart manually or automatically to reflect the changes. If you enter data by using the data-entry window of the Chart Editor module, all updates and changes are made in the Chart Editor module. Unlike information in a spreadsheet, you cannot perform calculations on data you enter manually in the Chart Editor.

Suppose that one of your spreadsheets contains cells showing your monthly net income. The income figures are based on several calculations that use data from other cells, such as gross receipts, salary expense, tax expense, and so on. This spreadsheet graphs the results of the formulas you created to calculate your net income. Because you cannot enter formulas when you use the Chart Editor's manual data entry feature, you must enter the final figures you want to chart. In this example, you would need to know what your monthly net income is to enter the data into the Chart Editor; however, if you import the data from the Spreadsheet into the Chart Editor, you can rely on the Spreadsheet to perform the calculations for you.

Entering Data Manually

To create a chart from data you enter manually, click the Data button or choose Chart Data from the Edit menu. WindowWorks displays the Chart Data Entry dialog box, which resembles a spreadsheet. It contains 150 rows and four columns into which you can enter numbers.

In the top row, you can enter a title for each column, and in the left-most column, you can enter a title for each row. The Chart Editor displays each column title in the chart's legend and displays the row titles as the labels for the *clusters* or bars along the horizontal axis.

Figure 9.11 shows the Chart Data Entry window, with values and labels for a sample high-low-close chart.

To enter data into a cell, click the cell you want and type a number or title. You also can move between cells by pressing the Tab key to move from left to right, Shift-Tab to move from right to left, and the up- and down-arrow keys to move up or down, respectively. Double-clicking a cell highlights all the data in that cell, which is useful for copying, moving, or replacing data, and for deleting information—rather than pressing the Backspace key to delete one character at a time.

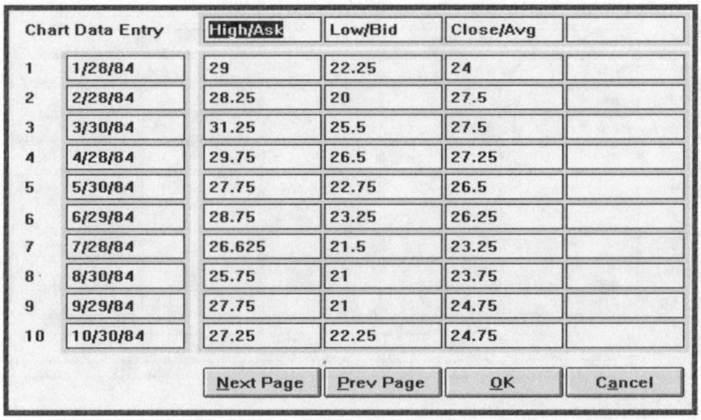

Chart Data Entry		High/Ask	Low/Bid	Close/Avg	
1	1/28/84	29	22.25	24	
2	2/28/84	28.25	20	27.5	
3	3/30/84	31.25	25.5	27.5	
4	4/28/84	29.75	26.5	27.25	
5	5/30/84	27.75	22.75	26.5	
6	6/29/84	28.75	23.25	26.25	
7	7/28/84	26.625	21.5	23.25	
8	8/30/84	25.75	21	23.75	
9	9/29/84	27.75	21	24.75	
10	10/30/84	27.25	22.25	24.75	

Next Page Prev Page OK Cancel

FIG. 9.11

The Chart Data Entry window, with a sample high-low-close chart.

T I P

Because the Chart Data Entry window is actually a dialog box, you cannot choose commands from the menu while the Chart Data Entry window is visible. WindowWorks beeps when you attempt to choose from the menu. However, you can cut, copy, and paste data by using the keyboard equivalents for each of these Edit menu commands. To cut data from a cell, select the cell and press Shift-Delete; to copy data from a cell, select the cell and press Ctrl-Insert. After you cut or copy data, you can move to a different cell and press Shift-Insert to paste the copied or cut data into that cell.

You can enter up to 29 characters in a cell, but the Chart Editor displays only 10 at one time. When you enter the eleventh character, the cell scrolls so that the new characters you enter are visible.

Also, the Chart Editor displays only 10 rows at a time, which make up a *Page*. You can enter a maximum of 15 pages of numbers, but if you really need to enter 150 rows of numbers, you probably should use the Spreadsheet module, which is better suited for entering and managing large amounts of data.

If you fill a page, click the Next Page button to display 10 more rows; click the Prev Page button to display the preceding 10 rows.

When creating a chart, considering the difference between rows and columns is important. How you *group* your data into rows and columns determines the appearance of your chart. Columns are the *categories* into which you divide your data. A group is a single row of data.

If you enter four rows and two columns of numbers in the Chart Data Entry dialog box for a bar chart (see fig. 9.12), the Chart Editor displays the bars in four groups, each containing two categories (see fig. 9.13).

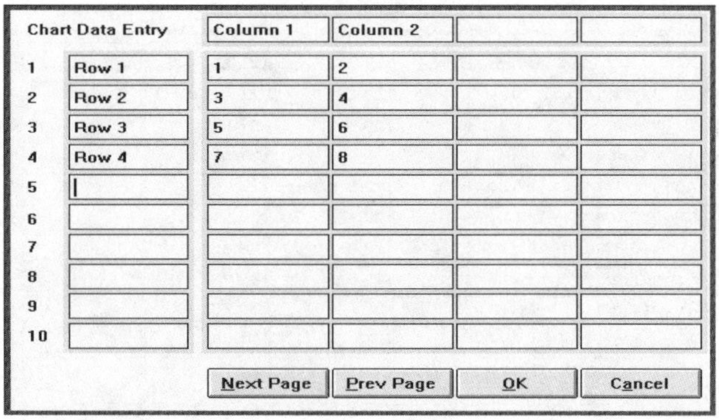

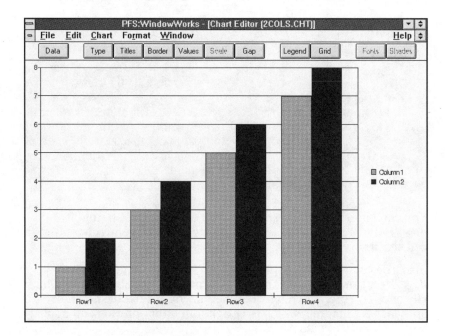

FIG. 9.12

A Chart Data Entry dialog box with four rows and two columns of data.

FIG. 9.13

A bar chart with four groups containing two categories.

If you enter the same data in two rows and four columns of numbers (see fig. 9.14), the Chart Editor displays the bars in two groups, each containing four categories (see fig. 9.15).

In bar charts, categories are separated by different shading patterns, and groups of data are separated by gaps.

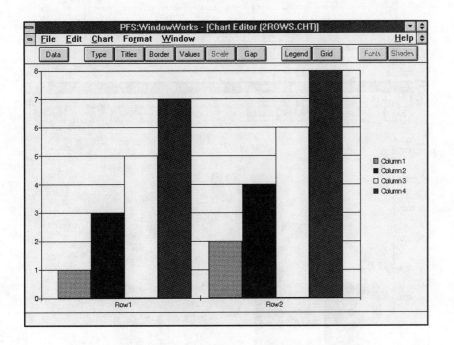

Chart Data Entry		Column 1	Column 2	Column 3	Column 4
1	Row 1	1	3	5	7
2	Row 2	2	4	6	8
3					
4					
5					
6					
7					
8					
9					
10					

Next Page   Prev Page   OK   Cancel

FIG. 9.14

A Chart Data Entry dialog box with two rows and four columns of data.

FIG. 9.15

A bar chart with two groups containing four categories.

Suppose that you want to chart the market value of two properties over a period of four years. Each property is a category, so enter the name of the first property as the title of the first column and the name of the second property as the title of the second column. Each year is a group of data, so enter the year as the title of the first four rows. Next, you enter the market value of each property for each year. Figure 9.16 shows an example of what your Chart Data Entry dialog box may look like after you enter the property data.

Clicking the OK button tells the Chart Editor to use the values you entered to create a chart. The default chart type for new charts is Bar.

You easily can change the chart type, however; see the section "Changing the Chart Type," further in this chapter. Based on the data shown in figure 9.16, the Chart Editor displays the bar chart shown in figure 9.17.

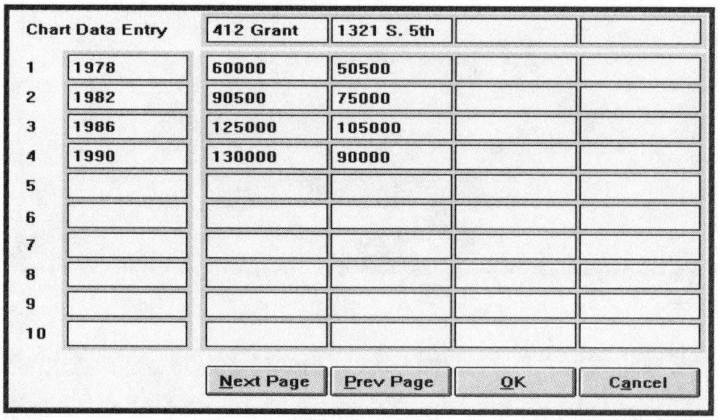

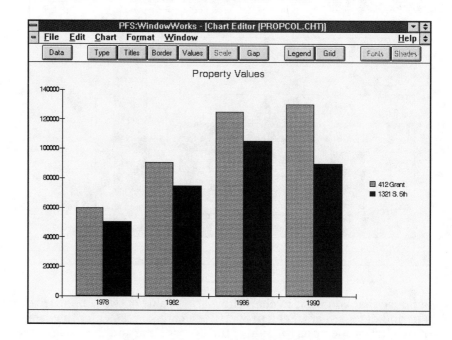

FIG. 9.16

The Chart Data Entry dialog box containing property data.

FIG. 9.17

A sample bar chart of property values.

If you reverse the order of rows and columns—creating a column instead of a row for each year and a row instead of a column for each property—the Chart Editor would display the chart shown in figure 9.18.

Notice that the Chart Editor displays column titles in the chart legend and displays row titles along the chart's horizontal axis.

 NOTE In pie and exploded pie charts, the Chart Editor displays row titles as the chart legend, as discussed further in this chapter.

After you create a chart in the Chart Editor, you can edit the chart at any time by clicking the Data button on the control strip to return to the Chart Data Entry window.

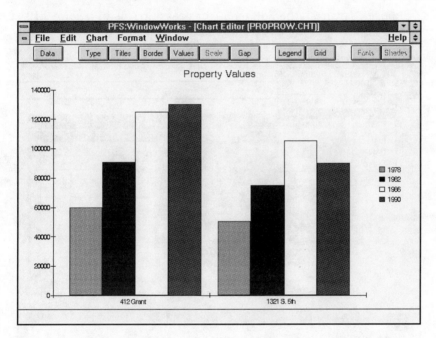

FIG. 9.18

The property values bar chart with row and column data reversed.

Importing Data from the Spreadsheet

The second way to create a chart is to import data from the Spreadsheet module—the better method if you want to chart a large amount of data, if you need to perform calculations on the data, or if you want to chart data you already entered in the Spreadsheet module. (Refer to Chapter 7, "Creating a Spreadsheet," for details about creating and editing spreadsheets.)

The following steps explain how to import data from the Spreadsheet to create a chart:

1. Open the Spreadsheet module.

2. In a new spreadsheet, enter the data you want to chart, or open an existing spreadsheet that contains the data.

3. Select the rows and columns of data you want to chart. Click the letter at the top of a column to select the entire column. Click a number at the left of a row to select the entire row. Refer to Chapter 7 for details on selecting data in the Spreadsheet module.

4. Choose Copy from the Edit menu, or press Ctrl-Insert. Figure 9.19 shows the Edit menu and a spreadsheet with selected data.

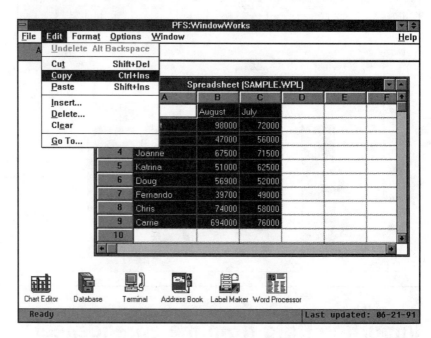

FIG. 9.19

The Edit menu, with selected spreadsheet data from SAMPLE.WPL.

5. Open the Chart Editor module by clicking the Chart Editor icon or by choosing Chart Editor from the Window menu. Whether you leave open, minimize, or close the Spreadsheet module does not matter.

6. If the Chart Editor's workspace is empty, choose Paste from the Edit menu (or press Shift-Insert) to paste the selected data from the Spreadsheet. If the workspace is not empty, choose New from the File menu before pasting the data.

The Chart Editor displays the Data Link dialog box (see fig. 9.20), which displays the name of the spreadsheet file you are *importing*, or copying, and the *source* of the file, such as the Spreadsheet module.

FIG. 9.20

The Data Link
dialog box.

The Data Link dialog box enables you to indicate whether you want to *hot-link* the chart with the original data in the Spreadsheet. Hot-linking data between one module and another means that the data is automatically updated in one module when you edit the data in the original module. In this example, hot-linking the two files means that every time you modify the data in the part of the spreadsheet you copied to the Chart Editor, the chart is modified to reflect the new data.

7. If you want to hot-link your chart to the spreadsheet file so that your chart automatically is updated to reflect changes to the spreadsheet data, turn on the Auto Refresh option—click the Auto Refresh toggle box to display an X (refer to fig. 9.20). If you do not want your chart to automatically reflect updates to the spreadsheet data, leave the Auto Refresh toggle box empty. Your data is still linked, and you can update the chart at any time with the Refresh Now option.

8. Click OK.

    The Chart Editor displays a bar chart that represents the data you copied from the Spreadsheet (see fig. 9.21). You now can format the chart or modify the chart type; see the following section, "Formatting the Chart," for a detailed discussion on formatting charts and modifying chart types.

If you want to edit the chart data, you can edit it from the Chart Data Entry window, as you learned in the preceding section, or you can edit it from the Spreadsheet. To maintain linked data, you must return to the Spreadsheet module to edit the data. If you use the Chart Data Entry window to edit data you imported from the Spreadsheet, the chart can no longer be linked to the original spreadsheet file. For example, if you copy data from cells in the Spreadsheet and paste them to the Chart Editor—with or without Auto Refresh turned on—and then attempt to use the Chart Data Entry window to edit the data, WindowWorks displays a warning message (see fig. 9.22). Breaking the link means that any further changes you make to the data in the Spreadsheet module are not reflected in the Chart; you must reimport the data to update the chart. If you do not want the data linked to the Spreadsheet, edit the data in the Chart Data Entry window; click the Data button on the control strip.

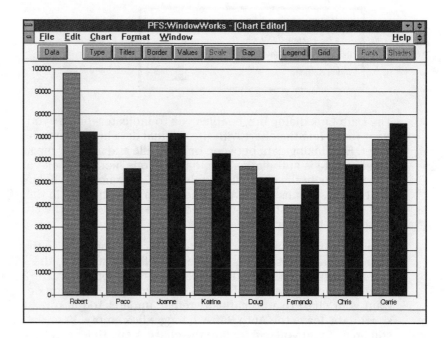

FIG. 9.21

A bar chart based on data from SAMPLE.WPL.

Even if you choose not to turn on the Auto Refresh option when you paste data from the Spreadsheet, the data is linked. You can turn on the Auto Refresh option later, creating a hot-link, by choosing Link from the Edit menu. The Chart Editor displays the Data Link dialog box, just as it does when you paste Spreadsheet data. You also can leave Auto Refresh turned off and refresh the data manually by choosing Refresh Now from the Edit menu.

FIG. 9.22

The warning message displayed when you attempt to edit imported data.

Formatting a Chart

After you create a chart, by entering data in the Chart Editor or by copying data from the Spreadsheet module, you are ready to format the chart to look exactly as you want it to look. You also are ready to change the chart type. You can add a grid, legend, or border; display the values associated with the chart elements; change the scale and spacing; add titles; and even change the shading of the chart or the fonts of the legend and labels.

Changing the Chart Type

The best way to determine which chart type best suits your current project is to quickly view your data as represented by each type of chart. First, enter your data and view the chart. Then click the Type button on the control strip, or choose Chart Type from the Chart menu. The Chart Editor displays the Chart Type dialog box (see fig. 9.23), which lists the available chart types.

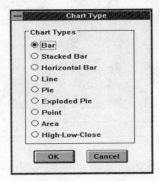

FIG. 9.23

The Chart Type dialog box.

Bar is the default chart type for all new charts. To display the current data as a chart type other than Bar, choose another chart type from the Chart Type dialog box, and click OK. The Chart Editor expresses the data in the new chart type. You can use this method to view your data in all nine chart types to determine the most appropriate type for your data. You can change the chart type any time, without affecting your data. A pie chart, however, displays only the first column of data.

Adding a Legend to Your Chart

When the Chart Editor first displays a chart, it does not display a *legend*—a key displayed to the right of your chart to indicate the meanings of the shades and patterns of your graph elements (see fig. 9.24). A chart's legend includes the titles of the columns in your data. If you want to display a legend with your chart, click the Legend button on the control strip, or choose Legend from the Chart menu.

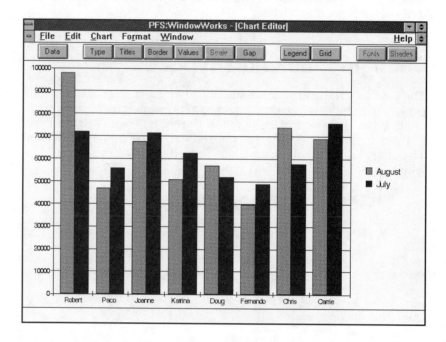

FIG. 9.24

A bar chart with a legend based on data from SAMPLE.WPL.

The Legend button on the control strip is a toggle button; click it once to turn on the legend option (display the legend), click it again to turn off the option (remove the legend). The button does not indicate whether the legend is on or off. The Legend option on the Chart menu, however, displays a check mark when you turn on the option.

If you turn on the option, but the Chart Editor does not display the legend, you probably need to go into the Chart Data Entry window (or to the source spreadsheet) and add column titles.

Displaying Chart Values

If the absolute numbers you enter in the Chart Data Entry window are pertinent to the display of your chart (rather than needing to show a general trend or approximate numbers), you can display the data values on the chart. The following steps explain how to display data values:

1. Click the Values button on the control strip or choose Data Values from the Chart menu. The Chart Editor displays the Data Values dialog box (see fig. 9.25).

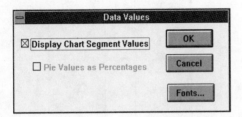

FIG. 9.25

The Data Values dialog box.

If the current chart type is not a pie chart, the only option available in the Data Values dialog box is the Display Chart Segment Values option.

2. Turn on the Display Chart Segment Values option (click the toggle box to display an X) to add the numerical values from the Chart Data Entry window to the appropriate chart elements.

Figure 9.26 shows a bar chart with the data values turned on.

3. You can control the appearance of the data values by setting the font characteristics. Click the Fonts button in the Data Values dialog box. The Chart Editor displays the Character dialog box (see fig. 9.27), which enables you to choose typeface, type size, and type style.

4. The fonts available with the currently selected printer are listed in the Face selection list. The currently selected font is highlighted in the Face text box. If these fonts are not the fonts you want to use, exit the Character dialog box and the Data Values dialog box (press Escape twice, or click Cancel twice), choose Printer Setup from the File menu, and choose the correct printer or printer driver.

5. Choose a type size from the list, or type a size in the Size text box. (If you are using the Publisher's Powerpak printer driver, you can enter any size font; you do not have to choose one from the list.)

6. Choose the attributes you want to apply to the data values: Bold, Italic, or Underline. You can choose as many of these attributes as you want. If you don't want any of these attributes, click Normal.

7. Click OK to confirm your font choices. The Chart Editor displays the Data Values dialog box.

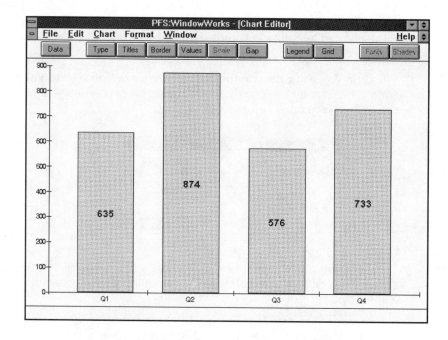

FIG. 9.26

A bar chart with
the data values
turned on.

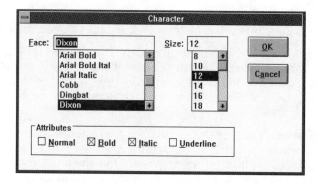

FIG. 9.27

The Character
dialog box.

8. Click OK to display the data values. The Chart Editor displays the chart, showing the data values in the specified font characteristics.

   To turn off the values, click the Values button, and again click the Display Chart Segment Values button to toggle off this option. Click OK to exit the window.

If the current chart type is a pie chart and the Display Chart Segment Values option is turned on, the option Pie Values as Percentages also is available in the Data Values dialog box. If you turn on this option (the toggle box displays an X), the Chart Editor displays values as percentages rather than the absolute numerical values you entered in the Chart

Data Entry window, which means that it displays the percentage of the total pie that each pie slice constitutes (see fig. 9.28). You can set the font characteristics for the percentage values the same way you modify numerical data values.

This percentage value display is useful for some pie charts. For example, suppose that you want to present last year's sales of your three products. In the Chart Data Entry window, you can enter Product 1, Product 2, and Product 3 as the row titles, enter the sales figures for each, and choose the chart type Pie, with the values displayed as percentages. You then can see what percent of your total sales each of the three products constituted, rather than having to guess at the percentage by eyeballing the size of each pie slice or by calculating it yourself from the total sales figures.

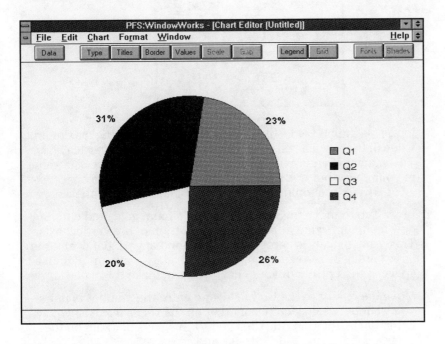

FIG. 9.28

A pie chart with the option Pie Values as Percentages turned on.

Changing the Vertical Scale

You can change your chart's *scale*, the incremental values used for reference on the y-axis (the vertical axis). If the Chart Editor displays your chart with a lot of unused space above it or with more incremental values listed on the vertical axis than you think are necessary for clarity, you should change the chart's scale. The following steps explain how to change the vertical scale:

1. Select the y-axis (vertical axis) by clicking it. The Chart Editor displays a small box, called a *selection handle*, at each end.

2. Click the Scale button on the control strip, or choose Scale from the Chart menu. If the Scale button is grayed, which indicates that it is not a currently available option, you probably have not selected the axis.

   After you click the Scale button, the Chart Editor displays the Scale dialog box (see fig. 9.29), which shows the chart's current scaling values.

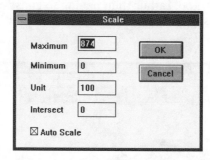

FIG. 9.29

The Scale dialog box.

3. In the Maximum field, enter a new value to specify the maximum value of the vertical axis, the value at the top of the vertical axis. The value you enter should be greater than the largest data value in your chart, but not so much larger that a lot of extra space exists between the top point on the chart and the top of the axis.

4. Press Tab to move the cursor to the Minimum field, and enter a new minimum value, the value at the bottom of the vertical axis. This value usually is zero; however, if none of your data values are anywhere near zero and you don't want a large amount of unused space at the bottom of your chart, you can make this value larger.

5. Move the cursor to the Unit field, and enter the number of units you want between each tick marker on the vertical axis. If you enter **100** as the Unit, the Chart Editor displays markers on the vertical axis at 100, 200, 300, 400, and so on.

   The Unit value should factor evenly into the total distance of the vertical axis (the Maximum value minus the Minimum value). If the Maximum is 1000 and the Minimum is 0, a good Unit value would be 200 [(1000 – 0) / 200 = 5] or 500 [(1000 – 0) / 500 = 2]. A Unit value of 300 would make your graph uneven [(1000 – 0) / 300 = 3 1/3], so WindowWorks would change the Maximum value to 1200, which is evenly divisible by 300.

6. Move the cursor to the Intersect field, and enter the value at which you want the vertical axis to intersect the horizontal axis. This value usually is zero, but if you change the Minimum value, you also may want to change the Intersect value.

Consider experimenting with different points of intersection. Changing the intersection point can have some interesting effects. If you make the intersection point 200, for example, and some of the data values in your chart are less than 200, the Chart Editor displays those portions of the chart below the horizontal axis, creating a very different looking chart.

Clicking the Auto Scale button in the Scale dialog box clears all values from the Maximum, Minimum, Unit, and Intersect fields, leaving WindowWorks to scale the chart automatically.

7. Click OK to confirm your scaling choices. The Chart Editor displays the same chart, but scales it according to the specified values.

Using figure 9.26 as an example, if you change the Maximum value to 1000 and the Unit value to 200, the Chart Editor displays the chart shown in figure 9.30.

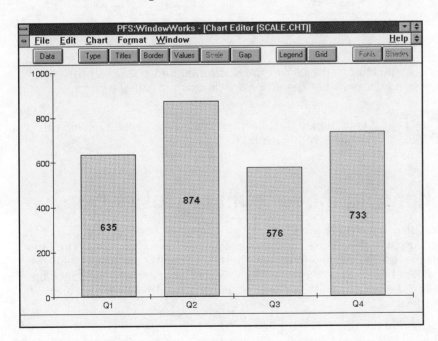

FIG. 9.30

A chart with a Maximum value of 1000 and a Unit value 200.

If you change the Maximum value to 2000, the Chart Editor displays the chart shown in figure 9.31.

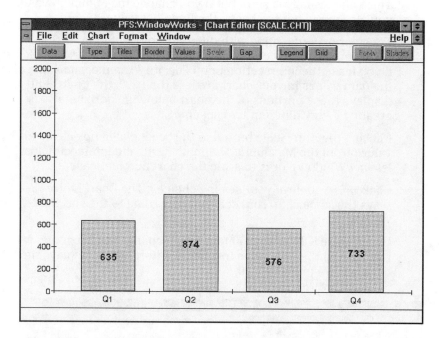

FIG. 9.31

A chart with a Maximum value of 2000 and a Unit value of 200.

If you choose the chart type Horizontal Bar, you select the horizontal axis rather than the vertical axis to scale the chart.

NOTE   If you choose the chart type Pie or Exploded Pie, no scale exists for you to scale.

Changing the Amount of Cluster Gap

You also can modify the *Cluster Gap*—the space between the chart bars or bar clusters—to change the appearance of your bar chart. The Cluster Gap is applicable only to bar charts, horizontal bar charts, and stacked bar charts. Increasing the Cluster Gap increases the space between the bars or clusters by decreasing the width of the bars and clusters.

To modify the Cluster Gap, click the Gap button on the control strip or choose Cluster Gap from the Chart menu. The Chart Editor displays the Cluster Gap window (see fig. 9.32), which indicates the gap setting of the current bar chart.

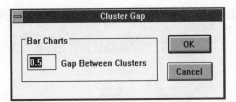

FIG. 9.32

The Cluster Gap
dialog box.

The cluster gap setting represents the ratio of the gap to the width of the bars. The default setting, 0.5, indicates that the gap is half as wide as the width of a single bar. If the setting is 1, the gap is as wide as the bar width. A setting of zero means no gap exists between bars.

To modify the cluster gap, enter a new setting in the Gap Between Clusters text box, and click OK. The Chart Editor displays the new chart, showing the specified gaps.

Using figure 9.30 as an example, which shows the default cluster gap of 0.5, if you change the gap setting to 0, the Chart Editor displays the chart shown in figure 9.33. If you change the cluster gap to 1.5, the Chart Editor displays the chart shown in figure 9.34.

Adding Titles

You can add a main title to your chart, and you can add titles to the horizontal and vertical axes. The following steps explain how to add titles to your chart:

1. Click the Titles button on the control strip, or choose Titles from the Chart menu. The Chart Editor displays the Chart Titles dialog box (see fig. 9.35), containing text boxes that enable you to enter titles for the chart itself (Main), the vertical (y) axis, and the horizontal (x) axis.

2. Type the title of your chart in the Main Title text box. The Chart Editor displays the Main Title at the top and center of the chart area.

3. Click the Fonts button in the Main Title field. The Chart Editor displays the Character dialog box, enabling you to select the title's font, text size, and attributes. Choose a typeface from the Face selection list, choose a type size from the Size list, and choose text attributes from the Attributes field.

4. Click OK to confirm your Character choices.

5. Repeat steps 2, 3, and 4 to specify a title in the Y-Axis text box. The Chart Editor displays the y-axis title vertically, to the left of your chart's vertical axis.

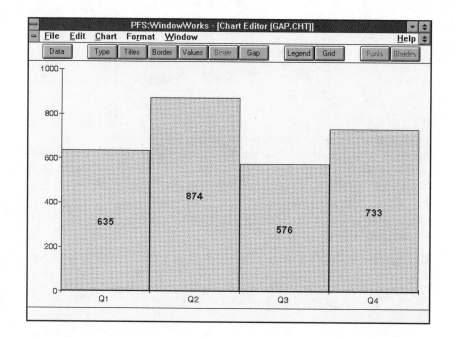

FIG. 9.33

A chart with a
Gap Between
Clusters value
of zero.

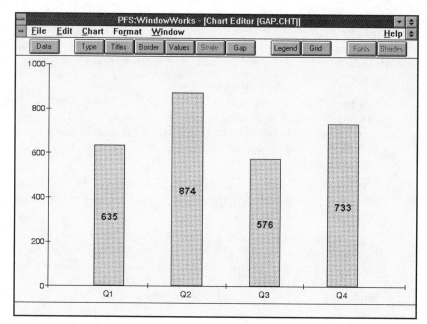

FIG. 9.34

A chart with a
Gap Between
Clusters value
of 1.5.

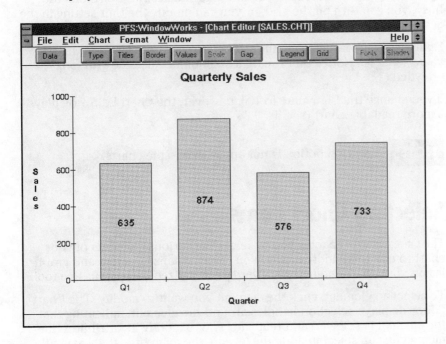

Chart Titles

Main Title
Quarterly Sales   Fonts...

Y-Axis Title
Sales   Fonts...

X-Axis Title
Quarter   Fonts...

OK
Cancel

6. Repeat steps 2, 3, and 4 again to specify a title in the X-Axis Title text box. The Chart Editor displays the x-axis title along the bottom of your chart's horizontal axis.

   Adding titles is optional. You can leave the title text boxes blank, enter only one title, or enter all three titles.

7. Click OK to confirm your title choices. The Chart Editor displays your chart with the specified titles. Figure 9.36 shows the chart displayed after adding the titles from figure 9.35.

PFS:WindowWorks - [Chart Editor (SALES.CHT)]

File Edit Chart Format Window   Help

Data   Type Titles Border Values Scale Gap   Legend Grid   Fonts Shades

Quarterly Sales

635 874 576 733

Q1 Q2 Q3 Q4

Quarter

NOTE In a pie chart, the only title the Chart Editor displays is the main title. If you create a horizontal bar chart, the axes are reversed; the Chart Editor displays the y-axis title along the horizontal axis (the y-axis) and displays the x-axis title vertically along the x-axis.

Adding a Grid

You can display a grid that corresponds to the incremental unit settings specified in the Scale dialog box. The grid helps you identify where your chart elements lie in relation to the unit values, and it also can add an interesting graphic effect to your chart.

To view the grid, click the Grid button on the control strip or choose Grid from the Chart menu. The Grid option is a toggle switch: click or choose it once to turn on the grid; click or choose it again to turn off the grid. The Grid button does not change appearance when you toggle the option; the menu command, however, displays a check mark when the option is on.

If the appearance of the grid on your chart makes the chart look too busy, you can turn off the grid, or you can modify the Unit setting in the Scale dialog box to make fewer grid lines.

Figure 9.37 shows a chart with the Grid option turned on and the Unit value set at 50. Notice that the tightly set units make the grid look crowded.

If you change the Unit value to 100, however, the Chart Editor displays a more readable chart (see fig. 9.38).

 NOTE The Grid option is not applicable to pie charts.

Selecting Chart Items

The Chart Editor enables you to select the various elements of your chart to edit them individually. You can customize the text and graphics on your chart and make it a very personalized and persuasive tool.

To select an element, click the element you want to modify. The Chart Editor displays selection handles around the element, indicating that the element is selected and ready for you to modify its attributes. Elements you can select include the legend, the main title, the y-axis title, the x-axis title, the y-axis (including its labels), the x-axis (including its labels and values), a series of data (from any chart except pie charts), or a pie chart segment.

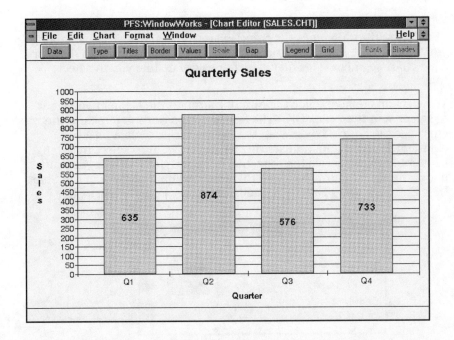

FIG. 9.37

A chart with the Grid option turned on and a Unit value of 50.

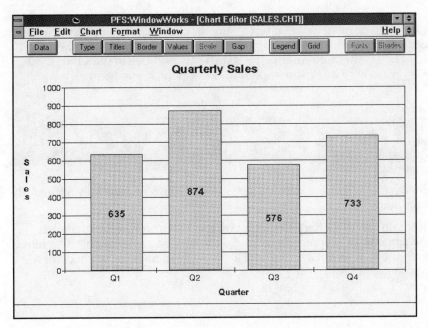

FIG. 9.38

A chart with the Grid option turned on and a Unit value of 100.

You also can choose Select from the Chart menu to select an element. The Chart Editor displays the Select dialog box (see fig. 9.39), enabling you to select the legend, vertical or horizontal axis, a series of data, or a pie chart segment. This dialog box does not enable you to select titles.

To select an element, click the option button of the element you want to select, and then click OK. (The Series option doesn't appear if the chart is a pie chart.) If you want to select a series of data on a bar chart, click Series and indicate the series you want to select by typing its number in the Series text box. In a bar chart, for example, the number of the series corresponds to the data's column number in the Chart Data Entry window. The first column of data is series 1, and so on.

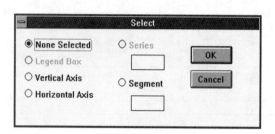

FIG. 9.39

The Select dialog box.

If you want to select a pie chart segment, click Segment and specify the segment you want to select by entering its number in the Segment text box. The segment number is the data's row number in the Chart Data Entry window. The first row of data is segment 1, and so on.

T   I   P   When selecting a series, simply clicking the bar, point, line, or area you want to select is easier than using the Select dialog box.

You cannot select the data values, grid, or border when they appear on your chart.

After you select a chart element, you can edit some of its attributes. You can edit the type style of any of the text you select, including labels along the horizontal and vertical axes, scale of an axis, or shade of a data segment.

T I P

The Select dialog box is intended primarily for people who do not have a mouse and, therefore, cannot click chart elements, such as a bar or axis. If you do not use a mouse, however, purchasing one is highly recommended. Using any Windows program without a mouse is very tedious.

Changing Character Attributes

When you select a chart element that contains text (legend, titles, and horizontal and vertical axes labels), you can change that element's typeface and text attributes.

Click the Fonts button on the control strip, or choose Fonts from the Format menu. The Fonts option is not available until you first select a text element, such as a title, legend, or axis. The Chart Editor displays the Character dialog box to enable you to choose the typeface, size, and attributes for the selected text. Click OK to confirm your choices and display your chart with the selected element's new character attributes. You now can select another text element and repeat this process.

To modify the character attributes of your chart's data values, you must return to the Data Values dialog box. You cannot select data values. Click Values, or choose Data Values from the Chart menu. After the Chart Editor displays the Data Values dialog box, click the Fonts button, modify the character attributes, and click OK.

Changing Shades and Fill Patterns

After you select a series of data from a bar, line, area, point, or high-low-close chart or a segment from a pie or exploded pie chart, you can modify the pattern or shade with which the series or segment is filled.

First select the element you want to modify, and then click the Shades button on the control strip or choose Shades from the Format menu. The Shades option is not available until you first select a series or a segment. The Chart Editor displays the Shades dialog box (see fig. 9.40), which enables you to specify a fill pattern.

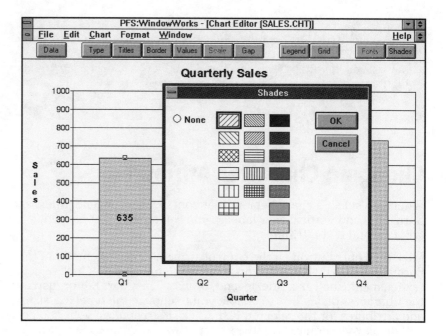

FIG. 9.40

The Shades dialog box, with a chart in the background.

Click the shade or pattern with which you want to fill the selected element. The Chart Editor displays a box around the shade you choose. If you want the element to be empty, click the None button. Click OK to display the chart with its new pattern. Figure 9.41 shows the chart displayed after modifying the shade in Series 1, as specified in figure 9.40. Repeat this process for any other series or segments you want to change.

Adding a Border

A final touch you can add to your chart before printing it or incorporating it into a Word Processor document is a *border*, which the Chart Editor displays as a box around your chart.

To add a border, click the Border button on the control strip or choose Border from the Chart menu. The Chart Editor displays the Lines dialog box (see fig. 9.42), which enables you to choose a border style.

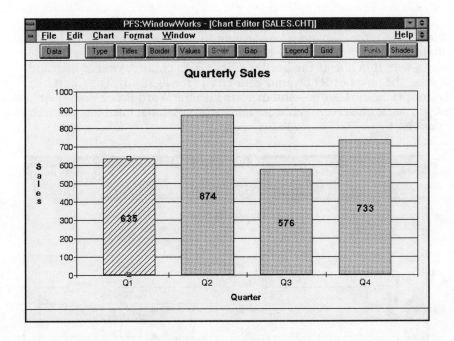

FIG. 9.41

A chart with the shade of Series 1 modified.

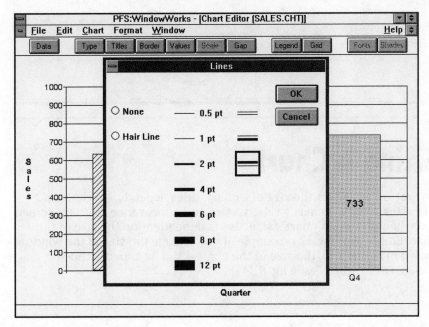

FIG. 9.42

The Lines dialog box, with a chart in the background.

Click the line style you want displayed as a border around your chart. The Chart Editor displays a box around the style you choose. To turn off the border, click the None button. Click the Hair Line button to display a very thin line as the border. Click OK to confirm your choice and display the new border around your chart (see fig. 9.43). The Chart Editor prints the border—and exports it to the Word Processor—just as you see it on-screen. A border adds a professional finishing touch to your chart.

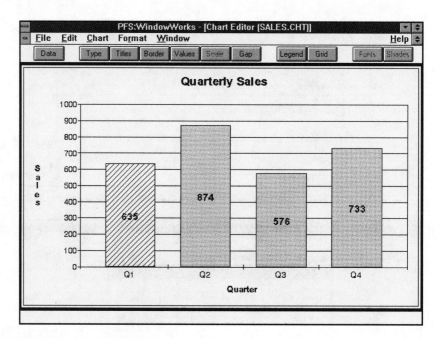

FIG. 9.43

A chart with a border.

Sizing a Chart

Several factors affect the size of a chart; titles, legends, borders, and font sizes change a chart's relative size and appearance, both on-screen and when printed. A chart's size also is dependent on the size of the Chart Editor window. For example, if you change the size of the window shown in figure 9.43, the size of the chart—and its aspect ratio—changes accordingly (see fig. 9.44).

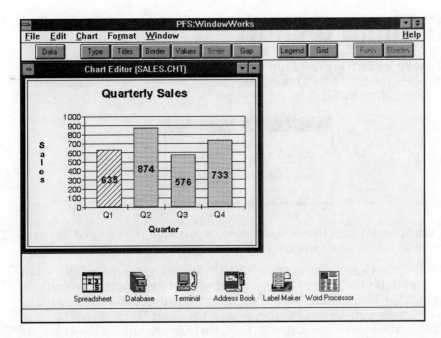

FIG. 9.44

A resized chart.

To resize a chart, simply use the mouse to resize the Chart Editor window. The Chart Editor automatically resizes the chart and its elements (titles, legends, and so on) to ensure visibility of all of the chart's elements. If your chart is complex and contains a lot of elements, such as numerous tick marks on an axis, shrinking the chart may make it unattractive—or worse, unreadable.

Saving a Chart

To save a chart, choose Save from the File menu. When you first save the chart, the Chart Editor displays the Save As dialog box to enable you to name the chart and specify the drive and directory in which you want to save the chart. You do not need to enter a file name extension when saving a chart; WindowWorks automatically adds the extension CHT. For subsequent saves, the Chart Editor does not display the Save As dialog box but simply saves the updated chart under its current file name.

If you want to save your chart under a different name, or if you make changes you want to save as a different chart, choose Save As and specify a different file name or directory or both.

Printing a Chart

To print a chart, choose Print from the File menu. The Chart Editor displays the Print Chart dialog box (see fig. 9.45), which contains two options: Maintain Size and Fit To Page.

Click Maintain Size, the default option, if you want the printout of your chart to be the same size as the chart displayed on-screen.

Click Fit To Page if you want the Chart Editor to resize the printed chart so that it fills the page in at least one direction (horizontally or verti-cally). The Chart Editor does not distort the aspect ratio of your chart as it appears on-screen; in other words, the Chart Editor doesn't change the chart's proportions. The Chart Editor expands the chart as much as possible within the page, while maintaining the chart's propor-tions.

Chapter Summary

In this chapter, you learned two methods of using the Chart Editor module to create charts: with data you copy from the Spreadsheet (us-ing the standard Copy command) or with data you enter directly in the Chart Editor. You learned to use the Auto Refresh option to link your chart to the Spreadsheet module, making automatic updates to your chart possible.

The Chart Editor also enables you to customize your charts by adding a legend, creating titles, displaying data values, and adding grid lines and a border. With ease, you can change the character formatting attributes (font, size, style) of any text item in a chart and change the fill patterns that identify chart segments (bars, pie segments, and so on). This chap-ter also explained how to change the scale of your chart, how the Chart Editor scales it for you, and how to change the size of your chart by resizing the Chart Editor window.

In this chapter, you also learned how easily you can print charts and copy them from the Chart Editor for integration to the Word Processor. (Refer to Chapters 6, 18, and 19 for information on integrating charts with the Word Processor.)

The
Database

PART

III

OUTLINE

Creating a Database

A database is an organized collection of information. A phone book, checkbook, and dictionary are examples of databases. The WindowWorks Address Book module, for example, is a specialized database for storing names, titles, addresses, phone numbers, and personal notes. Databases are composed of records. Each record in a database functions much like an index card; each database file functions as the container for the collection of index cards.

In the Database module, you create *forms* for the information you intend to store and enter records by using the forms you designed. You can perform several operations on the records, analyze the data in a variety of ways, and print a hard-copy *report* of your database information.

After you design your database and enter records, you can use the information in several ways: you can view each record; search for specific data in a record; add, edit, or remove records; print reports by using defined criteria; merge records into the Word Processor or Label Maker modules; and perform calculations on the data.

The Database module is an excellent tool for storing lists of primarily *text-based* information. Information that involves a great deal of numerical data on which calculations are performed should be stored in the Spreadsheet module. Lists of information based on names and addresses should be stored in the Address Book module. But to store a list of information for the items of your butterfly, stamp, or hubcap collection, use the Database module; to catalog the inventory of your bait and tackle shop or to keep a record of the titles and dates of articles you have published, use the Database module.

Using the Database Module

The basic operation of the Database module involves three steps:

1. Design your form.

    Plan the appearance of the form by determining what information to include and the length and name of each field. Determine the order in which the information is entered and the fields that will be used as index keys.

2. Save the form as a Database file.

    Give the form a file name. Saving and naming your form enables you to open it and enter records. When you save a form, you also have the option of creating index files for arranging the order in which records are displayed.

3. Enter the records.

    Type information into the form. Each completed form creates a *record*. You can create as many records as needed. After you enter the records, you can retrieve them and generate reports.

Reviewing the Database Window

Open the Database module by double-clicking the Database icon or by selecting Database from the Window menu. When the Database window appears, a blank workspace and the message No Database Open are displayed. This message indicates that you must create a new database file or open an existing file (see fig. 10.1). Notice that the status bar also displays the message No Database Open.

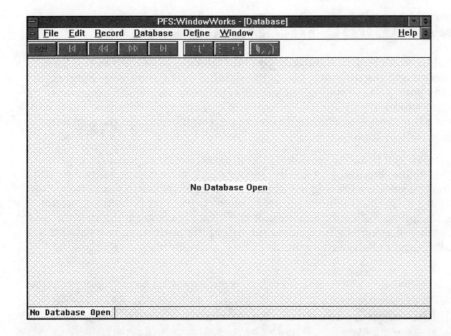

_File   _Edit   _Record   _Database   Defi_ne   _Window   _Help_

No Database Open

No Database Open

FIG. 10.1

Database
Window at
start-up.

The Database window consists of a menu bar, control strip, workspace, and status bar. If you used the WindowWorks Address Book module, you may recognize many of the buttons on the control strip. The Database buttons used for moving up and down through a record, adding a new record, and switching to record update mode are similar to the buttons that appear on the Address Book control strip.

The Database module has two modes of operation. The *definition*, or alter, mode is used to create or edit a form for a database. The *update mode* is used to enter and edit records using a database form that you created and for generating reports on your data.

The Database status bar displays the name of the currently open database, the name of the mode of operation (define database mode or update database mode), the current record number, the number of active records in the database, the total number of records created, and the current index field.

You see the blank screen with the message No Database Open. Choose New from the File menu to create a new database form in the definition mode, or choose Open to work on a previously created database in the update mode.

Designing the Database

Before you create a database, you must decide what information to record and the intended use of the database. The time you spend planning your form simplifies the creation process and makes your database a more useful tool. Although you can change a database later, you save time and aggravation if you create a well-organized database the first time around.

To give you practice creating a database, a business scenario is provided. Imagine that you are the owner of a bicycle shop. As owner, you want to create a catalog list of all the mountain bikes in your shop. You plan a form that includes model number, price, component set, frame size, and an indication of whether the frame set is assembled. Your catalog also may include notes regarding the performance level of the bike, target customer, available colors, and manufacturer's name.

T I P   Don't get carried away when you are designing your database form. The fields you create appear on every record. Although you don't have to complete every field in every record, your database isn't effective if several blank fields are left. Create only as many fields as you are going to use. Having more fields in your database than you really need wastes disk space and also will take longer when searching for a specific record.

Creating a New Database

To create a new form for a new database, choose New from the File menu, or press Ctrl and N. A blank Database Definition screen appears (see fig. 10.2). The status bar reflects that you are in Define mode with the message Define Database. The Create Text button, Create Field button, and Edit Record button, which enables you to switch to Update mode, are the only active buttons on the control strip; the other buttons are grayed.

Because you see three available buttons on the control strip, you know that in this mode you have three options only: you can enter a text label, create a field, or exit the definition mode and switch to update mode.

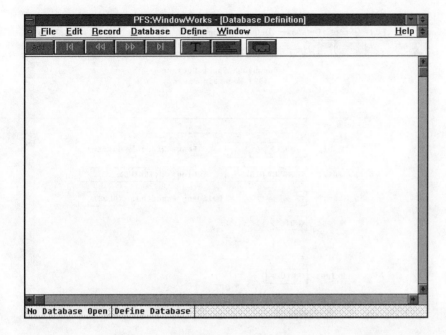

FIG. 10.2

The Database
Definition screen.

Text refers to any text that appears on a form but is not part of the data. Text is for display purposes only and can include the form title, field labels, and any necessary information or instructions that appear on the form.

A *field* is the rectangular blank in which information is entered. You must define the size and placement of each field, the type of information to be entered (characters, numbers, dates, etc.), and any qualifications that the data must meet (see fig. 10.3).

Adding Fields

The first action you take to create a database is to place the first field. To place a field on your form, follow these steps:

1. Click the Create Field button.

    The cursor changes to a cross hair.

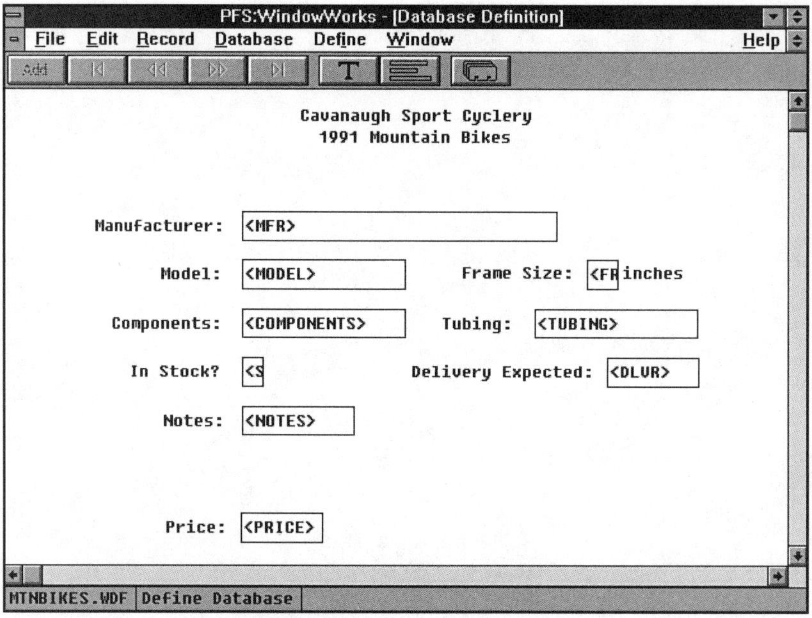

FIG. 10.3

A database form with text for labels, title, instructions, and several different fields.

T I P Alternatively, you can choose Create Field from the Define menu (or press Ctrl-C) to add a field to your database screen, but this method does not enable you to use the mouse to specify the location of the field. The Create Field command displays the Edit Position dialog box for specifying the horizontal and vertical location of a field. If you prefer the dialog box for setting the location of a field, use this command. Using the Create Field button is the best, and certainly the easiest method, for adding fields. You always can access the Edit Position dialog box after placing a field if you need to specify exact coordinates, for example. Refer to the section "Editing and Deleting Fields" for details about the Edit Position dialog box.

2. Move the cross hair cursor to the approximate on-screen location of the field, and click.

   The Field Definitions dialog box appears (see fig. 10.4).

   The Field Definitions dialog box is used to tell WindowWorks what type of information must be entered in this field. This dialog box contains important information because WindowWorks treats different types of data differently.

3. Type a field name in the Field Name box.

   The field name is used as a reference to identify the field. Field
   names do not appear on the final database form; they are displayed only while you are defining the database. If you want field
   names to appear on the final form, use the text tool to add field
   labels. In most cases, the field name and text label you add are the
   same. For example, if you define a field named *mfr*, you would
   probably create a text label, such as Manufacturer or mfr.

   Field names must consist of letters and numbers and are limited
   to 10 characters. Although field names cannot contain any punctuation marks or spaces, they can contain underscores. Last name
   is an acceptable field name, for example.

4. Select a field type from the Field type pull-down menu (see
   fig. 10.5). If your field entries contain mostly text, you can accept
   the default field type of Character and proceed to the next step.
   To specify a different field type, however, refer to the next
   section, "Specifying Field Types."

5. Enter the field's *width*, the maximum number of characters the field can contain, in the Field Size box.

   Field Size is predetermined by the type of field designated. (Refer to the descriptions of each field type.) You can enter any number from 1 to 254 as the field size for a Character field type. Remember, however, that the field size also determines how the field appears on-screen. Fields containing more than approximately 70 characters do not fit in the window. (You can enter information although the field exceeds the width of the screen, however.)

6. In the Decimals box, enter the number of decimal places, up to 16, to be displayed. This option is available only if you designate a Numeric field.

7. Enter a qualifier, if necessary, in the Field Qualifier box.

   This is an advanced concept. To enter a qualifier, refer to the section "Specifying Field Qualifiers."

8. Click OK to close the dialog box.

   The field you defined appears in your database definition screen. The field name you specified appears within brackets inside the field (see fig. 10.6).

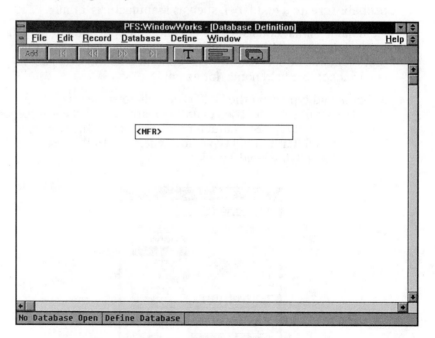

FIG. 10.6

Database Definition screen with a MFR field.

Specifying Field Types

The field type is used to indicate the type of information accepted in a field and the format in which the data is displayed. You must specify a field type for each field placed in your database. Descriptions of each field are discussed in the following sections.

Specifying Character Fields

Most of the fields in your database will be Character fields. Character fields can contain information containing text, numbers, punctuation, and spaces. A field for a last name is a Character field, as is a field for a phone number. If you are creating the database for the mountain bikes in your bicycle shop, the manufacturer and model fields are Character fields.

Don't confuse fields that consist predominantly of numbers, such as phone numbers, zip codes, or apartment numbers, with the Numeric field type choice. The phone number, zip code, and apartment number fields are best defined as Character fields.

Specifying Numeric Fields

A Numeric field contains only numbers that can contain decimal points but no other punctuation or characters. These numbers can be used in mathematical calculations. A phone number, although predominantly composed of numbers, is more appropriately a character field because the Numeric field would not accept the hyphen in 438-5004 or the slash and hyphen in 619/853-1212.

In a numeric field, all initial zeros are dropped, and the specified number of decimal places is displayed. If you specify 3 decimal places in a Numeric field and enter 005.5, WindowWorks changes it to 5.500. (Because of the displayed decimal points, apartment numbers and zip codes should be defined as character fields. With the numeric field, for example, Apartment 5 is displayed as 5.0000 and the zip code 01660 becomes 1660 or 1660.00.)

 NOTE The only time you should designate a field as a Numeric field is when you intend to perform calculations on the field data.

For your mountain bike database, make the price of each bike a Numeric field so that you can add the price field to a sales tax field for a total price. Numeric fields answer the questions "how much?", "how many?", "how big?", and so on.

A numeric field can contain as many as, but no more than, 18 characters, and specified Decimal places are included in the 18 characters.

When you determine the Field Size of a Numeric Field, the Field Size represents the total length of the entry, including decimal places and the decimal point. *Decimals* are the number of places to the right of the decimal point. This number must be at least 2 less than the total field size because your total field size must allow one space for one character to the left of the decimal point and one space for the decimal point. If you want 4 decimal places to be displayed, your Field Size must be at least 6. If you specify the Field Size at the maximum of 18, decimals cannot exceed 16.

 NOTE   WindowWorks displays an error message when you try to enter invalid lengths in the Field Size and Decimals boxes and tells you to increase the Field Size specification.

Specifying Date Fields

The Date field type is used for entering dates in the 12/25/90 or 12-25-90 form. The Date field is always eight characters long.

The Delivery Expected field is a date field. Date fields are useful for performing certain types of calculations. For example, if you had two date fields in your database, the first one could be Date Ordered. You could add a week to the date in the Date Ordered field to determine the value of the second date field Date Executed.

Specifying Logical Fields

A Logical field is used for True/False entries and is only one character long: T for True; F for False; Y for Yes; N for No. T, F, Y, and N are the only characters that can be entered into a Logical field.

If you are creating the database for your bike shop and need a field to indicate whether each model is in stock, for example, you can use the Logical field type and enter Y or N for each record.

Specifying Memo Fields

The Memo field is a great addition to a database form because you use this field to enter any information, such as notes or descriptions, to be included with each record but not to any other field. You may discover that you need to include a Memo field in almost every database you create. The Memo field can hold up to 5000 characters. Memo fields contain a small scroll bar at the right that enables you to view any text that does not fit within the field's bounding box. The size of the field displayed is determined by the Field Size specification.

Because Memo fields can be so large, the data within them is not stored in the same file as the rest of the database. Keep this in mind when performing functions, such as copying and pasting entire records. When a record is copied, all information except for data in Memo fields will be copied to the Windows Clipboard.

If you are entering records for the different types of bikes in your shop, you can use the memo field to note the performance characteristics of each frame type, for example.

Editing and Deleting Fields

You easily can change any of the attributes you defined for a field. If you double-click the field, the Field Definitions dialog box appears with the Name, Field Type, Field Size, and any Qualifiers you defined. Press Tab to move through the options, making any necessary changes. Click OK, and the modified field appears in the definition window.

To remove a field, double-click the field and click the Delete button in the Field Definitions dialog box.

Adding Text

After you create a field, you can add a text label. Text labels usually contain the field name or some description of the field, making the type of data required obvious to the person entering records. Text labels, however, are not mandatory. You can create a database form with fields only and no text labels.

A single text label often describes several fields. If you have fields for Street, City, State, and Zip, for example, you may want to create a single text label called Address. Text labels, however, do not have to correspond to actual fields. You can use text labels as titles, instructions, warnings, and so on. You can place text labels anywhere within the database form.

To add text to the database form, follow these steps:

1. Click the Text button on the control strip.

   The cursor changes to an I-beam.

   You also can use the menu command (choose Create Text from the Define menu) or keyboard shortcut (press Ctrl-T) for adding text. In most cases, however, the Text button is the easiest way to place and position text.

2. Move the I-beam to the approximate location of the text, and click.

   The Text dialog box appears (see fig. 10.7).

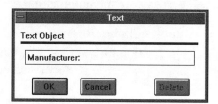

3. In the Text Object box, type the text you want to appear on your form.

   The text can include letters, numbers, spaces, punctuation, and characters. Although you can enter as many as 254 characters in your text, the text only displays one line of approximately 70 characters. More characters than this may exceed the width of your screen. If you need to make text longer than one line, you must enter each line as a separate text item.

4. Click OK.

   The text appears in the form window.

Editing and Deleting Text

To edit any text you entered, double-click the text item. The Text dialog box appears with the text currently selected in the Text Object box. Type the new text, or use the arrow keys to edit the existing text. Click OK, and the revised text appears in the definition window.

To remove the text item altogether, double-click the text and click the Delete button in the Text dialog box.

T I P

Under most circumstances, the best way to edit text is to double-click the text and edit it in the Text dialog box. If you need to set the position for the text or edit multiple text items, you can use the Edit Text command from the Define menu. Refer to the following sections for details about using the menu commands for positioning text and fields.

Moving Text and Fields

You can move text and fields in two ways. If you are good at "eyeballing" where the text or field should be placed on your form, you can use the easy method: click the text or field, and drag it with the mouse to the new position. If you use this technique to move text, be certain that you place the cursor on the text and not one of the handles of the bounding rectangle. Moving the handles changes the size of the bounding rectangle but does not affect the position of the text.

If approximating the location isn't accurate enough to suit your needs, you can specify the exact position for each field and text item. In this example, you edit a field; however, the steps are the same for editing text.

To specify the location of a field, perform the following steps:

1. Choose Edit Field from the Define menu.

   The Edit Field dialog box appears with a selection list of all fields created for this database (see fig. 10.8).

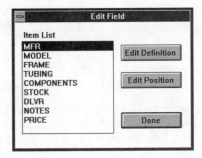

FIG. 10.8

The Edit Field dialog box.

2. Select the field that you want to position by clicking the field name or by using the arrow keys to move through the list until your selection is highlighted.

3. Click the Edit Position button.

    The Position dialog box appears (see fig. 10.9).

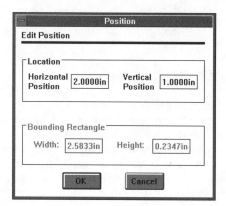

FIG. 10.9

The Position
dialog box.

4. In the Horizontal Position box, enter the distance (in inches) that the field should be indented from the left edge of the Database window.

    The *Horizontal Position* is the distance between the left edge of the Database window and the left edge of the selected field box.

5. In the Vertical Position box, enter the distance (in inches) that the field should be placed down from the top of the Database window.

    The *Vertical Position* is the distance between the top edge of the Database window and the top edge of the selected field box.

6. Click OK.

    The Edit Field selection dialog box reappears. You can select another field from the list and repeat the Edit Position process (steps 3, 4, 5, and 6) for each field you want to position.

    To edit the text items or fields you are positioning, select the item and click the Edit Definition button. The Field Definition or Text dialog box appears. Edit the text or field, and click OK to return to the Edit dialog box.

7. Click Done when you finish editing your fields.

    This method for setting positions can ensure that your fields align neatly and are spaced evenly.

Figure 10.10 was created by positioning the fields and text in vertical and horizontal alignment. Each field has a horizontal position of 2.0000in; the vertical positions of the fields are .5000in, 1.0000in, 1.5000in, and 2.0000in. Each text item has a horizontal position of 1.0000in and vertical positions of .5000in, 1.0000in, 1.5000in, and 2,0000in. These settings ensure that the text and field items are vertically aligned and that the text items are horizontally aligned with the corresponding field.

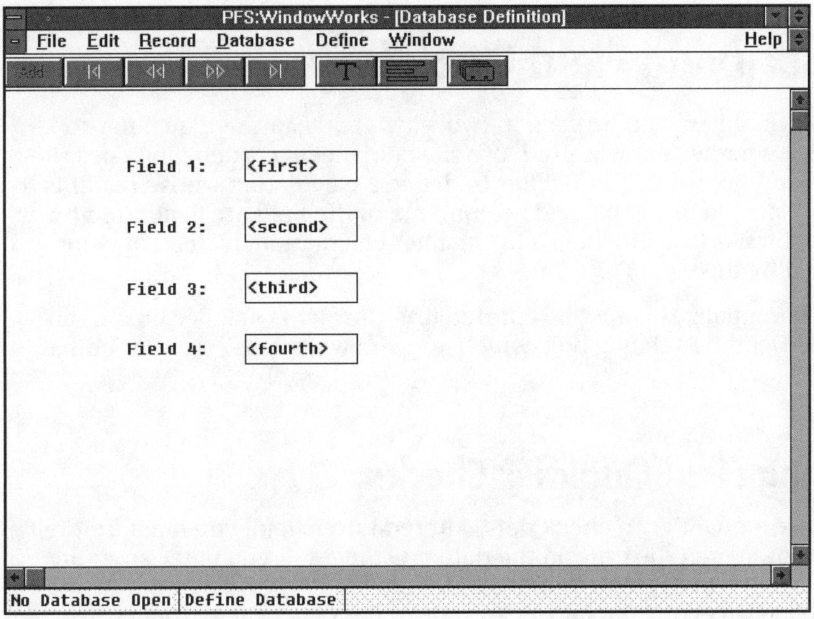

FIG. 10.10

Database with the four fields aligned.

Sizing Fields

The size of a Character field or Numeric field is determined by the Field Size specification in the Field Definitions dialog box. To make the field larger, increase the entry in the Field Size box. Numeric fields have a maximum field size of 18.

The size of a Logical field is fixed at one character because you can enter T, F, Y, or N only. The size of a Date field is fixed at eight characters because dates can only be in the 08-12-62 format. Any field defined as a Logical or Date field cannot be resized.

The size of a Memo field can be adjusted with the mouse, after the field has been placed in the definition window. To use the mouse to adjust the size of a Memo field, perform the following steps:

1. Click the memo field.

   Black selection handles appear around the field.

2. Move the cursor to the handle on the right end of the field.

3. Press and hold the mouse button and drag the mouse to stretch the memo field to the desired size.

   Memo fields can hold 5,000 characters.

Specifying Field Qualifiers

Field Qualifiers can be used in two ways. You can use a qualifier to check whether data entered into the field meets certain limits or criteria and you can use a qualifier to define a calculation whose result is to be displayed in the field. (The contents of the field are generated by WindowWorks using the Field Qualifier calculation, instead of being typed by the user.)

All field qualifiers must be entered into the Field Qualifier box in the Field Definition dialog box, which appears when you create or edit a field.

Using Field Qualifier Checks

To use a qualifier to check data entered into a field, you must first tell WindowWorks the criteria the data must meet. If you enter anything outside the acceptable bounds of the defined criteria, WindowWorks displays an error message. This type of data check is particularly useful in preventing people from unknowingly entering unacceptable data.

If you have a Size field in your database for the size of each mountain bike and you know that the maximum frame size for any bike is 30 inches, you can enter a field qualifier into the definition for the Size field. If a size greater than 30 inches is entered into the field on any record, an error message is displayed and the entry is not accepted.

The format or *syntax* for entering a field qualifier depends on the type of field. In all cases, you type the name of the field, an operator (see table 10.1), and the data limit. Data limits are formatted differently for the different field types. The *operators* or *logical operators* that you can use to define a field qualifier check are shown in table 10.1.

Table 10.1. Operators

Operator	Usage
<	Less Than
>	Greater Than
=	Equal To
<=	Less Than or Equal To
>=	Greater Than or Equal To
<>	Not Equal To

Operators in Character Fields

In a Character field, the data limit is enclosed in double-quotation marks. To compile a database of information on models belonging solely to the bicycle manufacturer Trek, place a field qualifier check on the mfr field so that Trek is the *only* name that can be entered. Type **mfr="Trek"** in the Field Qualifier box for the mfr field. Remember to enclose character field tests in double-quotation marks.

Operators in Numeric Fields

In a Numeric field, the data limit is entered as a number. If you have a price field for entering the estimated selling price of your assembled bikes, and you know that the minimum price for any frame set is $350, you want to accept only those prices equal to or above 350. Type **price>=350** in the Field Qualifier box for the Price field. Only prices greater than or equal to $350 are accepted.

Operators in Date Fields

For a Date Field, the date limit is enclosed in single quotation marks. If you have a delivery date field and you want to enter bikes delivered after December 31, 1990 only, type **dlvr>'12-31-90'** in the Field Qualifier box for the dlvr field. Remember to enclose the date in single quotation marks.

Operators in Logical Fields

In the Logical Field, to limit the responses to T for True or Y for Yes, the data limit is 1; to limit the responses to F for False or N for No, the data limit is 0. You can create a Yes/No logical field to indicate whether each bike is in stock. To include only bikes that are in stock, limit the response to Y for Yes. Type **stock=1** in the Field Qualifier box for the stock field. (For Logical Fields 1 means T for True and Y for Yes, and 0 means F for False and N for No.)

Using Field Qualifier Calculations

You also can use Field Qualifiers to define calculations to perform on data in your database. The result of the calculation appears in the field; therefore, you do not have to enter manually the data into a field for which a calculation is defined.

All Field Qualifier Calculations are indicated by an equals sign (=) in the Field Qualifier box of the Field Definitions window. Following the equals sign, type the field names and mathematical operators that define your calculation. The mathematical operators that you use to define a calculation are shown in table 10.2.

Table 10.2. Mathematical Operators

Mathematical Operator	Usage
+	Addition
-	Subtraction
*	Multiplication
/	Division
^	Exponent

If you have a FRAME COST field that contains the base price of a frame set and a COMP COST field that contains the cost of any component set, you may need a TOTAL field that contains the sum of the frame cost and comp cost for a total selling price. Type the following in the Field Qualifier box:

=FRAME_COST+COMP_COST

You also can perform calculations on date fields. For example, you could have a field called ORD DATE for the date you ordered the merchandise. You know that all the merchandise is delivered within 2 weeks; therefore, your DLVR field would have as its qualifier =ORD_DATE + 14.

Figure 10.11 shows a finished MTNBIKES database record.

```
┌──────────────────────────────────────────────────────────────┐
│         PFS:WindowWorks - [Database [MTNBIKES.WDF]]      ▼ ▲  │
│  ─  File  Edit  Record  Database  Define  Window    Help  ▲  │
│  ┌────┬───┬───┬───┬───┬──────┬─────┬─────┬──────┐           │
│  │Add │ |◁│◁◁ │▷▷ │ ▷|│  (¹   │  :  │ ₁,) │          ▲    │
│  └────┴───┴───┴───┴───┴──────┴─────┴─────┴──────┘           │
│                   Cavanaugh Sport Cyclery                    │
│                   1991 Mountain Bikes                        │
│                                                              │
│      Manufacturer:  ┌─────────────────────────────┐         │
│                     │KHS                          │         │
│                     └─────────────────────────────┘         │
│            Model:  ┌──────────────┐  Frame Size:  ┌──┐       │
│                    │Montana Team  │               │22│inches │
│                    └──────────────┘               └──┘       │
│       Components:  ┌──────────────┐    Tubing:  ┌────────────┐│
│                    │Deore XT      │             │Tange Prestige││
│                    └──────────────┘             └────────────┘│
│        In Stock?  ┌─┐        Delivery Expected: ┌────────┐   │
│                   │n│                           │08-01-91│   │
│                   └─┘                           └────────┘   │
│            Notes:  ┌────────────────────────────────┐▲      │
│                    │"The Montana Team is a pro-class XT│     │
│                    │equipped off-road racing bike that uses │ │
│                    │resilient Ritchey logic and Tange │▼     │
│                    └────────────────────────────────┘       │
│            Price:  ┌────────┐                                │
│                    │ 445.00 │                         ▼      │
│                    └────────┘                                │
├──────────────────────────────────────────────────────────────┤
│MTNBIKES.WDF│Update│Record:1, Active:2, Total:2│No Active Index│
└──────────────────────────────────────────────────────────────┘
```

FIG. 10.11

A sample mountain bike data record.

Saving a Database Definition

After you position and edit your fields and labels and add additional text for a title or instructions, you are ready to save the database form. To save the database form, follow these steps:

1. Click the Edit Records button on the control strip, or choose Edit Records from the Database menu.

   A dialog box with the message Save This Definition? appears.

> **NOTE** You save a definition by making changes and switching to Edit Records mode when WindowWorks asks whether you want to save. There is no Save command as such.

2. Click Yes.

   The Save As dialog box appears (see fig. 10.12).

3. Type a file name into the file name box; the example uses MTNBIKES. Do not type an extension. WindowWorks assigns the extension WDF to each database file.

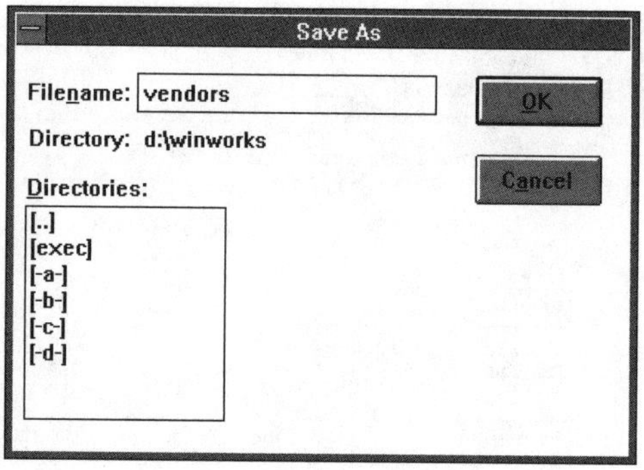

FIG. 10.12

The Save As
dialog box.

The Database Filenames dialog box appears for the entry of Index
file names (see fig. 10.13). If you decide not to create index files
now, you can create them later. See the section "Creating
Indexes."

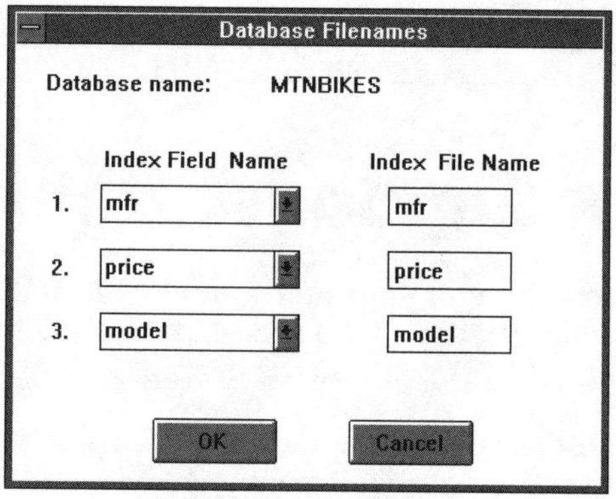

FIG. 10.13

The Database
Filenames dialog
box.

4. Select an index field name from each scroll list.

   You can index the database by using any of the fields you defined.
   If you indexed the file on the manufacturer name field, for example, the records are displayed in alphabetical order on the mfr
   field.

5. Type a file name in each Index File Name box, as specified in
   figure 10.13.

6. Click OK.

Creating Indexes

WindowWorks enables you to create index files when you save a database definition. Unfortunately, because no command exists to create index files, you must go into database definition to create index files.

Index files are used to change the order of records. Imagine how difficult it would be to find a book in a library without an index on titles or author names. Index files do not change the records themselves—just the order in which they are preserved. For the MTNBIKES database, for example, you could create an index of manufacturers. Records whose <MFR> fields begin with an A would come before those beginning with a B, for example.

To create or change index files for an existing database, perform the following steps:

1. With a database in update mode, choose Alter from the Database menu.

   Choosing Alter takes you into define mode, which enables you to add or change fields, field names, text labels, and so on.

2. Click the edit records button on the control strip, or choose Edit Records from the Database menu to return to update mode.

   WindowWorks displays a dialog box asking whether you want to save changes, regardless of whether any changes were made.

3. Click Yes.

   The Database Filenames dialog box appears (refer to fig. 10.13). From this dialog box you can create three index files. The three pull-down menus on the left side of the dialog box enable you to select fields to index. If you have not created index files for a database, the name of the first field you defined appears in all three menus.

4. Select up to three fields for which to create index files from the three pull-down menus. You can create up to three index files, with each using a single field from the database as a key.

   You enter file names for each index file in the three entry boxes to the right of the dialog box. You may want to name your index files by their corresponding field names. If you are indexing on a field named mfr, for example, enter **mfr** as the name for the index file. WindowWorks automatically appends the extension IDX to the name you enter.

> **CAUTION:** This is a very important step and one that many people forget to perform. Your indexed fields will not be saved unless you give them file names.

5. Enter an eight character name for each index file you create.

   To create a single index file, choose the field and enter an index file name. Do not enter file names in the remaining file name boxes. Although all three pull-down menus show index fields, index files are created only when you enter a name in the file name box. An empty file name box tells the program not to create an index file.

6. Click OK when you are satisfied with your index files.

   WindowWorks creates the index files you specified and returns you to the database in update mode. The records in your database are still indexed in record number order, the order in which the records were entered, from first to last. You can select one of the indexes you created by choosing the Set Index command from the Database menu.

Setting an Index

Using the Set Index command from the Database menu to choose an index file changes the order in which records are displayed in your database. If an index file is created by using a Character field, records are displayed in alphabetical order. If the index file is created by using a Numeric field, records are displayed in ascending order on the Numeric field.

To select an index file, perform the following steps:

1. Choose Set Index from the Database menu.

   The Set Index dialog box appears (see fig. 10.14). You can choose one of as many as four indexes. The Record # index is always an option. This index displays all records in a database in record number order.

   Index files created earlier appear in this dialog box. The file you select determines the record order when you press the Next or Previous record buttons.

FIG. 10.14

The Set Index
dialog box.

2. Select an index, and click OK.

The dialog box is closed and the database is re-indexed in the order of the index file you selected.

To turn off a particular index, choose Set Index from the Database menu; then select the Record # option. This option displays records in the order in which they were entered.

Opening a Database

After you create and save a database form with a file name, you can open the database form from the Database module. Choose Open from the File menu, or press Ctrl-O. The Open dialog box appears (see fig. 10.15).

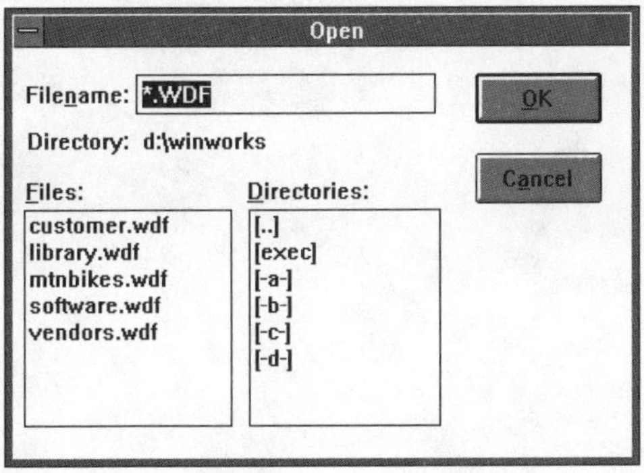

FIG. 10.15

The Open dialog box.

The Files list displays the names of all database files with a .wdf extension. Select a file and click OK. The database appears with the first record displayed.

If some of the text or fields in the database are cut off at the edge of the Database window, you can use the mouse to grab the borders of the Database window and resize it. You also can click the Maximize button on the Database title bar to maximize the window. All fields become visible.

Chapter Summary

Creating a useful database is a simple process; in fact, the key to a successful database is keeping it simple. Spend time designing the database to meet, but not exceed, your needs. A simple database is more useful than a complex database that contains irrelevant or poorly organized information. Plan your database carefully. You will run into nothing but trouble if you have entered 200 records, and then discover that you need to change a character field to a date field, and that the order of the fields is wrong. Careful planning and design can keep this problem from happening to you.

The key to creating a useful database is using the WindowWorks commands judiciously. Add only as many fields and text as necessary. Too many fields make completing each record a burden and retrieving information difficult. Use the Memo field to enter information relating to only a few records. Keep text labels, titles, and instructions brief, but descriptive, and don't overuse field qualifiers and calculations. All of these features, if used wisely, enhance your database.

The next chapter discusses entering and editing records.

Entering and Editing Data

After you have created a database form with which you are satisfied, you are ready to begin the process of entering the information that is to be stored in the database. You fill out one of your database forms for each record you are entering. When you have created a few records, you can begin moving through the database to view or edit individual records. At any time after you have created your database form, you can go back and enter more records, delete records, edit the information on the records, change the order of your records, or alter the database form itself.

If you already have used the WindowWorks Address Book module, entering, editing, and finding records in the Database module will be familiar, because the Address Book is really a database that uses a specialized form that cannot be altered.

Entering Records

When you have finished creating your database form in the database definition screen, click the Edit Records button, save the database definition, and create the index file names for the database. (Review Chapter 10 for details about saving your database definition and naming the index files.) After you click OK in the Database Filenames dialog box, a blank database form appears, ready for you to fill out. This blank form is the first record in your database (see fig. 11.1).

```
┌────────────────────────────────────────────────────────────────┐
│ ─          PFS:WindowWorks - [Database  [BIKES.WDF]]       ▼ ▲  │
│ ─   File   Edit   Record   Database   Define   Window   Help ▲  │
│ ┌────┬───┬────┬────┬────┬─────┬─────┬───────┐                   │
│ │Add │ I◄│ ◄◄ │ ▷▷ │ ▷I │  ' │  : │  ║.) │                   │
│ └────┴───┴────┴────┴────┴─────┴─────┴───────┘              ▲    │
│                   CAVANAUGH SPORTS CYCLERY                      │
│                     1991 Mountain Bikes                         │
│                                                                 │
│          Manufacturer: ┌─────────────────────────────┐         │
│                        └─────────────────────────────┘         │
│                Model:  ┌──────────────┐  Frame Size: ┌─┐ inches │
│                        └──────────────┘              └─┘        │
│           Components:  ┌──────────────┐  Tubing: ┌────────────┐ │
│                        └──────────────┘          └────────────┘ │
│            In Stock? ┌─┐   Delivery Expected: ┌─────────┐       │
│                      └─┘                      │ 01-01-80│       │
│                Notes:  ┌─────────────────────────┐ ▲           │
│                        │                         │ ║           │
│                        │                         │ ║           │
│                        └─────────────────────────┘ ▼           │
│                Price:  ┌─────────┐                              │
│                        │  0.00   │                         ▼    │
│ ◄ ▓▓▓▓▓▓▓▓▓▓▓▓▓▓▓▓▓▓▓▓▓▓▓▓▓▓▓▓▓▓▓▓▓▓▓▓▓▓▓▓▓▓▓▓▓▓▓▓▓▓▓▓▓ ►     │
│ BIKES.WDF │ Update │ Record:7, Active:6, Total:7 │ Index: mfr   │
└────────────────────────────────────────────────────────────────┘
```

FIG. 11.1

Blank record.

When the blank form appears, the cursor is blinking in the top blank field, ready for you to create a record. To create a record, follow these steps:

1. Type the information that completes the first field, and press Tab to move to the next field (or click the next field). Pressing Tab moves you to the next field from the top field down.

NOTE   Pressing Enter after completing a field also moves you to the next field, except in the case of a memo field. Pressing Enter when filling out a memo field moves the cursor to a new line. Pressing Tab always moves you to the next field, as does clicking the field to be completed. Enter and Tab are probably more practical choices.

2. Continue entering the data for each field and moving to the next field.

   You do not have to complete every field on the form; you can skip over any that do not apply to the record. Next time you view the record, it will appear with exactly the information that you complete. You can always return to the record and complete any unfinished fields later.

   Date and Numeric fields already contain data when you are filling a blank record. Date fields on the blank record appear with a six-digit default date already entered, providing you with an example of the correct date format to follow; you don't have to enter the dashes—just type the six digits of the date, and WindowWorks will put in the dashes when you complete the field. The date that appears on the blank record is also the earliest date that can be entered—01-01-80. You can enter any date starting from 1-1-00. WindowWorks will not accept any dates before January 1, 1900, which is the Julian date day one.

   Numeric fields appear with a default value of zero and display the correct number of decimal places so that you know the format to follow when you are entering a value in the field. WindowWorks always displays the decimal places regardless of whether you type values for them.

   When you Tab to move to a date or numeric field, the default data is automatically selected (highlighted); so you just begin typing to replace the data with the correct information for the field.

3. When you have completed all the information, click the Add button on the control strip, or press Ctrl-A, or choose Add from the Record menu.

   Figure 11.2 shows a completed record.

   Another blank record appears for you to complete. The record that you just completed is automatically saved when you move to another record; you do not need to save each record.

4. Continue filling and adding records to your database.

At any time during the record creation and addition process, you can browse through the records you have created, edit any of the records, copy and paste records, reorder the records by indexing, alter the database form, or exit the module completely, as described in the following sections.

```
┌─────────────────────────────────────────────────────────────┐
│        PFS:WindowWorks - [Database  [BIKES.WDF]]          ▾ ▴│
│─ File  Edit  Record  Database  Define  Window       Help │▾│
│ Add │  I◁ │ ◁◁ │ ▷▷ │  ▷I  │  ◠⌐  │  ⌐:  │ ⌐,⌐ │           │▴│
│                 CAVANAUGH SPORTS CYCLERY                  │▴│
│                   1991 Mountain Bikes                     │ │
│                                                           │ │
│        Manufacturer: │Mongoose                         │  │ │
│                                                           │ │
│              Model: │IBOC Pro DX      │  Frame Size: │20│ inches │ │
│                                                           │ │
│         Components: │Deore DX        │  Tubing: │Tange MTB   │ │ │
│                                                           │ │
│           In Stock? │y│   Delivery Expected: │01-01-80  │ │ │
│                                                           │ │
│              Notes: │Chromo Stem, Seat Post, Bar      │▴│  │ │
│                     │Gel Seat                         │ │  │ │
│                     │Teal Green Marble/Black          │▾│  │ │
│                                                           │ │
│              Price: │  650.00 │                          │ │
│                                                           │▾│
│◂│◼                                                      ◼│▸│
│BIKES.WDF │ Update │ Record:6, Active:5, Total:7 │ Index: mFr │
└─────────────────────────────────────────────────────────────┘
```

FIG. 11.2

A completed
record.

Browsing Records

You can move through the records you have created one at a time, or
you can skip directly to the first or last record in the database.

To move to the record immediately preceding the current record, click
the Previous button on the control strip (or press Ctrl and PgUp or
choose Previous Record from the Record menu).

To move to the record immediately following the current record, click
the Next button on the control strip (or press Ctrl and PgDn or choose
Next Record from the Record menu).

To move to the first record in the database, click the First button on
the control strip (or press Ctrl and Home or choose First Record from
the Record menu).

To move to the last record in the database, click the Last button on the
control strip (or press Ctrl and End or choose Last Record from the
Record menu).

As you move through the records, note that the database is organized
in the order that you entered the records, until you set an index (to set
an index, refer to the Indexing section). In other words, the first record
that you entered is record 1, the second record you entered is record 2,

and so on. Unlike the Address Book, the Database module does not alphabetize your entries automatically because, in the Database module, you can decide which field you want to use as an index.

Looking at the status bar at the bottom of your Database window should help clarify any confusion over the ordering of the records (see fig. 11.3). Before you have set an index for the database to use as a key for sorting, the entry on the far right on the status bar shows that there is No Active Index. Until you select an index, the records are sorted in the order in which they were entered.

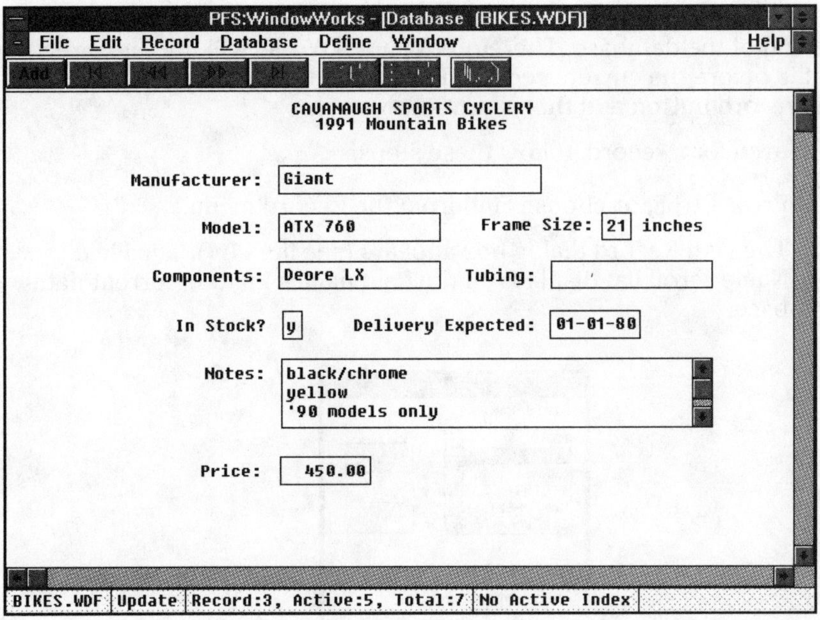

FIG. 11.3

The status bar indicates record information.

The status bar also tells you the current record number, the number of active records, and the total number of records in the database. The Record is always the number of the current record in the order of record entry, no matter what your index is currently set to. The Active number is the total number of records that you have entered, minus any records that you have removed from the database. The Total number is the total number of records that you have entered into this database since its creation or since you last purged the database; refer to the section "Purging the Database". As you move through the records, note how the status bar reflects the movement.

Finding Records

After you have entered quite a few records, you may find it somewhat tedious to move through the records one at a time, or to search from the beginning or end of the database to find the record you are looking for. At this point, you should use Find Record to move directly to the record of your choice. With the Find Record function, you select a field to search and enter the text that you want to search for. WindowWorks searches every record for that text in the specified field and displays the first record that it finds with the text.

WindowWorks starts the search at the current record and looks until the end of the database. Therefore, WindowWorks will not find a record that is before the current record. The best action to take is to click the first record button and then start your search.

To search for a record, follow these steps:

1. Press Ctrl-F, or choose Find from the Record menu.

   The Find Record dialog box appears (see fig. 11.4). The Field Name scroll list displays all the field names in your current database.

FIG. 11.4

The Find Record dialog box.

2. Choose the field that you want to use to search. If, for example, you want to search your database of mountain bikes for a particular bike model, select the model field from the scroll list.

3. Press Tab or click the Field Contents box to move the cursor. Type the text that you want to search for. If you want to search for a particular bike model called a Rockhopper Comp, type **Rockhopper Comp** in the Field Contents box.

If you cannot remember the exact name, type part of it, and WindowWorks will find it, as long as the portion you type appears within the field. If you cannot remember Rockhopper Comp, you could just enter **Rockhopper** or even **rock** as the field contents, and WindowWorks will find every record that has this text in the model field.

You also can use the wildcards * and ? in the Find operation.

4. Press Enter or click Find.

The first record containing the specified text is displayed. If you want to see another record meeting the specified criterion, press Ctrl-F again; the same field name and field contents appear as default selections. Click Find, and the next record with those field contents appears.

Editing Records

You can edit any or all the information entered in the record fields. You can complete fields that were left blank when the record was created or update any completed fields. You can copy data from a field on one record to a field on another record, or you can copy an entire record to another record. Records can be added to or deleted from the database at any time.

Copying and Pasting Records

You easily can copy all the information in a record into a new or existing record. This feature can save you a great deal of retyping, if you have several records containing the same or similar information. To use this feature, follow these steps:

1. Find the record that you want to copy.

2. Choose Copy Record from the Edit menu.

3. Move to the record into which you want to copy the information.

   If you are copying the information into an existing record, move to that record by using the Next and Previous buttons on the control strip, or use the Find Record option.

   If you are copying the information into a new record, click the New button on the control strip.

4. Choose Paste Record from the Edit menu.

The information appears in the appropriate fields on the selected record.

> **CAUTION:** If you are copying into an existing record, any existing information will be replaced with the data being copied.

The data in memo fields is not copied using the Copy Record and Paste Record procedures. You can copy each memo field individually. To copy the information from one field to another, or from one field to a different record, follow these steps:

1. Move the cursor to the field to be copied and select the information so that it is highlighted. (If you press Tab to move through the fields, the information is selected for you.)

2. Choose Copy from the Edit menu. (Be certain that you choose Copy rather than Copy Record.)

3. Move the cursor to the field into which you want to copy the information: on the current record, another existing record, or a new record.

4. Choose Paste from the Edit menu (not Paste Record).

The selected information appears in the new field.

Deleting Records

You can remove records from the database one at a time, or you can remove groups of records. Records that are removed from the database can be retrieved, as long as you have not purged the database; you can use the Remove functions to temporarily remove some records from the active database.

Removed records maintain their original record number and are added into the total number of records in the database; therefore, having large numbers of removed records can become confusing and cumbersome. If this is the case, and you do not need the removed records again, follow the instructions for purging the database.

To remove the current record, follow these steps:

1. Choose Remove Record from the Record menu. A message appears for confirmation of the deletion.

2. Press Enter, or click Yes to remove the record from the active database.

The record is still added to the total number of records, and it maintains its record number, but you cannot view or print the record. Basically, the removed record is just an invisible record.

You can also remove a group of records. To remove a group of records, you must specify criteria for a particular field. For example, in your database of mountain bikes, you could remove all the records for bikes produced by a manufacturer that you are no longer planning to use or you could temporarily remove all records for bikes that you do not currently have in stock. To remove a group of records, follow these steps:

1. Choose Remove Records from the Record menu or press Ctrl-R.

   The Remove Records dialog box appears (see fig. 11.5).

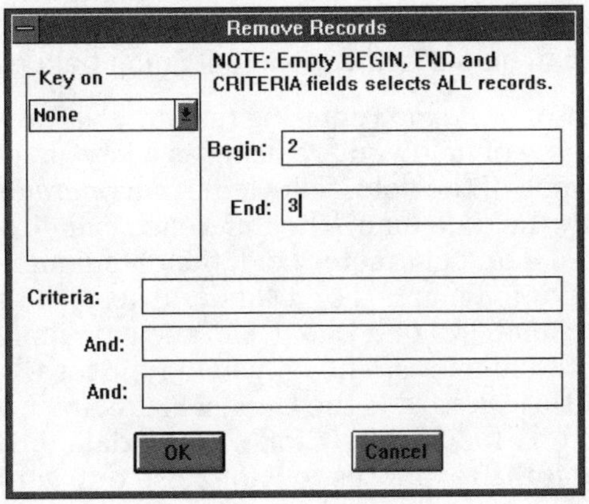

FIG. 11.5

The Remove Records dialog box.

2. In the Key on scroll list, select the field name that you will use to specify criteria for record removal.

   The Key on scroll list contains the field names that you specified as index fields when you saved your database form definition. If you want to remove all records for bikes manufactured by Schwinn, for example, you select the mfr field because you are going to specify criteria that applies to that field. If you want to remove all records for bikes that are not currently in stock, you select the stock field.

   If you are removing certain record numbers, select None in the Key on list because the data in the fields are not relevant to your removal criteria.

3. If you are removing certain record numbers or if you are removing a group of records whose key field contents are consecutive, enter the beginning record number or field contents into the Begin

box. If, for example, you are removing record numbers 3 through 7, type **3** in the Begin box. If you are removing records whose price field contents are between 500.00 and 1000.00, type **500.00** in the Begin box.

4. Type the end record number or field contents in the End box. If, for example, you are removing record numbers 3 through 7, type **7** in the End box. If you are removing records whose price field contents are between 500.00 and 1000.00, type **1000.00** in the End box.

5. If you need to specify more detailed criteria for removal of records, you can complete any or all three Criteria boxes with logical tests for field contents. The logical tests that you can use to specify records for removal are the same as those that you can use when defining field qualifiers in the database definition screen. Refer to Chapter 10 for details about the various types of tests that can be performed when defining field qualifiers.

The format or *syntax* for entering test criteria varies, depending on which type of field you are using as a key. In all field types, you type the name of the field, followed by an *operator* (see table 11.1), followed by the data limit. The difference is in how the data limit is formatted. For a character field, the data limit is enclosed in double-quotation marks. For a Numeric field, the data limit is just typed as a number. For a Date Field, the date limit is enclosed in single quotation marks. The only field type for which the syntax seems a little awkward is the Logical Field; if you want to limit the responses to T for True or Y for Yes, the data limit is 1. If you want to limit the responses to F for False or N for No, the data limit is 0.

Table 11.1. Operators

Operator	Usage
<	Less Than
>	Greater Than
=	Equal To
<=	Less Than or Equal To
>=	Greater Than or Equal To
<>	Not Equal To

If, for example, you want to remove all records in which the mfr field displayed Schwinn, you enter a character field test on the mfr field contents (see fig. 11.6).

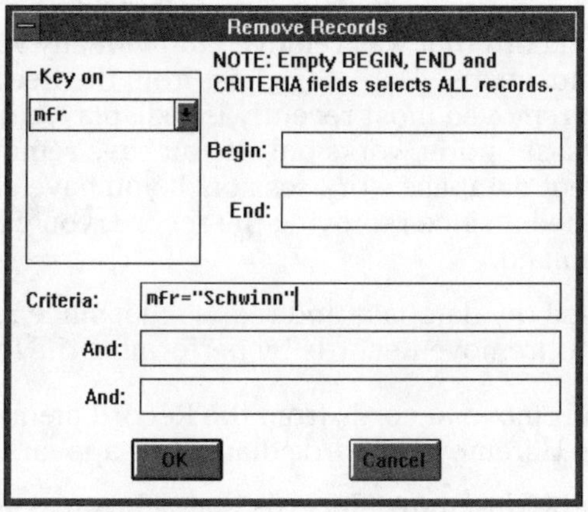

FIG. 11.6

Remove record window with mfr as selected field, and mfr="Schwinn".

If you want to remove all records in which the price field displays a value greater than $1,000.00, you enter a numeric field test on the price field contents, as shown in figure 11.7.

6. Click OK. Any records that meet the specified criteria are removed from the database.

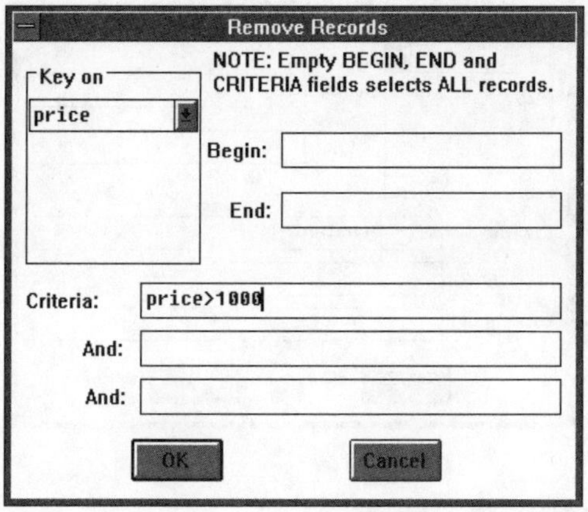

FIG. 11.7

Remove Records dialog box with price as selected field, and price>1000.

Unremoving Records

You can unremove any or all the records that you have removed, making them available for viewing and printing again.

To unremove a record that was removed individually with the Remove Record command, choose Unremove Last from the Record menu. The record that you removed most recently is redisplayed in the database. The Unremove Last option works only if you have removed the record during the current database work session. If you have closed the database and reopened it since removing the record, you cannot unremove it with this command.

If you have closed the database and reopened it since removing the record, use the Unremove Records by performing the following steps:

1. Choose Unremove Records from the Record menu, or press Ctrl-U. The Unremove Records dialog box appears (see fig. 11.8).

2. Complete the Unremove Records dialog box just as you completed the Remove Records dialog box. Select a key field name, enter a beginning and ending limit for the key field contents, and specify any criteria that must be met by records being unremoved. Any removed records that meet the criteria specified in the dialog box are redisplayed in the database.

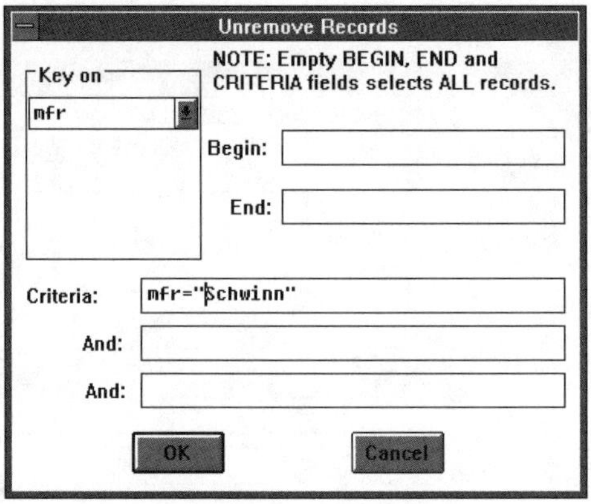

FIG. 11.8

The Unremove Records dialog box.

Purging the Database

If you do not want the removed records to remain in the database as invisible space holders—your database can get large and the record numbering confusing if all your removed records remain—you can purge the database of all removed records. Your database will contain only those records that are currently active. When you purge the database, the remaining records are renumbered consecutively in the order of entry, and the total number of records is reduced to include only those records that are active in the database. These changes are reflected on the status bar. The removed records are removed from your hard disk when the database is purged (reducing the size of the file containing your database), and you cannot get the records back.

To purge your database of records you previously removed, choose Purge from the Database menu. This command is gray and unavailable if your database does not contain removed records. When asked Are you sure? click OK or Cancel. Remember that *after you purge records from a database, they cannot be recovered.*

Indexing

Because it is usually not useful to organize your database records by the order in which they were entered, you can sort your database by the contents of a particular field. If you do not set a new index for sorting, your records will remain sorted by record number.

> If you are not sure how your records are sorted, look at the status bar. The status bar displays the name of the field that is currently being used as the index. If the records are sorted by record number, the status bar displays the message No Active Index.
>
> **T I P**

Changing the sorting index is simple, and as you become comfortable with using the database, you will find it handy to change the order of your database records from time to time. Follow these steps:

1. Choose Set Index from the Database menu, or press Ctrl-I.

   The Set Index dialog box appears (see fig. 11.9).

FIG. 11.9

The Set Index dialog box.

2. From the Field Name list, select a field name to use as the index for sorting your records.

    The field names on the list are those that you selected as index fields when you saved your database definition. Record # appears on the list as the default selection for sorting. If you want different field names to appear on the list of index fields, you must follow the instructions for changing the database definition, selecting different index fields, creating different index file names, and saving the new database definition. There is, unfortunately, no shortcut for changing the index fields.

3. Click OK.

    Your database is sorted according to the contents of the field that you selected as the index field.

 **NOTE** You cannot use a logical (Y/N) field or a memo field as an index.

If you select price as the index field in your mountain bike database, your records are sorted with the lowest priced bike record (the record with the lowest number in the price field) first, and the highest priced bike record (the record with the highest number in the price field) last.

If you select mfr as the index field in your mountain bike database, your records are sorted alphabetically according to the contents of the mfr field.

Changing the Database Definition

As you are using your database form to enter records and data, you may discover that your form design does not quite suit your needs. You can return to the database definition screen at any time and modify the database form by using the same techniques you used to create the form in the first place.

To modify your database form, follow these steps:

1. Choose Alter from the Database menu. The Database Definition screen appears, with all the fields and text elements displayed just as you created them (see fig. 11.10).

2. Make any changes needed to fine-tune your database form. You can use the Field and Text buttons to add fields and text elements to your form, or use the Edit Field and Edit Text options to modify the existing elements.

    You also can double-click a field or text item to edit it.

3. Click the Edit Records button, press Ctrl-E, or choose Edit Records from the Database menu.

4. Click Yes in the Save Database Definition dialog box to redefine your database form based on your changes.

5. Select Index Fields and Create Index Filenames in the Database Filenames dialog box.

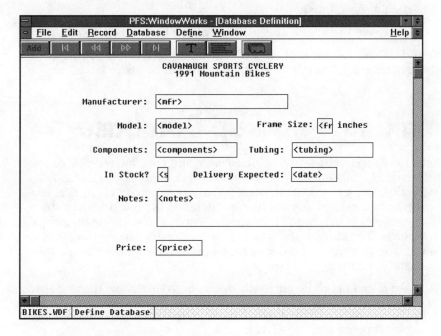

FIG. 11.10

Database Definition screen with complete database form.

If you have changed the name of any of the existing fields or added a new field, a dialog box appears in which you must specify what data from the completed records is to be placed into the newly defined field (see fig. 11.11).

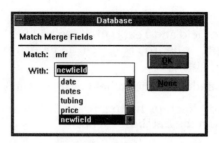

FIG. 11.11

Match Merge
Fields dialog
box.

The name of the previously defined field that contained data appears in the Match line. You must select a currently existing field name from the With list so that all data from the previous field is matched to the new field name. Select None if you do not want the data merged into a new field.

6. Complete the Match Merge Fields dialog box and click OK.

Your database records appear with the modified database form. You also can delete fields, but any data in them will be lost.

Making a Backup Database

Because your database can be quite large and entering records can be extremely time-consuming, WindowWorks enables you to easily make a backup of your database file. With a backup database file, you are protected against any inadvertent deletion of your original database, recreating that perfect database form, and reentering hundreds of records. You should perform this backup operation anytime that you have made changes or additions to your database that would be unpleasant to restore.

To make a backup of the currently open database, follow these steps:

1. Choose Backup from the File menu. The Select Directory dialog box appears (see fig. 11.12).

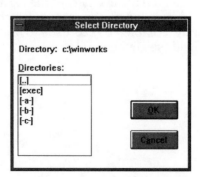

FIG. 11.12

Select Directory
dialog box.

2. Click a drive letter and the directory name for your database backup. You must select a different directory from the one containing your original database, which probably is the WindowWorks default directory.

3. Click OK when the selected directory for the backup appears in the Directory line. Your database backup is created automatically.

You cannot rename the database; you can only change the directory in which the backup copy resides. If you want a copy with a different name, you must perform the renaming from a DOS prompt. If you have a database named MTNBIKES.WDF, for example, you could back it up manually from a DOS prompt by typing **COPY MTNBIKES.* MTNBACKU.*** and then pressing Enter. This procedure copies all the associated files—.WDF, .DBF, and .DBT—as well as any report files.

Chapter Summary

Your database can be a simple and useful tool if you become comfortable with the basic operation and maintenance of the database file. Entering records should be an easy task.

If you find yourself moving through a large database one record at a time using the Previous, Next, First, and Last buttons, you should learn to use the Find function to move directly to the record you need. This option is handy for quickly looking up any information on any record.

You also should be familiar with removing and unremoving records and purging the removed records from the database so that your database contains exactly the information that you need. Monitor these functions carefully so that you do not inadvertently lose data or clutter your database and hard disk with data you don't need. Making a backup of your database can help you keep the right information available at all times.

With the information in this chapter, you have all the requisite tools to use your database as it appears on-screen. In the next chapter, you can acquire the tools for printing reports and hard copies of your database.

Creating Database Reports

W hen you select Print from the File menu of the Database module, what actually prints is not your database as it appears on your screen as you enter records, but rather a database "report." The report that you see when you print is the WindowWorks default database report if you have not defined another report. Default is not automatically selected; you must choose Default. If this report gives you the information that you need, you may not need to learn to create database reports as they are described here. If, however, you need to see different information when you print your database, or if you want a printout that is formatted differently, you can use this chapter to learn to design your own custom database reports.

The database report creation process is similar to the database form creation process—you use the Text tool to enter text labels, and you use the Field tool to enter field references. Although the database form creation process is an intuitive and elegant way to design a workable form, the report creation process is a rather clumsy way to do something that is relatively simple. If you have pulled your hair out trying to create reports in the Database module—you're not alone—you should read through this chapter.

Creating a New Report

When you create a report, you are in essence creating another form for your database. You created one to use when you entered data, now you must create one to use when you print. If you keep this in mind while trudging through the following process, you may find the report process a bit more manageable.

To create a new report, follow these steps:

1. After you open the designated database, choose Report from the Database menu. The Report dialog box appears (see fig. 12.1). Any reports you have created are displayed here. One report, Default, always appears in this list. The Default report cannot be deleted or changed. The Default report displays and prints records using the same field layout and design as your data entry form.

FIG. 12.1

The Report dialog box.

2. Click the New button. The Define Report dialog box appears (see fig. 12.2).

3. Enter a name up to 10 characters long—you can include spaces—for the report in the Report Name field. The name you enter is used to identify the report and appears for selection in the Report dialog box (see fig. 12.1).

4. Enter a title for the report in the Report Title field. Entering a Report Title tells WindowWorks to create a title page—containing nothing else but the title—when you print the report. Report titles can be up to 192 characters long. You can enter any characters, including spaces, extended characters, and punctuation, but you cannot use carriage returns or tabs. Report titles do not appear when you view your reports on-screen (this would require too much space). The Report Title prints in the center of a page, in a small plain font, and is not in any way impressive.

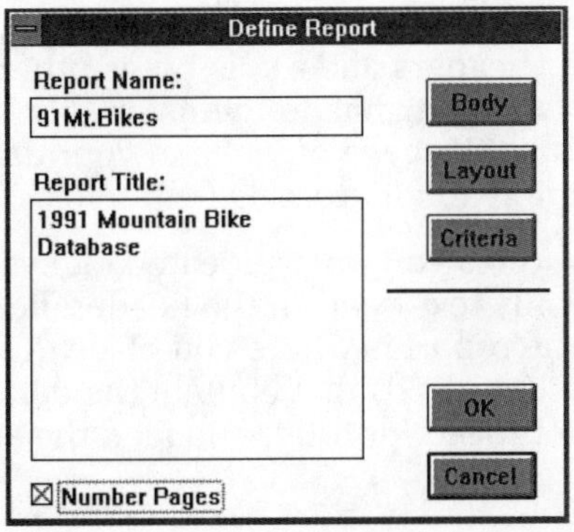

FIG. 12.2

The Define
Report dialog
box.

5. Click the Body button. The report body window appears (see
fig. 12.3). This window is where you create the report and any
headers and footers to be printed with the report.

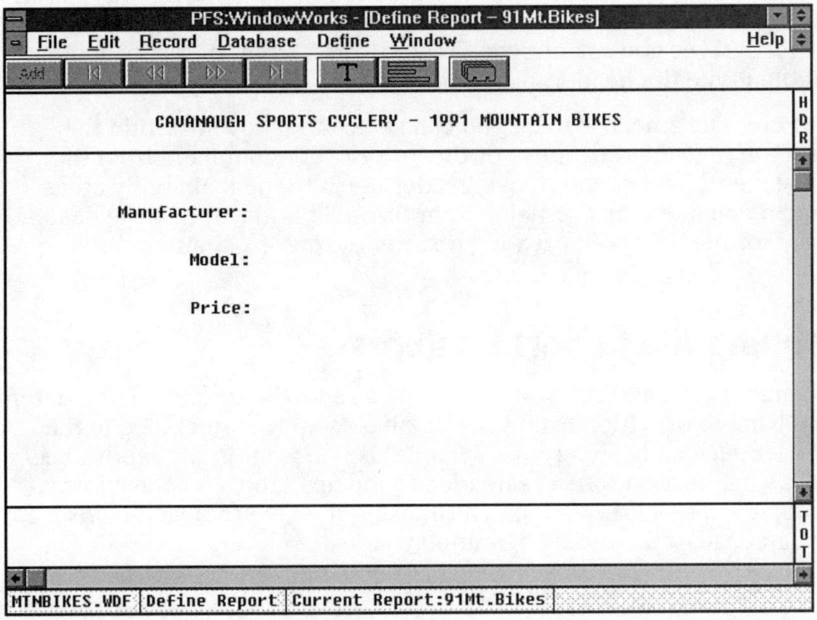

FIG. 12.3

The Define
Report window
with header and
Text labels.

Defining the Body

You define the body of a report in the same way you defined the database itself—you insert text items using the Text tool and fields using
the Field tool; you also can use menu command equivalents. The

window is somewhat different from the database definition window because it has areas for headers and totals but is otherwise the same. You create text items (including header items) and fields (including footer fields) just as you did when you defined your database. (See Chapter 10 for information about creating text items and fields.)

The header is used for items you want repeated on every page of the report. You can place only text items in the header; field items are not allowed. The body of the report is where you place the fields (and corresponding text labels, if desired) that contain the data you want in the report. The footer area is used for totals—in fact, the area is called TOT to indicate this.

Defining the Header

A header is text that is repeated at the top of every page in a report. A header item is simply a text item that appears in the header (HDR) area. You cannot put fields in the header area. You create the header text by clicking the Text tool, clicking the I-beam in the header area, and typing the header. Or, you can choose Create Header from the Define menu, and then type the header.

After creating a header item, you can select and move it within the header area using the mouse or the Edit Header command from the Define menu. You cannot move header items to the main body area, nor can you move text or fields from the main body area to the header area. (For details about creating text items, refer to Chapter 10.)

Defining the Report Contents

You must perform three tasks to create a report's contents. First, determine what information from your database you want included in the report. Specifically, determine what fields you want in the report. Second, using the Text tool, create identifying text labels for the information that will be in the report. Third, using the field tool, add fields from the database to the report definition window.

To add a text label to a report, perform the following steps:

1. Click the text tool from the control strip (or choose Create Text from the Define menu), and click anywhere within the main body area. The familiar Text dialog box appears.

2. Type your text and click OK. You can move the text label with the mouse, or edit its position by choosing Edit Text from the Define menu.

To add a field to the report, perform the following steps:

1. Click the Field tool from the control strip (or choose Create Field from the Define menu), and click anywhere in the main body area. The Report Field dialog box appears (see fig. 12.4).

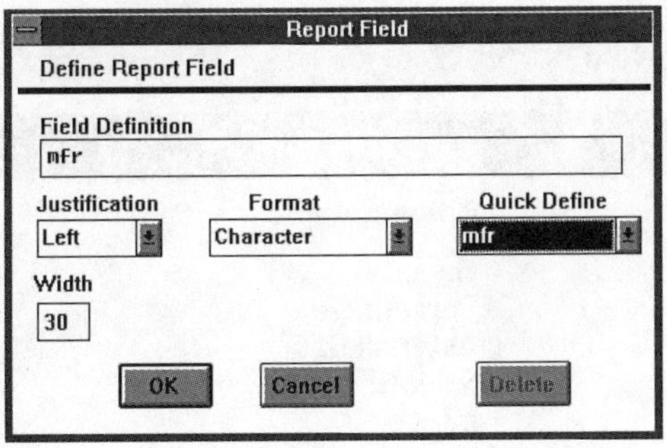

Report Field
Define Report Field

Field Definition
`mfr`

Justification   **Format**   **Quick Define**
`Left`   `Character`   `mfr`

Width
`30`

[OK]   [Cancel]   [Delete]

FIG. 12.4

The Report Field dialog box.

2. Choose a field from the Quick Define pull-down menu; the field is added to the Field Definition box.

   The data type of the field you select determines the default, or initial, selection of the Format menu. Formats determine how WindowWorks displays and prints the selected field. Depending on the field type, you can choose other formats from the Format menu (see table 12.1).

   If you choose a format that doesn't match the field type—such as choosing the date format mm/dd/yy for a character type field—WindowWorks displays an error message when you attempt to close the dialog box.

3. If necessary, select a different format for the field from the Format menu. You can, for example, change the format of a numeric field from General to $1,234.56. The field will be displayed and printed with a dollar sign and two decimal places. Refer to table 12.1 to determine which formats are appropriate for the selected field.

4. Choose an alignment option from the Justification menu. The choices are Left, Center, and Right. This determines how the field contents are aligned within the field bounding rectangle.

5. Optionally, change the width of the bounding rectangle by typing a different number in the box.

   If the field contents exceed the width, only a portion of the field contents are displayed and printed. The initial value is the actual width of the field as specified in the database definition. By leaving the width value at its default, field contents will never be truncated in a report.

6. Click OK. The field appears in the report body.

7. Drag the field to the desired location, or choose Edit Field from the Define menu to enter its position from a dialog box.

8. Repeat this process for each field you want included in the report.

Table 12.1. Field Formats

Field Type	Available Formats
Character	Character*
Numeric	General* Percentage Asterisk Bar Scientific Integer .# .## .### .#### $1,234.56 1,234.56 $1,234 1234
Numeric (Version 1.1 only)	0.0 0.00 0.000 0.0000 $#,##0.00 #,##0.00 $#,##0 #,##0
Date	mm/dd/yy* mm-dd-yy Mon dd, yy Mon dd, yyyy Month dd, yy Month dd, yyyy mm-yyyy dd-mm dd-mm-yy dd-mm-yyyy dd Mon yy dd Mon yyyy dd Month yy dd Month yyyy yymmdd yyyymmdd

Field Type	Available Formats
Memo	Memo*
Logical	True/False*
	Yes/No

* Default format for selected field type.
Version 1.0 does not enable all these date formats.

Defining the Footer

You can create fields in the footer totals area for totaling numeric data. In figure 12.5, the report will display values for the Price field. You can then set up a footer to display the total of all values in the Price fields of the displayed records. Totals for each page appear in the footer at the bottom of that page. The total on the last page is the grand total for all values in the selected numeric format.

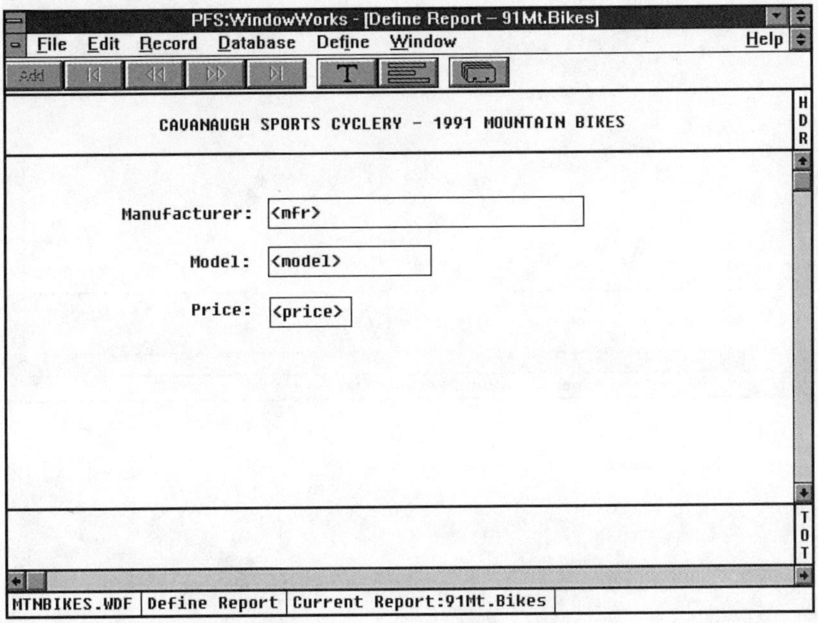

FIG. 12.5

The Define Report window with report fields and text labels.

To create a footer that includes a total from one of the fields that appears in the report, perform the following steps:

1. Click the Field Tool and click in the footer (TOT) area of the Define Report screen. The Report Field dialog box appears.

2. Select a numeric field from the Quick Define list. If there are no numeric fields in your database, no fields will appear in this list.

3. Optionally, select a different numeric format from the Format list.

4. Set the Justification and Field Width as necessary.

5. Click OK. The field appears in the footer area of the Define Report screen.

6. Using the Text tool, add a text label, such as **TOTAL:**, to the footer field (see fig. 12.6).

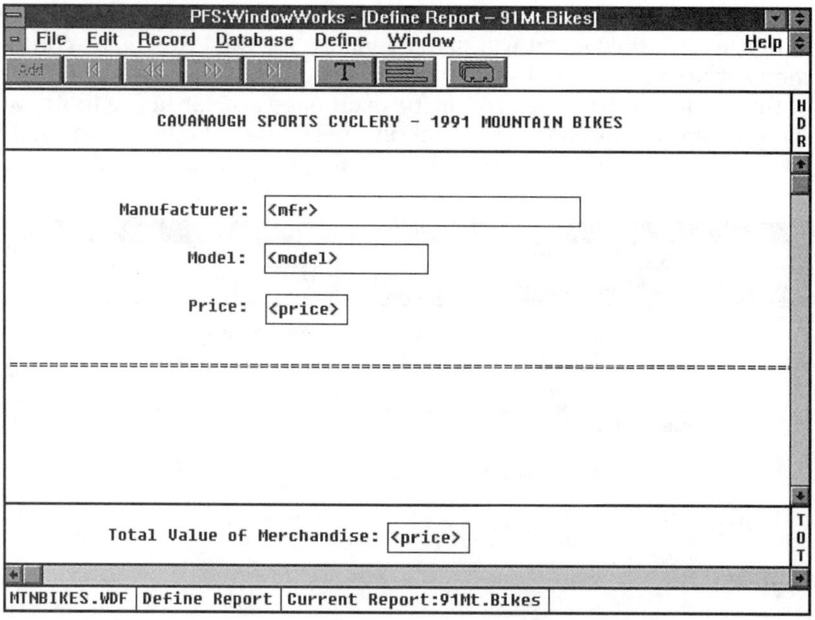

FIG. 12.6

The Define Report screen with footer definition.

T I P   In figure 12.6, a horizontal line has been added beneath the last field included in the report. This line was actually entered as text; it is really just a long string of equal signs (=). This can be a helpful technique if you find that your report prints one record after the next without enough space to differentiate where one record ends and the next begins. This line serves as a divider between the records on the report. Try it with dashes, asterisks, or even plus signs.

Leaving the Define Report Window

When you are done creating your header, body, footer text, and field definitions for your report, click the Edit Record button, or choose Edit Records from the Database menu. (This is the same process you use to exit the Database Form Definition window.) A prompt appears asking whether you want to save the report definition. Click OK. The Define Report dialog box reappears. Although this dialog box may look like it is prompting you for a file name, it is really just presenting you with the options found on the buttons: Body, Layout, and Criteria.

Defining the Page Setup

You probably are familiar with page setup throughout the WindowWorks modules. The Report Definition process uses this process but calls it *layout* instead of *page setup*; it is the same process.

1. Click the Layout button in the Define Report dialog box. A Page Setup window appears (see fig. 12.7).

2. Set the page size, orientation, and margins for the report you want to print.

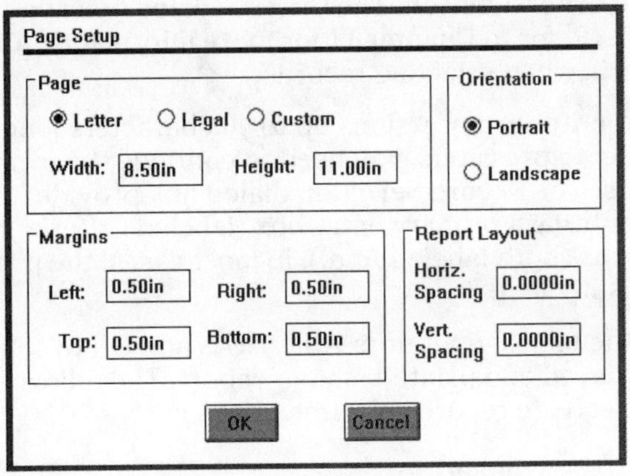

FIG. 12.7

The Page Setup dialog box.

3. If you are ambitious, experiment with the Report Layout values. Any number that you enter into the Horizontal Spacing field causes the report to split itself into two columns. The Vertical Spacing value can be used to increase the amount of space between one record and the record below it.

This feature can be problematic. The best way to approach this task is to align the fields on the left margin, one above the other, when you define the body of the report. If the fields aren't too long, WindowWorks splits the data into two columns using the Horizontal Spacing value you have entered as the distance between the columns. If you enter a value for Horizontal Spacing that is small enough for WindowWorks to display more than two columns across, it will do so. Three or four columns, however, require that your data fields be fairly short.

Selecting Records

Record selection criteria are stored with individual reports as are body and layout attributes.

To enter criteria for a report, follow these steps:

1. Choose Report from the Database menu. The Report dialog box appears, displaying a list of reports that you have created, along with the Default report format.

2. Select the Report to be edited from the list.

3. Click the Edit button. The Define Report dialog box appears.

4. Click the Criteria button. The Criteria dialog box appears (see fig. 12.8). (Refer to Chapter 11 for more information about entering criteria when selecting records.)

You can enter criteria expressions up to 40 characters long. If you want to create longer expressions, you need to continue the expression in the And: boxes. The Record Selection dialog box provides three boxes for entering criteria: a primary entry box (labeled Criteria:) and two additional boxes (both labeled And:). In most cases, the primary criteria boxes are sufficient.

You can use the logical operators AND, NOT, and OR to select records you want displayed and printed in your report. The following operators can be used to create record selection criteria:

Operator	Description
AND	Logical AND. For example, the criteria *(price>500) AND (price<1000)* selects all records whose price field is greater than 500 and less than 1000.
NOT	Logical negative. For example, the criteria *NOT* (mfr="Trek") selects all records except those whose mfr field equals Trek.

Operator	Description
OR	Logical inclusive OR. For example, the criteria expression *(components="Deore DX") OR (components="Deore LX")* selects only those records whose components field contains the strings Deore DX or Deore LX.

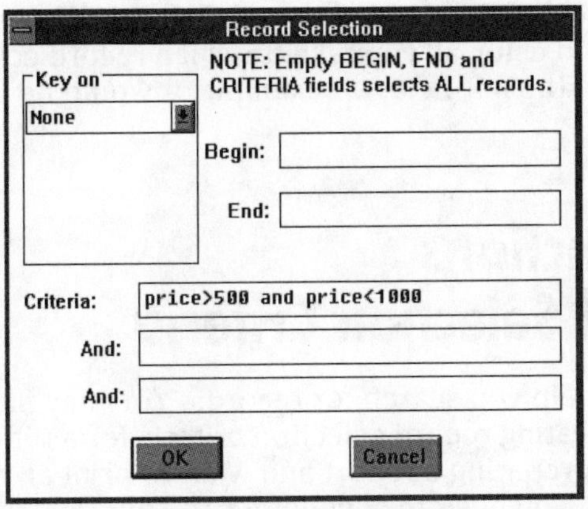

FIG. 12.8

The Record Selection criteria dialog box.

You can use parentheses to separate parts of an expression, but they are not required. Operators can be entered in either upper- or lower-case. You must separate operators with spaces.

You can combine operators to create more complex criteria. For example, the expression *price>500 AND NOT mfr="Trek"* would select all records whose *price* field contains values greater than 500, except those records whose *mfr* field equals Trek.

Unfortunately, WindowWorks does not give you an error message if you enter criteria incorrectly. For example, if you entered operators without spaces before and after them, WindowWorks would display the message No Records Meet Current Selection Criteria when you attempt to view or print the report. In actuality, records may meet the criteria, but you did not enter spaces before and after the operators.

Using Functions in Reports

The Database module uses the same functions as the Spreadsheet module but also has some additional functions. You can use these functions to help you select records or even to define fields.

Using Functions in Field Definitions

You can use field names as arguments for functions. For example, entering ROUND(price+price*0.075,2) in the Field Definition box (see fig. 12.4) tells WindowWorks to calculate sales tax on the price field, rounding the result to two decimal places. Entering UPPER(mfr)—where mfr is a character field in the database—tells WindowWorks to display and print the mfr field using all capital letters; if a record contained the string Bianchi in the mfr field, for example, it would be displayed as BIANCHI.

Using Functions in Record Selection Criteria

Functions also help you search for records. You may find functions helpful when creating record selection criteria for a report. If, for example, you are preparing a report and want to print all records whose mfr field is Trek, you need to account for the different ways in which the string Trek could have been entered; Trek, TREK, and trek all represent the same manufacturer, but the database treats them differently. In other words, if you enter *mfr="Trek"* as your record selection criteria, WindowWorks will not find records with TREK or trek in the mfr field. But, by using the function UPPER(), you can compensate for any differences in the way data was entered in the mfr field; the criteria UPPER(mfr)="TREK" converts data in the mfr field to uppercase, and then looks for the string TREK; the data is converted for reporting purposes only; the data is not physically changed.

Using Math Functions

See Chapter 8, "Entering Formulas and Functions," for a complete list of mathematical functions you can use with the database. Function syntax is the same for both the Spreadsheet and Database modules.

Using Date Functions

See Chapter 8, "Entering Formulas and Functions," for a complete list of date functions you can use with the database. Function syntax is the same for both the Spreadsheet and Database modules.

Using Conversion Functions

The following list contains the conversion functions that can be used in reports:

- *ASC(character)*. Converts a character (or the left-most character of a character string) to its ASCII code equivalent. For example, ASC(Sean) returns the number 83, the ASCII code equivalent of the letter S.

- *CHR(number)*. Converts an ASCII code (number) to the character it represents on an ASCII chart. For example, CHR(83) returns S.

- *STRING(number)*. Converts number (including any numeric fields) to a text string.

- *VAL(character)*. Converts text (character) to a number. For example, VAL(2) returns the number 2.00.

Using String Functions

The following list contains the string functions that can be used in reports:

- *AT(character1,character2)*. Checks whether the first string (character1) is contained in the second (character2). If it is not, then it returns 0; otherwise it returns a number indicating the character position at which the first string starts in the second.

- *LEN(character)*. Computes the length of a text string (character), including spaces.

- *LOWER(character)*. Converts all characters to lowercase.

- *SPACE(number)*. Produces a string containing the number of spaces you specify.

- *TRIM(character)*. Removes all trailing blanks from a character string.

- *UPPER(character)*. Converts all characters to uppercase.

Editing Existing Reports

To edit an existing report, follow these steps:

1. Choose Report from the Database menu. The Report dialog box appears, displaying a list of reports that you have created, along with the Default report format.

2. Select the Report to be edited from the list.

3. Click the Edit button. The Define Report dialog box appears, enabling you to edit the body, layout, or criteria for the report.

4. When you are finished editing, click the Edit Records button, save the report definition, and exit from the Report window.

Viewing Reports On-Screen

To view an existing report, follow these steps:

1. Choose Report from the Database menu. The Report dialog box appears, displaying a list of reports that you have created, along with the default report format.

2. Select the report to be viewed from the list.

3. Click the View button. The report appears, displaying all headers, data, totals, and text labels that you specified in the Report Definition window.

4. When you are finished viewing the report, click the Edit Records button to return to the database.

Printing Reports

To print a custom report, follow these steps:

1. Choose Print from the File menu. The Print Report dialog box appears, with a list of existing reports (see fig. 12.9).

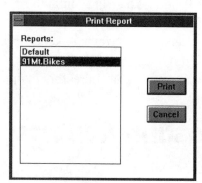

FIG. 12.9

The Print Report dialog box.

2. Select a report from the list and click Print.

   WindowWorks prints the report on the printer selected in the
   Windows control panel.

Chapter Summary

The process of creating database reports is similar to creating a database—you create fields and enter text labels just as you did when you
defined your database. You can optionally enter record selection criteria to tell WindowWorks which records you want included in the report. A default report exists and cannot be deleted or changed. Reports
can be viewed on-screen or printed.

Other Modules

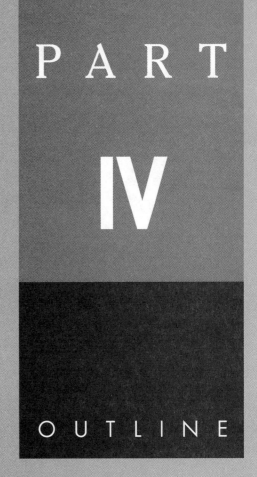

PART

IV

OUTLINE

Setting Up Your System for Terminal

Although Terminal may sound like an ominous module, using terminal actually is simple. The WindowWorks Terminal is used for communications or transferring information from one computer to another. Only a Hayes-compatible modem and a phone line are required for a wealth of information to be at your fingertips. You can log on to such services as CompuServe or GEnie, check your e-mail (electronic mail) for messages, download or retrieve a new game or paint program, check stock quotes, chat with a communications partner, or send a package of information in a data file. (Using Terminal to log on to services is covered in Chapter 14.)

When communicating via the Terminal, you and your communications partner must speak the same language; your modem settings, emulation, and protocols must match so that you can understand each other.

PC communications require essentially two components: hardware and software. The following section provides an overview of the hardware. The remainder of the chapter discusses using the software, which is the Terminal module.

Reviewing Communications Hardware

To use the WindowWorks Terminal module, you need a Hayes-compatible modem and an available serial communications (COM) port. This section discusses the hardware required for Terminal.

The Modem

The word *modem* is short for *mo*dulator/*dem*odulator. A modem is a device that takes the digital signals from the communications port of your PC, changes these signals into analog signals to enable them to travel through the phone lines, and converts the pulses back again to digital signals at the receiving computer.

Hayes Microcomputer Products, Inc., established the industry standard for modem commands just as IBM established the industry standard for PCs. A modem that is Hayes-compatible understands the Hayes Standard AT Command Set. The Hayes Standard AT Command Set is a modem command language used to configure operating parameters of the modem, as well as initiation and termination of communications. The letters AT represent *at*tention, the Command Set's way of getting the modem's attention so additional commands can be sent. You can type these commands directly from your keyboard, or you can use software, such as WindowWorks, to issue the commands for you.

Two types of modems exist: internal and external. An *internal modem* is a card that resides within your computer. Internal modems usually are cheaper than external modems and don't take up space on your desk or computer table. Internal modems lack some of the conveniences that you find in external modems, however, such as reset switches and volume control.

An *external modem* resides outside your computer and is easier to install than an internal modem. An external modem is connected to the computer by a cable plugged into the D-shaped RS-232 port. (RS-232 refers to the type of pin configuration that is the Electronics Industry

Association standard for modems. This configuration has 25 pins; each pin understands a specific signal.) External modems have indicator lights on the front panel that enable you to monitor the activity of the modem. Most external modems have a reset switch and a volume control on the rear or side panel.

The Serial Communications Port

Two types of data transmission ports exist: parallel and serial communication. A *parallel port* sends several bits or bytes of data simultaneously as though the data were travelling in parallel lines. Many printers accept data from a parallel port. *Serial communication ports*, however, transmit data sequentially, one bit or byte at a time in a single line. Pointing devices, such as a mouse or graphics pencil, certain printers, fax boards, and modems are examples of serial devices.

A *port* is an address inside your computer. Each port has a unique name so that data can be delivered to a particular port. Parallel ports are called LPT followed by a number from 1 to 3 (LPT1, for example). Serial ports are called COM followed by a number from 1 to 4 (COM1, for example).

Each serial port can be connected to one device at a time, and the port address must be correct for data to be transmitted. If you use both a mouse and a modem, you must have two available serial ports. If, for example, you set up your computer system so that your mouse is connected to COM1, your modem must reside on COM2. When you use the WindowWorks Terminal, you must tell Terminal that your modem is connected to COM2.

Setting Up Your System

For successful terminal communications, you must match your modem settings to the settings of your communications partner. Imagine calling for a taxicab in Brazil. The dispatcher answers the phone in Portuguese, but you speak English. If you and the dispatcher do not speak a common language, you're going to have a difficult time requesting a taxi. The same is true when communicating with a computer. If you and your communications partner do not speak the same language, you'll have a difficult, perhaps impossible, time transmitting intelligible data.

Most remote computer systems (electronic bulletin boards or services) publish their *parameters*, the items that comprise this language, in addition to their phone numbers. For example, the number for Channel One, a subscription bulletin board service (BBS) on the East Coast, is

617 354 8873, 300/1200/2400/9600, 8, N, 1

The phone number you dial to reach the service is (617) 354-8873. Baud rates accepted are 300, 1200, 2400, or 9600. Data bits or word length is eight bits, no parity, and one stop bit. These terms are defined in the section "Setting Up Your Modem."

If you call Channel One and your settings don't match, garbage characters appear on-screen. To alleviate this problem, you must set up your modem to match the settings of your communications partner.

Setting Up Your Modem

Before beginning your first communications session, you must configure Terminal to your hardware and the hardware of your communications partner. To configure Terminal, choose Modem Settings from the Options menu, or click the Setup button on the control strip. You see the Communications Settings dialog box (see fig. 13.1).

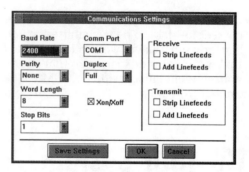

The Communications Settings dialog box.

Most of the settings in this dialog box must match exactly the settings of your communications partner or the service to which you connect. The current settings are displayed at the bottom of the Terminal screen when the COM port is connected.

Baud Rate

Baud rate refers to a modem's speed: the rate at which a modem can translate digital computer signals into analog telephone signals and back again. The baud rate of a modem is expressed in *bits per second* (bps). WindowWorks supports modem speeds from 300 to 19200 bps. Although a lower baud rate modem is less expensive to purchase, transmitting data takes much longer. The time required to transmit data can be significant when long distance charges are incurred or when an on-line service that charges by the minute is used. Currently, 2400-baud modems are the most commonly used.

Your baud rate setting must match the baud rate setting of your communications partner. This setting controls the speed at which WindowWorks talks to your modem. If you have a 2400-baud modem and connect to a service that supports 1200 baud transfers only, you see garbage on-screen. To solve this problem, you must change your modem setting to 1200 baud.

Parity

Parity is a form of error checking. You can set the parity of your system to odd, even, or none. Odd and even parity settings make the system add the 1s and 0s of the seven bits used to transmit a character and then add an eighth bit.

If the sum of the seven bits is even and your parity setting is odd, the system adds a 1 to make the sum odd; if the parity setting is even, a 0 is added. If the sum of the seven bits is odd and the parity setting is odd, the system adds a 0 to remain odd; if the parity setting is even, a 1 is added to make the sum even.

Set the parity to *none* to enable the computer to transmit characters in the standard ASCII character set. The eighth bit is transmitted as data, not as an error check. Parity must be set to none for binary file transfers.

Your parity setting must match the parity setting of your communications partner.

Word Length

Word length, or the number of *data bits*, tells the receiving computer how large each character is that you transmit. This value can be 7 or 8. Seven is used with a parity setting of 1 or 0; 8 is used with a parity setting of none.

This setting must match your communications partner's setting.

Stop and Start Bits

A *stop bit* signals the receiving computer that a character has been transmitted. Stop bits are the timing unit between characters; they are not actually bits. You set your computer to send 1 or 2 stop bits; 1 is the most common and is the default. A *start bit* tells the receiving computer how many bits will be transmitted before the end of the character is reached.

This setting must match the setting of your communications partner.

COM Port

The *Communications port* (COM Port) is the address where your modem resides. Because you may have other devices, such as a mouse, connected to a COM port, you must tell WindowWorks which port to send communications data. Usually, this address is COM1 or COM2. WindowWorks supports addresses up to COM4; however, most people don't have four serial devices. If you configure WindowWorks for the wrong communications port, you receive an error message when you try to initialize the port.

Duplex

Duplex, or echo, determines which typed characters you see on-screen. If you set the Duplex to Half, you see both the characters you type and the characters typed by your communications partner. If you set the Duplex to Full, you see only characters typed by your partner. For remote systems that echo the characters you type back to you, you must set your Duplex to Full; otherwise, you see two of every character you type.

The Echo button on the control strip is used to toggle between Full and Half duplex.

Xon/Xoff

Xon/Xoff is a data flow control mechanism. Xon/Xoff is a software handshaking method. *Handshaking* is the exchange of control characters indicating that the modem is ready to receive data, that the data is sent, and that the data has been received. Handshaking can be controlled through hardware or software.

Turn on Xon/Xoff (make sure the check box is checked) so that the WindowWorks Terminal pauses if it communicates faster than the other computer. After the other computer catches up with the data exchange, the Terminal sends a go-ahead signal to the remote computer.

This setting must match that of your communications partner.

Options

You must know how the computer system with which you're communicating handles the end of a line. Some systems send linefeeds, other systems do not. If Add Linefeeds is activated as you are receiving and if the sending computer also sends linefeeds, an extra line appears between each line of text. If this happens, turn off Add Linefeeds. If you don't have either box checked and an extra line appears, check the Strip Linefeeds box. This option handles linefeeds for text you type or receive while chatting.

You may need to experiment with the Strip and Add Linefeeds options for receiving and transmitting. In most cases, all options remain unchecked.

Saving Your Communications Settings

After you configure these settings to suit your typical communications session, save the setup by clicking the Save Settings button. If you click OK without saving the setup, you must repeat these steps the next time you use these settings.

Choosing a Terminal Type

The WindowWorks Terminal enables your computer to act like, or *emulate*, a mainframe computer or other terminal. Many on-line services are hosted by mainframe computers. Mainframes use special commands, or *control characters*, to display special characters on-screen, clear the screen, and so on. The keyboard of a mainframe also is mapped differently than a PC keyboard. Choosing a terminal emulation causes your PC screen and keyboard to perform like the keyboard and screen of the host to which you're connected. The default terminal type is ANSI. If you are sending files to another PC, you probably need to use this emulation.

358

To choose a terminal type, select Terminal Settings from the Connect menu or click the Emulate button. The Terminal Setup dialog box appears (see fig. 13.2). Terminal types are explained in this section.

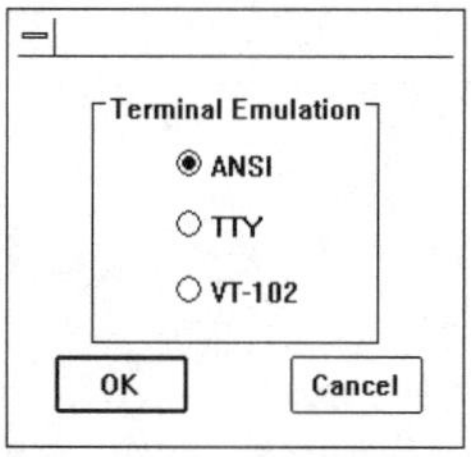

FIG. 13.2

The Terminal Setup dialog box.

ANSI

ANSI emulation is a subset of the DEC VT-100 series terminal codes. ANSI is used most commonly by electronic bulletin board services to control the output of on-screen text.

TTY

TTY stands for Teletype and is a standard *dumb* terminal. Choosing this emulation causes your computer to send formatting codes for carriage returns, backspaces, and tab characters only. TTY does not recognize any special screen characters and does not remap the keyboard.

VT-102

A *VT-102* is a Digital Equipment Corporation terminal type. VT-102 is the most commonly available emulation on microcomputers, such as VAXes and UNIX workstations.

Setting File Transfer Preferences

File Transfer Preferences are protocols for sending information. A *protocol* is a formal set of rules or conventions that controls the timing and format of a data exchange between two computers. Most protocols include an error checking mechanism to check the accuracy of the transmitted data. Choose the fastest and most reliable protocol that your communications partner supports.

You can set a default protocol by selecting File Transfer Preferences from the Connect menu (see fig. 13.3). No equivalent control strip button exists.

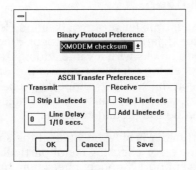

FIG. 13.3

The File Transfer Preferences dialog box.

Setting a default protocol is not necessary. Each time you send or receive a file in the WindowWorks Terminal, you have the opportunity to select an appropriate transfer protocol. This section discusses the available protocols.

ASCII Text

The ASCII transfer protocol is the same format as ASCII text in the WindowWorks Word Processor. ASCII files consist of characters without formatting codes or attributes. ASCII files are transferred *as is*, with no error checking mechanism. Using ASCII is the slowest and least sophisticated way to transfer data. You probably will use this protocol only as a last resort if that is the only protocol your communications partner supports.

Although ASCII files consist of text characters only and can be opened by almost any word processing program, differences exist in the way some ASCII file formats handle linefeeds and carriage returns. In a particular ASCII file, for example, a blank line may exist between each line of text, or the text may run together without paragraph breaks. If ASCII files are displayed like this, you must change the Transmit and Receive preferences.

Check the Strip Linefeeds option in the Transmit block to strip linefeeds from an ASCII text file being sent. If your communications partner requires a time delay between lines sent, you can issue the delay in tenths of a second.

Check the Strip Linefeeds or Add Linefeeds options in the Receive block to remove or add linefeeds as you receive a file.

Xmodem Checksum

The *Xmodem checksum* transfer protocol is among the oldest and most widely used and is the default transfer protocol. Xmodem checksum sends data in 128-byte blocks with a value adding the number of bits in the package. If the receiving computer checks the sum value to be the same as the value sent, the sending computer is enabled to forward another block. Errors, which are caused by line noise resulting from bad connections, can be caught and corrected.

This method of file transfer is slow because of the small amount of data sent at a time, and the error checking is not particularly precise. Because many systems support Xmodem checksum, however, it is a popular binary file transfer protocol.

Xmodem CRC

Xmodem CRC is an update to the original Xmodem checksum protocol. CRC stands for Cyclic Redundancy Check, a very advanced mathematical way of making a checksum. Xmodem CRC sends data in much larger 1024-byte blocks; therefore, Xmodem CRC is much faster, and the error checking is much more reliable.

Ymodem Batch

Ymodem is a newer version of the Xmodem CRC protocol. Ymodem uses 1024-byte transfers and CRC error checking. The batch indicates that multiple files can be transferred without user intervention. File names are included by the sending system; you don't need to name a file yourself.

The binary transfer protocols (Xmodem checksum, Xmodem CRC, and Ymodem) use all eight bits as data bits; therefore, you must set the parity option to none.

Using the Dial List

The Dial List is a useful tool if you call particular communications partners frequently. The *Dial List* enables you to store phone numbers and parameters, as well as log on scripts or other instructions. This section discusses adding and removing entries.

Adding New Entries

To create a list of frequently called communications partners, perform the following steps:

1. Select Dial List from the Connect menu (see fig. 13.4).

The Dial List.

2. Click the Dial List Name box. Type the name as it should appear in the Log On dialog box.

    Because the name you enter is the only item that appears in the Log On dialog box, make sure the name is descriptive.

3. Press Tab to move to the Phone Number box, and enter the phone number.

    You can enter the number with or without punctuation (commas or hyphens between digits). Be sure to add a 9 at the beginning of the number if dialing 9 is required to get an outside phone line.

4. Press Tab to move to the User ID box, and enter your ID in the User ID box. (This step is optional.)

5. Press Tab to move to the parameters boxes, and change the Baud Rate, Parity, Word Length, and Stop Bits settings as necessary.

    If the host you're dialing requires a user name, you may want to include the user name in your log-on script.

6. Choose a log on script from the Log-On Script box by clicking the Select Script button.

The log-on script issues commands to the modem by using the Hayes AT Command Set and the WindowWorks Terminal Scripting Language. Usually, the default DIAL.SCR script is used in the WINWORKS\EXEC directory. The WindowWorks Scripting Language is covered extensively in the WindowWorks User's Guide.

7. Click the Save button to save your Dial List settings before closing the dialog box.

   If you don't save the changes, the parameters you enter do not appear in the Log On dialog box.

8. Click the Quit button when you finish adding entries in the Dial List dialog box.

The Dial List holds as many as 30 entries. When you first set up your dial list, you probably want to include more than one entry. To add successive entries, click the New button at the bottom of the Dial List dialog box. The most recently entered contact moves down the list to make room for the new entry. Follow the preceding steps to enter as many entries as you need. Remember to click the Save button before you quit so that all your information is saved.

Removing Entries

You may have entries that you call infrequently and want removed from your dial list. To remove an entry from the dial list, perform the following steps:

1. Highlight the appropriate name in the Dial List list box to select the entry to be removed.

2. Click the Remove button at the bottom of the dialog box.

   WindowWorks asks whether you are sure you want to remove the entry.

3. Choose OK to remove the entry, or choose Cancel to leave the entry in the dial list.

4. Click the Save button before you quit so that the removed entries do not remain on the list.

Chapter Summary

In this chapter you learned to set up the WindowWorks Terminal to work with your hardware. The most important thing to remember in terminal communications is that you and your communications partner must speak the same language. Communications parameters, such as baud rate, parity, word length, and stop bits, as well as your chosen transfer protocol and terminal emulation, must coincide.

The next chapter illustrates how to dial, automatically or manually, another computer; how to send and receive data; and how to terminate the communications session.

Communicating with the Terminal

After you configure the parameters of your hardware and software to match the parameters of your communications partner or host service (as explained in Chapter 13, "Setting Up Your System for Terminal") you're ready to communicate by using the Terminal. This chapter introduces using Terminal to dial the phone number of another computer, answer calls from another computer, transmit and receive data, and disconnect from the remote computer.

Dialing

You can dial your partner's number in several ways. If you created a dial list, you can instruct WindowWorks to dial the number for you. You also can use the Dial command to dial the number manually. You can enter a command sequence according to the Hayes AT Command Set, in addition to the number to be dialed.

Before dialing a number with the WindowWorks Terminal, you must activate the serial communications port. Make sure that you have told the program to which port your modem is connected (see Chapter 13 for information on designating a modem). Click the Com Port button on the control strip, or choose Connect to Port from the Connect menu. If the Com Port button is reverse video (white on black) and all of the control strip buttons are activated, you are connected.

Autodialing from the Dial List

Perhaps the quickest and easiest method of dialing your communications partner is through the Dial List. See Chapter 13 for instructions on creating a Dial List. You can use the Dial List to connect to any service. This chapter uses Channel One as an example. Throughout this chapter are instructions for accessing the Channel One. If you're using the Dial List, add Channel One as an entry. Channel One's parameters are 617 354 8873, 300/1200/2400/9600, 8, N, 1.

To access your dial list, choose Log On from the Connect menu, or click the Log On button on the control strip. The Log On dialog box appears with your list of dial entries. Choose Channel One from the list and click OK. If you have an external modem, you see the indicator lights flash. The modem dials the phone number. After a series of strange buzzes and bleeps, you hear a ring or a busy signal. If the phone rings, a connecting sound soon follows, and a CONNECT message appears on-screen.

After a few seconds, Channel One prompts you to choose the language you want to communicate in. (See the later section concerning transmitting data.)

You can cancel a dialing attempt at any time by pressing your keyboard's Esc key or clicking the Cancel button on the control strip.

Dialing Manually

If you did not create a dial list, you can enter manually a phone number. WindowWorks offers a dial command to dial for you. You also can type directly all commands from the keyboard.

Using the Dial Command

To dial manually a phone number, choose Dial from the Connect menu, or click the Dial button on the control strip. The Dial dialog box appears (see fig. 14.1).

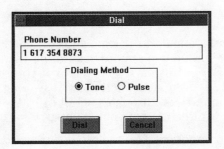

FIG. 14.1

The Dial dialog box.

Enter Channel One's phone number. Commas and hyphens are optional; however, a second delay is added for each punctuation mark in the phone number. Choose Tone or Pulse as the dialing method. If you have a touchtone phone, you can choose either dialing method, but Tone is faster. If you have a rotary dial phone, you must choose Pulse as the dialing method.

After you enter the phone number and dialing method, click the Dial button. The modem dials the number; you hear the familiar beeps and buzzes of the modem until a connection is made. To cancel the dialing attempt, press Esc on your keyboard or click the Cancel button on the control strip.

Using the Hayes AT Command Set

To avoid menus and dialog boxes in dialing a communications partner, you can enter the appropriate commands directly to the Terminal screen. Be certain that the Com Port is activated and that you set up the parameters for Channel One in the Communications Dialog box; click the setup button on the control strip or choose Modem settings from the Options Menu. Then follow these steps:

1. With the cursor flashing in the Terminal window, type

   ATDT 617 354 8873

   (ATDT stands for ATtention Dial Tone and is followed by Channel One's phone number.)

2. Press Enter.

The modem dials the phone number you entered. You can cancel the dialing attempt at any time by pressing Esc or clicking the Cancel button on the control strip.

Answering

The WindowWorks Terminal was designed for the communications user who primarily logs on to a remote host rather than a "live" communications partner. For this reason, no menu or control strip command for answering your modem line exists. Answering your modem line, however, is simple to do through a script or by typing the Command Set commands directly from your keyboard.

You can instruct your modem to answer in one of two ways. You can wait until the phone rings and then type the appropriate commands, or you can type a sequence that indicates the number of rings the modem must wait before connecting.

Manual Answering

To manually initiate an answer command, your modem must be on and the Com Port activated. The cursor should be flashing in the Terminal window.

When the telephone rings, pick up the receiver. If you hear a high-pitched tone, a modem is trying to connect with your modem. Type **ATA** and press Enter. Hang up the phone receiver; you are connected to the other modem.

Auto Answering

You can set up WindowWorks to answer the call after a set number of rings. Your modem must be on and the Com Port activated. The cursor should be flashing in the Terminal window.

Type **ATS0=*x***. X indicates the number of rings before the modem picks up the line. If you want the phone to ring three times, for example, type **ATSO=3**.

When a call comes into your phone line, the modem intercepts the call after the designated number of rings.

Transmitting Data

After you make a connection, you may want to exchange data with your communications partner or the host service. You can transmit data in two ways. You can type text directly from the keyboard, or you can upload a text or binary file. The method you choose depends on the type and amount of data you intend to send.

Sending Text Typed from the Keyboard

Whether you're communicating *real time* (chatting) with another person or just leaving a message for someone on an electronic bulletin board, you may need to type text that indicates to your partner that a good connection is made or that you're sending a data file.

When you type text directly from your keyboard, your communications partner receives the message on the other end of the line.

 NOTE If too many or too few characters are displayed, you may be using an inappropriate duplex setting. Click the Echo button on the control strip to toggle the duplex setting between Full and Half. (The current setting is indicated on the status bar.)

If your message is more than a few lines long, you may want to type the text in the word processor while you're off-line and copy the text to the Windows Clipboard. During a communications session, you can choose Paste to Modem from the Edit menu to paste the copied text. Your communications partner sees the same message whether the text was typed directly or copied from the Clipboard. Only text can be pasted to the modem, however; you cannot paste objects from the Clipboard during a communications session.

When you log on to Channel One, Channel One prompts you to choose a language and indicate whether to display in color. You then must enter your first name, last name, and other miscellaneous information. Channel One does not enable you to continue until you answer these questions. After you have responded to all queries, press Enter.

A list of many languages appears with instructions for choosing one. This screen asks you to press Y or N. Type the message from the keyboard, and you see it on-screen. Pressing Enter sends the message.

Sending Text Files

You can send text files by using any protocol supported by your communications partner; however, the selected protocol must match the protocol of your communications partner. Chapter 13, "Setting Up Your System for Terminal," lists complete descriptions of all transfer protocols supported by WindowWorks.

To send a file, you first must make a connection with the receiving computer. After you have made a connection and you're ready to send (upload) the file, choose Send File from the File menu or click the Send button on the control strip. The Send File dialog box appears (see fig. 14.2).

The Send File dialog box.

The protocol you chose in the File Preferences dialog box appears in the Send File dialog box. If you haven't chosen another default, ASCII is the default protocol. To change the default protocol, pull down the File Transfer Protocol menu and select a protocol from the list. In most cases, you will choose Xmodem checksum or Xmodem CRC. After the correct protocol is selected, click OK.

After you click OK, the Transmit File dialog box appears (see fig. 14. 3). Choose the file you want to upload. The file begins uploading as soon as you click the OK button. Channel One prompts you for your next action.

Sending Complex Files

When sending files more complex than simple text, the protocol you choose becomes more important. Binary files, such as compressed files, tend to be larger than text files. You should consider the time needed to transfer the file as well as the error checking mechanism used by the protocol.

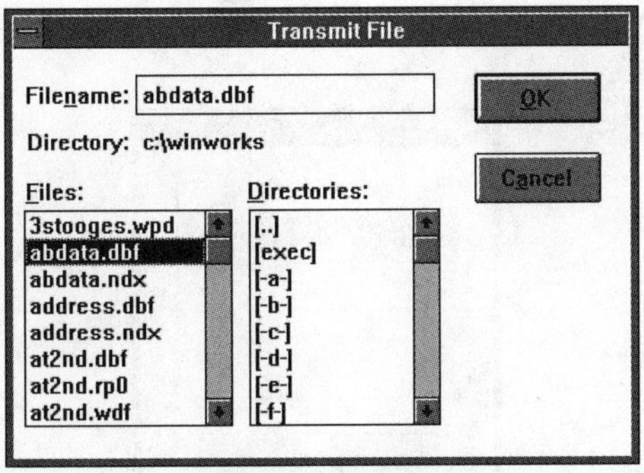

FIG. 14.3

The Transmit File dialog box.

You cannot use ASCII to transfer a binary file. However, Xmodem checksum, Xmodem CRC, and Ymodem batch can transfer binary files. Xmodem checksum sends data in small chunks and the error checking mechanism is simple, but most systems support this protocol. Xmodem CRC sends data in larger chunks and the error checking mechanism is more reliable than the error checking of Xmodem checksum. Ymodem batch also sends data in larger chunks and enables you to send multiple files simultaneously.

You should choose the most sophisticated protocol supported by your system and your communications partner's system.

Receiving Data

Receiving data is as easy as sending data. Again, the file transfer protocols of both computers must match.

After you make a connection and you're ready to receive (download) the file, choose upload Receive File from the File menu or click the Receive button on the control strip. The Receive File dialog box appears (see fig. 14.4).

When you open this dialog box, the protocol you chose in the File Preferences dialog box appears. If you haven't chosen another default, ASCII is the default. Pull down the File Transfer Protocol menu and select a protocol from the list. In most cases, you will choose Xmodem checksum or Xmodem CRC.

After you click OK, the Save As dialog box appears (see fig. 14.5). Type a name for the file being downloaded. Because you are saving a *copy* of the file from the host computer, you can save it with its original name or any other name you choose—as long as a file with that name does not already exist in the WINWORKS directory.

The download process begins as soon as you click the OK button.

Capturing a Communications Session

Long distance charges and on-line fees for bulletin board services can be expensive. To minimize the actual time you spend on-line, you may want to *capture* your communications session to read after you disconnect.

The Capture Session command begins capturing on-screen data when you choose the command. Assign a file name to the captured data so you can load the data into the word processor to be read later. If you want to capture only certain parts of your session, you can temporarily pause the capture and restart it to continue the file.

To capture a communications session, follow these steps:

1. Connect to the service from which you intend to capture data.

2. Choose Capture from the File menu when you want the captured text file to begin.

You can determine whether the Capture command is activated by pulling down the File menu. The Capture command is activated if a check mark appears beside Capture Session. You also can read the message on the status bar at the bottom of the Terminal screen. The screen will indicate that Capture is on.

During the session, you can temporarily disable the Capture feature by choosing Pause Capture from the File menu. Choose Resume Capture to reactivate the capture.

3. After you capture as much of the session as you need, choose Capture Session from the File menu.

   The Save As dialog box appears.

4. Assign a file name to your captured communications session and click OK.

   You can open the captured file in the WindowWorks word processor. Choose ASCII (.txt) as the file type.

Disconnecting

Most bulletin board services have some sort of disconnect command. To disconnect from Channel One, choose G for goodbye. (This method of disconnecting is common to many bulletin boards). If no other method to disconnect from your communications partner exists, choose Hangup from the Connect menu, or click the Hangup button on the control strip.

Handling Communications Errors

If you run into problems connecting to a remote computer, read through the following list for troubleshooting ideas:

■ Be certain that all hardware connections are set up properly. Check whether the modem cable is attached to the modem and the computer. Check the phone jacks to see whether the telephone line is connected properly.

■ Be certain that the correct COM port is selected. Check the Communications Settings dialog box (choose Modem Settings from the Options menu) to make sure the correct COM port is selected.

■ Be certain that you and your communications partner are using the same settings. The following items, located in the Communications Settings dialog box, must match for both the WindowWorks Terminal and the remote computer:

Baud Rate (300, 600, 1200, 2400, 4800, 9600, or 19200)

Parity (none, odd, or even)

Word Length (7 or 8)

Stop Bits (1 or 2)

Xon/Xoff (this feature toggles on or off)

■ Check the settings of your communications partner, BBS, or other remote computer, and set up the WindowWorks Terminal accordingly.

■ Be certain that you have selected a file transfer protocol supported by your communications partner. Choose the File Transfer Preferences command from the Options menu. WindowWorks supports ASCII, Xmodem Checksum, Xmodem CRC, and Ymodem Batch protocols.

Chapter Summary

Communicating with the WindowWorks Terminal is a process that involves dialing the remote computer manually or automatically; answering the call of a remote computer; transmitting (uploading) or receiving (downloading) data; and disconnecting from the remote computer.

Using the Address Book

You use WindowWorks Address Book module to create and update a personalized list of addresses, phone numbers, and other information about business associates, friends, and colleagues. Any or all of this information in the Address Book can be printed or merged into the Label Maker module to create address labels. You also can merge the address book information with a document in the Word Processor to create customized copies of the standard documents.

The Address Book is really just a specialized and simplified database used for maintaining personalized address files. The WindowWorks Address Book module works similarly to the Database module but on a limited scale. The menu options and control strip have many of the same command options and work in the same way as the Database module. Unlike the databases that you create in the Database module, however, WindowWorks has defined the fields and form layout for the address book database. You only have to enter data.

Understanding the Address Book Window

The first time you open the Address Book module, the Address Book window appears with a blank address record in the workspace (see fig. 15.1).

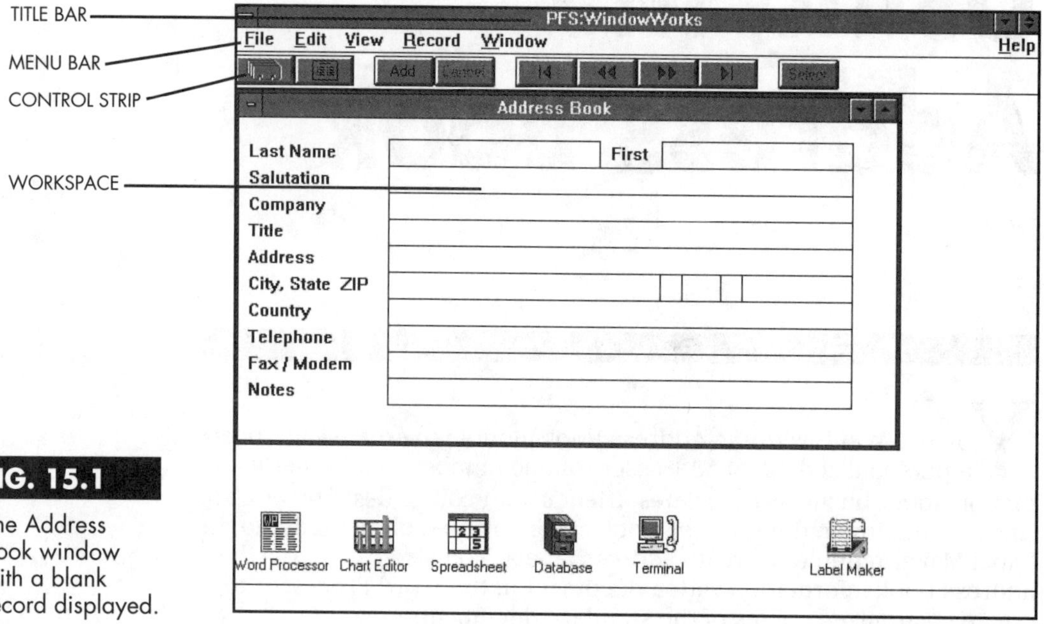

TITLE BAR

MENU BAR

CONTROL STRIP

WORKSPACE

FIG. 15.1

The Address Book window with a blank record displayed.

After you create an address book database and close the Address Book module, you can reopen it. When you reopen the Address Book module, the window appears as it did when you last closed it, if you did not exit WindowWorks. However, if you have exited and reopened WindowWorks since using the Address Book module, the Address Book window appears with a list of all entries in your address book database. To access the record forms, click the Record icon on the control strip or choose View Record from the View menu.

The Address Book window has elements found in all WindowWorks modules: a title bar, a menu bar, a control strip containing shortcut buttons for the commands used most often, and a workspace. The workspace displays the selected address book entry or the list of all entries in the address book database.

Creating Your Address Book Database

To start your personal address book database file, type address information in the blank record form that appears when you open the Address Book module. (This section assumes that you are in View Record mode.) You do not have to type the entries in alphabetical order; WindowWorks alphabetizes your entries.

Entries are made at the location of the cursor; therefore, the cursor must be in the correct field. Moving through fields is easy and can be done in the following ways:

- Move the mouse to the field and click.
- Press Enter.
- Press Tab. Pressing Shift-Tab moves to the previous field.
- Press the down-arrow key. The up-arrow key moves to the previous field.

To create records in your database, perform the following steps:

1. Type the last name of the person in the Last Name field. (Be sure the cursor is in the last name field.)

   Do not put a comma between the last name and the first name, as you would if you were writing the name (Cavanaugh, Sean, for example). WindowWorks thinks that the comma is part of the name and will print interesting, albeit incorrect, names, such as *Sean, Cavanaugh*.

2. Move to the field labeled First and type the first name.

3. Complete the remaining fields.

   You do not have to complete all fields. In fact, you can use the address book for a collection of last names and phone numbers only.

4. Enter any notes or reminders about this entry in the Notes field at the bottom of the record.

   The Notes field is handy for noting where or when you met someone, what days or times you can reach them, or when you last spoke to them.

When you finish entering information, your screen may resemble figure 15.2, which shows a completed address book record.

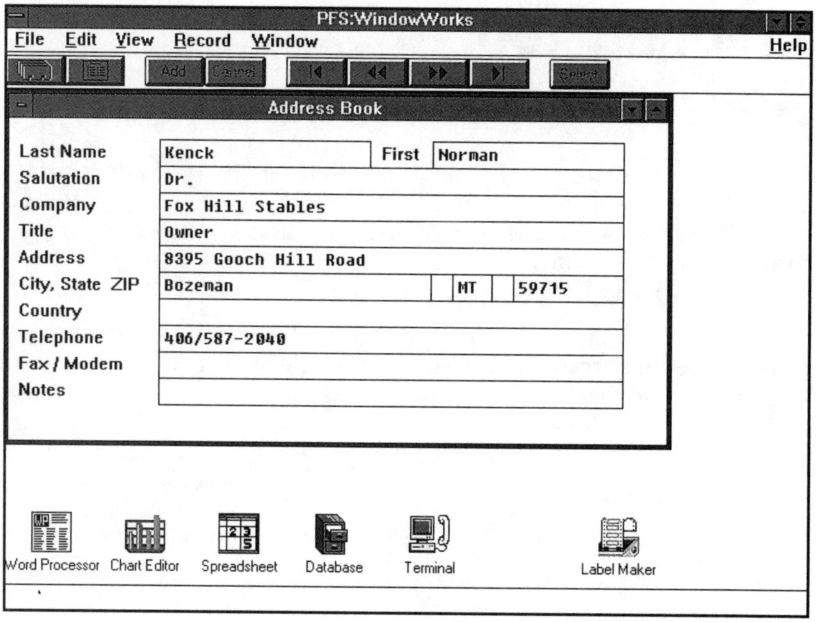

FIG. 15.2

A completed
address book
record.

Adding Records

You can add a blank form in three ways:

- Choose Add from the Record menu.
- Press Ctrl-A.
- Click the Add button on the control strip.

When you use one of these three methods to move to a blank form, the record you just entered disappears. Saving each entry before moving on to a new one is not necessary. When you exit the Address Book module, WindowWorks saves all changes to your address book database.

Enter the necessary information on the blank form, move to another blank form, and continue this process until you have entered all of the records.

If you begin entering a record that you realize was entered earlier or is not needed, click the Cancel button on the control strip. A blank form reappears.

Moving through the Records

You can move through records in the address book database in three ways:

- The movement buttons on the control strip.
- The Keyboard shortcuts, using the Ctrl key.
- The Record menu options.

With these methods, you can move up or down through the records one record at a time by using the Next or Previous option. You can move directly to the first or last record in the database with the First or Last option.

Remember that your database is organized alphabetically, not in the order that you enter records. When you select the Previous option, you move to the record that alphabetically precedes the current record; you do not move to the record that you entered most recently. If you select the First option, you move to the record that occurs first alphabetically in your database, not the first record that you created.

> Use the First and Last options to find not only the first or last record in the address book database, but also any record near the beginning or end of a long database. If you are viewing a record near the end of your database and want to move to the fourth record in the file, for example, you can select the First option and then select the Next option three times to move to the fourth record. Using the First or Last option is usually much faster than selecting Previous or Next to move through the entire list one record at a time.

T I P

You can move through the database by using the Previous, Next, First and Last buttons on the control strip. Click the Previous button to view the record that alphabetically precedes the current record. Click the Next button to view the record following the current record. Click the First button to view the first record in your database. Click the Last button to view the last record in the database.

You also can perform the functions of the First, Last, Previous, and Next buttons with the Record menu. Choosing Next, Previous, First, or Last from the Record menu is the same as clicking the corresponding button on the control strip.

Convenient keyboard shortcuts also exist for the following options:

Key combination	Move to which record
Ctrl-PgUp	Previous record
Ctrl-PgDn	Next record
Ctrl-Home	First record
Ctrl-End	Last record

Searching for a Record

If your address book database is extensive, moving to a particular record by using the Previous, Next, First, and Last options may be tedious. You can use the Find option to search for text within the record you want to find.

To use the Find option from the Record menu, perform the following steps:

1. Choose Find from the Record menu, or press Ctrl-F.

   The Find Entry dialog box appears.

2. In the Search For Text box, enter the text for which you want to search (see fig. 15.3).

   You do not have to search for a last name. You can search for any text that occurs in the record. In the figure, for example, the search command searches only for the first name Sean. The text you search for does not have to be a complete word or field entry.

3. Click the Case Sensitive toggle box (so that an X appears) to search for the text matching upper- and lowercase. The Case Sensitive option is on. To search for any occurrence of the text, regardless of case, be sure that Case Sensitive is turned off (no X in the box).

4. Click OK.

   WindowWorks searches all fields of all records for the entered text. The record containing the first occurrence of the entered text appears. You can edit or view the record.

5. Choose Find Next from the Record menu, or press Ctrl-N to continue the search for other occurrences of entered text.

WindowWorks continues the search and displays the next record containing the entered text. Continue this process until you find the record you want or until WindowWorks does not find any more occurrences of the text.

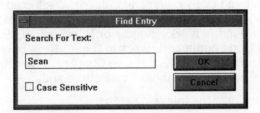

FIG. 15.3

Find Entry dialog box searching for Sean.

The Find Next feature remembers the text for which you last searched, even if you exited the module since conducting a search. To repeat your last search, choose Find Next instead of re-entering text in the Find dialog box.

T I P

Editing a Record

You can edit easily any information in a record. To edit records, perform the following steps:

1. Move through the records until the record you intend to edit is displayed.

2. Use the Tab or Enter key to move to the appropriate field.

   The current field is highlighted.

3. Edit text in any of the following ways:

   To replace all existing text in a field, type the new text when the field is highlighted.

   To modify existing text, use the left- and right-arrow keys to move through the text. Insert or delete text by using the Del and Backspace keys.

4. To abandon your edits and return to the previously saved information in the record, click the Cancel button on the control strip or choose Cancel Edits from the Edit menu.

Copying and Moving Text

You can copy or move text between fields, records, WindowWorks modules, and Windows programs by using the Cut, Copy, and Paste options. The Cut and Copy commands place the selected text on the Windows clipboard. From the Windows clipboard, the text can be pasted into any WindowWorks module or Windows application. The Cut, Copy, and Paste commands work in the Address Book as they do in the Word Processor module. Refer to Chapter 2, "Creating a Document," for more information about these commands.

To copy text, perform the following steps:

1. Select the text from the field by holding down the mouse button and dragging the mouse over the text. You also can press Shift while you use the arrow keys or mouse clicks to highlight the text. Refer to Chapter 2 for details about selecting text.

2. Choose Copy from the Edit menu, or press Ctrl-Ins.

3. Place the cursor in the field or record where the copied text should appear.

   You also can copy text to another WindowWorks module or a Windows program; however, you first must open the Window-Works module or Windows program and place the cursor there.

4. Choose Paste from the Edit menu.

   The selected text appears in both its original position in an address book field and its pasted location.

To move text, follow the steps for copying text, but choose the Cut command instead of the Copy command. If you move text, the selected text is moved from its original position in an address book field to its pasted location.

Deleting a Record

You can delete an entire record without deleting the text from each field. When the record is visible, Choose Delete from the Record menu or press Ctrl-R. The current record is removed, and the next record in the database is visible.

WindowWorks does not display one of those "are you sure you want to do this?" messages before the record disappears; however, you can correct a mistaken deletion. WindowWorks provides an Undelete command to retrieve the last record deleted, even if you closed and reopened the module since the deletion. To retrieve a record, choose Undelete from the Record menu, or press Ctrl-U.

> **CAUTION:** Although you can retrieve a record with the Undelete command after you close the WindowWorks module, the record is lost forever if you close WindowWorks.

Viewing the List of Records

You can view your WindowWorks Address Book records in two ways. With Record View, the default, one record at a time is displayed. With List View, a list of all records in your database is displayed. This list displays the First and Last Name fields only of each record.

To switch to List View, click the List icon on the control strip or choose View List from the View menu. The list appears, displaying an alphabetical listing of all names in your address book database. The current record is highlighted (see fig. 15.4).

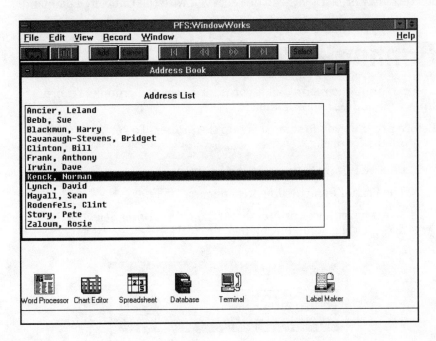

FIG. 15.4

The Address List.

You can use this address list to select a record and avoid searching through individual records. Use the up- and down-arrow keys to move through the list. If the list extends beyond the window, use the scroll bar to view the remainder of the list. When the record you want to view is highlighted, you can see the complete record by double-clicking the entry, clicking the View Record icon, or choosing View Record from the View menu.

From the address list, you also can access a blank record form. To add a blank record, press Ctrl-A, click the Add button on the control strip, or choose Add from the Record menu. Accessing a blank record form returns you to the Record View mode where you can type information for the new record. You cannot type any information in the address list; you must return to the Record View mode to make any additions or modifications to the address book database.

You can remove a record from the address list without returning to the Record View mode, however. Choose Delete from the Record menu, or press Ctrl-R. The highlighted record is removed, and the next entry in the list becomes selected. An entry removed from the list also is re-moved from the Record View mode. You can retrieve the most recently deleted entry by pressing Ctrl-U or choosing Undelete from the Record menu. Until you exit WindowWorks, the last entry deleted within Record View or List View can be retrieved with the Undelete command.

Printing Records

You can print one record, all records, or a selected group of records from your address book database.

Before printing, you first must set up the printer. To set up the printer, perform the following steps:

1. Choose Printer Setup from the File menu.

   The Printer Setup dialog box appears.

2. Select a printer or printer driver from the Printer Selection List and click the Setup button (see fig. 15.5).

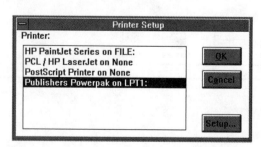

FIG. 15.5

The Printer Setup
dialog box.

3. Set appropriate printer options and click OK.

4. Click OK again in the Printer Setup dialog box.

To print one record, perform the following steps:

1. The record to be printed must be the current record.

   In Record View, move through the records until the record is displayed.

   In List View, use the up- and down-arrow keys to highlight the record.

2. Choose Print from the File menu.

   The Print dialog box appears (see fig. 15.6).

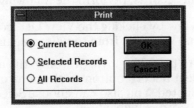

3. Select the Current Record option by clicking the option button next to Current Record or using the arrow keys to move up to Current Record.

4. Click OK.

   The current record is printed. The printout includes the first and last names on the record, a list of all field names in the address book database, and any information within each field (see fig. 15.7).

To print all records, perform the following steps:

1. Choose Print from the File menu.

   The Print dialog box appears.

2. Select the All Records option by clicking the option button next to All Records or using the arrow keys to move up to All Records.

3. Click OK.

   The entire address book database is printed in alphabetical order.

```
Norman Kenck

Telephone            406/587-2040
Fax / Modem
Company              Fox Hill Stables
Title                Owner
Address              8395 Gooch Hill Road
City, State          Bozeman, MT
ZIP                  59715
Country
Notes
```

FIG. 15.7

Sample printout
of a record.

To print selected records, you first must select the records. To select
and print only certain records, perform the following steps:

1. Switch to List View by clicking the View List icon on the control
   strip or choosing View List from the View menu.

2. Select records to print by moving through the address list and
   clicking the Select Record button on the control strip when a
   record is highlighted. You also can choose Select from the Record
   menu when a record is highlighted.

   A plus sign (+) appears next to the selected entry. You can select
   any number of entries on the database list. If you select an entry
   by mistake, highlight the entry and again click Select or choose
   Select from the Record menu. The record becomes unselected
   (the plus sign disappears). Figure 15.8 shows the address book list
   with records selected.

3. Choose Print from the File menu.

   The Print dialog box appears.

4. Select the Selected Records option by clicking the option button
   next to Selected Records or by using the arrow keys to move to
   Selected Records.

   The records you selected in the address book list are printed.

Merging Records with a Word Processor Document

After you create your address book database, you can merge this database information with a Word Processor document and print a copy

of the document for any or all of the names on your address book records. You may want to refer to Chapter 5 for more details about Print Merging; however, the following steps can get you started if you are familiar with Print Merging and the field names of the address book.

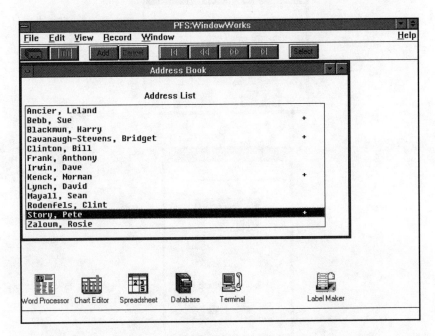

FIG. 15.8

The Address
Book list with
items selected.

To merge records with a word processor document, perform the following steps:

1. To merge one or more records that are not alphabetically contiguous with the Word Processor document, select the records to be merged from the Address Book module.

   To merge records that are alphabetically contiguous, such as records 4, 5, 6, and 7, make a mental note of the numerical position of these records in the list. You must count the positions yourself to determine the position number because WindowWorks doesn't number records.

2. Open the Word Processor module.

3. Position the cursor where you intend to insert an address book field, and choose Merge Field from the Insert menu.

4. Select Use Address Book in the Merge File Type dialog box and click OK (see fig. 15.9).

The Merge Field dialog box with a scroll list of the field names in the address book records appears (see fig. 15.10).

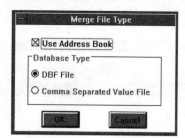

FIG 15.9

The Merge File Type dialog box.

FIG. 15.10

The Merge Field dialog box.

5. Select the field name to be inserted at the cursor position and click OK.

   The field name appears in brackets at the cursor position. If your document is a letter that begins Dear {FNAME}, the first name from each selected address book record is substituted for {FNAME} when the letters are printed (see fig. 15.11).

6. Repeat this process to insert other address book fields at other cursor locations.

   After merging the first field, the Merge File Type dialog box doesn't reappear because WindowWorks knows that you are merging the address book. For subsequent fields, the Merge Field dialog box appears as soon as you select Merge Field from the Insert menu.

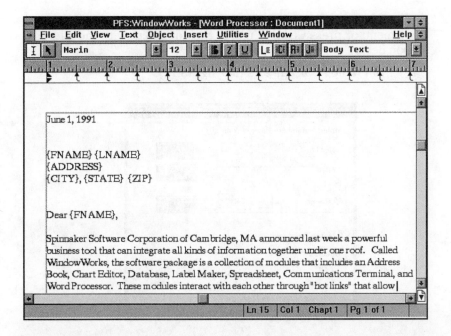

FIG. 15.11

A document with merged fields.

T I P

You may want to select the Collapse White Space option in the Merge Field dialog box (refer to fig. 15.10). When this option is on, WindowWorks compensates for any entries that lack information rather than leave an empty space. If you have not specified a company name on one record, for example, but you have merged the company name field, WindowWorks does not print the letter with a blank where the company name field appears. WindowWorks eliminates, on the letter, any blank space created by blank fields in the address book.

T I P

Remember to place spaces between fields because the Word Processor positions fields exactly where you specify in relationship to the rest of the document. To merge the First Name and Last Name fields from the address book, for example, you must insert the First Name field, press space bar, and insert the Last Name field. A document that shows Dear{FNAME}{LNAME} prints as DearJohnSmith when merged. A document that shows Dear {FNAME} {LNAME} prints as Dear John Smith.

7. After fields are inserted in the document, choose Print from the File menu or press Ctrl-P to merge the document with the address book fields.

The Print dialog box appears (see fig. 15.12).

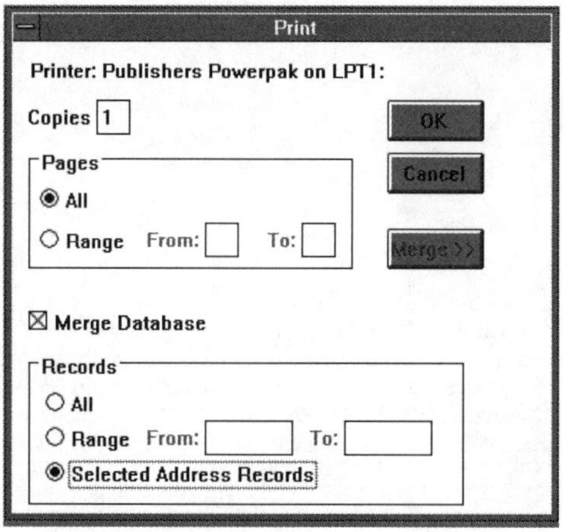

FIG. 15.12

The Print dialog box with merge options.

8. Click the Merge button.

9. Make a selection in the Records list in one of the following ways:

Select All to print one copy of the document for each record in the address book.

Select Range to print a group of contiguous records. Enter the first record number to be merged in the From box; enter the last record number to be merged in the To box. (To merge the first two address book records with your document, for example, type 1 in the From box and 2 in the To box.)

Select Selected Address Records if you marked one or more records in the Address Book module.

10. When the Print dialog box appears, the Merge Database option is selected. To print the document as it appears on-screen, with field names in brackets, click Merge Database to turn off the merge option. (Turning off the Merge option produces the same result as printing without clicking the Merge button in the Print dialog box.)

11. Click OK.

The contents of the address book fields replace the field names when the document is printed.

You also can merge the address book records with address labels. Refer to Chapter 16, "Using the Label Maker," for details.

Chapter Summary

The WindowWorks User's Guide compares the Address Book module to a Rolodex. Although the address book records do look conveniently like a Rolodex card, this comparison is misleading; the Address Book can do much more for you than a Rolodex. If you use the Address Book to do for you only what your Rolodex does, you are missing several very useful features.

You can use Cut, Copy, and Paste to edit an address or phone number field in the address book, for example, without retyping the other information on the record. You can avoid additional retyping by using these commands to copy and move fields between records, modules, and programs.

Moving through your address book is a giant leap from licking your index finger and flipping through Rolodex cards. You have menu, keyboard, and control strip methods of accessing the Next, Previous, First, or Last records in your list. The Find and Find Next commands make searching through an extensive list quick and easy. If your list is short, the List View may be the most convenient way to quickly find a record.

Keeping your address book updated requires only a few seconds of maintenance. Use Add to produce instantly a blank record ready for an entry; use Delete Record to remove a record that you no longer need.

When you need a portable hard copy version of your records, printing records is a simple matter of selecting the records to print. You can have a clean printout of the latest update. To use your address book records in a document or in labels, you can merge the records into the Word Processor or Label Maker modules. If you become familiar with these features, you may never find yourself retyping an address stored in your address book.

If you learn to use all the features of the Address Book, you may find that, behind that pile of business cards and "While You Were Out" notes that have been your contact lists for so long, sits an incredibly organized and efficient person.

Using the Label Maker

With the Label Maker, you can print addresses directly onto standard- and legal-size envelopes and onto address labels. You can enter the addresses for the labels one at a time in the Label Maker window, or you can use addresses stored in your WindowWorks Database or Address Book. The WindowWorks Label Maker module makes printing envelopes and address labels a simpler process than typing them or using your existing software.

If you have Version 1.0 of WindowWorks, it is very difficult and time-consuming to get the module to print. The only variations that seem to work with some degree of consistency are printing standard size envelopes (stationery size: 6 1/2 inches by 3 5/8 inches), printing one label at a time, or using tractor-feed labels. The legal size envelope (business size: 9 1/2 inches by 4 1/8 inches) does not print well with a standard laser printer, and printing a whole sheet of labels is an absurd process with any printer.

NOTE Version 1.0 problems have been corrected in Version 1.1. Spinnaker will gladly send new program disks, free of charge, to any Version 1.0 user.

Understanding the Label Maker Window

When you open the Label Maker, WindowWorks displays a blank label form in the Label Maker window (see fig. 16.1), which contains fields in which you specify the name and address of both the sender and the recipient. The label form is divided into two sections: From, for the sender's name and address, and Send To, for the recipient's name and address.

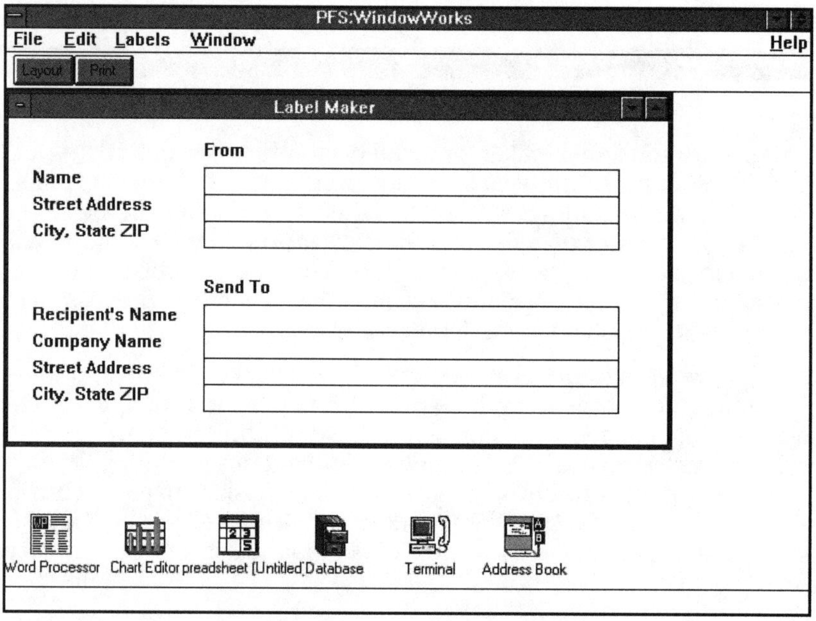

FIG. 16.1

A blank label form.

Before printing, choose Printer Setup from the File menu. WindowWorks displays the Printer Setup dialog box (see fig. 16.2). Choose a printer or printer driver from the Printer selection list, and click Setup. Make sure that all printing settings are correct. Click OK twice to confirm your choices and exit from Printer Setup.

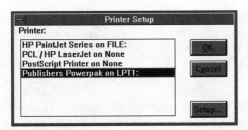

FIG. 16.2

The Printer Setup dialog box.

Entering Addresses

If you are not using addresses stored in your WindowWorks Database or Address Book, you can directly enter addresses, one at a time, to blank label forms. The following steps explain how to enter addresses manually:

1. When you first open the Label Maker window, the cursor is in the Name field of the From section of the blank label form. Type the name of the sender in the Name field.

2. Move to the next field. You have four choices for moving to the next field in the Label Maker:

    ■ Press Tab (or Shift-Tab to move to the preceding field).

    ■ Press Enter.

    ■ Press the down-arrow key (or the up-arrow key to move to the preceding field).

    ■ Click the field to which you want to move the cursor.

3. Enter the sender's address in the Street Address and City, State ZIP fields.

    When you print a label or sheet of labels, WindowWorks does not print the address information you enter in the From section; therefore, you can skip right to the Send To section of the label form. You need to fill out the From section only if you are printing envelopes and want the sender's name and address printed on the envelope.

4. Move to the Recipient's Name field in the Send To section of the form, and complete the remaining fields with the recipient's company name and address.

T I P   If you do not enter a company name, WindowWorks inserts a blank
line between the name and address on the label or envelope. The
text always prints exactly as it appears on the form. A simple trick to
prevent this blank line from printing is to enter the recipient's name
in the Company Name field (see fig. 16.3). WindowWorks doesn't
know whether the name you enter is a person's name or a company
name, so you can type whatever you want in the fields.

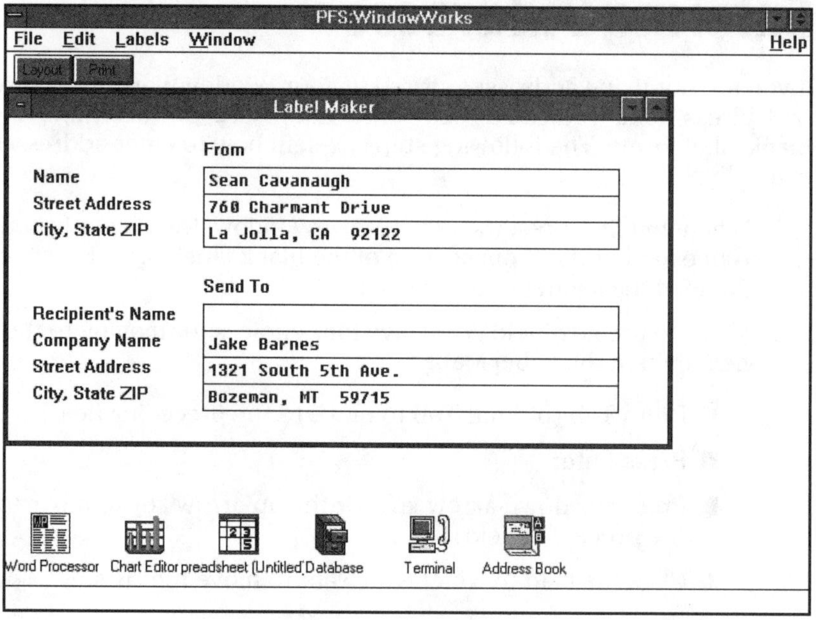

FIG. 16.3

A Label Maker
form with the
recipient's name
moved to the
Company Name
field.

Editing Addresses

To edit label form fields, you can use either the Delete and Backspace
keys to delete individual characters; or select text and then use the
keyboard or the Edit menu to cut, copy, and paste the selected text.

When you move to a field, WindowWorks automatically selects, or highlights, all the text in the field. To replace the text, simply start typing;
WindowWorks replaces the selected text with your new entry. You also
can choose Delete from the Edit menu or press Delete. To edit a portion
of the text, use the left- and right-arrow keys to move the cursor to the
character that needs editing, and delete or add text as necessary.

The Windows Clipboard enables you to use the Copy command to copy
text from one field to another field, to another WindowWorks module,

and even to another Windows program. To copy text from one field and paste it in another field, select the field, choose Copy from the Edit menu or press Ctrl-Insert, move the cursor to another field or to another module or program, and choose Paste from the current Edit menu or press Shift-Insert. The text remains in the Label Maker field from which you copied it and is copied to the new location.

To move text, you must select the text you want to move, choose Cut from the Edit menu or press Shift-Delete, move the cursor to another field, module, or program, and choose Paste from the Edit menu or press Shift-Insert. WindowWorks removes the text from the field from which it was cut and displays it in the new location.

Printing Envelopes

After you enter a sender's and a recipient's name and address, you are ready to print an envelope. The following steps explain how to print an envelope:

1. Choose Layout from the Labels menu or click Layout on the control strip.

   WindowWorks displays the Layout dialog box (see fig. 16.4).

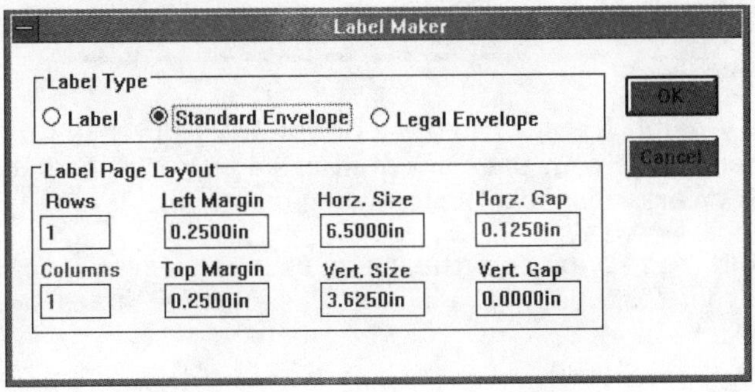

Label Maker
Label Type
○ Label   ⊙ Standard Envelope   ○ Legal Envelope
OK   Cancel
Label Page Layout

Rows	Left Margin	Horz. Size	Horz. Gap
1	0.2500in	6.5000in	0.1250in

Columns	Top Margin	Vert. Size	Vert. Gap
1	0.2500in	3.6250in	0.0000in

FIG. 16.4

The Layout dialog box.

2. Choose Standard Envelope as the Label Type if you want to print a standard-size envelope (6 1/2 inches by 3 5/8 inches). Choose Legal Envelope to print a legal-size envelope (9 1/2 inches by 4 1/8 inches). Use the left- and right-arrow keys to move to the appropriate envelope size, or click the option button next to the selected size.

3. Click OK.

4. Insert an envelope into your printer.

 NOTE Before inserting an envelope, try printing on a piece of paper so that you can test where your printer head starts printing. Read your printer documentation for specific instructions about feeding envelopes through your printer.

5. Choose Print from the File menu or click Print on the Tool Bar.

WindowWorks displays the Print dialog box (see fig. 16.5).

In the No. of Labels box, enter the number of labels—envelopes, in this case—you want to print with the specified address and return address.

```
┌─────────────────────────── Print ───────────────────────────┐
│                                                              │
│    No. of Labels  [1]                          ┌──────────┐  │
│                                                │    OK    │  │
│    ┌─Merge Records─────────────────┐           └──────────┘  │
│    │ ● All                         │           ┌──────────┐  │
│    │ ○ Range  [      ]  to [     ] │           │  Cancel  │  │
│    │                               │           └──────────┘  │
│    │ ○ Selected Address Records    │           ┌──────────┐  │
│    └───────────────────────────────┘           │  Merge...│  │
│                                                └──────────┘  │
└──────────────────────────────────────────────────────────────┘
```

FIG. 16.5

The Print dialog box.

If you use Version 1.1 and you use a dot-matrix printer to print a legal envelope and have your page orientation set to Portrait, as it should be, WindowWorks displays the following message:

```
Layout sizes exceed the page size currently selected
for your printer. The current settings in inches are:
   Width:   8.50
   Height: 11.00
Continue with print?
```

WindowWorks warns you that the horizontal size of a legal envelope (9 1/2 inches) is larger than 8 1/2 inches, which the Portrait setup expects. Click OK. If WindowWorks does not display this message, the orientation of your printer may be set to Landscape, in which case the envelope may not print out correctly.

While WindowWorks prints the envelope, a message alerts you that the program currently is printing a label. Don't panic; the message specifies labels regardless of the Label Type you choose in the Layout dialog box.

WindowWorks prints the envelope, placing the sender's address in the upper-left corner and appropriately centering the recipient's address according to the specified envelope size (see fig. 16.6).

```
Sean Cavanaugh
760 Charmant Drive
La Jolla, CA  92122




                    Jake Barnes
                    1321 South 5th Ave.
                    Bozeman, MT  59715
```

FIG. 16.6

An example of a printed legal envelope.

 NOTE If you use a Hewlett-Packard LaserJet or compatible printer, you may want to print labels for your envelopes rather than attempt guiding envelopes through the printer. In general, envelopes do not feed through laser printers or print as well as sheets of paper, due to the multiple layers of paper that comprise an envelope.

The following steps explain how to use the manual feed guides on the paper tray of a LaserJet or compatible printer to print a 9 1/2-inch by 4 1/8-inch business envelope:

1. Be certain that the Paper Size option in your Printer Setup dialog box is set to Letter size paper (8.5" x 11"), and the orientation is set to Landscape.

2. Click Layout on the control strip or choose Layout from the Labels menu, and select the option Legal Envelope.

   NOTE The zeros are inserted by default. You do not need to type them, but they will appear.

3. Change the Left Margin to at least **1.75** inches and the Top Margin to at least **2.25** inches.

4. Change the Horz. Size to **8.5** inches; leave the Vert. Size set at **4.125** inches.

5. Click OK.

6. Be certain that you adjust the paper tray's manual feed guides so that they fit envelopes, and position a 9 1/2-inch by 4 1/8-inch envelope between the guides.

7. Click Print on the control strip or choose Print from the File menu; then choose OK from the Print dialog box to print the envelope according to the information you entered on the label form.

T   I   P   If your printer feeds the envelope in an unusual way, you may discover that your envelopes print with the text somewhat out of place. You can adjust the Left and Top Margin settings in the Layout dialog box to correct this problem. For example, if the return address is too close to the top of your envelope, increase the Top Margin setting to **0.5000in** (or even more, if necessary). This adjustment can correct some discrepancies between printers.

Printing Labels

The Label Maker enables you to print both sheet-fed labels and tractor-fed labels. Be sure to use labels recommended for your particular printer. Read your printer documentation to learn how to feed labels through your printer.

After you enter a recipient's name and address, you can print a label or a page of labels. The following steps explain how to print a label:

1. Choose Layout from the Labels menu or click Layout on the Control Strip to display the Layout dialog box.

2. Choose Label as the Label Type.

3. In the Rows box, enter the number of rows (horizontal) of labels on your page. Press Tab to move to the Columns box, and enter the number of columns (vertical) of labels on your page.

4. Press Tab to move to the Left Margin box. Enter the distance, in inches, between the left edge of the page and the left edge of the labels, followed by **in** to specify inches; for example, type **0.5000in**. You can specify the distance in as many as ten thousandth's of an inch (four digits).

5. Press Tab to move to the Top Margin box, and enter the distance, in inches, between the top edge of the page and the top edge of the labels.

6. Press Tab to move to the Horz. Size box, and enter the width (horizontal), in inches, of each label.

7. Press Tab to move to the Vert. Size box, and enter the height (vertical), in inches, of each label.

8. Press Tab to move to the Horz. Gap box, and enter the distance, in inches, between the columns of labels. If your sheet of labels has only one column, press Tab again to skip this box.

9. Press Tab to move to the Vert. Gap box, and enter the distance, in inches, between the rows of labels. (On some sheets of labels, this distance is zero).

10. Press Enter or click OK to confirm your adjustments.

11. Choose Print from the File menu or click Print on the control strip to display the Print dialog box.

12. In the No. of Labels box, enter the number of sets of labels you want to print.

13. Click OK to print the label. (Be sure to insert labels into your printer before printing.)

Merging Address Book Records

WindowWorks enables you to merge any or all of your Address Book records with the Label Maker so that you can print each address on a label.

If you want to print labels from your entire address book—the address records saved when you last closed the Address Book—you can print directly from the Label Maker, without opening the Address Book.

If you want to print a label for only one record or a specified group of records from the Address Book, you first need to open the Address Book module and then select the address or addresses you want to print or note the numeric value of the range of records. (Refer to Chapter 15, "Using the Address Book," for details about creating and selecting Address Book records).

Before you can print the labels, you must follow the preceding 13 label-printing steps for layout of a page of labels. After you complete the layout process and select records from your Address Book (unless you are going to print all records or a range of contiguous records), you are ready to print labels from your Address Book records:

1. Choose Print from the File menu or click Print on the control strip to display the Print dialog box.

2. Click the Merge button to display the Merge File Type dialog box (see fig. 16.7).

3. Choose Use Address Book; click the option button to mark it with an X.

4. Click OK.

FIG. 16.7

The Merge File
Type dialog box.

5. From the Merge Records field in the Print dialog box, choose the group of records you want to print:

■ Click All to print one label of each record in your Address Book.

■ Click Selected Address Records to print one label of each selected record in your Address Book. If you want to print a selected group of address book records but haven't selected them, open the Address Book module, select the records, return to the Label Maker, and then print them.

■ Click Range to print labels of a contiguous group of address book records, such as the fourth, fifth, sixth, and seventh records. In the first Range box, type the number of the first record in the group you want to print, and in the second Range box, type the number of the last record you want to print. For example, to print the fourth, fifth, sixth, and seventh records, type **4** in the first Range box, and **7** in the second box.

6. In the No. of Labels box, type the number of sets of labels you want to print using the specified addresses.

7. Click OK.

Be sure to insert labels into your printer before printing. On each label, WindowWorks prints one address from the Address Book module.

Merging Database Records

You also can print labels from data stored in the WindowWorks Database module or in a *Comma Separated Value* database—an ASCII text file in which each entry is delineated by commas. (Refer to Chapter 18 for details about this file type).

Before you can use database records to print labels, you must indicate the page layout of the labels.

You do need not to open the Database module to merge your records with the address labels. After completing the layout of the labels, you can print labels from your database records:

1. Choose Print from the File menu or click Print on the control strip to display the Print dialog box.

2. Click the Merge button to display the Merge File Type dialog box.

3. Click DBF File to use a database from the WindowWorks Database module. Click Comma Separated Value File to use a database text file.

4. Click OK.

   WindowWorks displays the Open dialog box (see fig. 16.8), enabling you to choose the database file you want to use to print labels.

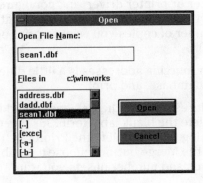

FIG. 16.8

The Open dialog box.

5. To specify the file you want to use, choose the directory and file name from the file selection list, or choose the directory and type the file name in the Open File Name text box.

6. Click Open.

7. Specify whether you want to merge all or part of the database:

   ■ Click All to print a label of each record in the database file.

   ■ Click Range to print a label of each record within a specified range in the database file. In the Range boxes, enter the numbers of the first and last records you want to print. For example, to merge only the first three records in the database, choose Range, type **1** in the first Range box, and type **3** in the second Range box.

8. In the No. of Labels box, type the total number of sets of labels you want to print using the specified records.

9. Click OK.

Before printing, make sure you have loaded labels into your printer. WindowWorks prints one label for each database record you specified.

Chapter Summary

The basic process for printing an envelope or label is simple: enter an address, indicate the layout, and print.

If the preceding summary is more abridged than you wanted, try the following summary: Type the sender's and recipient's name and address on the Label Maker's blank label form. Choose Layout from the Labels menu or click Layout on the control strip, and specify the size of label or envelope you want to print. Choose Printer Setup from the File menu, choose a printer or printer driver, and configure your printer settings. Choose Print from the File menu or click Print on the control strip. Specify the number of copies you want to print of the label or envelope, and click OK.

The basic process for merging addresses is a little different: indicate the layout, choose a database, and print.

If you are merging addresses from the Database or Address Book, you do not need to complete the blank label form. Just specify a format and size in the Layout dialog box, complete the Printer Setup as needed, and click Print. Click the Merge button, choose a database type, click OK, specify the records and number of sets you want to print, and click OK.

If these procedures work with your printer, you are in business; however, if you encounter problems, call the Spinnaker Software technical support staff, and they will send you a free program update.

PART

V

Integration

Integrating Data from Program Modules

Impressive and easy-to-use integration features make WindowWorks more than seven applications in one. *Integration features* enable you to take information from one module—such as a pie chart from the Chart Editor—and place the element into another module, such as the Word Processor.

Integration features offer even more. Integrated data is *linked*, meaning that changes you make to the source of the information are updated—manually or automatically—in the integrated document. You can write a memo in the Word Processor, build a spreadsheet in the Spreadsheet module, and then link the two elements by pasting a copy of the spreadsheet into your memo. The memo and the spreadsheet can be *hot-linked* so that every change you make to the spreadsheet is reflected automatically in the memo. You also can create a hot-linked chart based on the spreadsheet and paste the chart into the memo. You don't have to hot-link integrated information, however, and sometimes you will not want to. You can update linked data manually simply by choosing a single command.

All WindowWorks modules are integrated to a certain extent, but only three modules can exchange data through direct linking: the Spreadsheet, the Chart Editor, and the Word Processor. Although you can print merge data from the Database or Address Book with the Word Processor, this useful integration feature is not considered linking.

The four primary types of integration include the following:

- Creating charts by using numbers from a spreadsheet

- Pasting charts in a Word Processor document

- Pasting tables of data from a spreadsheet into a Word Processor document

- Print merging Database or Address Book data with a Word Processor document

No special commands exist for linking data between modules. You use the Copy and Paste commands (and the Paste Object command in the Word Processor) to link data among the Spreadsheet, Chart Editor, and Word Processor modules. You use the Merge Field and Set Database commands for integrating the Word Processor, Database, and Address Book.

Integration with Links

Integrating data by using links is one of WindowWorks' strongest and easiest-to-use features. You can link data among the Spreadsheet, Chart Editor, and Word Processor modules. Linking is as simple as copying information from one module and pasting it in another.

Copying Spreadsheet Data to the Chart Editor

You can copy selected cells from a spreadsheet and paste them into the Chart Editor to create a chart. To create a chart using Spreadsheet data, perform the following steps:

1. Open the Spreadsheet module.

2. Enter the data that you want to chart, or open an existing spreadsheet that contains the data.

3. Select a range of cells containing the numerical data you want to chart. Text you select—depending on its location in your spreadsheet—is used as column and row headings in the Chart Editor. If the text is contained within a range of numbers (not along the top and left sides of the range), the Chart Editor interprets the text as a zero value.

4. Choose Copy from the Edit menu. From the keyboard, press Ctrl-Ins. (Refer to Chapter 7 for details about creating and editing spreadsheets.)

5. Open the Chart Editor module by clicking the Chart Editor icon or by choosing Chart Editor from the Window menu. This process works whether you leave the Spreadsheet module open, minimize it, or close it. The information you copied remains on the Clipboard.

6. If the workspace in the Chart Editor window is empty, choose Paste from the Edit menu. From the keyboard, press Shift-Ins. If the workspace is not empty, choose New from the File menu before pasting the data.

   The Data Link dialog box appears. The Data Link dialog box displays the name of the Spreadsheet file that you are importing (copying) and the source of the file (the Spreadsheet module).

   The Data Link dialog box enables you to indicate whether you want to *hot-link* the chart with the original data in the Spreadsheet module. Hot-linking data between modules means that if you edit the data in the original module, the data in the linked module is updated automatically. In this case, hot-linking the two files means that every time you modify the information in the Spreadsheet module that you copied to the Chart Editor, the chart will be modified to reflect the new data.

7. If you want your chart to be hot-linked to the Spreadsheet file, check the Auto Refresh option. If you do not want the chart data updated automatically as the Spreadsheet data changes, leave the Auto Refresh box unchecked.

8. Click OK.

   WindowWorks displays a bar chart representing the data that was copied from the Spreadsheet module. You now can edit and format the chart just as you would modify a chart created directly in the Chart Editor. Refer to Chapter 9 for information on editing and formatting chart data.

You can edit chart data from the Chart Editor's Data window or from the Spreadsheet module. To maintain the data link, you should return to the Spreadsheet module to edit the data. If you edit data that came from the Spreadsheet module by using the Chart Editor's Data window, the chart no longer can be linked to the original Spreadsheet file.

If, for example, you copied cells from the Spreadsheet module and pasted them to the Chart Editor (with or without Auto Refresh) and then attempted to edit the Spreadsheet data in the Chart Editor, WindowWorks displays a warning message. By breaking the link, any further changes you make to the data in the Spreadsheet module will not be reflected in the Chart, and you will have to re-import the data to create an updated chart.

Until you see the warning message about breaking the link, the data is linked regardless of whether you selected Auto Refresh. If you did not select Auto Refresh, you can update the linked data manually by using the Refresh Now command. If you selected Auto Refresh, the data is updated automatically, If you break the link, you cannot update at all. You have made two separate data tables: one in the spreadsheet and one in the Chart Editor. (Refer to the later section "Updating Links.")

If you did not want the data linked to the Spreadsheet, edit the data in the Chart Editor's Data window. To access the Data window, click the Data button on the control strip.

Copying a Chart to the Word Processor

You can copy a chart from the Chart Editor and paste the chart into the Word Processor as a chart frame. If you created the chart by integrating data from the Spreadsheet module, pasting the chart into the Word Processor creates a three-way link.

To create a chart frame in a Word Processor document, perform the following steps:

1. Open the Chart Editor.

2. Create a chart that you want included in the Word Processor document or open an existing chart. (Refer to Chapter 9 for details about creating and editing charts.)

3. Choose Copy from the Edit menu.

4. Open the Word Processor by clicking its icon (if the Word Processor is not open already). From the keyboard, choose Word Processor from the Window menu. You can leave the Chart Editor module open, minimize it, or close it.

5. Choose Paste Object from the Edit menu.

   The Link dialog box appears and displays the name of the Chart Editor file you copied—the source.

   The Link dialog box enables you to indicate whether you want to hot-link the Word Processor chart with the original chart in the Chart Editor. Again, hot-linking data between modules means that chart data is updated automatically if edited in the original module. In this case, hot-linking the two files means that every time you modify the information in the Chart Editor, the chart in the Word Processor reflects the changes.

6. If you want the chart to be hot-linked, check the Auto Refresh option. If you do not want the chart data updated automatically as the original data changes, leave the Auto Refresh box unchecked.

7. Click OK.

   The frame tool appears.

8. Hold the left mouse button down. Drag the mouse to create a frame in which you want the chart to appear.

   The chart appears within the frame. You now can format the chart's object attributes (border lines, shades, and so on) and move or resize the chart.

Copying Spreadsheet Data to the Word Processor

You can copy selected cells from a spreadsheet and paste them into the Word Processor to create a table. To create a table in the Word Processor using Spreadsheet data, perform the following steps:

1. Open the Spreadsheet module.

2. Enter the data that you want to include in the table, or open an existing spreadsheet.

3. Select the range of cells that you want to appear in the Word Processor.

4. Choose Copy from the Edit menu. From the keyboard, press Ctrl-Ins. (Refer to Chapter 7 for details about creating and editing spreadsheets.)

5. Open the Word Processor module by clicking its icon or by choosing Word Processor from the Window menu. You can leave the Spreadsheet module open, minimize it, or close it.

6. Choose Paste Object from the Edit menu. (If you choose Paste, rather than Paste Object, the selected Spreadsheet data is imported as text—columns are separated with tabs and rows are separated with hard returns. Using the Paste command does not create a table and does not link the data in any way.)

   The Link dialog box appears and displays the name of the Spreadsheet file from which you are copying—the source.

   The Link dialog box enables you to indicate whether you want to hot-link the Word Processor with the original data in the Spreadsheet module. Hot-linking data between modules means that the data in one module is updated automatically if edited in the original module. In this case, hot-linking the two files means that every time you modify the Spreadsheet information that you copied to the Word Processor, the table changes to reflect the new data.

7. If you want your table to be hot-linked to the Spreadsheet file so that the table is updated automatically to reflect the current Spreadsheet data, check the Auto Refresh option. If you do not want the chart data updated automatically as the original data changes, leave the Auto Refresh box unchecked.

8. Click OK.

   WindowWorks displays the Frame tool.

9. Hold the left mouse button down. Drag the mouse to create a frame in which you want the table to appear.

   The table appears within the frame containing the data you copied from the Spreadsheet module. You now can format the text within the frame or modify the frame's object attributes (border lines, shades, and so on).

You can link data from new spreadsheets or charts that you have not yet saved; in other words, you can link data from files that are untitled. You even can set up a hot-link to untitled spreadsheets or charts, although this procedure is not recommended. If you link the Word Processor to an untitled file, the Word Processor is linked to whatever spreadsheet or chart happens to be open. If, for example, you create a chart linked to an untitled spreadsheet and then open a different spreadsheet (or create a new one), the chart is linked to the current spreadsheet—not to the original untitled spreadsheet. These rules also apply to tables or charts linked to the Word Processor.

If you're just creating a quick chart or table and don't plan to update the data link in the future, linking data from untitled files poses no problems. If, however, you plan to update your linked charts and tables, you should save and name chart and spreadsheet files before copying data from them.

Updating Links

Even if you choose not to turn on the Auto Refresh option when you integrate data between modules, the data is linked nevertheless. You can turn the Auto Refresh option on or off at any time by choosing the Link command. In the Word Processor, this command is located on the Object menu and remains grayed unless you select a chart or table object. In the Chart Editor, the Link command is located on the Edit menu. Choosing the Link command displays the Link dialog box that appeared when you initially pasted the data.

You can refresh data links manually at any time by choosing the Refresh Now command located on the Object menu in the Word Processor and on the Edit menu in the Chart Editor.

Suppose that you are working with Spreadsheet data that changes on a continual basis, but you want to create a chart that represents the data at a specific moment. Unless you want the chart to be updated whenever the Spreadsheet data changes, you should leave the Auto Refresh option off. If you later change your mind, you can turn the hot-link on or choose Refresh Now to bring the chart up-to-date.

Creating an Integration Example

In the following example, you create an integrated Word Processor document using data from the Spreadsheet and Chart Editor modules. Before proceeding, you need a spreadsheet containing numbers you want to chart and a Word Processor document in which you can assemble all the elements. If you need more information about individual modules, refer to their respective chapters.

To create an integrated word processor document, perform the following steps:

1. Double-click the Spreadsheet module icon, or choose Spreadsheet from the Window menu.

2. Open or create a spreadsheet file.

3. Select a range of cells you want to chart by clicking the first cell in the range and dragging to the last cell in the range.

   The cells are highlighted (see fig. 17.1).

4. Choose Copy from the Edit menu.

   You now can paste the data that you copied from the Spreadsheet module into the Chart Editor to create a chart based on Spreadsheet data.

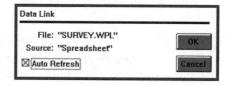

FIG. 17.1

Spreadsheet with range of cells selected.

5. Double-click the Chart Editor icon or choose Chart Editor from the Window menu.

6. Choose Paste from the Edit menu.

7. WindowWorks displays the Data Link dialog box (see fig. 17.2). All data shared by the Spreadsheet, the Chart Editor, and the Word Processor is linked. You can select the Auto Refresh check box to activate a hot-link so that any changes to the spreadsheet are automatically reflected in the chart; if Auto Refresh is checked and you edit the data in its original module, the data is updated automatically in other modules.

FIG. 17.2

Data Link dialog box.

Data Link

File: "SURVEY.WPL"
Source: "Spreadsheet"
☒ Auto Refresh

OK

Cancel

In the Chart Editor window, a newly created chart displays a graphic representation of the data you copied from the Spreadsheet module (see fig. 17.3). But you probably will want to add formatting, titles, and labels to your chart before placing it in your Word Processor document. (Refer to Chapter 9 for information about creating and formatting charts in the Chart Editor.)

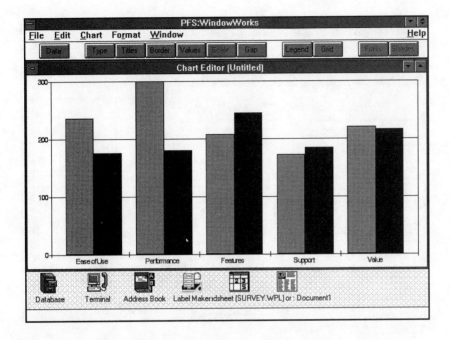

FIG. 17.3

New chart created by using data copied from Spreadsheet module.

You can add your chart to a Word Processor document by following these steps:

1. Choose Copy from the Chart Editor's Edit menu.

2. Choose Word Processor from the Window menu.

3. Choose Paste Object from the Word Processor's Edit menu.

    The Link dialog box appears.

4. Check the Auto Refresh box to create a hot-link and click OK.

    WindowWorks displays the Frame tool.

5. Hold down the left mouse button and drag the cursor to create a rectangle large enough for the chart (see fig. 17.4). When you release the mouse button, the chart appears within the frame. If necessary, you easily can resize the chart by clicking one of the selection handles that appears on its borders.

If you want to move or resize the chart and the black selection handles do not appear on its borders, you must select the chart. Click the Object button (the arrow icon) on the control strip or press the right mouse button to switch to Object mode. Then click the chart to select it for moving or resizing.

Notice that the text in your document automatically flows around the chart whenever the chart is moved or resized.

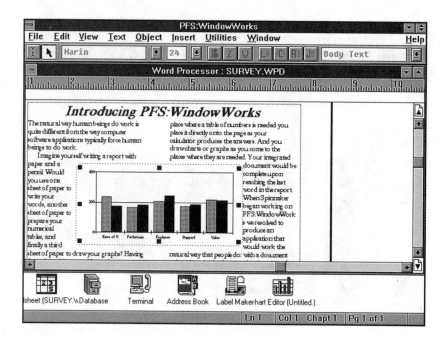

FIG. 17.4

Word Processor
document with
previously copied
chart.

Tiling the Modules

When you are working on a project that integrates data from several modules, you may want to view the modules simultaneously. WindowWorks enables you to tile the open modules so that you can view them side-by-side. To view all open modules at the same time, choose Tile from the Window menu.

With the modules tiled on-screen, you can see the effects of hot-links that you created between modules (see fig. 17.5). If, for example, you edit the data in a hot-linked Spreadsheet file, you instantly see the results when you select the other modules.

Select a cell in the Spreadsheet module that you charted in the Chart Editor and change the cell's value. Now click once in the Chart Editor window and watch the chart reflect your edit. Click once in the Word Processor window to see the chart updated.

Print Merging

You easily can merge Database or Address Book data with a Word Processor document and print a copy of the document for any (or all) of the records in your database.

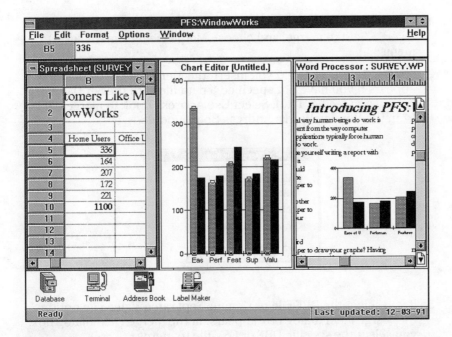

FIG. 17.5

Tiled Spread-
sheet, Chart
Editor, and
Word Processor
modules.

NOTE *Print merging* is the process of combining data from one or
more records of data with a word processor document and
printing one copy of the document for each selected record.

The most common use of the print merge feature is the printing of form
letters. Suppose that you recently have moved and want to send a letter to family and friends informing them of your new address. If you
have a database containing the names and addresses of your acquain-
tances—created by using the Address Book module, for example—
creating a form letter and merging the names and addresses is a snap.

Print merging involves telling the Word Processor which data file you
want to use and which fields from that data file you want to appear in
the document. When you insert a field in a document, the field name
appears in brackets—for example, {NAME}. But when you print the
document, the content of the field (for example, "Bridget Cavanaugh")
is substituted for the field name. A copy of the document then is
printed for each record in the database, and (in this example) the
{NAME} field is substituted for each record.

To print merge using the Word Processor and a data file, perform the
following steps:

1. Open the Word Processor, position the cursor where you want to insert a field to merge, and choose Merge Field from the Insert menu.

2. For the first merge field you insert, the Merge File Type dialog box appears if you have not specified a data file with the Set Database command (see fig. 17.6). Select Use Address Book to merge data from the WindowWorks Address Book module.

Merge File Type dialog box.

3. If you select the DBF File or Comma Separated Value File options, the Merge Field dialog box appears. In the Merge Field dialog box, you select the specific DBF or CSV file to merge.

NOTE DBF is a standard database file format, made popular and universal by such programs as dBASE and FoxBASE. DBF is the most common data file format. The WindowWorks database uses the DBF format.

CSV is an acronym for Comma Separated Value. CSV is a text file. Each field is separated by a comma; each record is separated by a carriage return.

The Merge Field dialog box contains a scroll list of field names available from the selected Address Book or DBF file (see fig. 17.7). If you are merging data from a CSV file, a number appears for each comma-separated item (or *field*) appearing on the first line (or *record*) of the CSV file. If, for example, the first line of a CSV file contains three comma-separated entries, the Merge Field list displays 1, 2, and 3 as available fields.

4. Select the field name that you want to insert at the cursor position, and click OK.

T I P

Select the Collapse White Space option from the Merge Field dialog box if you want WindowWorks to compensate for any entries that may not have information for a particular field (instead of leaving space for the information). If, for example, you are merging data from the Address Book and have not specified a company name in a particular Address Book record (but you have merged the company name field to occupy a line by itself), WindowWorks deletes from your document the blank line that would have been caused by the empty field. When the Collapse White Space option is selected, WindowWorks eliminates blank space in a document that otherwise would have been created by empty data fields.

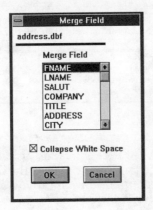

FIG. 17.7

Merge Field dialog box.

The inserted field name appears in brackets at the cursor position. If you use the Address Book, for example, your document can be a letter that starts out Dear {FNAME}, and the first name from each selected Address Book record will be substituted for {FNAME} when the letter is printed (see fig. 17.8).

5. Choose Merge Field from the Insert menu for each field you want included in the document.

After you merge one field, WindowWorks does not display the Merge File Type dialog box. You can merge only one data file with a Word Processor document at a time; in other words, you cannot simultaneously merge a Word Processor document with a DBF file and the Address Book. After you have merged one field, therefore, WindowWorks knows which data file you are merging. For subsequent fields, the Merge Field dialog box appears as soon as you select Merge Field from the Insert menu.

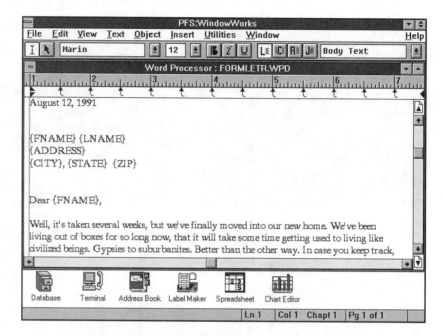

FIG. 17.8

Word Processor
document with
several Address
Book fields listed.

T I P

Remember to place spaces between fields just as you would between
words, because the word processor places the merged fields exactly
as you specify. If, for example, you want to merge the First Name and
Last Name fields from the Address Book, you should insert the First
Name field, press the space bar, and then insert the Last Name field.
If your document shows `Dear{FNAME}{LNAME}:` with no spaces, the
line prints as *Dear.JohnSmith:* when merged. If your document shows
`Dear {FNAME} {LNAME}:`, the line prints correctly as *Dear John
Smith:*.

You can format inserted merge fields just as you would format
regular characters. Simply select a merge field by double-clicking
and then change font, size, and so on as usual. All formatting controls that apply to regular text also apply to merge fields.

6. When all fields are inserted in the correct positions, choose Print
from the File menu (or press Ctrl-P) to merge the document with
the selected data file.

The Print dialog box appears (see fig. 17.9).

7. Click the Merge button (see fig. 17.10).

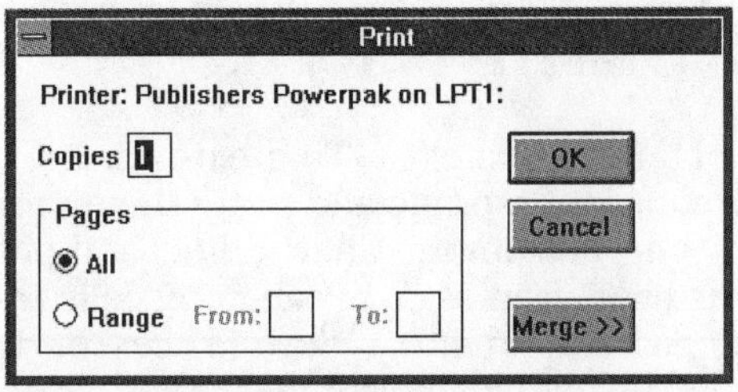

FIG. 17.9

Print dialog box.

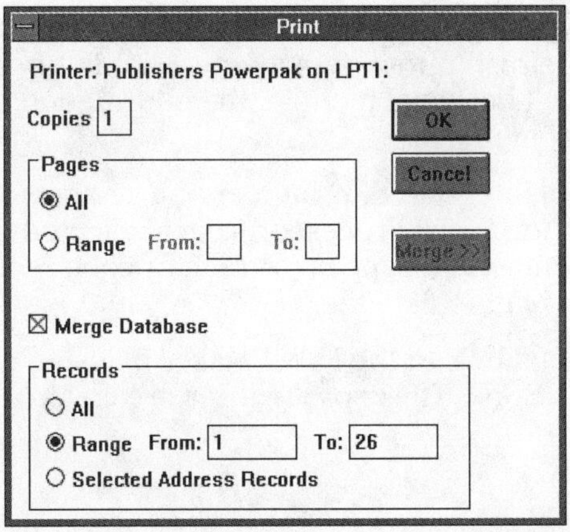

FIG. 17.10

Print dialog box
with merge
options.

8. Select All to print a copy of the document for each record in the selected data file. Alternatively, select Range to print a group of contiguous records. Enter the first record number to be merged in the From box and the last record number to be merged in the To box.

   If you are merging data from the Address Book, you can choose the Selected Address Records option to merge only those records you marked for selection in the Address Book. (See Chapter 15 for more information about using the Address Book module.)

   When this dialog box appears, the Merge Database option is selected. If you want to print the document as it appears on-screen (with the field names in brackets), click Merge Database to turn it off; this is the same as printing without clicking the Merge button in the Print dialog box.

9. Click OK.

   A copy of the document is printed for each record in the selected merge file—with the contents of the data file substituted for the field names you inserted.

Chapter Summary

Four main types of integration exist. To create charts, you can copy cells from the Spreadsheet module and paste them in the Chart Editor. You also can copy charts from the Chart Editor and paste them into the Word Processor as chart frames. You can copy cells from the Spreadsheet module and paste them into a Word Processor document to create table frames. Finally, you can print merge with the Word Processor by using data from Address Book, Database, or CSV files.

The first three types of integration link data between modules. You can select the Auto Refresh option to activate a hot-link, which means that if you edit data in its original module, the information is updated automatically in other modules.

The fourth type of integration, print merging, enables you to insert merge fields into the Word Processor from a selected data file. When you print the document, a copy is printed for each record—or selected range of records—in the data file.

You also can print labels in the Label Maker by using data merged from the Address Book. These procedures are covered further in Chapters 15 and 16.

Importing Data

Y̲ou may need to import data from files from different programs that you or someone else uses. This chapter explains how PFS:WindowWorks enables you to import from PFS:First Choice and Betterworking Eight-in-One. Specifically, this chapter provides a series of steps for importing word processor, spreadsheet, and database information from these two programs to the corresponding module in WindowWorks.

Importing Data from PFS:First Choice

You can import data from the PFS:First Choice word processor, spreadsheet, and database to the corresponding modules in PFS:WindowWorks.

Importing PFS:First Choice Word Processor Files

WindowWorks can open PFS:First Choice documents directly, without saving the documents in an intermediate format. To import a PFS:First Choice document into the WindowWorks word processor, perform the following simple steps:

1. Select the Open command from the WindowWorks Word Processor module's File menu.

   The Open dialog box appears.

2. Pull down the Type menu, and choose the PFS:First Choice Format option.

3. Change the drive/directory if necessary, and select a PFS:First Choice file to open.

   The document appears on-screen.

Importing PFS:First Choice Spreadsheet Files

The WindowWorks spreadsheet module cannot open PFS:First Choice worksheet files directly; you first must save your worksheets as WKS (Lotus 1-2-3) or WK1 (Lotus 1-2-3 version 1a) files in First Choice.

To import your worksheet file, perform the following steps:

1. In PFS:First Choice, save your worksheet as a WKS or a WK1 file.

2. In WindowWorks, select the Import command from the spreadsheet's File menu.

   The Import Worksheet dialog box appears.

3. Pull down the Type menu, and choose the Lotus 1-2-3 (WKS) or Lotus 1-2-3/2 (WK1) option.

4. Change the drive/directory if necessary, and select the file created in step 1.

   The spreadsheet appears on-screen.

Importing Comma-Delimited Files

Importing PFS:First Choice database files to the WindowWorks database requires that you use caution. WindowWorks cannot read First Choice database files directly. Before you import the database files into WindowWorks, you first must save the files as comma-delimited files in First Choice. Then you must create a new WindowWorks database definition whose fields are the same type, size, and, most importantly, in the exact same order as the fields in the comma-delimited file.

NOTE In a comma-delimited file, fields are set apart with commas, and records are separated by carriage returns.

Before importing the comma-delimited file, ensure that the fields adhere to the following rules:

■ Character fields must have quotation marks around them.

■ Date fields must be in the format 01-01-80. No quotation marks can be around date fields. Some programs save date fields in the format 19910812 (August 12, 1991). WindowWorks cannot interpret this format. You must change the format to 08-12-91, the format accepted by WindowWorks.

■ Logical fields must be in the format T, F, Y, or N and without quotation marks.

■ Numeric fields simply show the number; however, remember to consider decimal places when defining numeric fields.

■ Memo fields, which cannot be output in comma-delimited files, cannot be imported.

To import comma-delimited files into the WindowWorks Database, regardless of whether the comma-delimited files were created in PFS:First Choice, perform the following steps.

1. In PFS:First Choice, save your database as *comma delimited*.

T I P

After opening the comma-delimited file you output from the PFS:First Choice database in the WindowWorks word processor, tile the Word Processor and Database modules (choose Tile from the Window menu) to see the modules side-by-side.

2. In WindowWorks, create a *database definition* (data entry form), ensuring that the fields are in the same order as the fields in the comma-delimited file.

   If the first field in the comma-delimited file is a character field 30 characters long, for example, create a field, using the field tool with the character Field Type and a Field Size of at least 30. Define matching fields for each field in the comma-delimited file.

 **NOTE** Although fields must be in the correct order in the database definition window, defining fields in the correct order is difficult. Fields are ordered from top to bottom, then from left to right. However, you should avoid defining fields in left to right order. A top-to-bottom only layout is best. In other words, do not define fields side-by-side. The best way to determine field order is to set field positions using the Edit Field command. If the fields aren't in the same order as they are in the comma-delimited file, you cannot import the data. After you import the data from the comma-delimited file, you can rearrange the database.

3. Click the Edit Records button on the control strip, or choose Edit Records from the Database menu.

4. Select the Import command from the Database module's Database menu.

   The Import Database dialog box appears.

5. Change the drive/directory if necessary, and select the CSV (comma-delimited) file created in PFS:First Choice.

   A record is created in the database for each record from the comma-delimited file.

   The first record is blank; all other records follow.

Importing Data from BetterWorking Eight-in-One

You can import data from the Eight-in-One word processor, spreadsheet, and database to the corresponding modules in WindowWorks.

Importing Eight-in-One Word Processor Files

WindowWorks can open BetterWorking Eight-in-One documents directly, without saving the files in an intermediate format.

To import a BetterWorking Eight-in-One document into the WindowWorks Word Processor, perform the following steps:

1. Select the Open command from the WindowWorks word processor's File menu.

   The Open dialog box appears.

2. Pull down the Type menu, and choose the BetterWorking Format option.

3. Change the drive/directory if necessary, and select a file to open.

   The word processor document appears on-screen.

Importing Eight-in-One Spreadsheet Files

The WindowWorks Spreadsheet module cannot open Eight-in-One spreadsheet files directly; you first must save your spreadsheet as WKS (Lotus 1-2-3) or WK1 (Lotus 1-2-3 version 1a) files in Eight-in-One.

 NOTE Version 1.0 of WindowWorks cannot open 8N1 files directly. Version 1.1 *can* open 8N1.tpl files directly.

To import Eight-in-One spreadsheet files, perform the following steps:

1. Save your worksheet as a WKS or WK1 file in Eight-in-One.

2. Select the Import command from the WindowWorks spreadsheet's File menu.

   The Import Worksheet dialog box appears.

3. Pull down the Type menu, and choose Lotus 1-2-3 (WKS) or Lotus 1-2-3/2 (WK1).

4. Change the drive/directory if necessary, and select the file created in step 1.

Importing Eight-in-One (DBF) Files

Importing Eight-in-One database files to the WindowWorks database is a relatively simple process. Importing is a misleading term, however, because both the WindowWorks and Eight-in-One database modules use the same format: DBF, the dBASE standard for data files. More precisely, Eight-in-One data files are merged with WindowWorks data files. You must create a new database definition in WindowWorks before merging the DBF files.

To import Eight-in-One database files, perform the following steps:

1. In WindowWorks, re-create the definition (data entry form), using the same fields as those in your Eight-in-One file.

2. Select the Merge command from the Database module's Database menu.

3. Change the drive/directory if necessary, and select the Eight-in-One DBF file.

   You are prompted to match each merge field from the old database into the new definition.

4. Choose OK each time WindowWorks prompts you for the match field name if you defined the same fields in the same order for both databases.

   or

   Select the appropriate merge field name (this could be NONE) before choosing OK if you changed the order of the fields or the number of fields in the new database definition.

   The first record is blank; the other records follow.

Chapter Summary

This chapter provided the steps you need to import from PFS:First Choice and BetterWorking Eight-in-One to PFS:WindowWorks. Specifically, you learned to import from the First Choice word processor, spreadsheet, and database and the Eight-in-One word processor, spreadsheet, and database in the appropriate method for the corresponding WindowWorks module.

Installing PFS:WindowWorks

You can use the following three methods to determine whether you have WindowWorks Version 1.0 or Version 1.1:

- *Check the installation guide.* Turn to the section "Installing WindowWorks." If you are instructed not to be in Windows when you install, you have Version 1.0. If you are instructed to be in Windows when you install, you have Version 1.1.

- *Check the program disks.* Insert Disk 1 into your floppy drive, and type **DIR** at the appropriate prompt. If the last file in the disk directory is DISK1.ZIP, you have Version 1.0. If the last file in the disk directory is DISK1.PPK, you have Version 1.1.

- *Check the installation procedure.* Insert Disk 1 into your floppy drive. At the DOS prompt, but before starting Windows, type **A:INSTALL** or **B:INSTALL**, and press Enter. If the program begins to install, you have Version 1.0. If you are instructed to first start Windows, you have Version 1.1.

PFS:WindowWorks Version 1.0

If you have PFS:WindowWorks Version 1.0, perform the following steps:

1. Insert PFS:WindowWorks Disk 1 into drive A or drive B.

2. Start the installation process.

   You can use one of the following methods to start the PFS:WindowWorks installation process:

   ■ If you prefer using DOS, start from a DOS prompt or the DOS icon on your Microsoft Windows Program Manager, type **A:INSTALL** or **B:INSTALL**, and press Enter.

   ■ If you prefer using Windows, select the Run option from the File menu of the Windows Program Manager, type **A:INSTALL** or **B:INSTALL** on the command line, and press Enter.

   ■ If you want to know the names of all the files on the installation disk, open the Microsoft Windows File Manager, select drive A or drive B, and double-click the file named INSTALL.EXE.

   The PFS:WindowWorks installation program first prompts you to identify the drive from which you are installing PFS:WindowWorks.

3. If your PFS:WindowWorks disk is in drive A, press Enter. If the disk is in drive B, move the cursor down to the Drive B option, and press Enter.

   You then are prompted to identify the drive to which you are installing PFS:WindowWorks.

4. Press Enter to install the program on drive C, or move the cursor down to the appropriate drive letter, and press Enter.

   PFS:WindowWorks requires approximately 4M of disk space. If the selected drive does not have that much space available, select another drive or delete unnecessary files from the drive before installing PFS:WindowWorks.

   The installation program then inquires whether you want your AUTOEXEC.BAT file changed as part of the installation. Although this proposition may concern those of you who monitor carefully every line in your AUTOEXEC.BAT file, the change simply adds the WINWORKS directory to your path statement.

5. If you want to add the WINWORKS directory to your path statement, press Enter. If you want to edit your AUTOEXEC.BAT file yourself by using a text editor, or if you do not want WINWORKS listed in your path statement, move the cursor down to NO, and press Enter.

   The program files are copied into the WINWORKS directory on the selected drive.

6. When prompted, replace Disk 1 with Disk 2, and press any key to continue the installation.

   If for some reason you choose not to finish the installation at this point, press Esc to abort the process.

After all the PFS:WindowWorks files have been copied, a prompt appears and asks whether you want to install Publisher's Powerpak. Publisher's Powerpak is a superb printer and screen driver package that includes an outstanding font selection. Three type families are included with Powerpak, and an incomprehensible variety of additional fonts is available from Atech software. Installing Publisher's PowerPak is a great way to start building an outstanding font library.

To install Powerpak, perform the following steps:

1. When prompted to install Publisher's Powerpak, press Enter.

2. Replace Disk 2 with Disk 3, and press any key.

   The Powerpak files are copied into a Powerpak subdirectory within your Windows directory. The Powerpak installation procedure also adds some files to your Windows directory and modifies your Windows SYSTEM.INI file.

3. Restart Windows.

PFS:WindowWorks Version 1.1

To install WindowWorks Version 1.1, perform the following steps:

1. Start Windows.

2. Put Disk 1 in drive A or drive B.

3. Choose Run from the Program Manager's File menu, type **A:INSTALL** or **B:INSTALL**, and click OK. The Install screen appears (see fig. A.1).

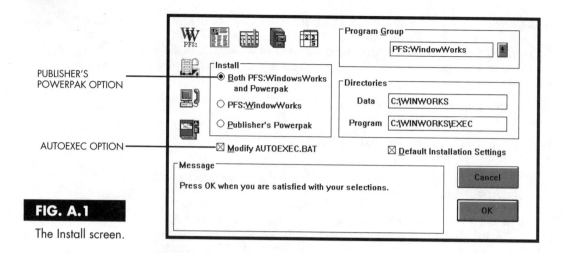

PUBLISHER'S POWERPAK OPTION

AUTOEXEC OPTION

The Install screen.

NOTE If WindowWorks detects that you have any active printer font screen drivers, a dialog box appears. This box tells you how to turn off the screen driver if you want to install Publisher's Powerpak. If you don't want to install Powerpak, you can continue with the installation procedure. However, Install PFS:WindowWorks will be the only available option; you cannot install Powerpak if you have another active screen driver.

4. If you do not want a new group created on your desktop for PFS:WindowWorks, type a new name for the group or select an existing group from the Program Group list.

5. If you do not want to install PFS:WindowWorks in a directory called C:\WINWORKS, enter another drive or directory name in the Directories box. You then can alter the path and name of the EXEC subdirectory. If you change the group or directory for installation and want to change back to the default, click the Default Installation Settings toggle box.

6. If you do not want to install Publisher's Powerpak for some reason—perhaps you already are a big fan of Adobe Type Manager or a similar program—select Install PFS:WindowWorks from the Install box. (See preceding section for a description of Publisher's Powerpak.)

7. If you do not want WindowWorks added to your path statement, click the Modify AUTOEXEC.BAT toggle box to turn off the option.

The installation program then inquires whether you want your AUTOEXEC.BAT file changed as part of the installation. Although this proposition may concern those of you who monitor carefully every line in your AUTOEXEC.BAT file, the change simply adds the WINWORKS directory to your path statement.

8. Click OK when you are ready to install WindowWorks.

9. Follow the on-screen instructions by inserting Disks 2 and 3 when prompted.

When the installation is finished, you are returned to the Program Manager. If you installed Publisher's Powerpak with WindowWorks, you must restart Windows.

Symbols

A

G

T

X-Z

Computer Books from Que Mean PC Performance!

Spreadsheets

1-2-3 Beyond the Basics	$24.95
1-2-3 Database Techniques	$29.95
1-2-3 for DOS Release 2.3 Quick Reference	$ 9.95
1-2-3 for DOS Release 2.3 QuickStart	$19.95
1-2-3 for Windows Quick Reference	$ 9.95
1-2-3 for Windows QuickStart	$19.95
1-2-3 Graphics Techniques	$24.95
1-2-3 Macro Library, 3rd Edition	$39.95
1-2-3 Release 2.2 PC Tutor	$39.95
1-2-3 Release 2.2 QueCards	$19.95
1-2-3 Release 2.2 Workbook and Disk	$29.95
1-2-3 Release 3 Workbook and Disk	$29.95
1-2-3 Release 3.1 Quick Reference	$ 8.95
1-2-3 Release 3.1 + QuickStart, 2nd Edition	$19.95
Excel for Windows Quick Reference	$ 9.95
Quattro Pro Quick Reference	$ 8.95
Quattro Pro 3 QuickStart	$19.95
Using 1-2-3/G	$29.95
Using 1-2-3 for DOS Release 2.3, Special Edition	$29.95
Using 1-2-3 for Windows	$29.95
Using 1-2-3 Release 3.1, + 2nd Edition	$29.95
Using Excel 3 for Windows, Special Edition	$29.95
Using Quattro Pro 3, Special Edition	$24.95
Using SuperCalc5, 2nd Edition	$29.95

Databases

dBASE III Plus Handbook, 2nd Edition	$24.95
dBASE IV PC Tutor	$29.95
dBASE IV Programming Techniques	$29.95
dBASE IV Quick Reference	$ 8.95
dBASE IV 1.1 QuickStart	$19.95
dBASE IV Workbook and Disk	$29.95
Que's Using FoxPro	$29.95
Using Clipper, 2nd Edition	$29.95
Using DataEase	$24.95
Using dBASE IV	$29.95
Using ORACLE	$29.95
Using Paradox 3	$24.95
Using PC-File	$24.95
Using R:BASE	$29.95

Business Applications

Allways Quick Reference	$ 8.95
Introduction to Business Software	$14.95
Introduction to Personal Computers	$19.95
Norton Utilities Quick Reference	$ 8.95
PC Tools Quick Reference, 2nd Edition	$ 8.95
Q&A Quick Reference	$ 8.95
Que's Computer User's Dictionary, 2nd Edition	$10.95
Que's Using Enable	$29.95
Que's Wizard Book	$12.95
Quicken Quick Reference	$ 8.95
SmartWare Tips, Tricks, and Traps, 2nd Edition	$26.95
Using DacEasy, 2nd Edition	$24.95
Using Managing Your Money, 2nd Edition	$19.95
Using Microsoft Works: IBM Version	$22.95
Using Norton Utilities	$24.95
Using PC Tools Deluxe	$24.95
Using Peachtree	$27.95
Using PROCOMM PLUS, 2nd Edition	$24.95
Using Q&A 4	$27.95
Using Quicken: IBM Version, 2nd Edition	$19.95
Using SmartWare II	$29.95
Using Symphony, Special Edition	$29.95
Using TimeLine	$24.95
Using TimeSlips	$24.95

CAD

AutoCAD Quick Reference	$ 8.95
Que's Using Generic CADD	$29.95
Using AutoCAD, 3rd Edition	$29.95
Using Generic CADD	$24.95

Word Processing

Microsoft Word Quick Reference	$ 9.95
Using LetterPerfect	$22.95
Using Microsoft Word 5.5: IBM Version, 2nd Edition	$24.95
Using MultiMate	$24.95
Using PC-Write	$22.95
Using Professional Write	$22.95
Using Word for Windows	$24.95
Using WordPerfect 5	$27.95
Using WordPerfect 5.1, Special Edition	$27.95
Using WordStar, 3rd Edition	$27.95
WordPerfect PC Tutor	$39.95
WordPerfect Power Pack	$39.95
WordPerfect 5 Workbook and Disk	$29.95
WordPerfect 5.1 QueCards	$19.95
WordPerfect 5.1 Quick Reference	$ 8.95
WordPerfect 5.1 QuickStart	$19.95
WordPerfect 5.1 Tips, Tricks, and Traps	$24.95
WordPerfect 5.1 Workbook and Disk	$29.95

Hardware/Systems

DOS Tips, Tricks, and Traps	$24.95
DOS Workbook and Disk, 2nd Edition	$29.95
Fastback Quick Reference	$ 8.95
Hard Disk Quick Reference	$ 8.95
MS-DOS PC Tutor	$39.95
MS-DOS 5 Quick Reference	$ 9.95
MS-DOS 5 QuickStart, 2nd Edition	$19.95
MS-DOS 5 User's Guide, Special Edition	$29.95
Networking Personal Computers, 3rd Edition	$24.95
Understanding UNIX: A Conceptual Guide, 2nd Edition	$21.95
Upgrading and Repairing PCs	$29.95
Using Microsoft Windows 3, 2nd Edition	$24.95
Using MS-DOS 5	$24.95
Using Novell NetWare	$29.95
Using OS/2	$29.95
Using PC DOS, 3rd Edition	$27.95
Using Prodigy	$19.95
Using UNIX	$29.95
Using Your Hard Disk	$29.95
Windows 3 Quick Reference	$ 8.95

Desktop Publishing/Graphics

CorelDRAW! Quick Reference	$ 8.95
Harvard Graphics Quick Reference	$ 8.95
Que's Using Ventura Publisher	$29.95
Using Animator	$24.95
Using DrawPerfect	$24.95
Using Harvard Graphics, 2nd Edition	$24.95
Using Freelance Plus	$24.95
Using PageMaker 4 for Windows	$29.95
Using PFS: First Publisher, 2nd Edition	$24.95
Using PowerPoint	$24.95
Using Publish It!	$24.95

Macintosh/Apple II

The Big Mac Book, 2nd Edition	$29.95
The Little Mac Book	$12.95
Que's Macintosh Multimedia Handbook	$24.95
Using AppleWorks, 3rd Edition	$24.95
Using Excel 3 for the Macintosh	$24.95
Using FileMaker	$24.95
Using MacDraw	$24.95
Using MacroMind Director	$29.95
Using MacWrite	$24.95
Using Microsoft Word 4: Macintosh Version	$24.95
Using Microsoft Works: Macintosh Version, 2nd Edition	$24.95
Using PageMaker: Macintosh Version, 2nd Edition	$24.95

Programming/Technical

C Programmer's Toolkit	$39.95
DOS Programmer's Reference, 2nd Edition	$29.95
Network Programming in C	$49.95
Oracle Programmer's Guide	$29.95
QuickC Programmer's Guide	$29.95
UNIX Programmer's Quick Reference	$ 8.95
UNIX Programmer's Reference	$29.95
UNIX Shell Commands Quick Reference	$ 8.95
Using Assembly Language, 2nd Edition	$29.95
Using BASIC	$24.95
Using Borland C++	$29.95
Using C	$29.95
Using QuickBASIC 4	$24.95
Using Turbo Pascal	$29.95

For More Information, Call Toll Free!

1-800-428-5331

*All prices and titles subject to change without notice.
Non-U.S. prices may be higher. Printed in the U.S.A.*

Find It Fast With Que's Quick References!

Que's Quick References are the compact, easy-to-use guides to essential application information. Written for all users, Quick References include vital command information under easy-to-find alphabetical listings. Quick References are a must for anyone who needs command information fast!

Teach Yourself
With QuickStarts From Que!

The ideal tutorials for beginners, Que's QuickStart books use graphic illustrations and step-by-step instructions to get you up and running fast. Packed with examples, QuickStarts are the perfect beginner's guides to your favorite software applications.

1-2-3 for DOS Release 2.3 QuickStart

Release 2.3

$19.95 USA

0-88022-716-8, 500 pp., 7 3/8 x 9 1/4

1-2-3 for Windows QuickStart

1-2-3 for Windows

$19.95 USA

0-88022-723-0, 500 pp., 7 3/8 x 9 1/4

1-2-3 Release 3.1 + QuickStart, 2nd Edition

Releases 3 & 3.1

$19.95 USA

0-88022-613-7, 569 pp., 7 3/8 x 9 1/4

dBASE IV 1.1 QuickStart,

Through Version 1.1

$19.95 USA

0-88022-614-5, 400 pp., 7 3/8 x 9 1/4

Excel 3 for Windows QuickStart

Version 3 fo rWindows

$19.95 USA

0-88022-762-1, 500 pp., 7 3/8 x 9 1/4

MS-DOS QuickStart, 2nd Edition

Version 3.X & 4.X

$19.95 USA

0-88022-611-0, 420 pp., 7 3/8 x 9 1/4

Q&A 4 QuickStart

Versions 3 & 4

$19.95 USA

0-88022-653-6, 400 pp., 7 3/8 x 9 1/4

Quattro Pro 3 QuickStart

Through Version 3.0

$19.95 USA

0-88022-693-5, 450 pp., 7 3/8 x 9 1/4

WordPerfect 5.1 QuickStart

WordPerfect 5.1

$19.95 USA

0-88022-558-0, 427 pp., 7 3/8 x 9 1/4

Windows 3 QuickStart

Ron Person & Karen Rose

This graphics-based text teaches Windows beginners how to use the feature-packed Windows environment. Emphasizes such software applications as Excel, Word, and PageMaker and shows how to master Windows' mouse, menus, and screen elements.

Version 3

$19.95 USA

0-88022-610-2, 440 pp., 7 3/8 x 9 1/4

MS-DOS 5 QuickStart

Que Development Group

This is the easy-to-use graphic approach to learning MS-DOS 5. The combination of step-by-step instruction, examples, and graphics make this book ideal for all DOS beginners.

DOS 5

$19.95 USA

0-88022-681-1, 420 pp., 7 3/8 x 9 1/4

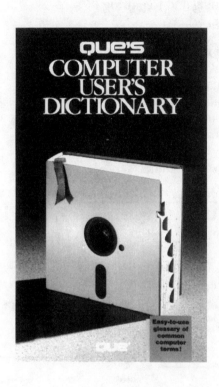

Enhance Your Personal Computer System
With Hardware And Networking Titles From Que!

Upgrading and Repairing PCs
Scott Mueller

This book is the ultimate resource for personal computer upgrade, maintenance, and troubleshooting information! It provides solutions to common PC problems and purchasing descisions and includes a glossary of terms, ASCII code charts, and expert recommendations.

IBM Computers & Compatibles

$29.95 USA

0-88022-395-2, 724 pp., 7 3/8 x 9 1/4

Hard Disk Quick Reference
Que Development Group

Through DOS 4.01

$8.95 USA
0-88022-443-6, 160 pp., 4 3/4 x 8

Introduction To Personal Computers, 2nd Edition
Katherine Murray

IBM, Macintosh, & Apple

$19.95 USA
0-88022-758-3, 400 pp., 7 3/8 Xx9 1/4

Networking Personal Computers, 3rd Edition
Michael Durr & Mark Gibbs

IBM & Macintosh

$24.95 USA
0-88022-417-7, 400 pp., 7 3/8 x 9 1/4

Que's Computer Buyer's Guide, 1992 Edition
Que Development Group

IBM & Macintosh

$14.95 USA
0-88022-759-1, 250 pp., 8 x 10

Que's Guide to Data Recovery
Scott Mueller

IBM & Compatibles

$29.95 USA
0-88022-541-6, 500 pp., 7 3/8 x 9 1/4

Que's PS/1 Book
Katherine Murray

Covers Microsoft Works & Prodigy

$22.95 USA
0-88022-690-0, 450 pp., 7 3/8 x 9 1/4

Using Novell NetWare
Bill Lawrence

Version 3.1

$29.95 USA
0-88022-466-5, 728 pp., 7 3/8 x 9 1/4

Using Your Hard Disk
Robert Ainsbury

DOS 3.X & DOS 4

$29.95 USA
0-88022-583-1, 656 pp., 7 3/8 x 9 1/4

To Order, Call:
(800) 428-5331 OR (317) 573-2500

Free Catalog!

Mail us this registration form today, and we'll send you a free catalog featuring Que's complete line of best-selling books.

Name of Book _____

Name _____

Title _____

Phone (___) _____

Company _____

Address _____

City _____

State _____ ZIP _____

Please check the appropriate answers:

1. Where did you buy your Que book?
   - ☐ Bookstore (name: _____)
   - ☐ Computer store (name: _____)
   - ☐ Catalog (name: _____)
   - ☐ Direct from Que
   - ☐ Other: _____

2. How many computer books do you buy a year?
   - ☐ 1 or less
   - ☐ 2-5
   - ☐ 6-10
   - ☐ More than 10

3. How many Que books do you own?
   - ☐ 1
   - ☐ 2-5
   - ☐ 6-10
   - ☐ More than 10

4. How long have you been using this software?
   - ☐ Less than 6 months
   - ☐ 6 months to 1 year
   - ☐ 1-3 years
   - ☐ More than 3 years

5. What influenced your purchase of this Que book?
   - ☐ Personal recommendation
   - ☐ Advertisement
   - ☐ In-store display
   - ☐ Price
   - ☐ Que catalog
   - ☐ Que mailing
   - ☐ Que's reputation
   - ☐ Other: _____

6. How would you rate the overall content of the book?
   - ☐ Very good
   - ☐ Good
   - ☐ Satisfactory
   - ☐ Poor

7. What do you like *best* about this Que book?

   _____
   _____

8. What do you like *least* about this Que book?

   _____
   _____

9. Did you buy this book with your personal funds?
   - ☐ Yes   ☐ No

10. Please feel free to list any other comments you may have about this Que book.

    _____
    _____
    _____

— que —

Order Your Que Books Today!

Name _____

Title _____

Company _____

City _____

State _____ ZIP _____

Phone No. (___) _____

Method of Payment:

Check ☐   (Please enclose in envelope.)

Charge My: VISA ☐   MasterCard ☐

American Express ☐

Charge # _____

Expiration Date _____

Order No.	Title	Qty.	Price	Total

You can **FAX** your order to **1-317-573-2583**. Or call **1-800-428-5331, ext. ORDR** to order direct.
Please add $2.50 per title for shipping and handling.

Subtotal _____

Shipping & Handling _____

Total _____

— que —

BUSINESS REPLY MAIL
First Class Permit No. 9918   Indianapolis, IN

Postage will be paid by addressee

11711 N. College
Carmel, IN 46032

NO POSTAGE
NECESSARY
IF MAILED
IN THE
UNITED STATES